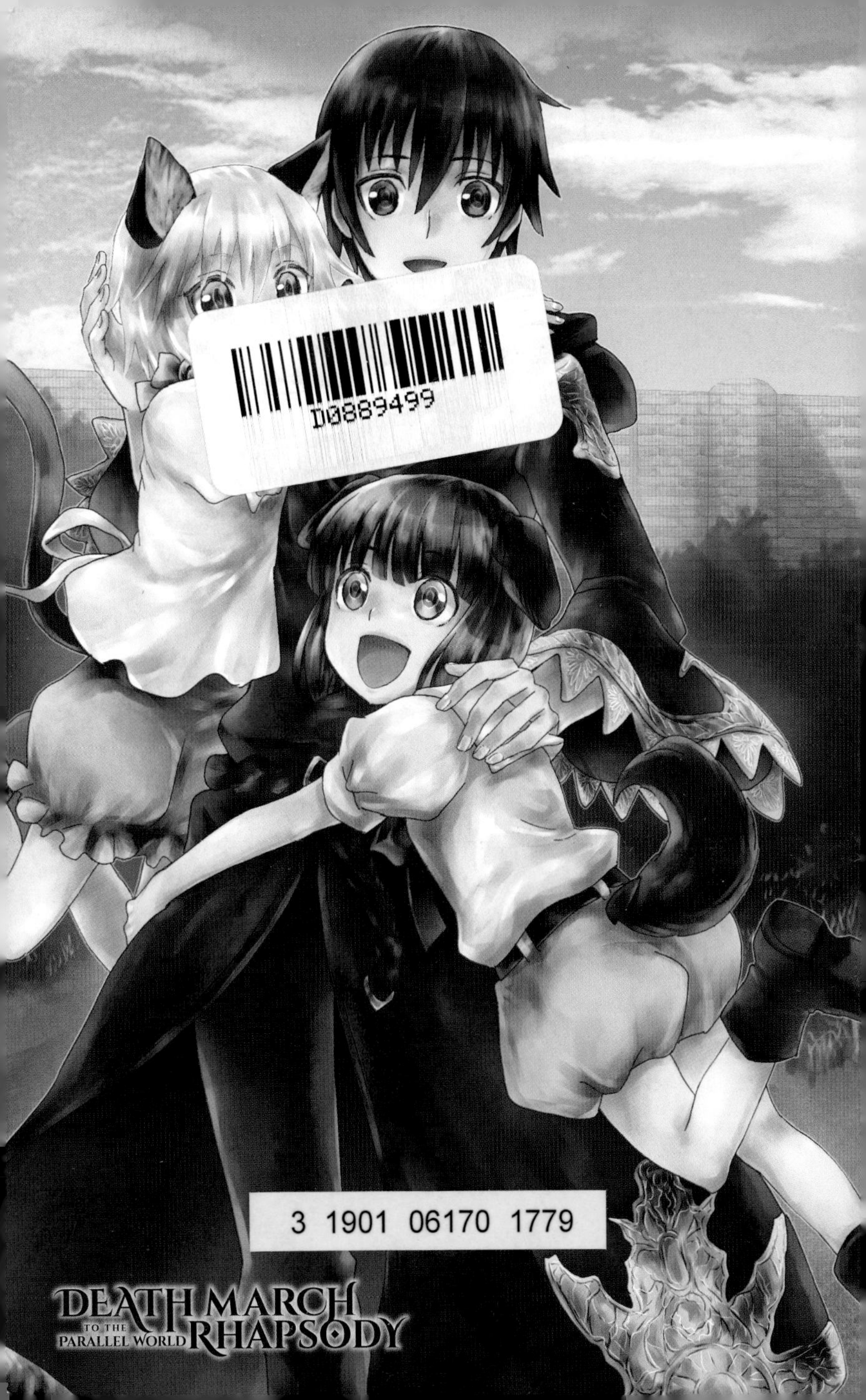
DEATH MARCH
TO THE PARALLEL WORLD
RHAPSODY

CONTENTS

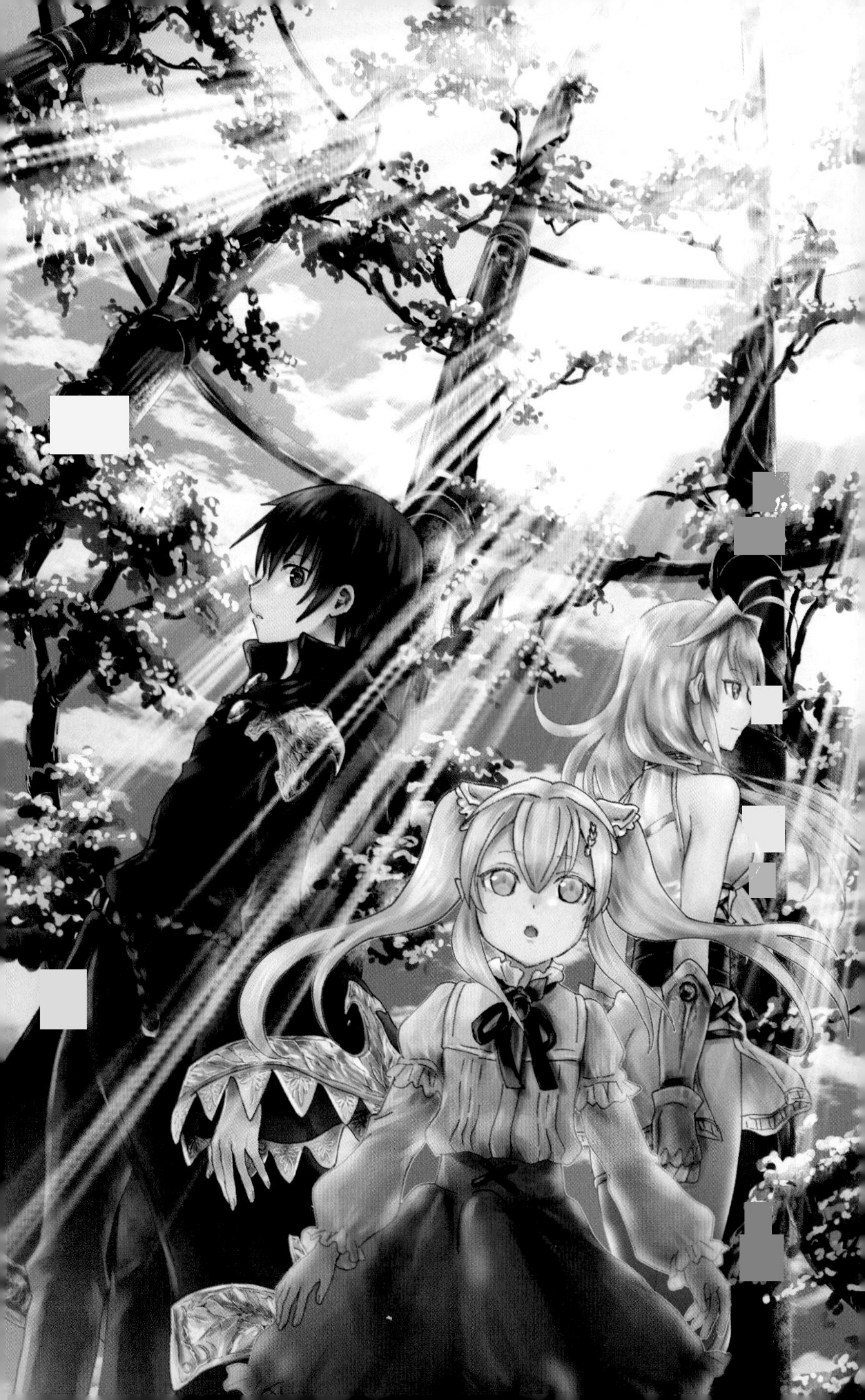

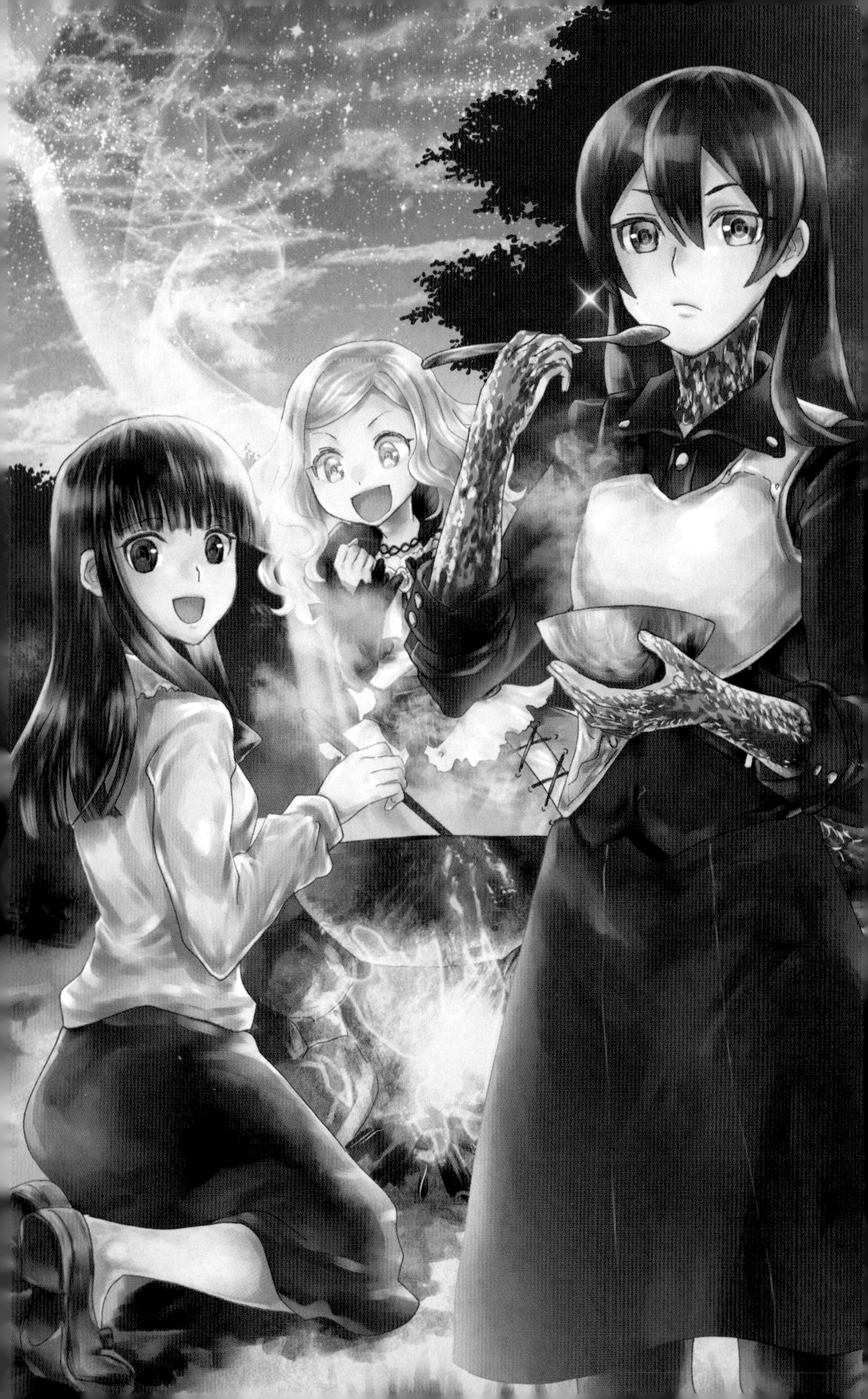

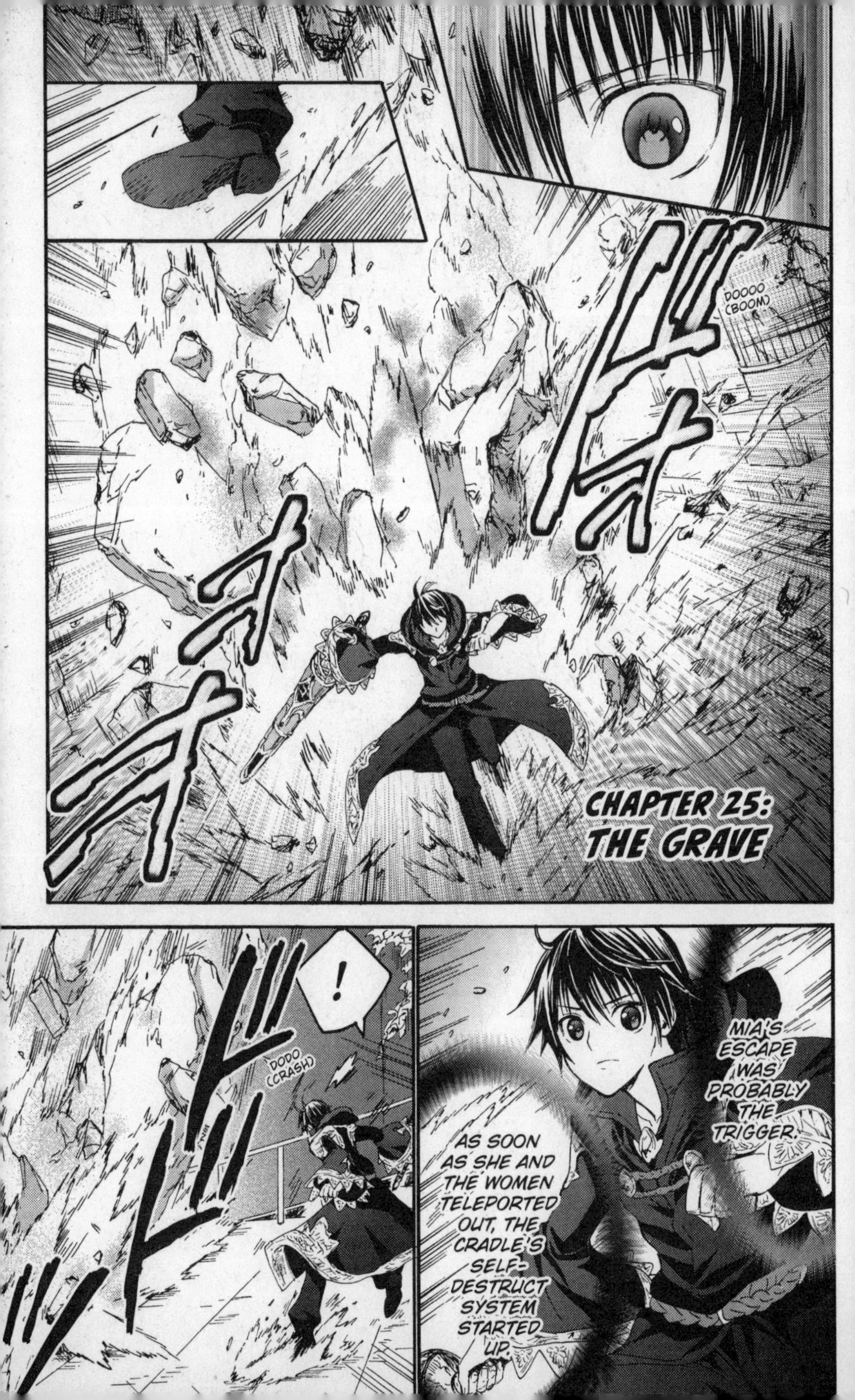
DOOOO (BOOM)
CHAPTER 25: THE GRAVE
MIA'S ESCAPE WAS PROBABLY THE TRIGGER.
AS SOON AS SHE AND THE WOMEN TELEPORTED OUT, THE CRADLE'S SELF-DESTRUCT SYSTEM STARTED UP.
!
DODO (CRASH)

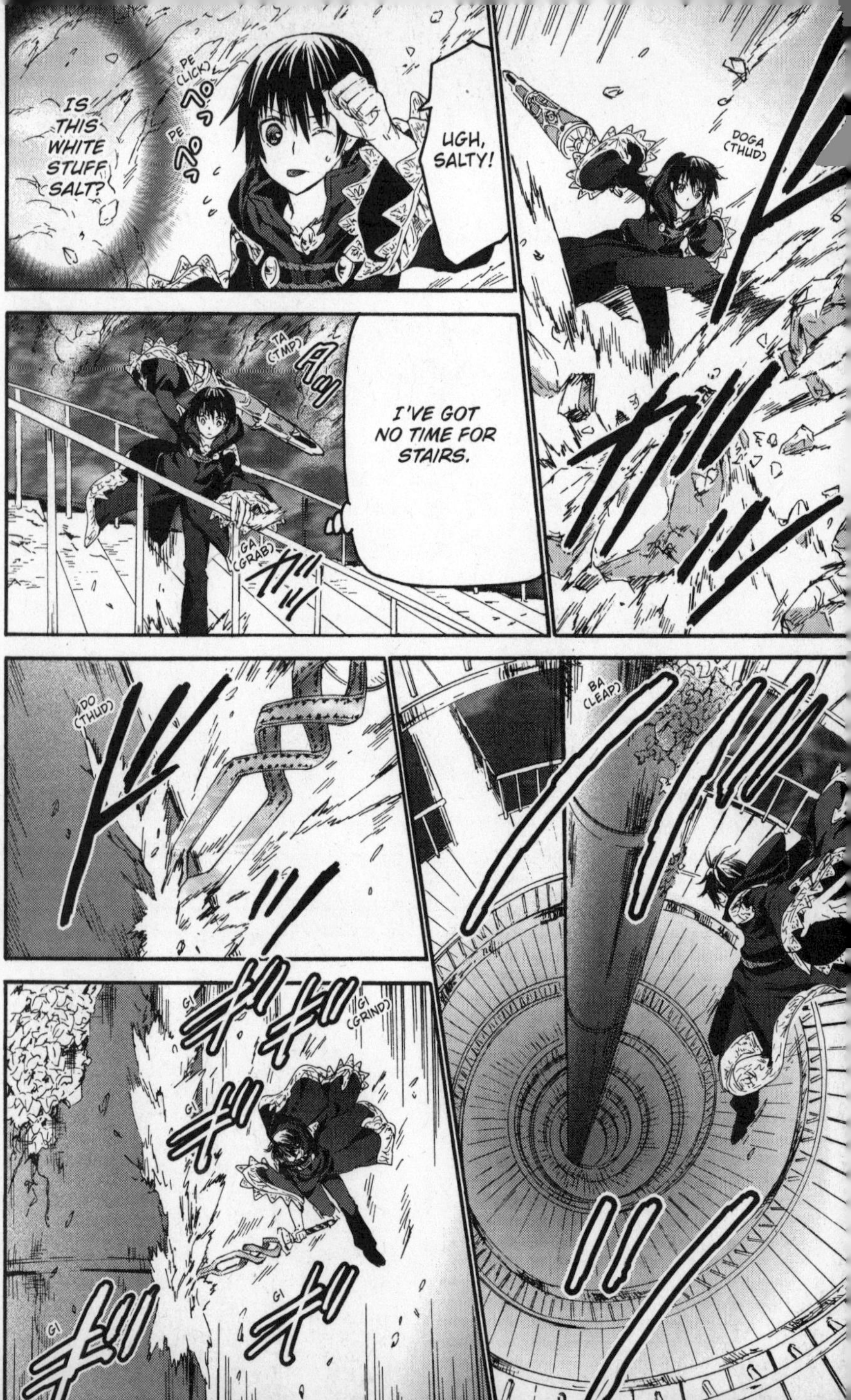

DOGA (THUD)
UGH, SALTY!
PE (LICK)
PE
IS THIS WHITE STUFF SALT?
I'VE GOT NO TIME FOR STAIRS.
TA (TMP)
GA (GRAB)
BA (LEAP)
DO (THUD)
GI (GRIND)
GI
GI
GI
GI

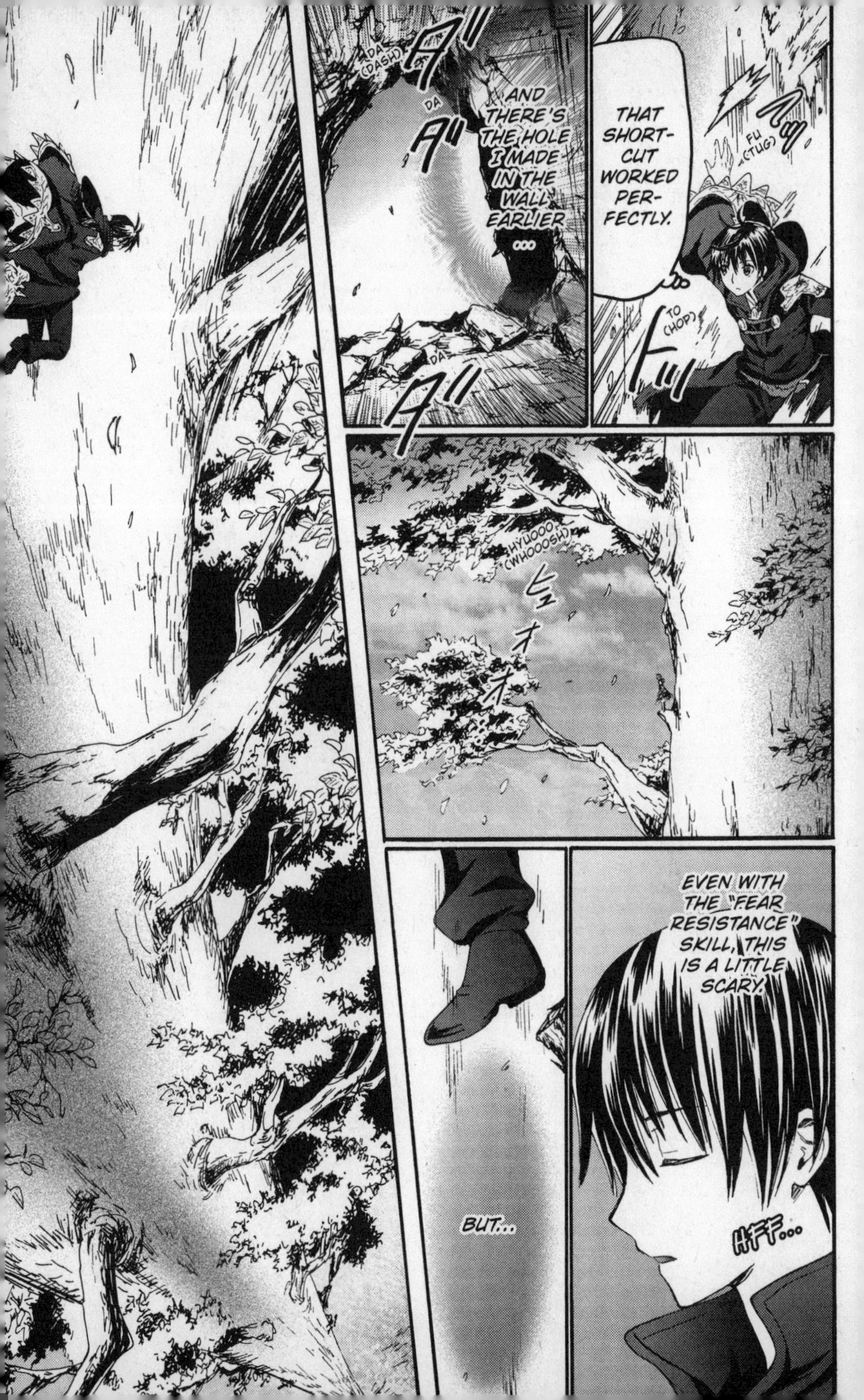
FU (TUG)
THAT SHORT-CUT WORKED PER-FECTLY.
TO (HOP)
DA (DASH)
DA
AND THERE'S THE HOLE I MADE IN THE WALL EARLIER...
DA
HYUOOO (WHOOOSH)
EVEN WITH THE "FEAR RESISTANCE" SKILL, THIS IS A LITTLE SCARY.
HFF...
BUT...

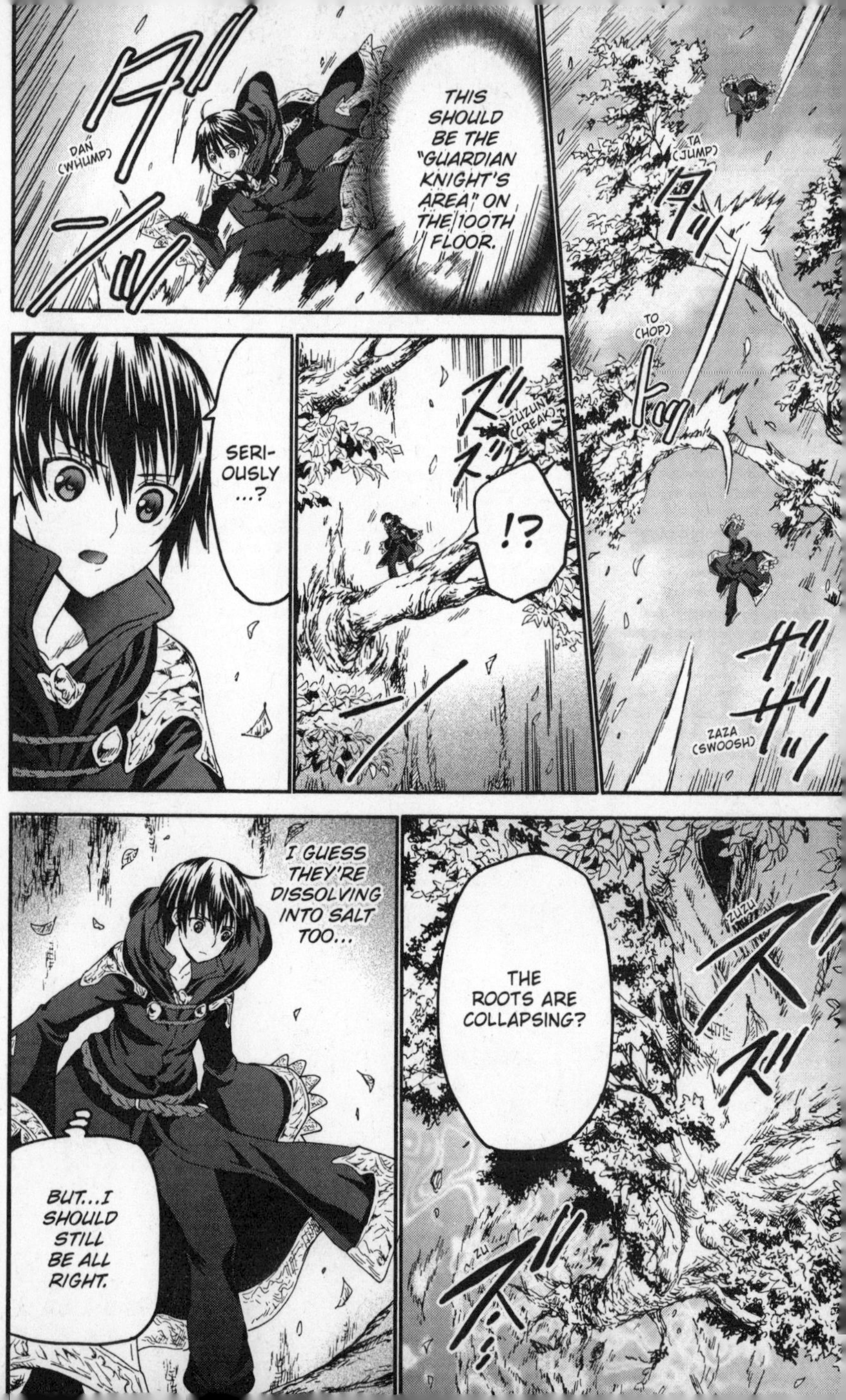
TA (JUMP)
TO (HOP)
ZAZA (SWOOSH)
DAN (WHUMP)
THIS SHOULD BE THE "GUARDIAN KNIGHT'S AREA" ON THE 100TH FLOOR.
ZUZUN (CREAK)
!?
SERI-OUSLY ...?
ZUZU
THE ROOTS ARE COLLAPSING?
ZU
I GUESS THEY'RE DISSOLVING INTO SALT TOO...
BUT...I SHOULD STILL BE ALL RIGHT.

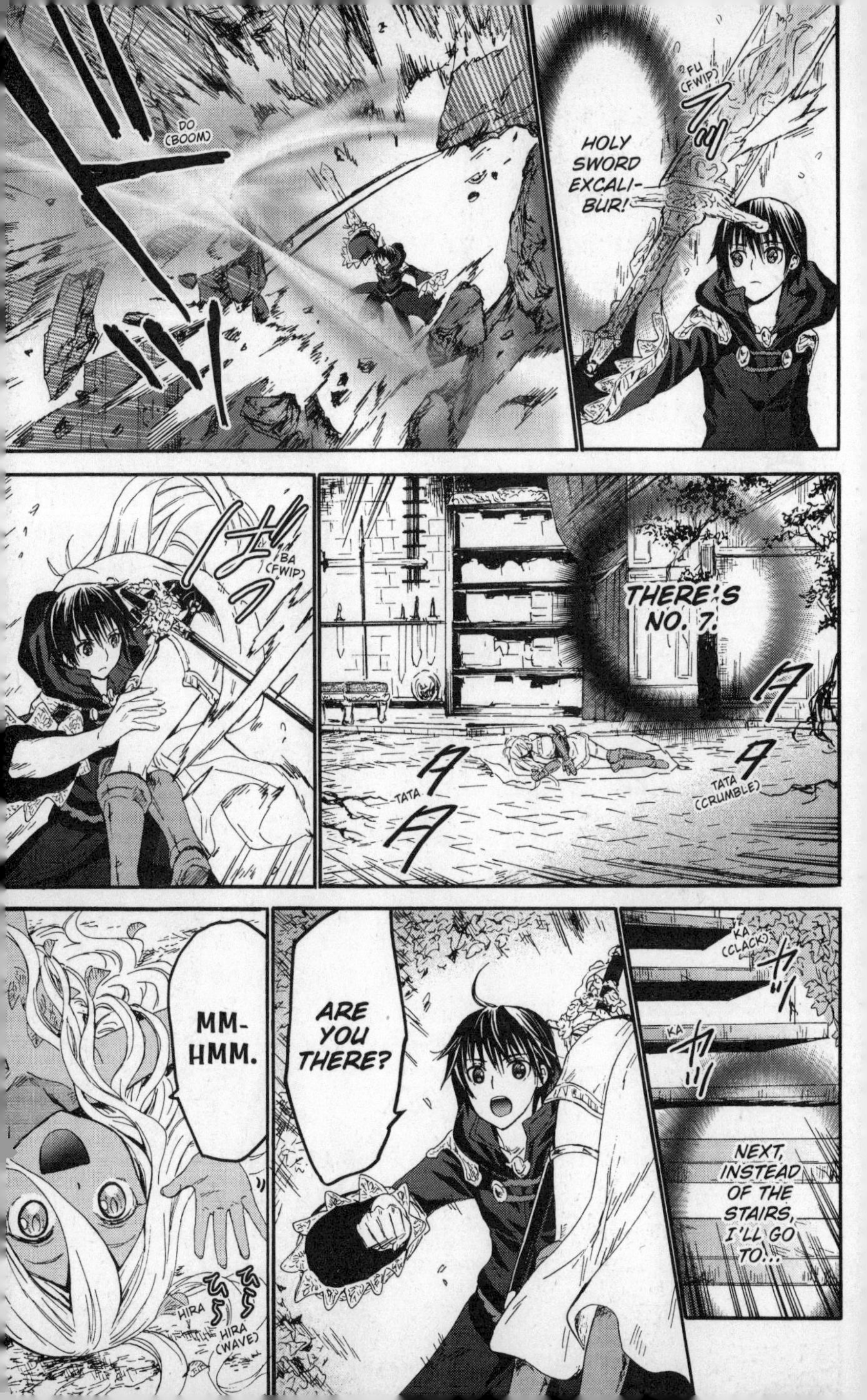
FU (FWIP)
HOLY SWORD EXCALI-BUR!
DO (BOOM)
THERE'S NO. 7.
TATA (CRUMBLE)
TATA
BA (FWIP)
KA (CLACK)
KA
NEXT, INSTEAD OF THE STAIRS, I'LL GO TO...
ARE YOU THERE?
MM-HMM.
HIRA HIRA (WAVE)

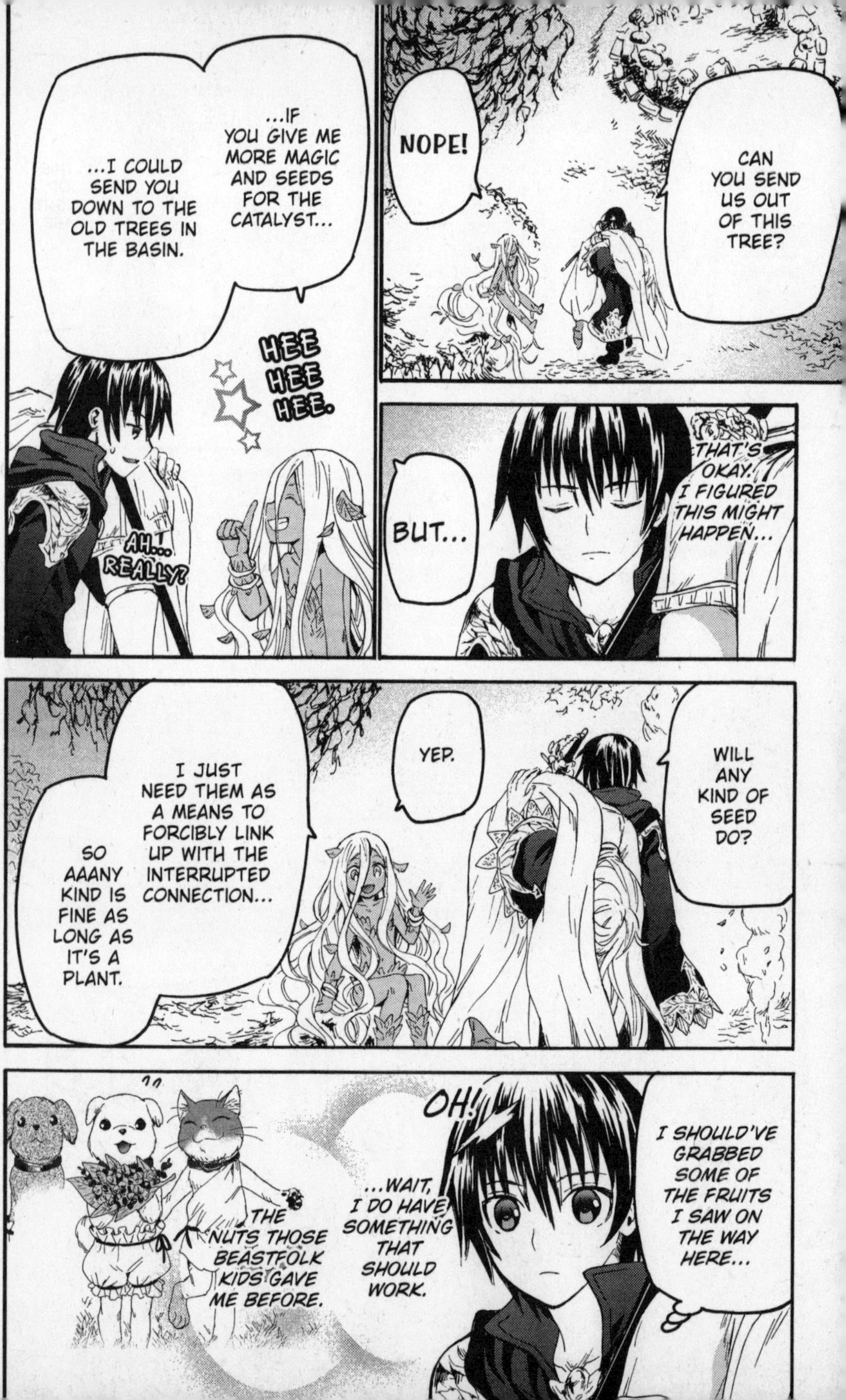
CAN YOU SEND US OUT OF THIS TREE?
NOPE!
THAT'S OKAY. I FIGURED THIS MIGHT HAPPEN...
BUT...
...IF YOU GIVE ME MORE MAGIC AND SEEDS FOR THE CATALYST...
...I COULD SEND YOU DOWN TO THE OLD TREES IN THE BASIN.
HEE HEE HEE.
AH... REALLY?
WILL ANY KIND OF SEED DO?
YEP.
I JUST NEED THEM AS A MEANS TO FORCIBLY LINK UP WITH THE INTERRUPTED CONNECTION...
SO AAANY KIND IS FINE AS LONG AS IT'S A PLANT.
OH!
I SHOULD'VE GRABBED SOME OF THE FRUITS I SAW ON THE WAY HERE...
...WAIT, I DO HAVE SOMETHING THAT SHOULD WORK.
THE NUTS THOSE BEASTFOLK KIDS GAVE ME BEFORE.

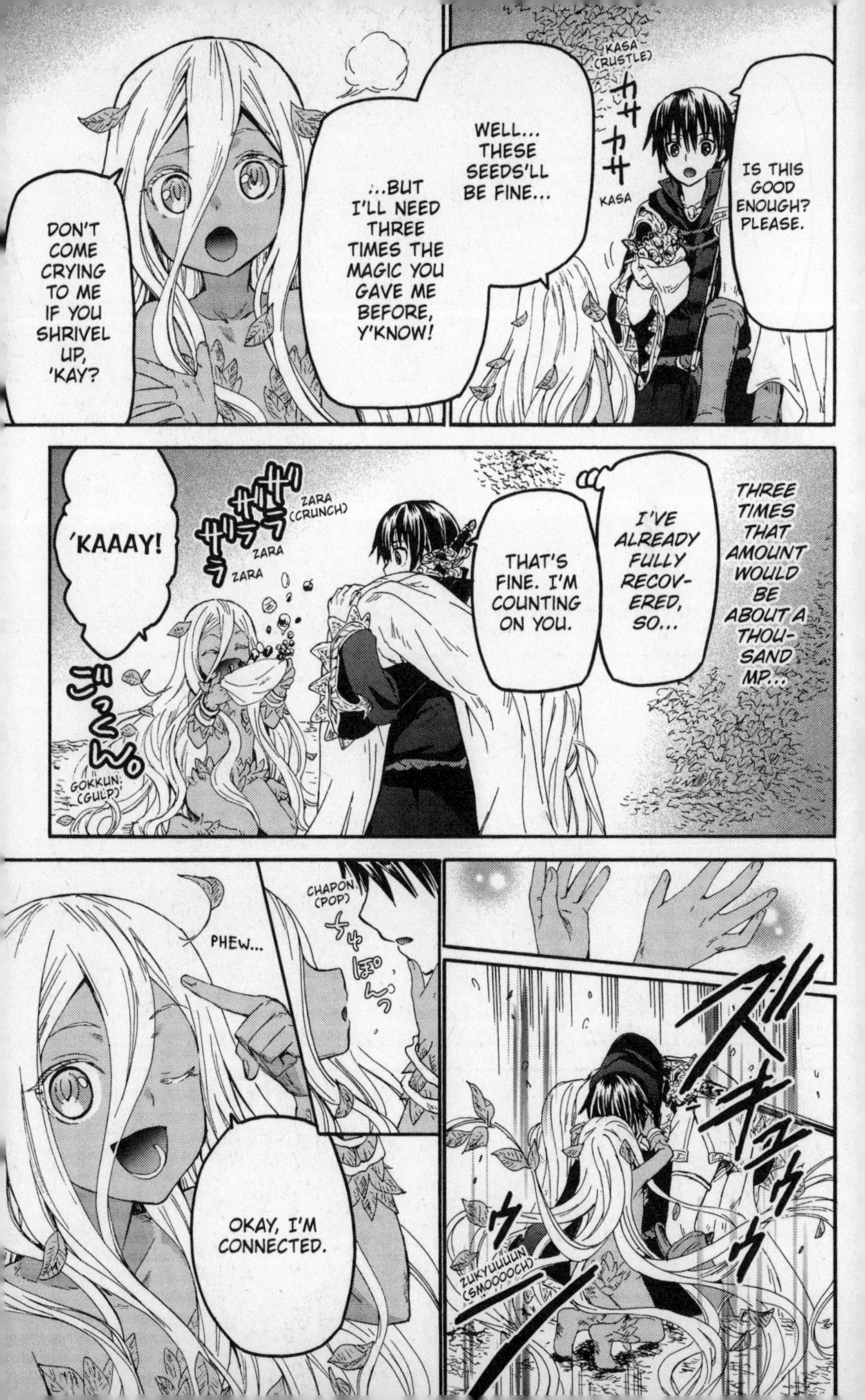

IS THIS GOOD ENOUGH? PLEASE.
KASA (RUSTLE)
カサカサ
KASA
WELL... THESE SEEDS'LL BE FINE...
...BUT I'LL NEED THREE TIMES THE MAGIC YOU GAVE ME BEFORE, Y'KNOW!
DON'T COME CRYING TO ME IF YOU SHRIVEL UP, 'KAY?
THREE TIMES THAT AMOUNT WOULD BE ABOUT A THOUSAND MP...
I'VE ALREADY FULLY RECOVERED, SO...
THAT'S FINE. I'M COUNTING ON YOU.
ZARA (CRUNCH)
ザラザラザラ
ZARA
ZARA
'KAAAY!
ごっくん。
GOKKUN (GULP)
ズギュウウウン
ZUKYUUUUN (SMOOOOCH)
CHAPON (POP)
ちゅぽんっ
PHEW...
OKAY, I'M CONNECTED.

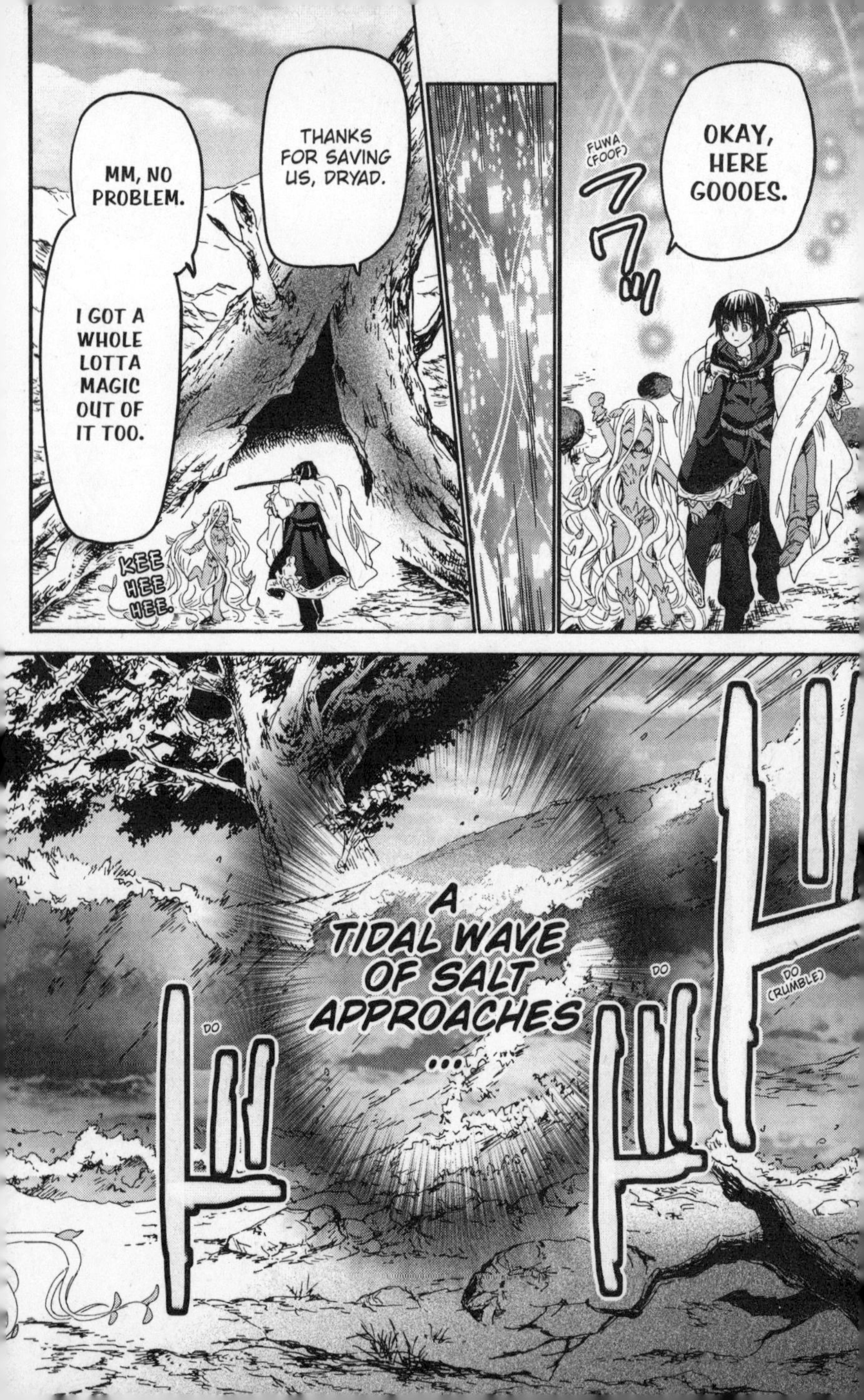
FUWA (FOOF)
OKAY, HERE GOOOES.
THANKS FOR SAVING US, DRYAD.
MM, NO PROBLEM.
I GOT A WHOLE LOTTA MAGIC OUT OF IT TOO.
KEE HEE HEE.
DO (RUMBLE)
DO
A TIDAL WAVE OF SALT APPROACHES...
DO

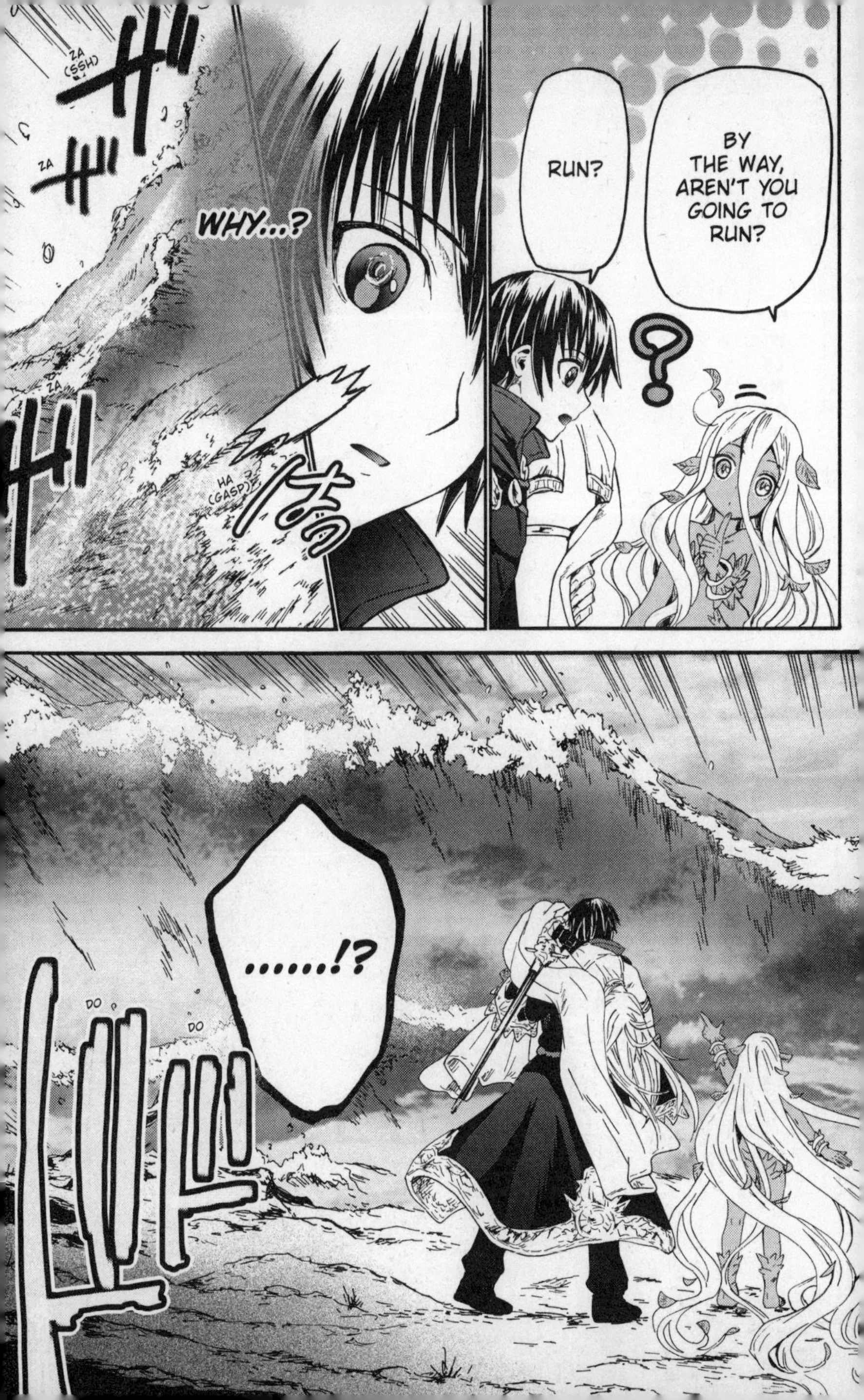
BY THE WAY, AREN'T YOU GOING TO RUN?
RUN?
ZA (SSH)
ZA
WHY...?
ZA
HA (GASP)
......!?
DO
DO

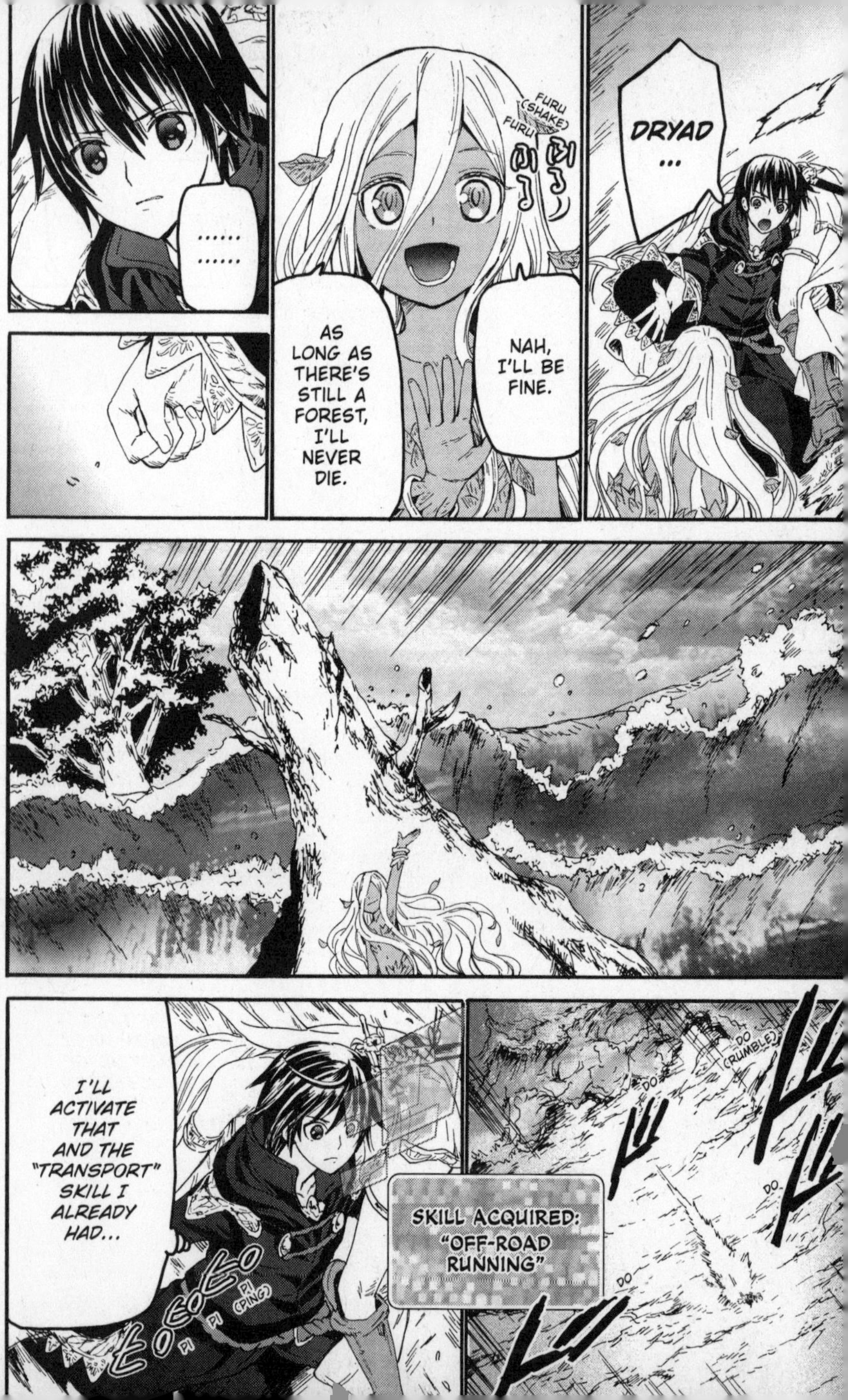
DRYAD ...
FURU (SHAKE) FURU
NAH, I'LL BE FINE.
AS LONG AS THERE'S STILL A FOREST, I'LL NEVER DIE.
....
DO (RUMBLE)
DO
DO
DO
SKILL ACQUIRED: "OFF-ROAD RUNNING"
PI (PING) PI PI
I'LL ACTIVATE THAT AND THE "TRANSPORT" SKILL I ALREADY HAD...

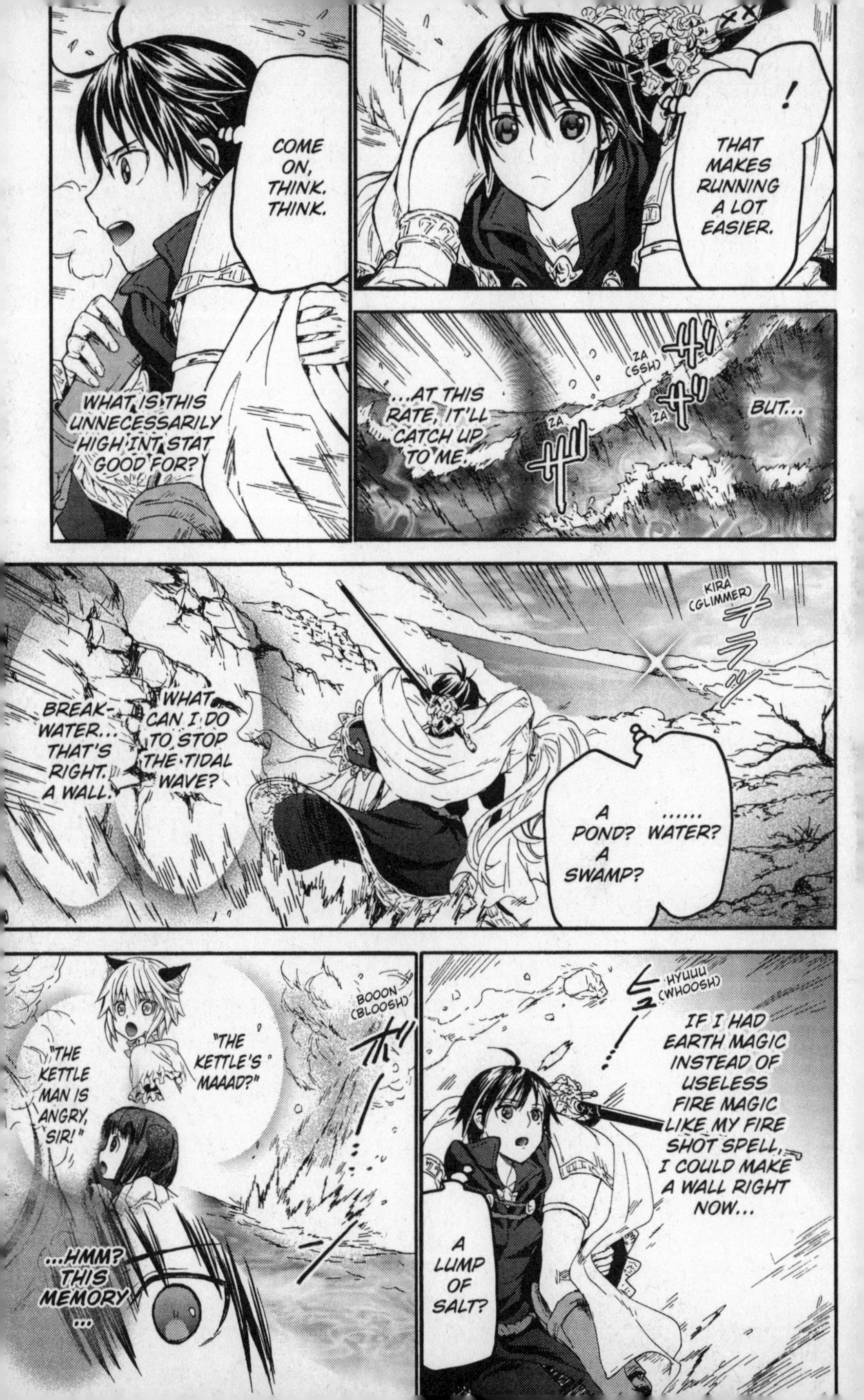
!
THAT MAKES RUNNING A LOT EASIER.
ZA (SSH)
ZA
ZA
BUT...
...AT THIS RATE, IT'LL CATCH UP TO ME.
COME ON, THINK. THINK.
WHAT IS THIS UNNECESSARILY HIGH INT STAT GOOD FOR?
KIRA (GLIMMER)
...... WATER?
A POND? A SWAMP?
WHAT CAN I DO TO STOP THE TIDAL WAVE?
BREAK-WATER... THAT'S RIGHT. A WALL.
HYUUU (WHOOSH)
IF I HAD EARTH MAGIC INSTEAD OF USELESS FIRE MAGIC LIKE MY FIRE SHOT SPELL, I COULD MAKE A WALL RIGHT NOW...
A LUMP OF SALT?
BOOON (BLOOSH)
"THE KETTLE'S MAAAD?"
"THE KETTLE MAN IS ANGRY, SIR!"
...HMM? THIS MEMORY...

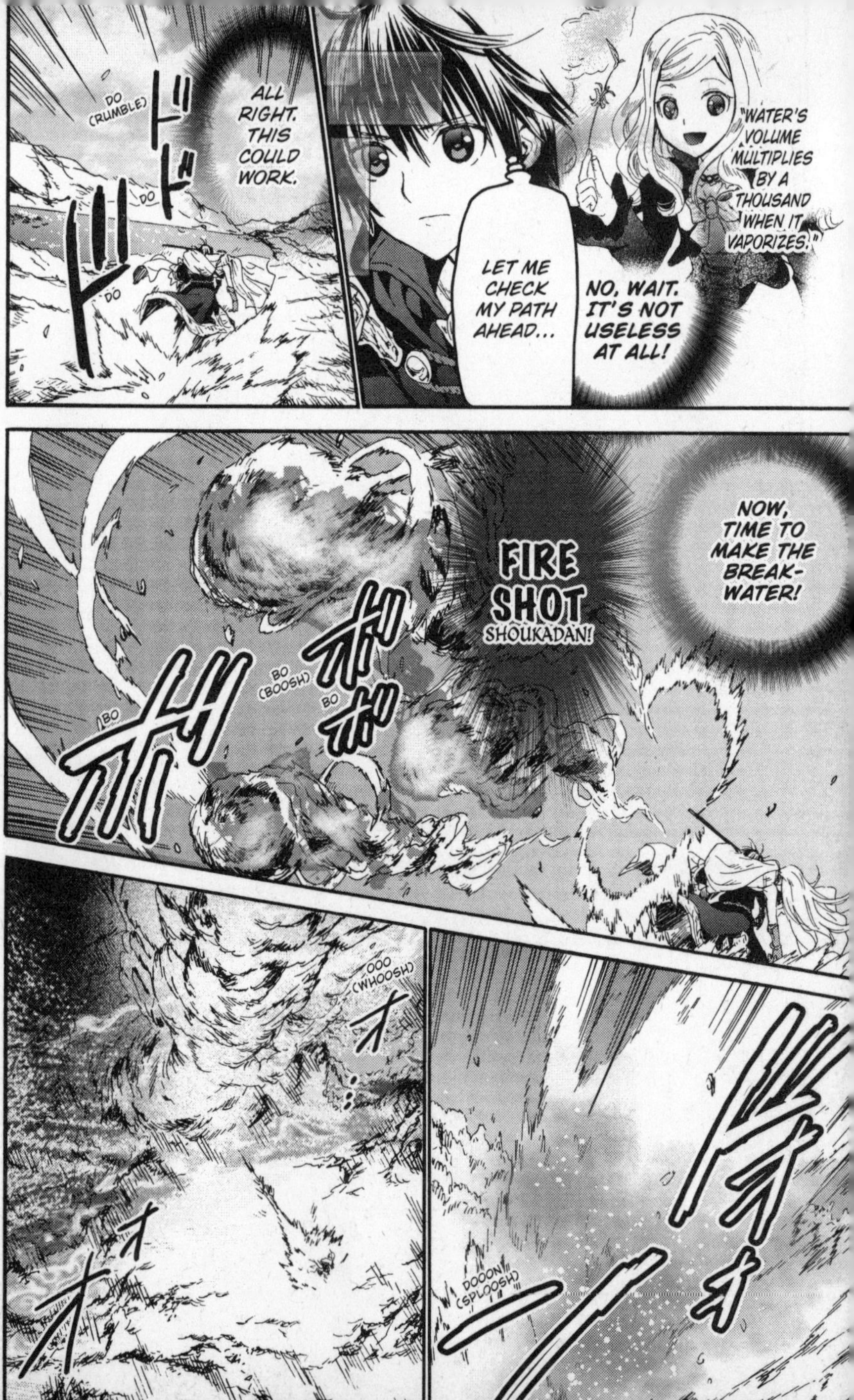
"WATER'S VOLUME MULTIPLIES BY A THOUSAND WHEN IT VAPORIZES."
NO, WAIT. IT'S NOT USELESS AT ALL!
LET ME CHECK MY PATH AHEAD...
ALL RIGHT. THIS COULD WORK.
DO (RUMBLE)
DO
DO
NOW, TIME TO MAKE THE BREAK-WATER!
FIRE SHOT
SHOUKADAN!
BO (BOOSH)
BO
BO
DOOON (SPLOOSH)
OOO (WHOOSH)

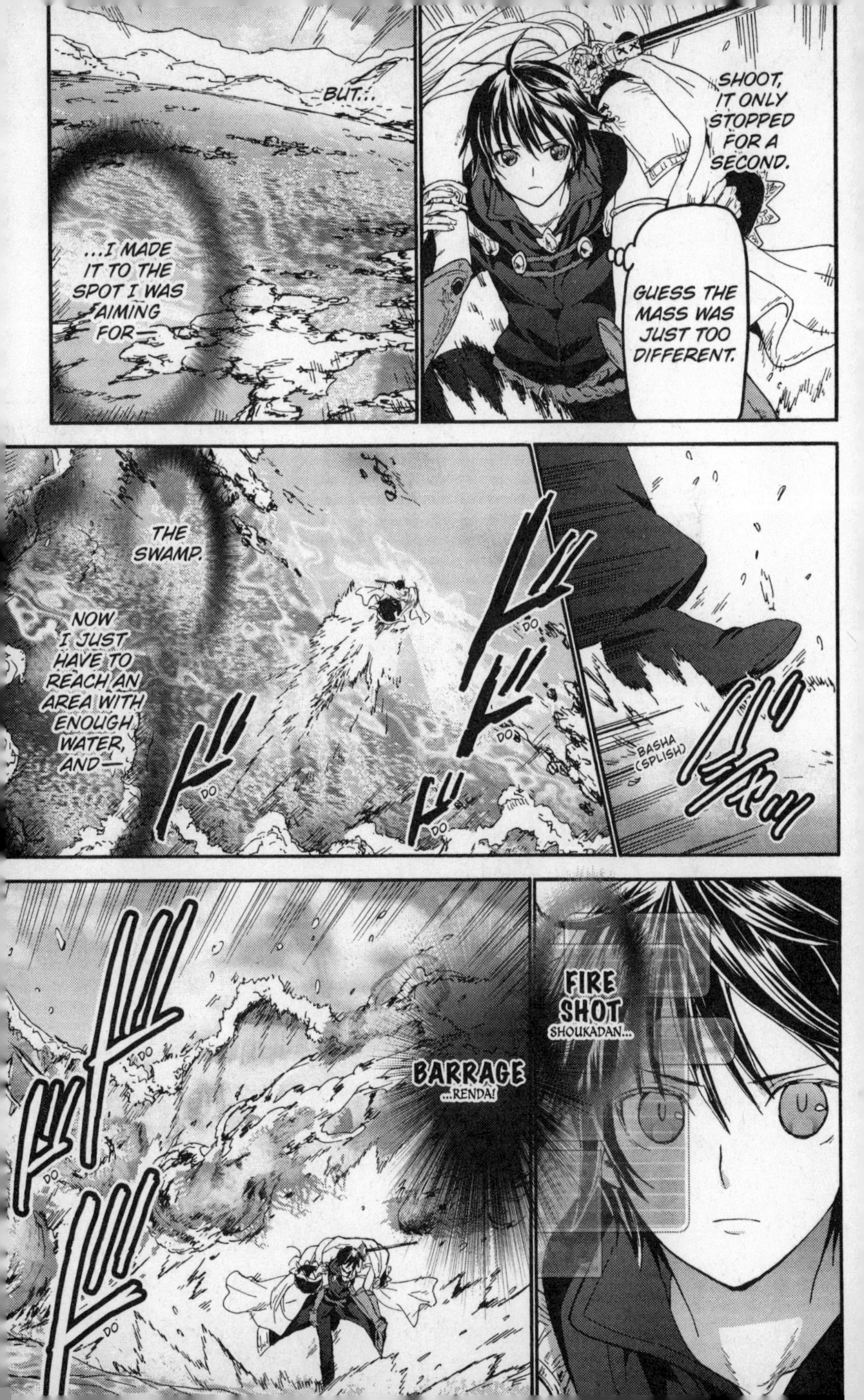
SHOOT, IT ONLY STOPPED FOR A SECOND.
GUESS THE MASS WAS JUST TOO DIFFERENT.
BUT...
...I MADE IT TO THE SPOT I WAS AIMING FOR—
BASHA (SPLISH)
DO
DO
DO
THE SWAMP.
NOW I JUST HAVE TO REACH AN AREA WITH ENOUGH WATER, AND—
DO
FIRE SHOT
SHOUKADAN...
BARRAGE
...RENDA!
DO
DO
DO

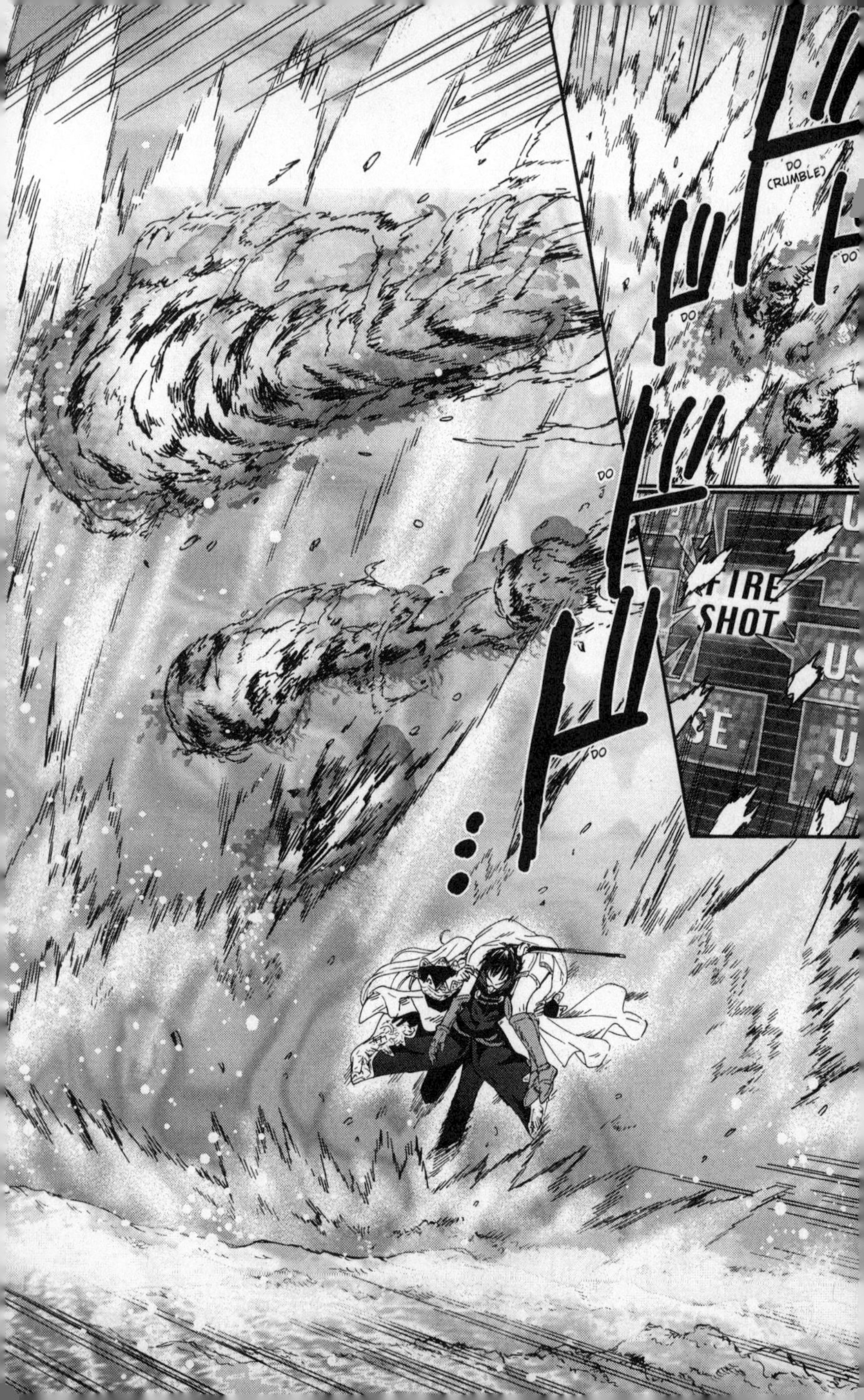
DO (RUMBLE)
DO
DO
DO
DO
FIRE SHOT
...

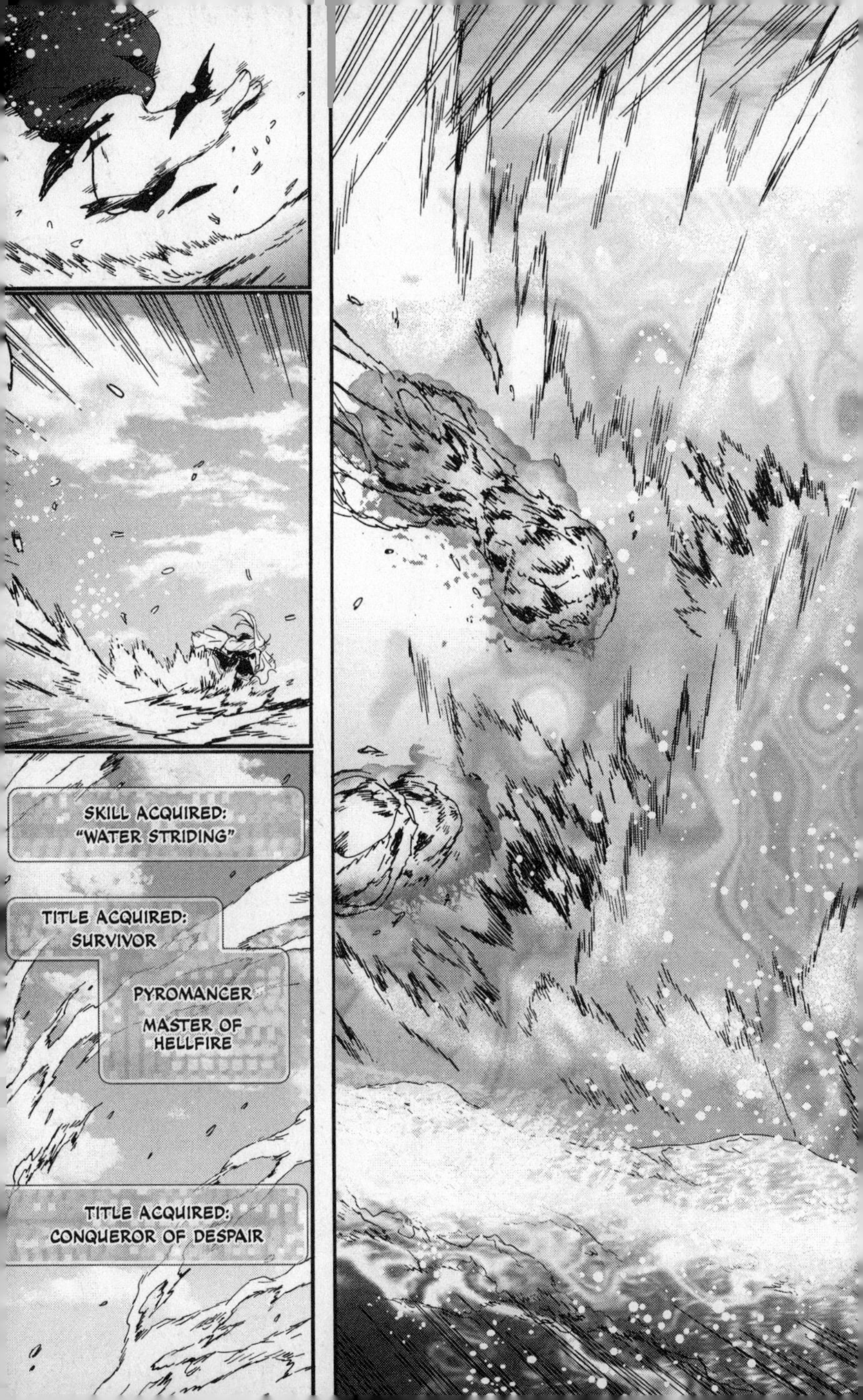
SKILL ACQUIRED:
"WATER STRIDING"
TITLE ACQUIRED:
SURVIVOR
PYROMANCER
MASTER OF
HELLFIRE
TITLE ACQUIRED:
CONQUEROR OF DESPAIR

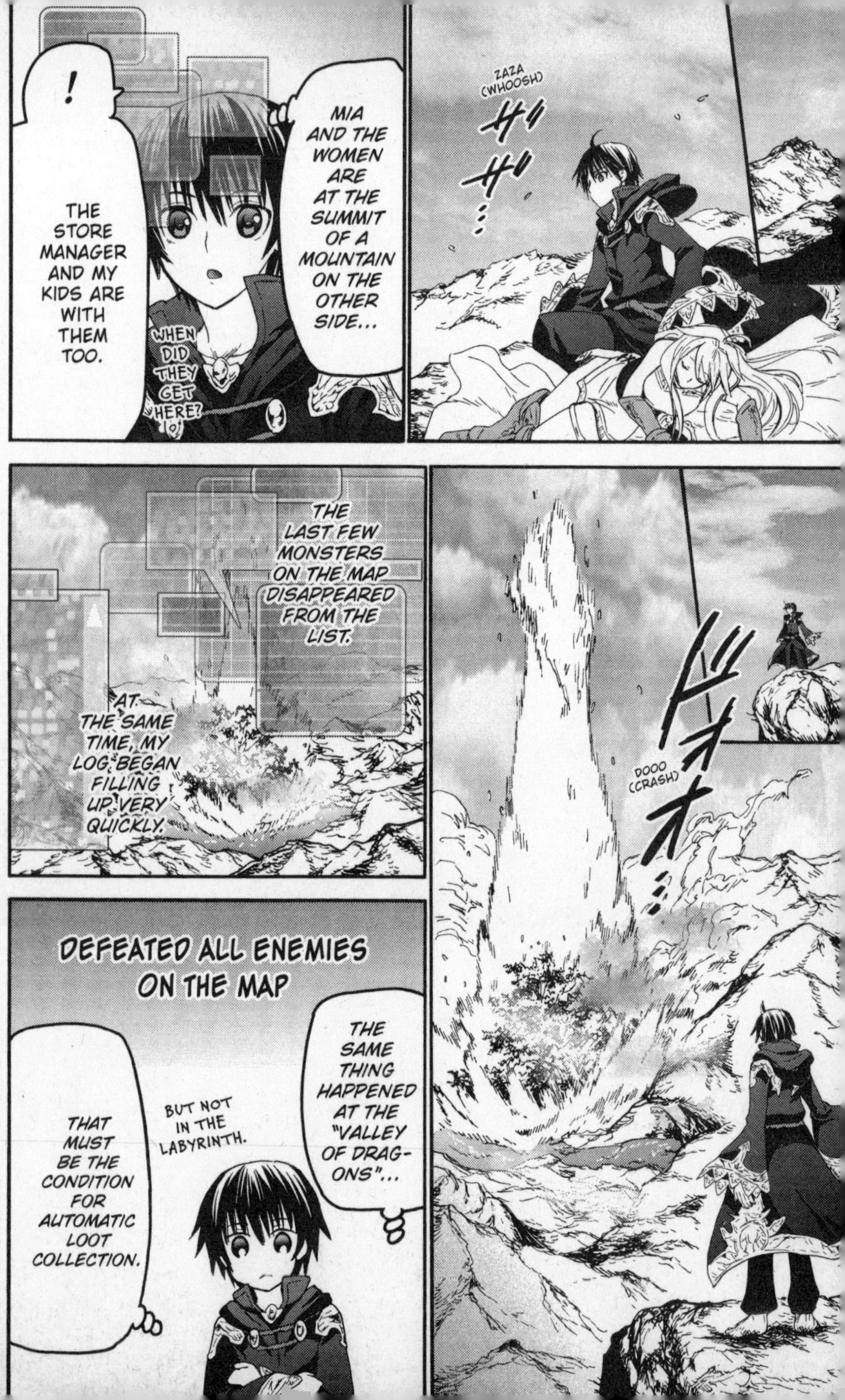
ZAZA (WHOOSH)
!
MIA AND THE WOMEN ARE AT THE SUMMIT OF A MOUNTAIN ON THE OTHER SIDE...
THE STORE MANAGER AND MY KIDS ARE WITH THEM TOO.
WHEN DID THEY GET HERE?
DOOO (CRASH)
THE LAST FEW MONSTERS ON THE MAP DISAPPEARED FROM THE LIST.
AT THE SAME TIME, MY LOG BEGAN FILLING UP VERY QUICKLY.
DEFEATED ALL ENEMIES ON THE MAP
THE SAME THING HAPPENED AT THE "VALLEY OF DRAG-ONS"...
BUT NOT IN THE LABYRINTH.
THAT MUST BE THE CONDITION FOR AUTOMATIC LOOT COLLECTION.

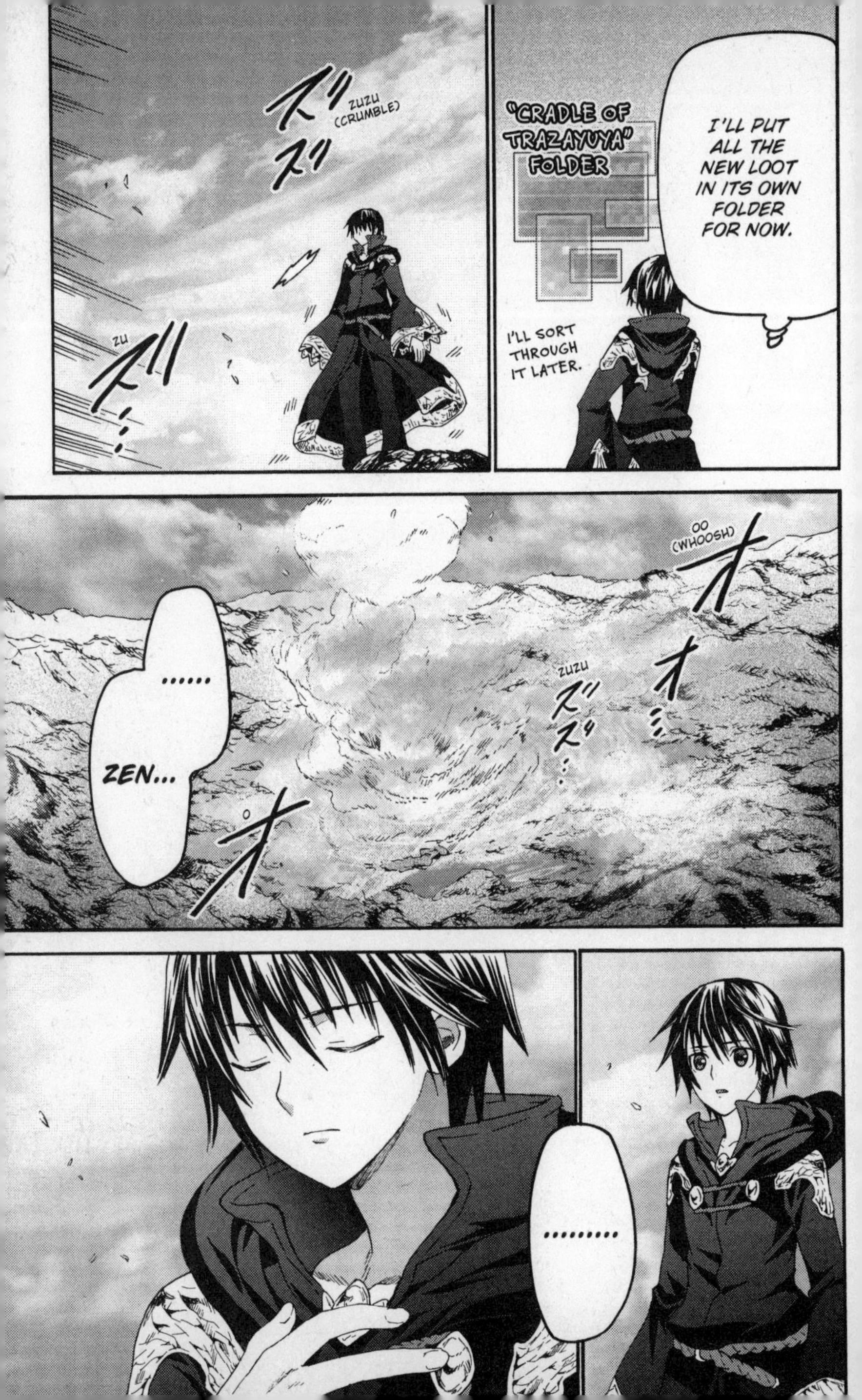
I'LL PUT ALL THE NEW LOOT IN ITS OWN FOLDER FOR NOW.
"CRADLE OF TRAZAYUYA" FOLDER
I'LL SORT THROUGH IT LATER.
ZUZU (CRUMBLE)
ZU
OO (WHOOSH)
ZUZU
......
ZEN...
....

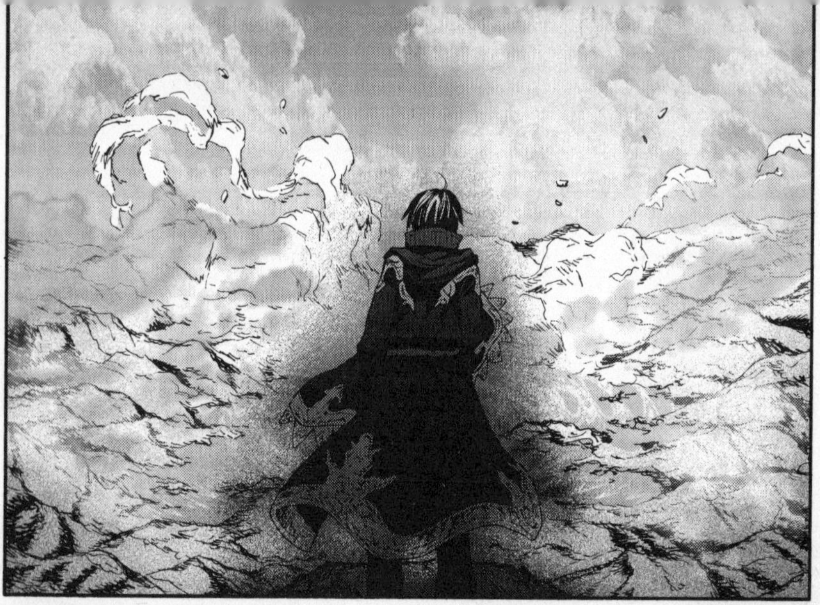

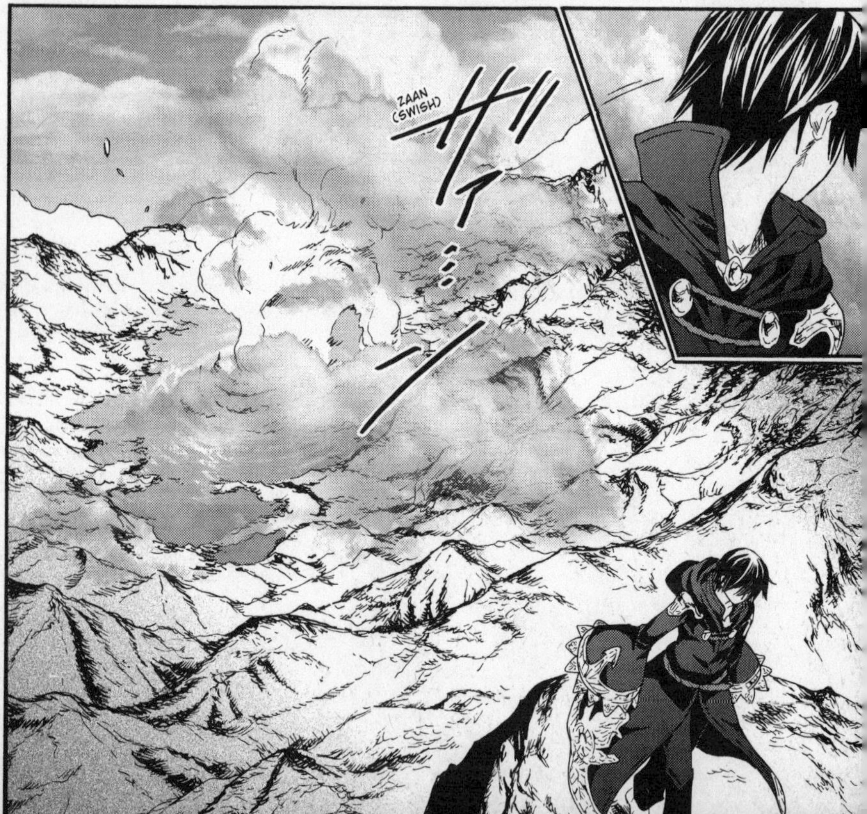
ZAAN (SWISH)

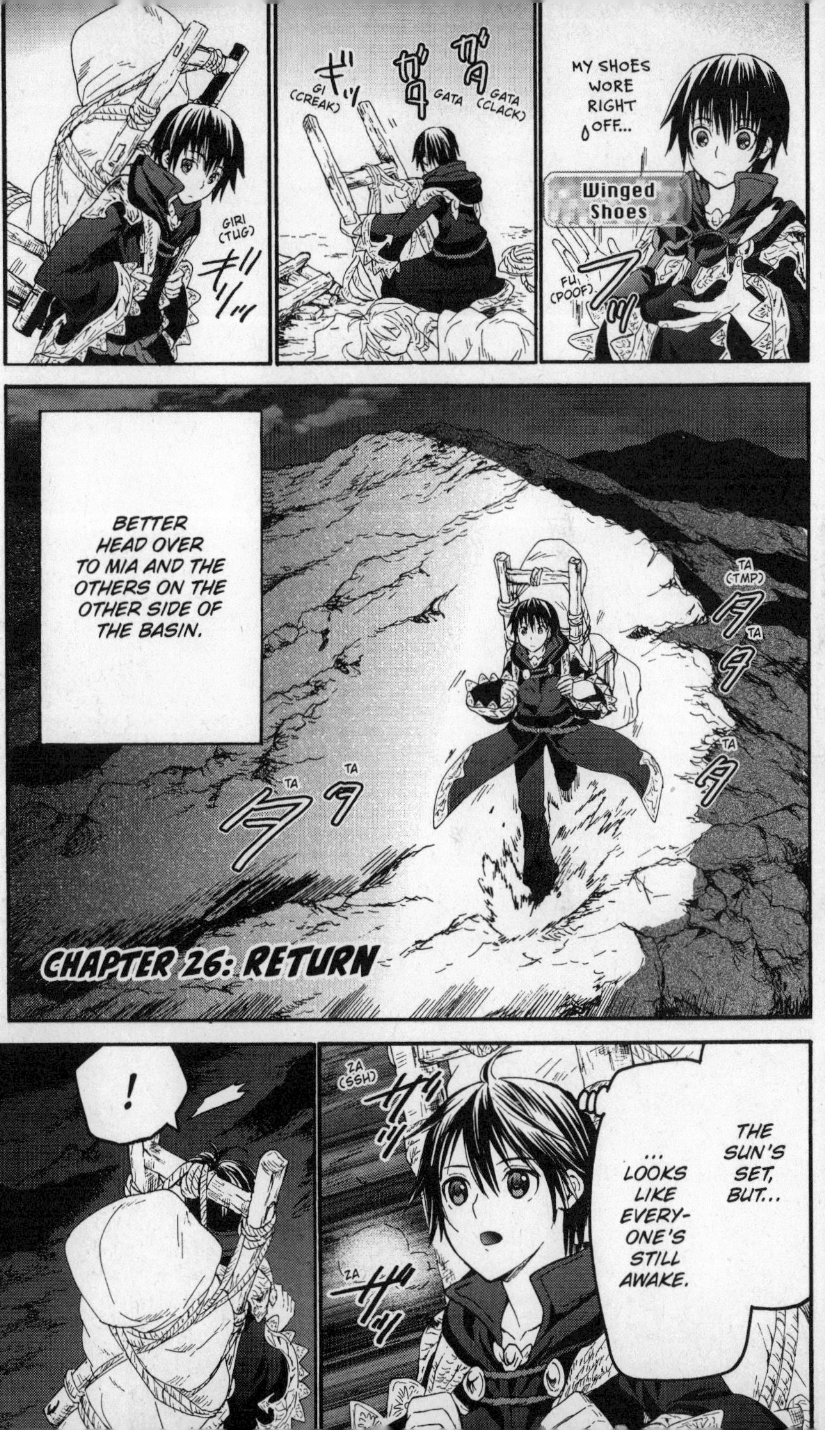
MY SHOES WORE RIGHT OFF...
Winged Shoes
FU (POOF)
GATA GATA (CLACK)
GI (CREAK)
GIRI (TUG)
BETTER HEAD OVER TO MIA AND THE OTHERS ON THE OTHER SIDE OF THE BASIN.
TA (TMP)
TA
TA
TA
TA
CHAPTER 26: RETURN
THE SUN'S SET, BUT...
...LOOKS LIKE EVERYONE'S STILL AWAKE.
ZA (SSH)
ZA
!

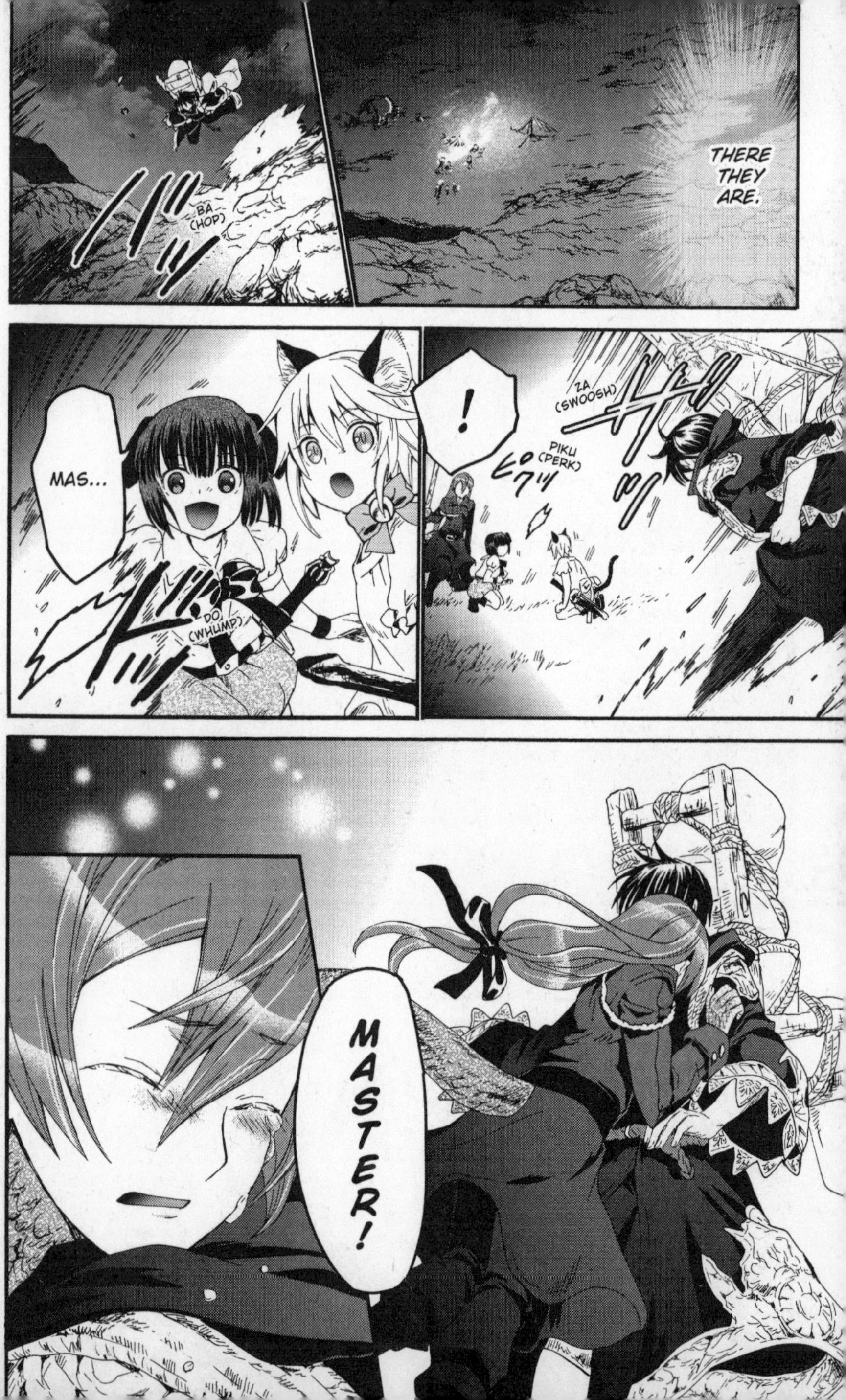
THERE THEY ARE.
BA (HOP)
ZA (SWOOSH)
PIKU (PERK)
!
MAS...
DO (WHUMP)
MASTER!

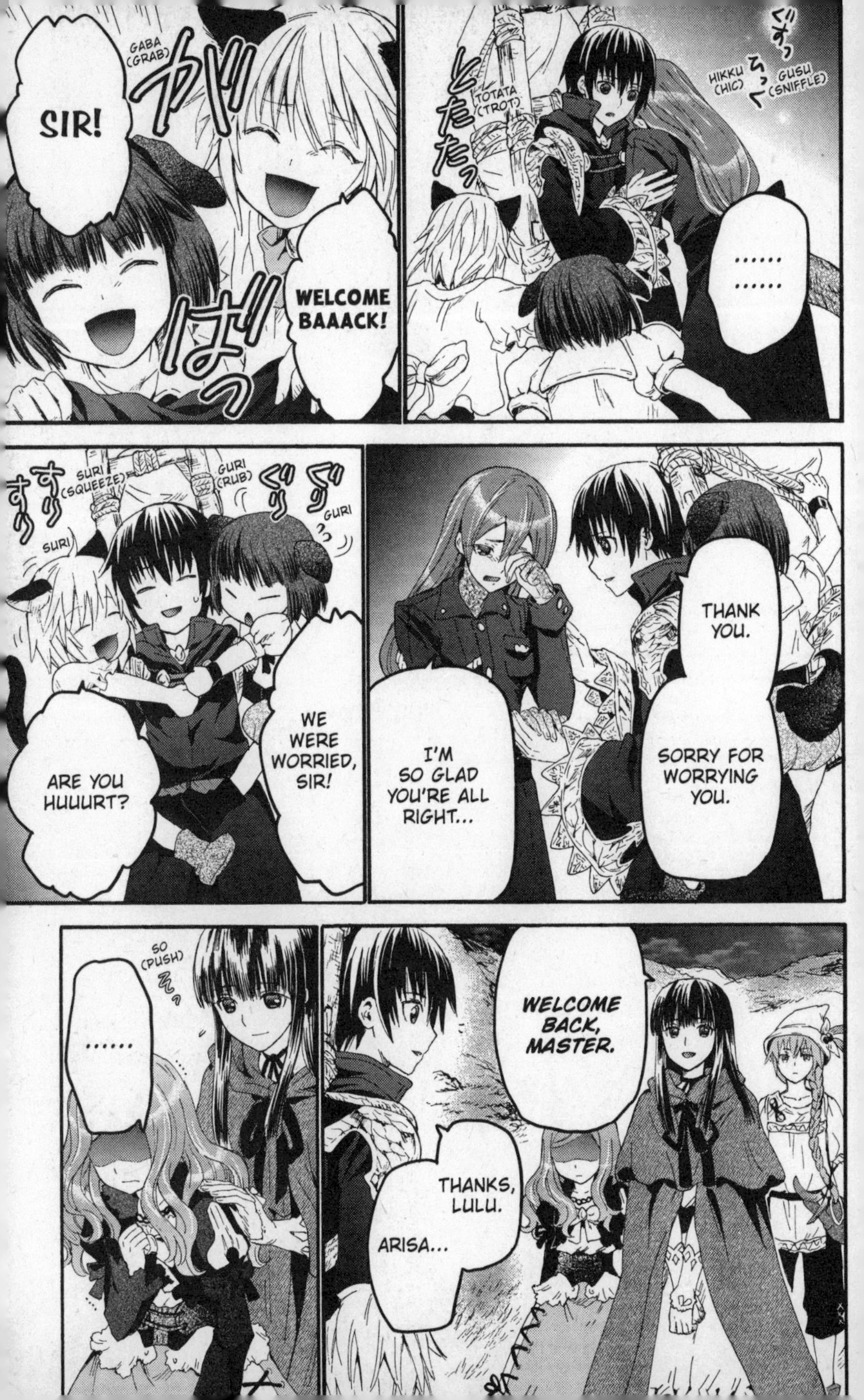
HIKKU (HIC)
GUSU (SNIFFLE)
TOTATA (TROT)
......
......
GABA (GRAB)
SIR!
WELCOME BAAACK!
THANK YOU.
SORRY FOR WORRYING YOU.
I'M SO GLAD YOU'RE ALL RIGHT...
GURI (RUB)
GURI
SURI (SQUEEZE)
SURI
WE WERE WORRIED, SIR!
ARE YOU HUUURT?
WELCOME BACK, MASTER.
THANKS, LULU.
ARISA...
SO (PUSH)
......

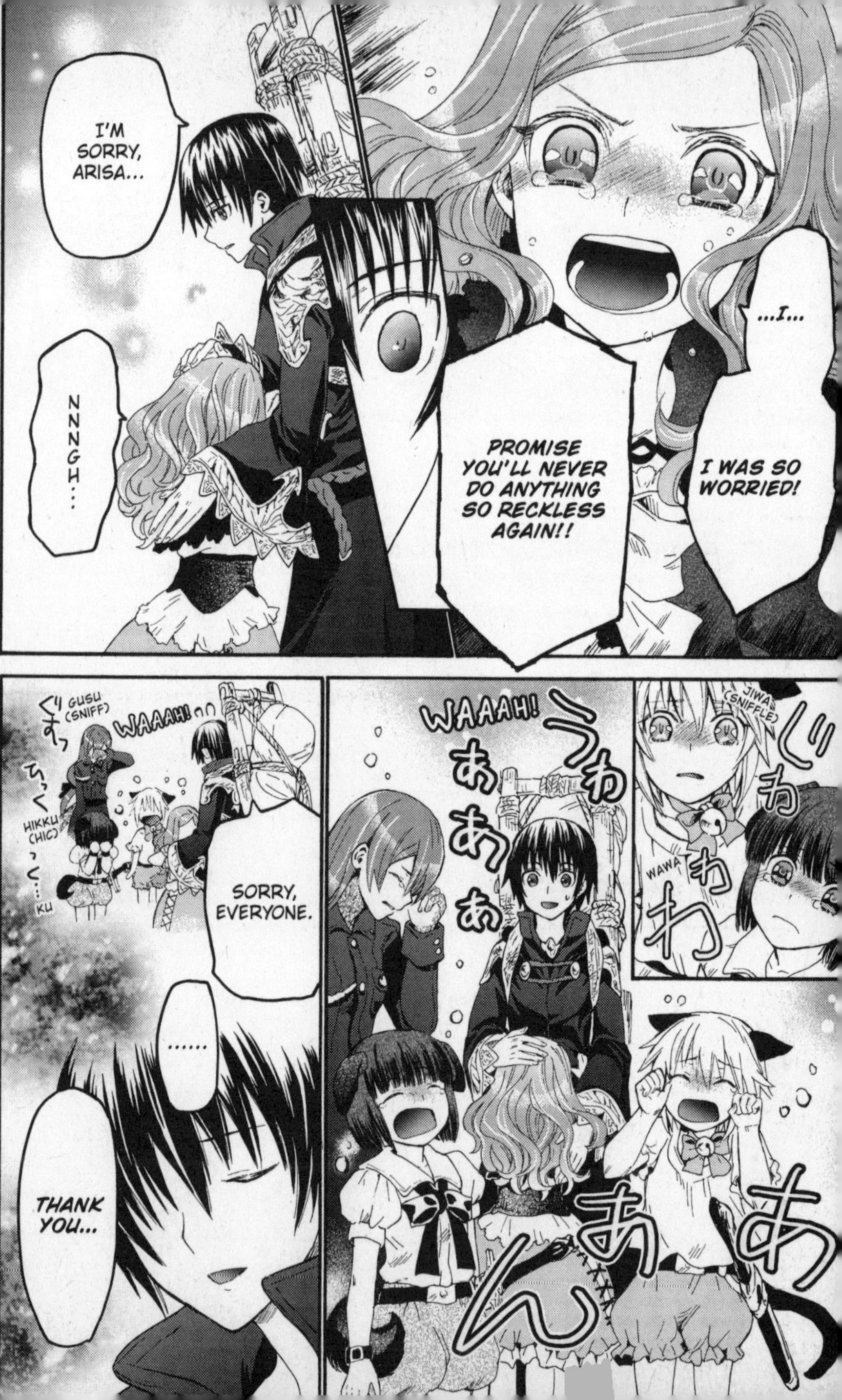
...I...
I WAS SO WORRIED!
PROMISE YOU'LL NEVER DO ANYTHING SO RECKLESS AGAIN!!
I'M SORRY, ARISA...
NNNGH...
JIWA (SNIFFLE)
WAWA
WAAAH!
GUSU (SNIFF)
WAAAH!
HIKKU (HIC)
KU
SORRY, EVERYONE.
......
THANK YOU...

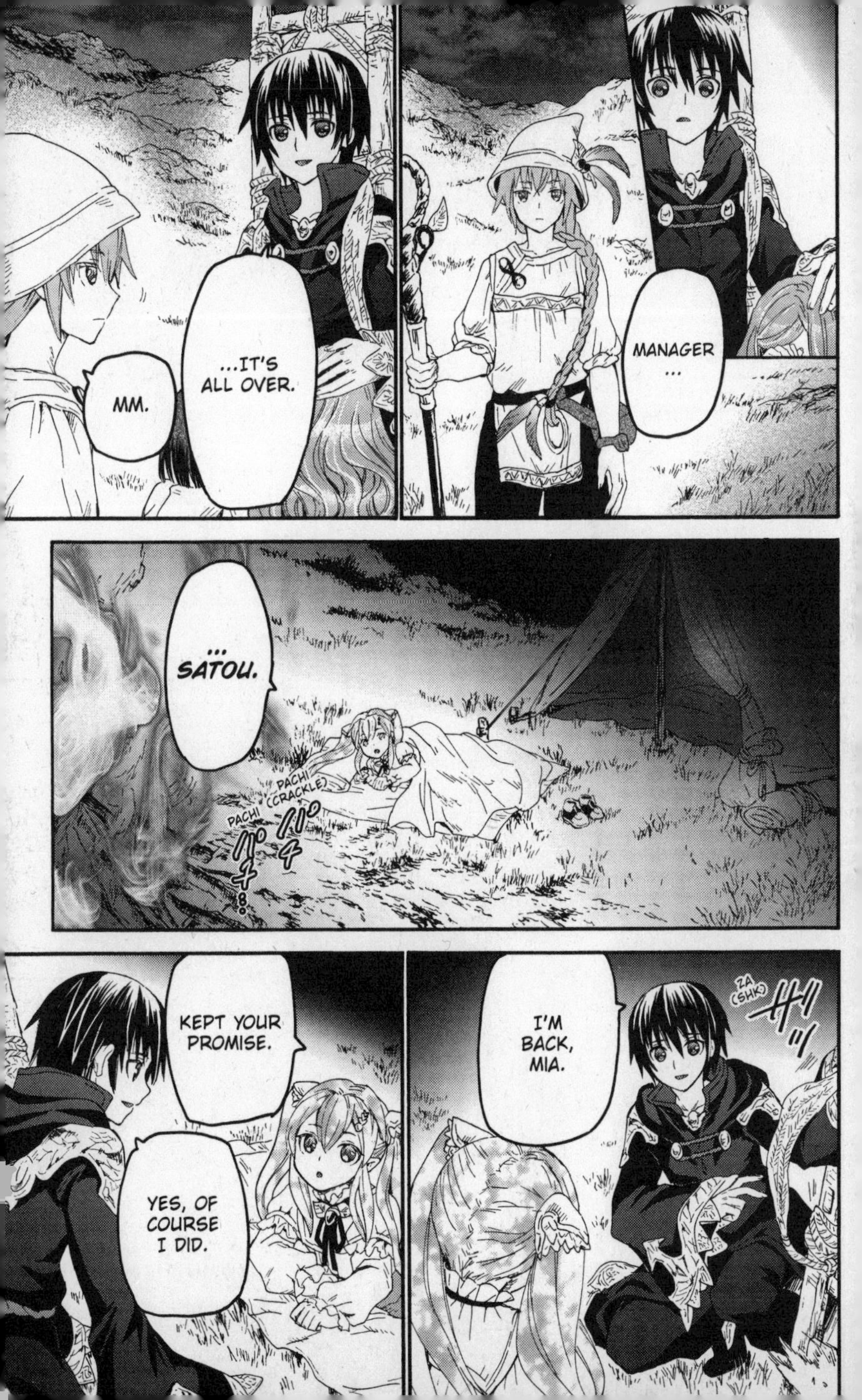
MANAGER...
...IT'S ALL OVER.
MM.
...SATOU.
PACHI (CRACKLE)
PACHI
ZA (SHK)
I'M BACK, MIA.
KEPT YOUR PROMISE.
YES, OF COURSE I DID.

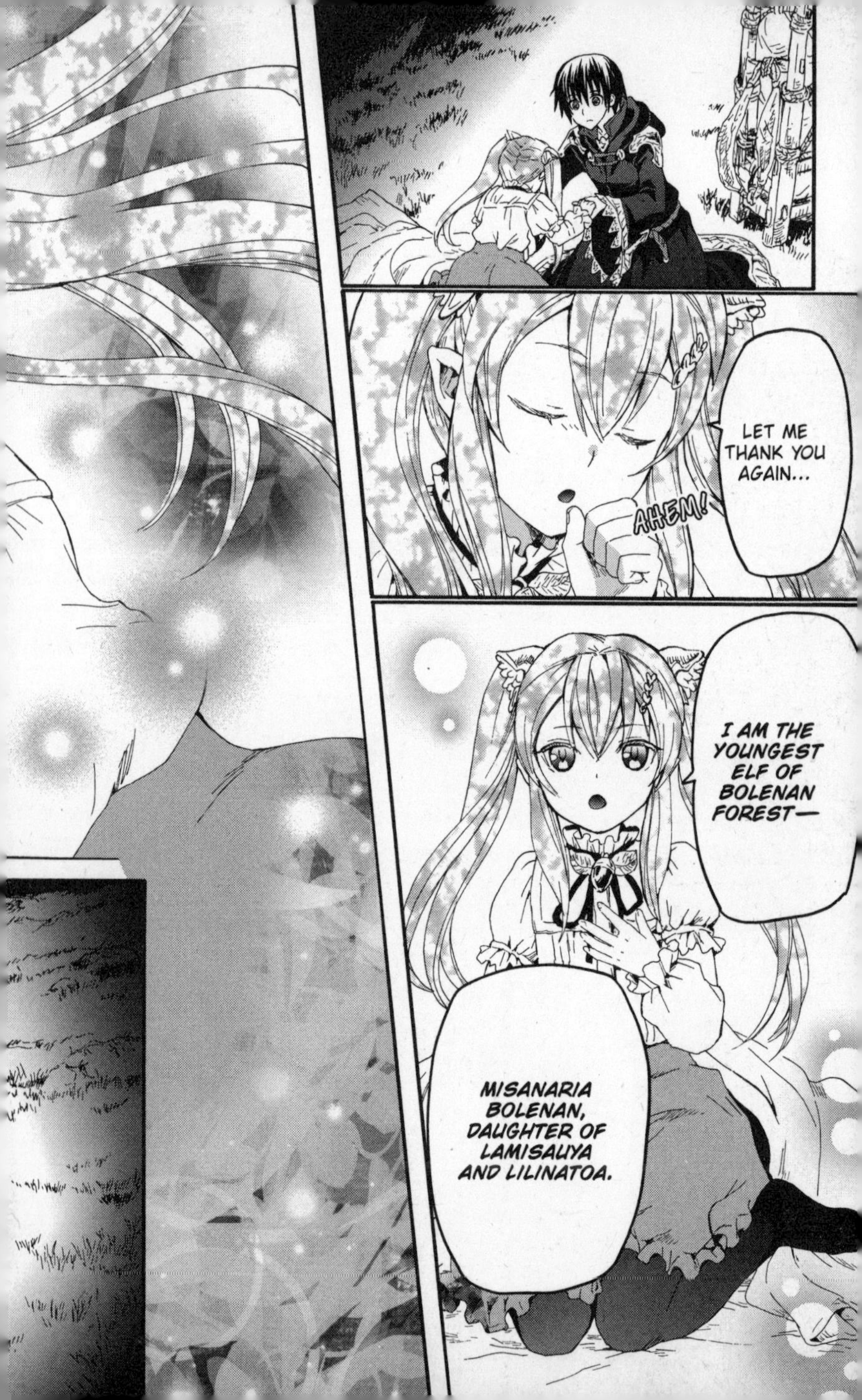
LET ME THANK YOU AGAIN...
AHEM!
I AM THE YOUNGEST ELF OF BOLENAN FOREST—
MISANARIA BOLENAN, DAUGHTER OF LAMISAUYA AND LILINATOA.

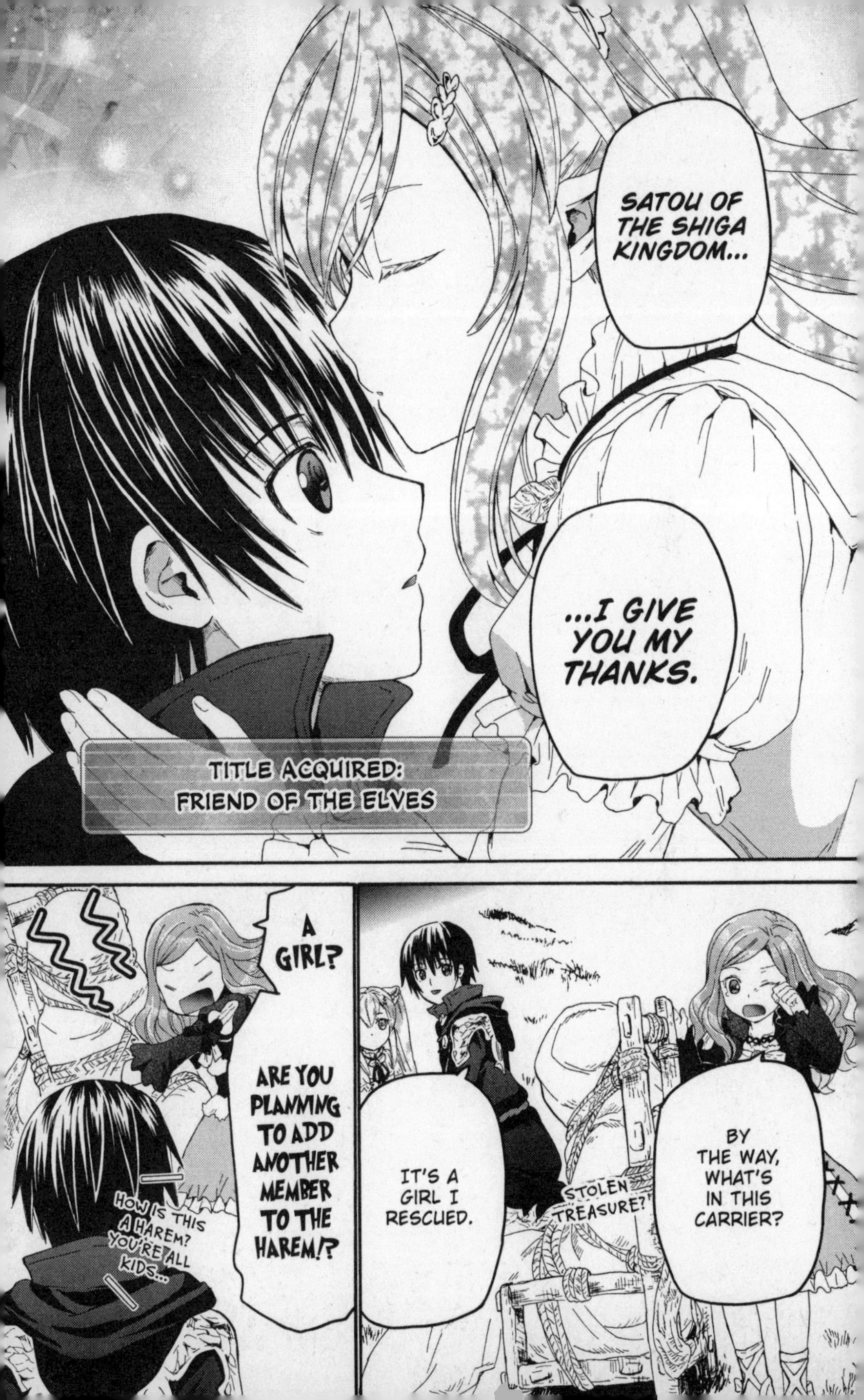
SATOU OF THE SHIGA KINGDOM...
...I GIVE YOU MY THANKS.
TITLE ACQUIRED: FRIEND OF THE ELVES
BY THE WAY, WHAT'S IN THIS CARRIER?
STOLEN TREASURE?
IT'S A GIRL I RESCUED.
A GIRL?
ARE YOU PLANNING TO ADD ANOTHER MEMBER TO THE HAREM!?
HOW IS THIS A HAREM? YOU'RE ALL KIDS...

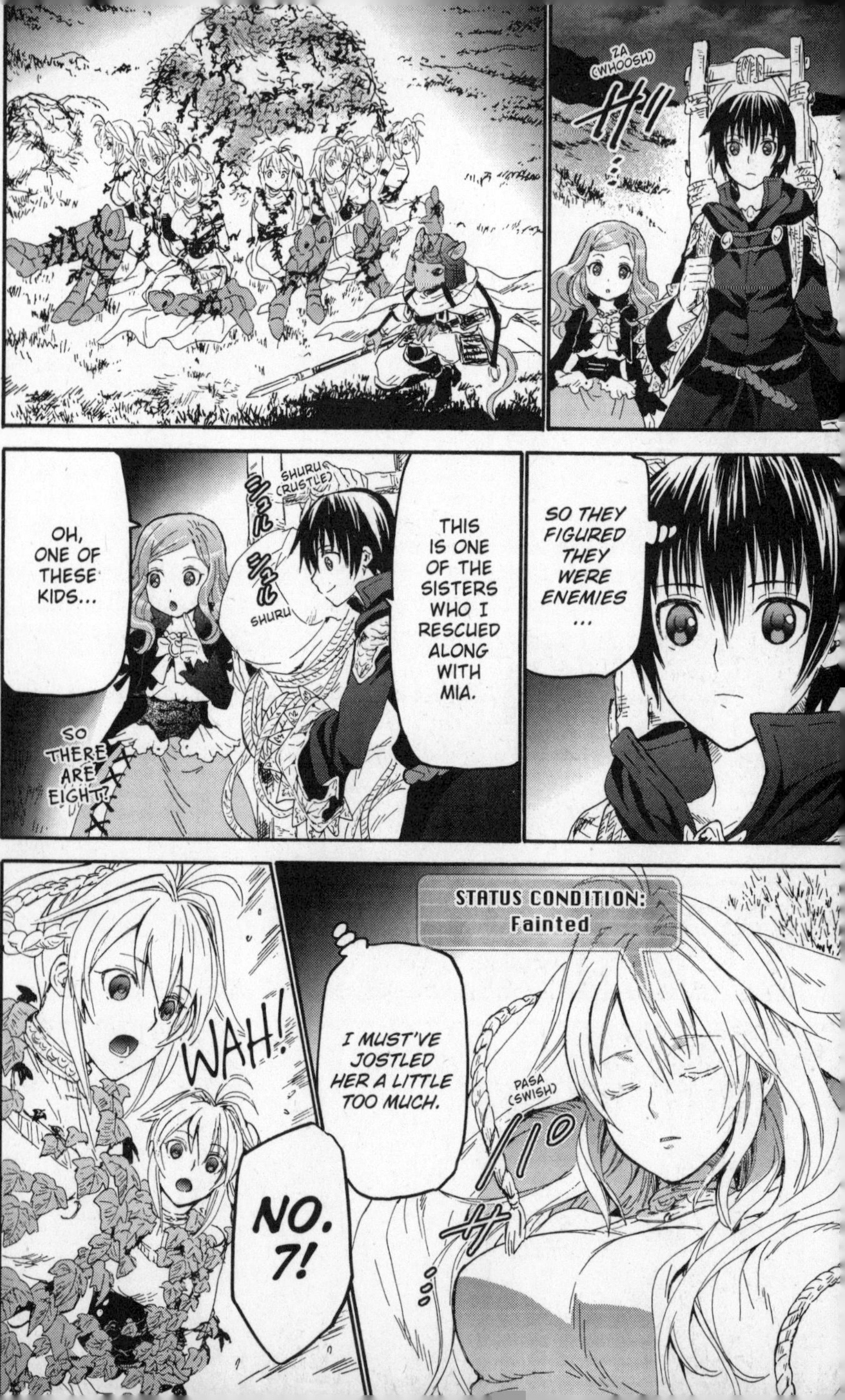
ZA (WHOOSH)
SO THEY FIGURED THEY WERE ENEMIES...
SHURU (RUSTLE)
THIS IS ONE OF THE SISTERS WHO I RESCUED ALONG WITH MIA.
SHURU
OH, ONE OF THESE KIDS...
SO THERE ARE EIGHT?
STATUS CONDITION:
Fainted
PASA (SWISH)
I MUST'VE JOSTLED HER A LITTLE TOO MUCH.
WAH!
NO. 7!

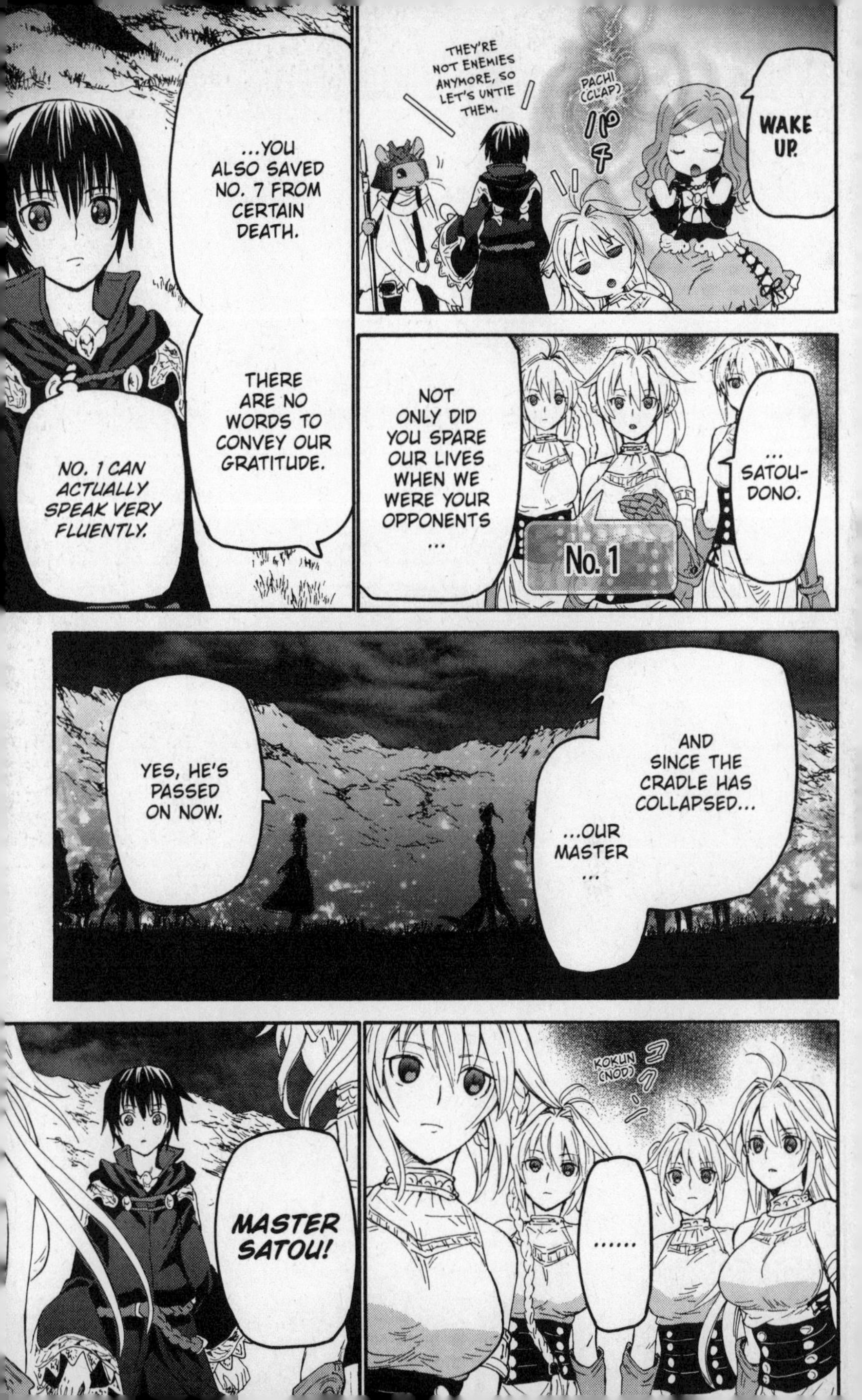
WAKE UP.
PACHI (CLAP)
THEY'RE NOT ENEMIES ANYMORE, SO LET'S UNTIE THEM.
...SATOU-DONO.
No. 1
NOT ONLY DID YOU SPARE OUR LIVES WHEN WE WERE YOUR OPPONENTS...
...YOU ALSO SAVED NO. 7 FROM CERTAIN DEATH.
THERE ARE NO WORDS TO CONVEY OUR GRATITUDE.
NO. 1 CAN ACTUALLY SPEAK VERY FLUENTLY.
AND SINCE THE CRADLE HAS COLLAPSED...
...OUR MASTER...
YES, HE'S PASSED ON NOW.
KOKUN (NOD)
......
MASTER SATOU!

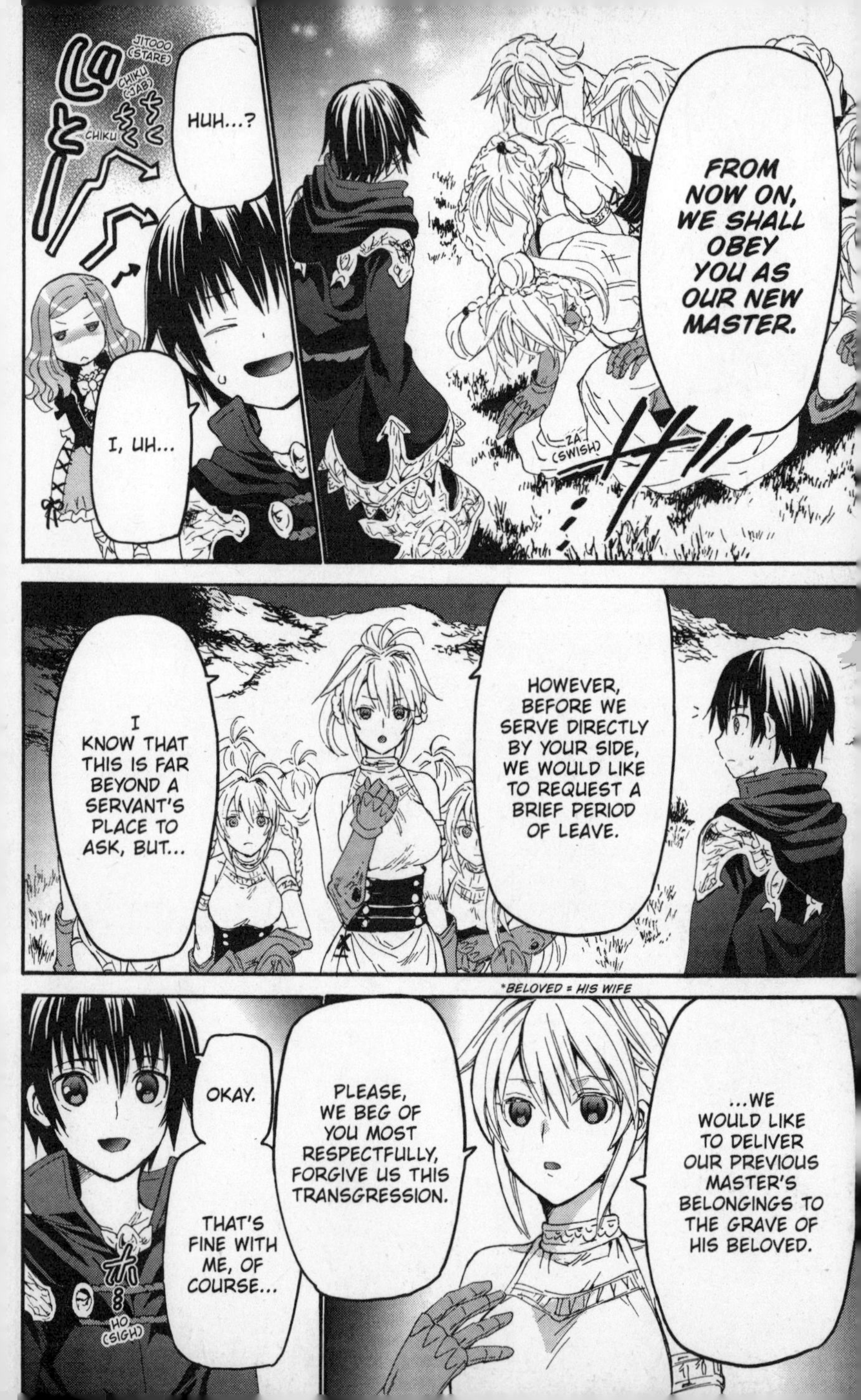
FROM NOW ON, WE SHALL OBEY YOU AS OUR NEW MASTER.
ZA (SWISH)
HUH...?
JITOOO (STARE)
CHIKU (JAB)
CHIKU
I, UH...
HOWEVER, BEFORE WE SERVE DIRECTLY BY YOUR SIDE, WE WOULD LIKE TO REQUEST A BRIEF PERIOD OF LEAVE.
I KNOW THAT THIS IS FAR BEYOND A SERVANT'S PLACE TO ASK, BUT...
*BELOVED = HIS WIFE
...WE WOULD LIKE TO DELIVER OUR PREVIOUS MASTER'S BELONGINGS TO THE GRAVE OF HIS BELOVED.
PLEASE, WE BEG OF YOU MOST RESPECTFULLY, FORGIVE US THIS TRANSGRESSION.
OKAY.
THAT'S FINE WITH ME, OF COURSE...
HO (SIGH)

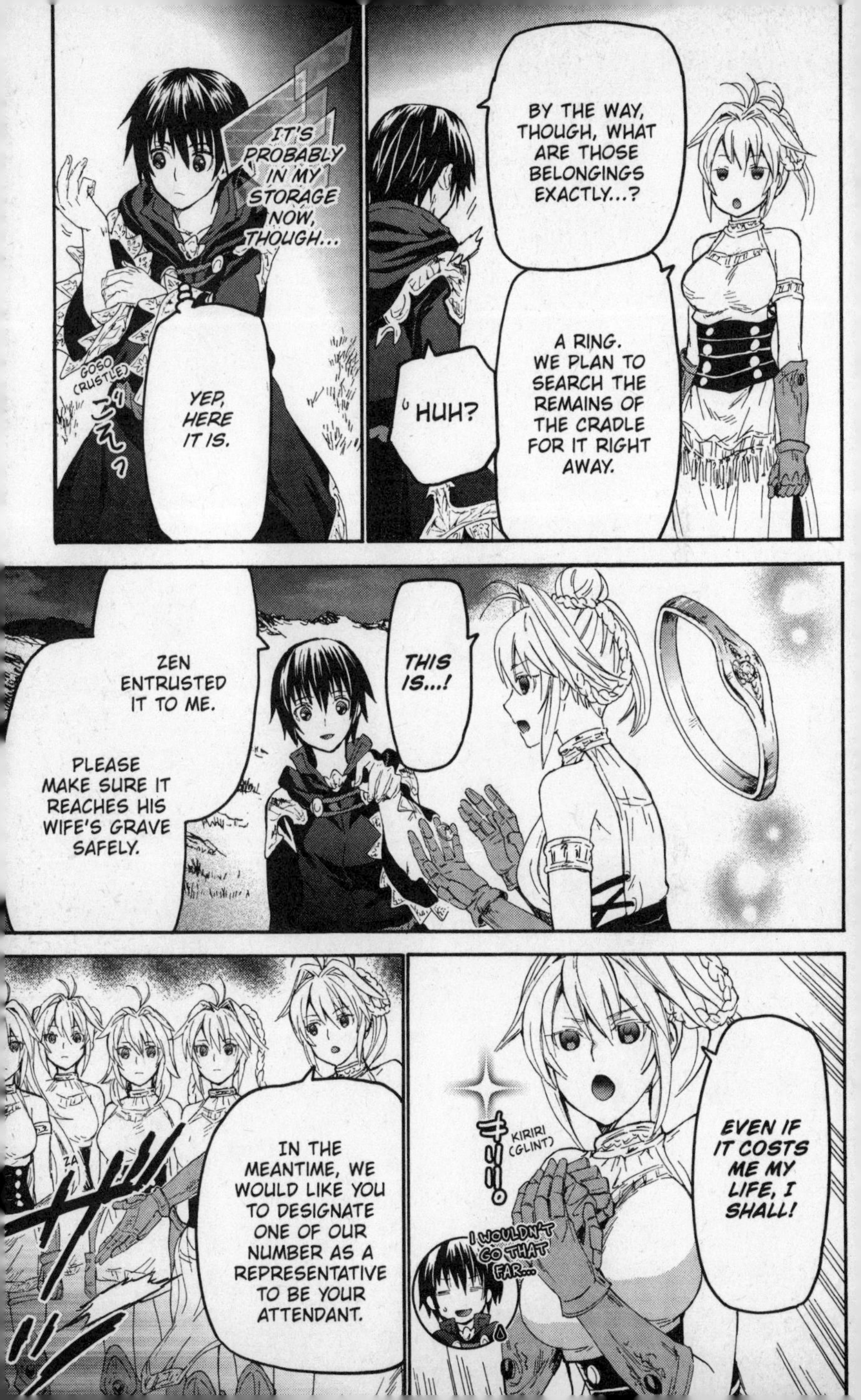
BY THE WAY, THOUGH, WHAT ARE THOSE BELONGINGS EXACTLY...?
A RING. WE PLAN TO SEARCH THE REMAINS OF THE CRADLE FOR IT RIGHT AWAY.
HUH?
IT'S PROBABLY IN MY STORAGE NOW, THOUGH...
GOSO (RUSTLE)
YEP, HERE IT IS.
THIS IS...!
ZEN ENTRUSTED IT TO ME.
PLEASE MAKE SURE IT REACHES HIS WIFE'S GRAVE SAFELY.
EVEN IF IT COSTS ME MY LIFE, I SHALL!
KIRIRI (GLINT)
I WOULDN'T GO THAT FAR...
IN THE MEANTIME, WE WOULD LIKE YOU TO DESIGNATE ONE OF OUR NUMBER AS A REPRESENTATIVE TO BE YOUR ATTENDANT.
ZA

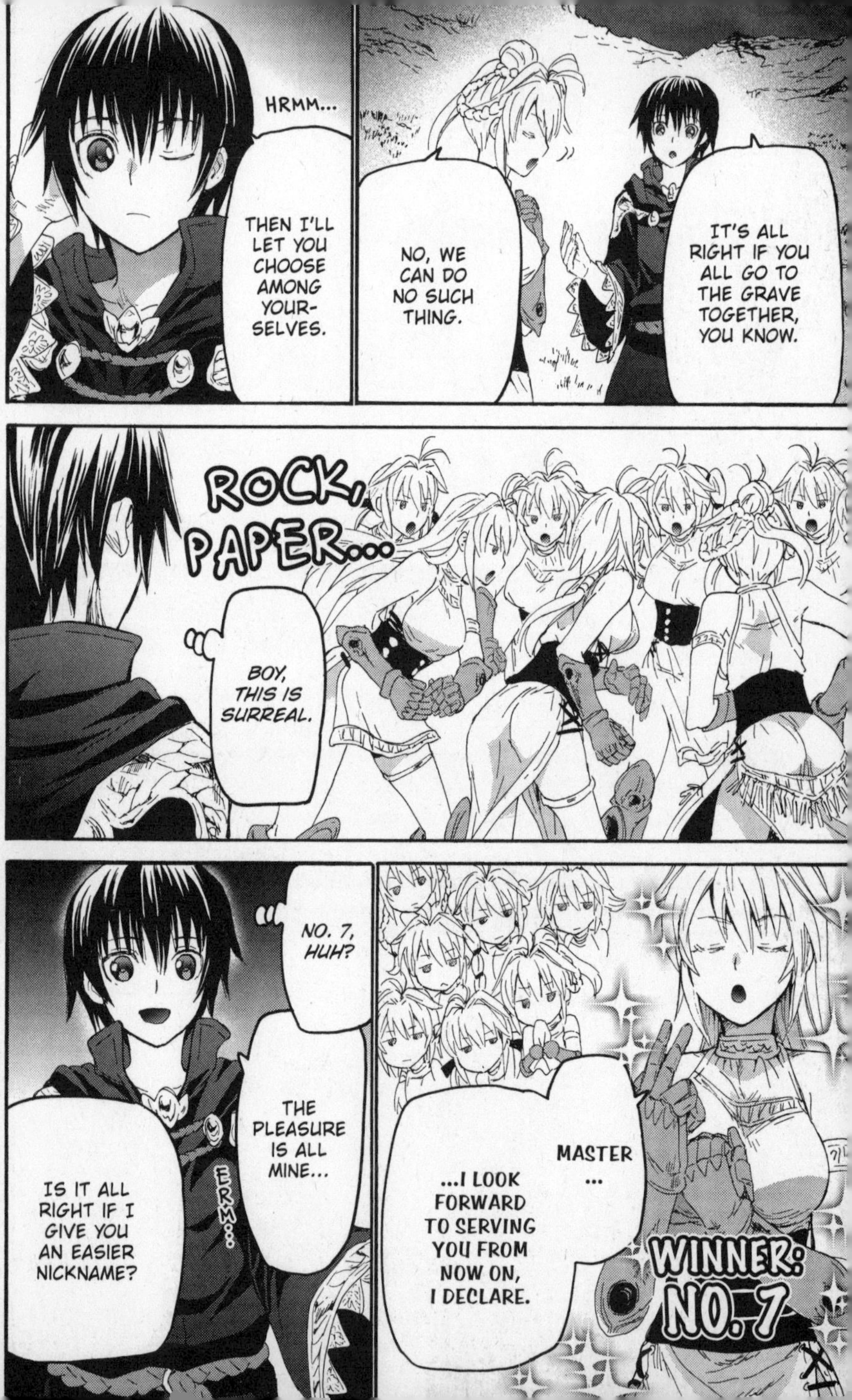
IT'S ALL RIGHT IF YOU ALL GO TO THE GRAVE TOGETHER, YOU KNOW.
NO, WE CAN DO NO SUCH THING.
HRMM...
THEN I'LL LET YOU CHOOSE AMONG YOUR-SELVES.
ROCK, PAPER...
BOY, THIS IS SURREAL.
MASTER...
...I LOOK FORWARD TO SERVING YOU FROM NOW ON, I DECLARE.
WINNER: NO. 7
NO. 7, HUH?
THE PLEASURE IS ALL MINE...
ERM...
IS IT ALL RIGHT IF I GIVE YOU AN EASIER NICKNAME?

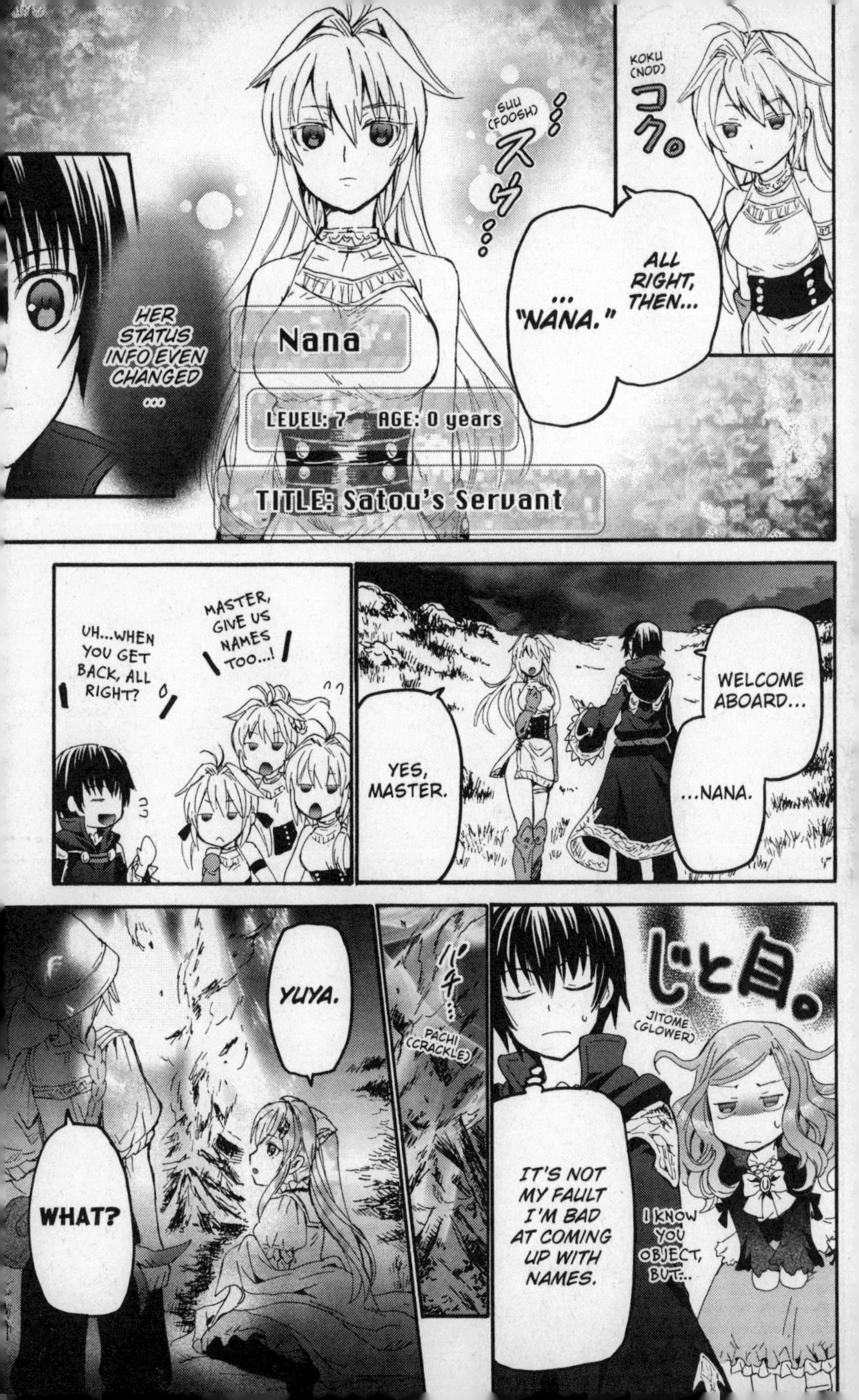
KOKU (NOD)
コク。
ALL RIGHT, THEN...
... "NANA."
SUU (FOOSH)
スゥ...
Nana
LEVEL: 7 AGE: 0 years
TITLE: Satou's Servant
HER STATUS INFO EVEN CHANGED...
WELCOME ABOARD...
...NANA.
YES, MASTER.
MASTER, GIVE US NAMES TOO...!
UH...WHEN YOU GET BACK, ALL RIGHT?
じと目。
JITOME (GLOWER)
I KNOW YOU OBJECT, BUT...
IT'S NOT MY FAULT I'M BAD AT COMING UP WITH NAMES.
パチ...
PACHI (CRACKLE)
YUYA.
WHAT?

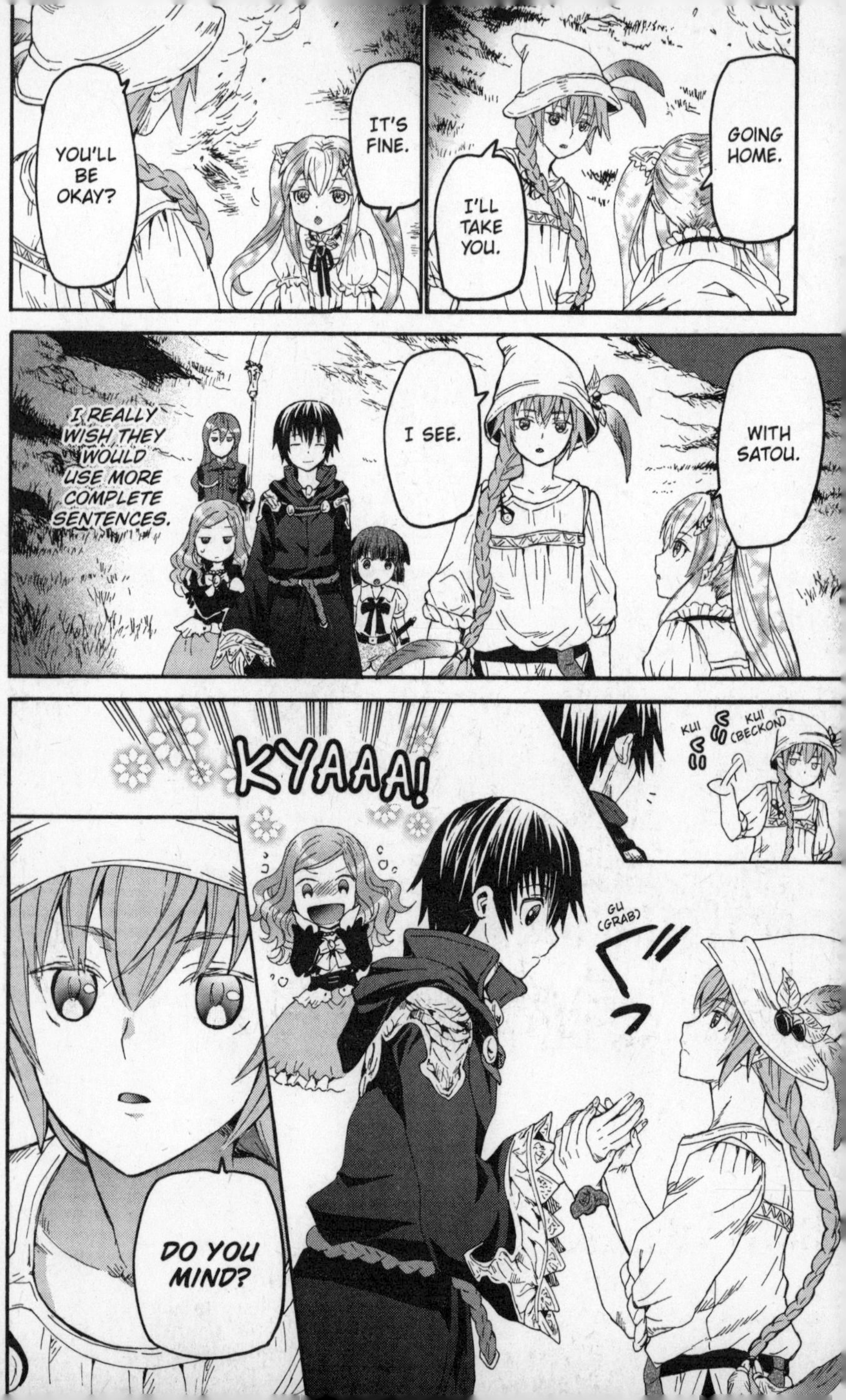
GOING HOME.
I'LL TAKE YOU.
IT'S FINE.
YOU'LL BE OKAY?
WITH SATOU.
I SEE.
I REALLY WISH THEY WOULD USE MORE COMPLETE SENTENCES.
KUI KUI (BECKON)
KYAAA!
GU (GRAB)
DO YOU MIND?

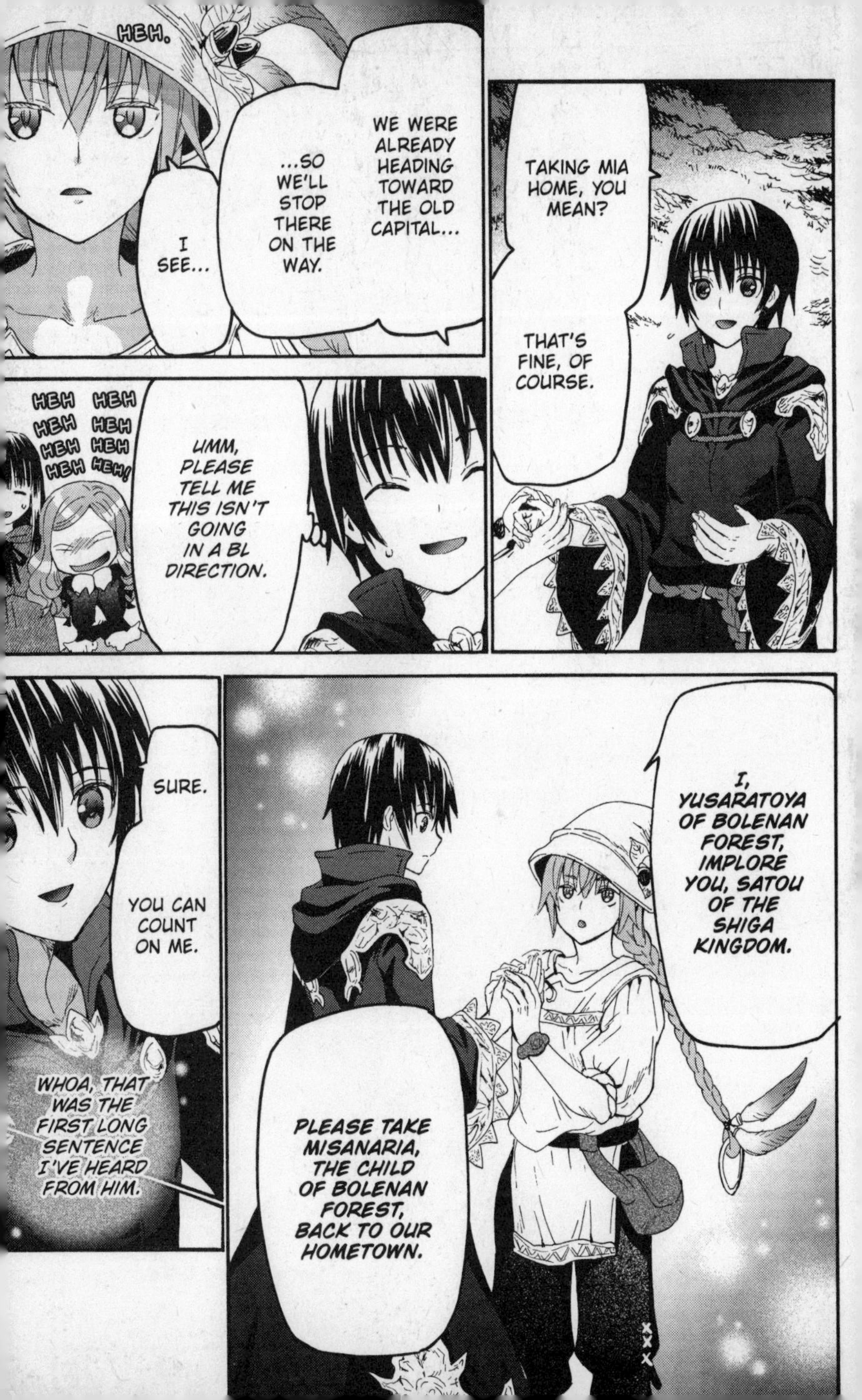
HEH.
I SEE...
WE WERE ALREADY HEADING TOWARD THE OLD CAPITAL...
...SO WE'LL STOP THERE ON THE WAY.
TAKING MIA HOME, YOU MEAN?
THAT'S FINE, OF COURSE.
UMM, PLEASE TELL ME THIS ISN'T GOING IN A BL DIRECTION.
HEH HEH HEH HEH HEH HEH HEH HEH!
I, YUSARATOYA OF BOLENAN FOREST, IMPLORE YOU, SATOU OF THE SHIGA KINGDOM.
PLEASE TAKE MISANARIA, THE CHILD OF BOLENAN FOREST, BACK TO OUR HOMETOWN.
SURE.
YOU CAN COUNT ON ME.
WHOA, THAT WAS THE FIRST LONG SENTENCE I'VE HEARD FROM HIM.

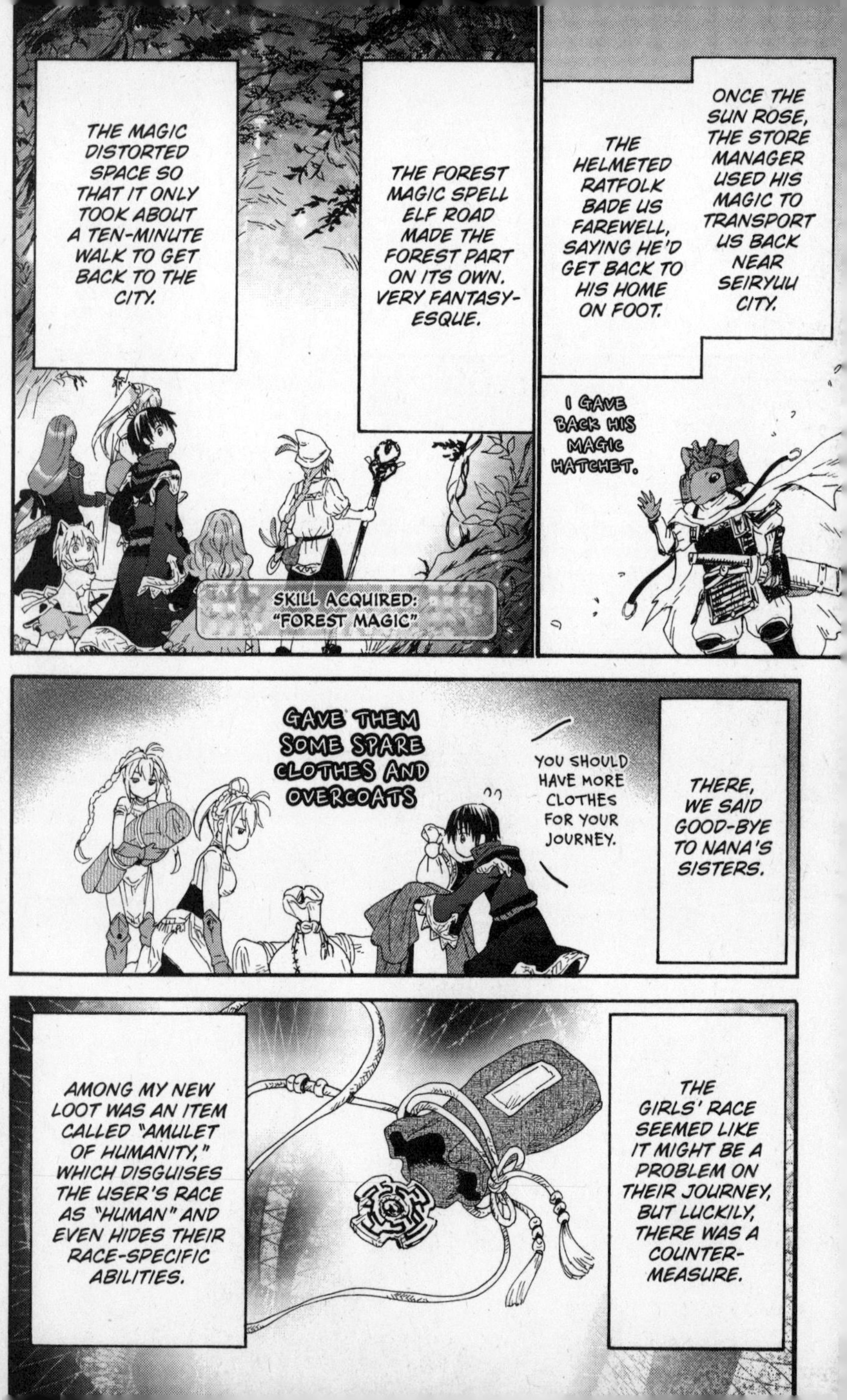
ONCE THE SUN ROSE, THE STORE MANAGER USED HIS MAGIC TO TRANSPORT US BACK NEAR SEIRYUU CITY.
THE HELMETED RATFOLK BADE US FAREWELL, SAYING HE'D GET BACK TO HIS HOME ON FOOT.
I GAVE BACK HIS MAGIC HATCHET.
THE FOREST MAGIC SPELL ELF ROAD MADE THE FOREST PART ON ITS OWN. VERY FANTASY-ESQUE.
THE MAGIC DISTORTED SPACE SO THAT IT ONLY TOOK ABOUT A TEN-MINUTE WALK TO GET BACK TO THE CITY.
SKILL ACQUIRED: "FOREST MAGIC"
THERE, WE SAID GOOD-BYE TO NANA'S SISTERS.
YOU SHOULD HAVE MORE CLOTHES FOR YOUR JOURNEY.
GAVE THEM SOME SPARE CLOTHES AND OVERCOATS
THE GIRLS' RACE SEEMED LIKE IT MIGHT BE A PROBLEM ON THEIR JOURNEY, BUT LUCKILY, THERE WAS A COUNTER-MEASURE.
AMONG MY NEW LOOT WAS AN ITEM CALLED "AMULET OF HUMANITY," WHICH DISGUISES THE USER'S RACE AS "HUMAN" AND EVEN HIDES THEIR RACE-SPECIFIC ABILITIES.

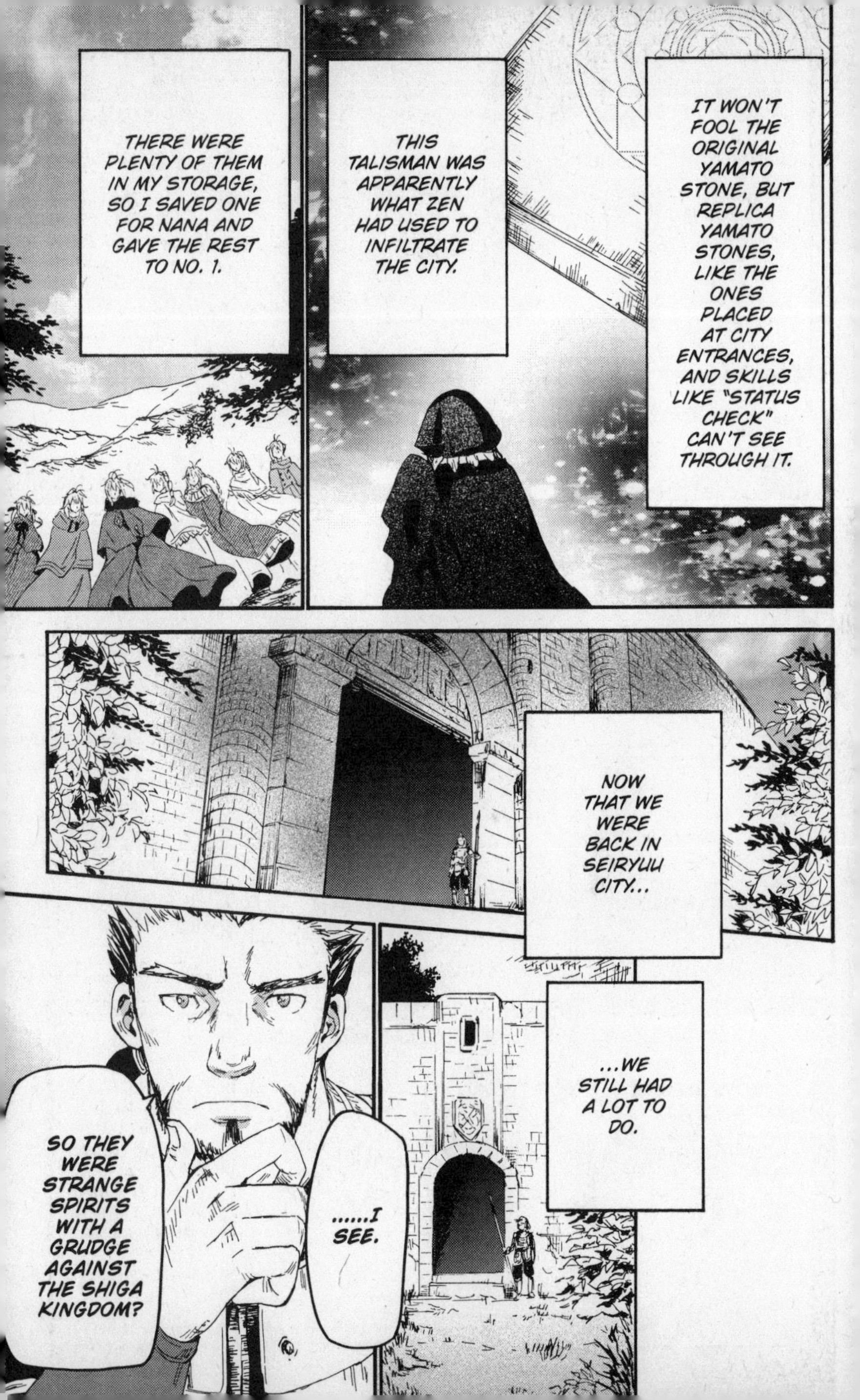

IT WON'T FOOL THE ORIGINAL YAMATO STONE, BUT REPLICA YAMATO STONES, LIKE THE ONES PLACED AT CITY ENTRANCES, AND SKILLS LIKE "STATUS CHECK" CAN'T SEE THROUGH IT.
THIS TALISMAN WAS APPARENTLY WHAT ZEN HAD USED TO INFILTRATE THE CITY.
THERE WERE PLENTY OF THEM IN MY STORAGE, SO I SAVED ONE FOR NANA AND GAVE THE REST TO NO. 1.
NOW THAT WE WERE BACK IN SEIRYUU CITY...
...WE STILL HAD A LOT TO DO.
......I SEE.
SO THEY WERE STRANGE SPIRITS WITH A GRUDGE AGAINST THE SHIGA KINGDOM?

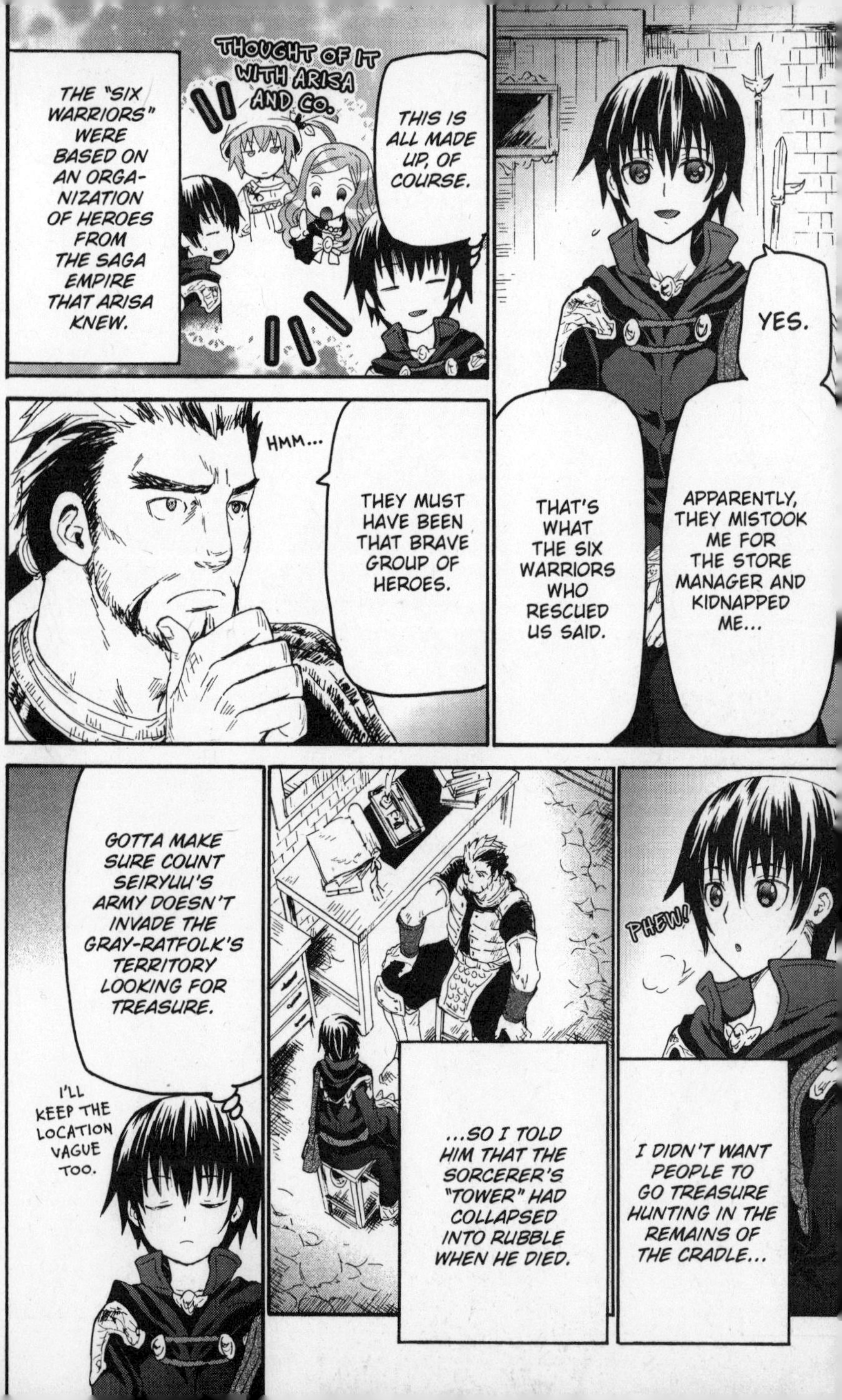
YES.
APPARENTLY, THEY MISTOOK ME FOR THE STORE MANAGER AND KIDNAPPED ME...
THAT'S WHAT THE SIX WARRIORS WHO RESCUED US SAID.
THIS IS ALL MADE UP, OF COURSE.
THOUGHT OF IT WITH ARISA AND CO.
THE "SIX WARRIORS" WERE BASED ON AN ORGA-NIZATION OF HEROES FROM THE SAGA EMPIRE THAT ARISA KNEW.
HMM...
THEY MUST HAVE BEEN THAT BRAVE GROUP OF HEROES.
PHEW!
I DIDN'T WANT PEOPLE TO GO TREASURE HUNTING IN THE REMAINS OF THE CRADLE...
...SO I TOLD HIM THAT THE SORCERER'S "TOWER" HAD COLLAPSED INTO RUBBLE WHEN HE DIED.
GOTTA MAKE SURE COUNT SEIRYUU'S ARMY DOESN'T INVADE THE GRAY-RATFOLK'S TERRITORY LOOKING FOR TREASURE.
I'LL KEEP THE LOCATION VAGUE TOO.

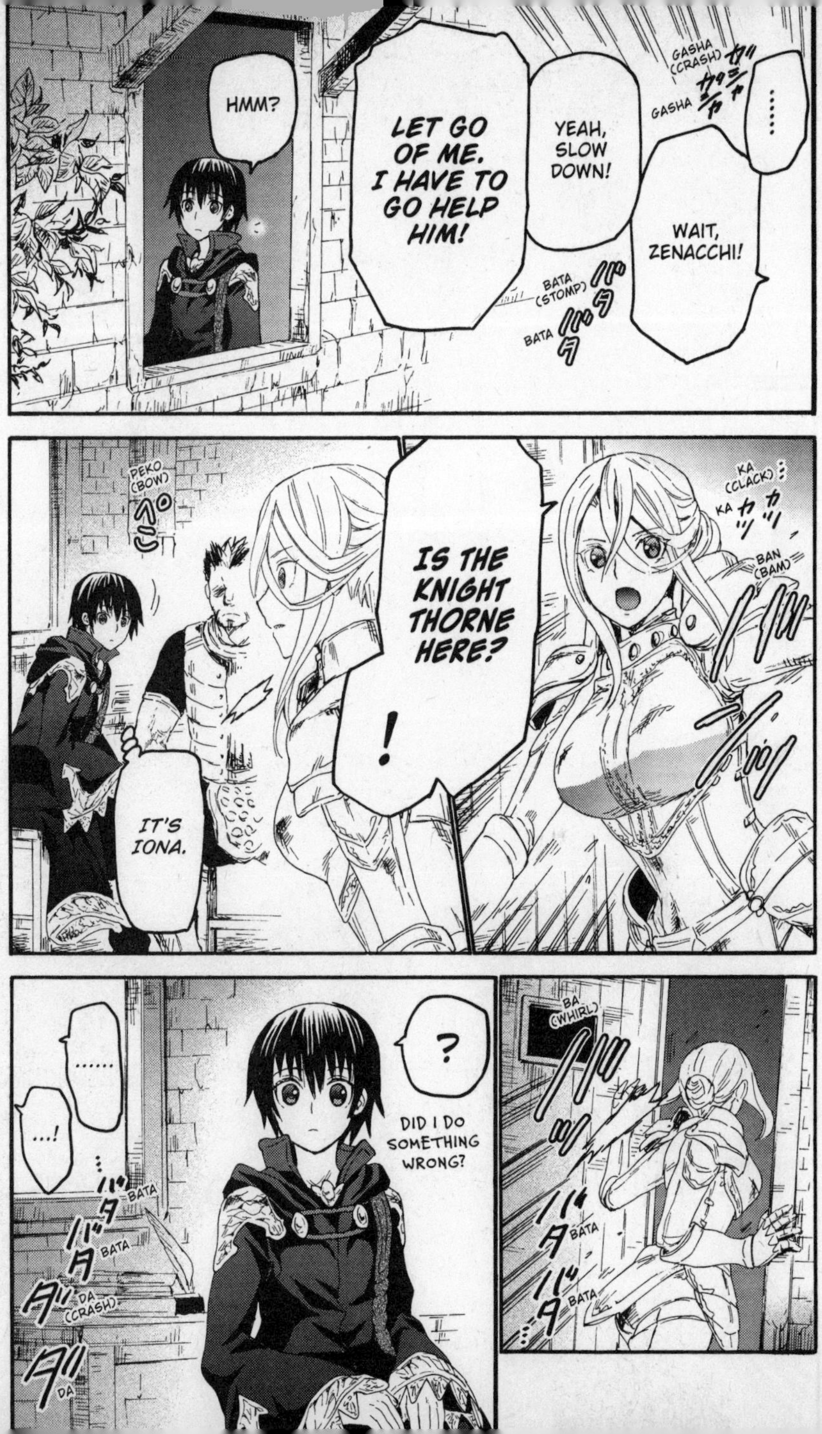
GASHA (CRASH)
GASHA
......
WAIT, ZENACCHI!
YEAH, SLOW DOWN!
LET GO OF ME. I HAVE TO GO HELP HIM!
BATA (STOMP)
BATA
HMM?
KA (CLACK)
KA
BAN (BAM)
IS THE KNIGHT THORNE HERE?
!
PEKO (BOW)
IT'S IONA.
BA (WHIRL)
BATA
BATA
?
DID I DO SOMETHING WRONG?
......
...!
BATA
BATA
DA (CRASH)
DA

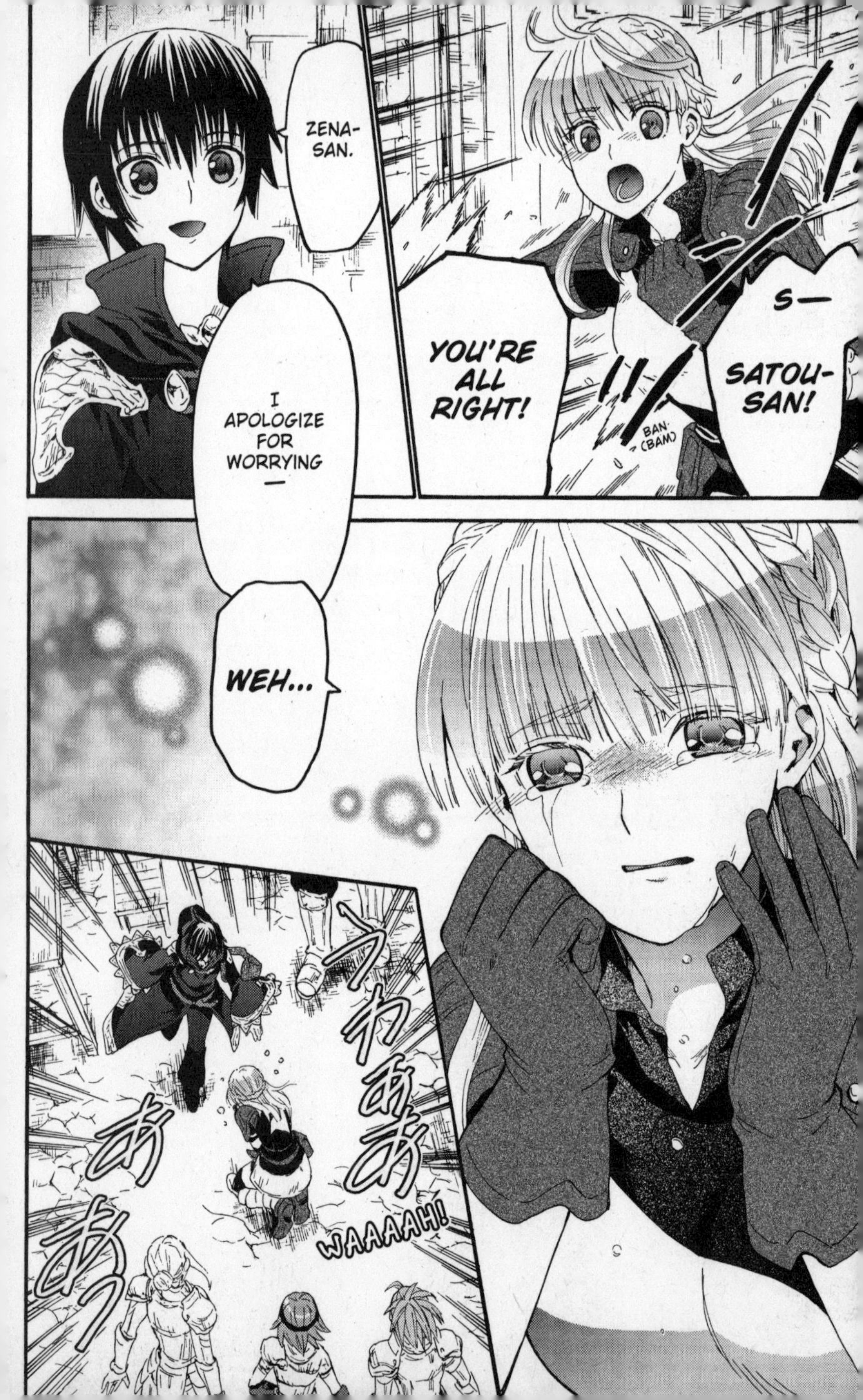
S—
SATOU-SAN!
YOU'RE ALL RIGHT!
BAN (BAM)
ZENA-SAN.
I APOLOGIZE FOR WORRYING—
WEH...
うわああああっ
WAAAAH!

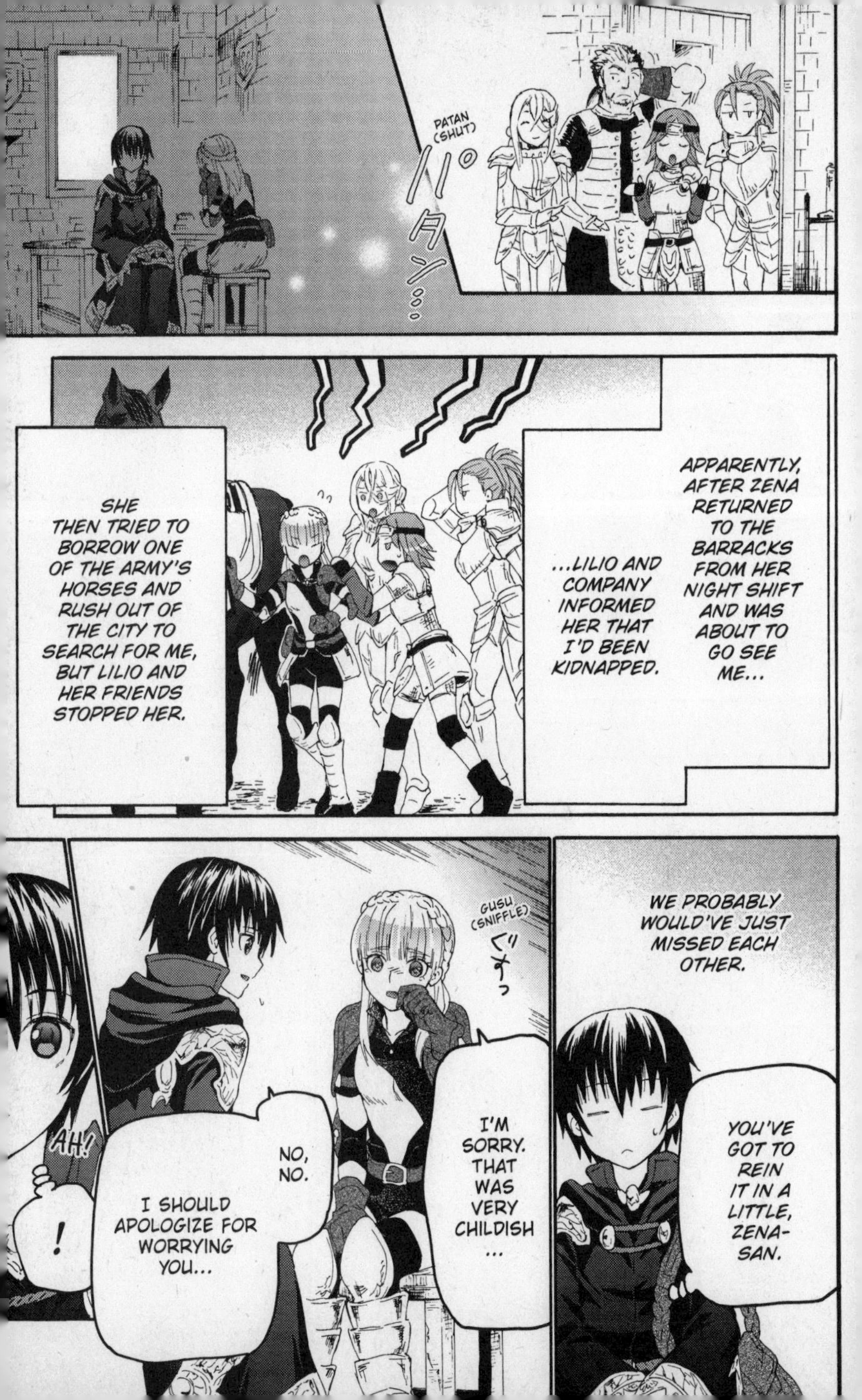
PATAN (SHUT)
パタン…
APPARENTLY, AFTER ZENA RETURNED TO THE BARRACKS FROM HER NIGHT SHIFT AND WAS ABOUT TO GO SEE ME…
…LILIO AND COMPANY INFORMED HER THAT I'D BEEN KIDNAPPED.
SHE THEN TRIED TO BORROW ONE OF THE ARMY'S HORSES AND RUSH OUT OF THE CITY TO SEARCH FOR ME, BUT LILIO AND HER FRIENDS STOPPED HER.
WE PROBABLY WOULD'VE JUST MISSED EACH OTHER.
YOU'VE GOT TO REIN IT IN A LITTLE, ZENA-SAN.
GUSU (SNIFFLE)
ぐすっ
I'M SORRY. THAT WAS VERY CHILDISH…
NO, NO.
I SHOULD APOLOGIZE FOR WORRYING YOU…
AH!
!

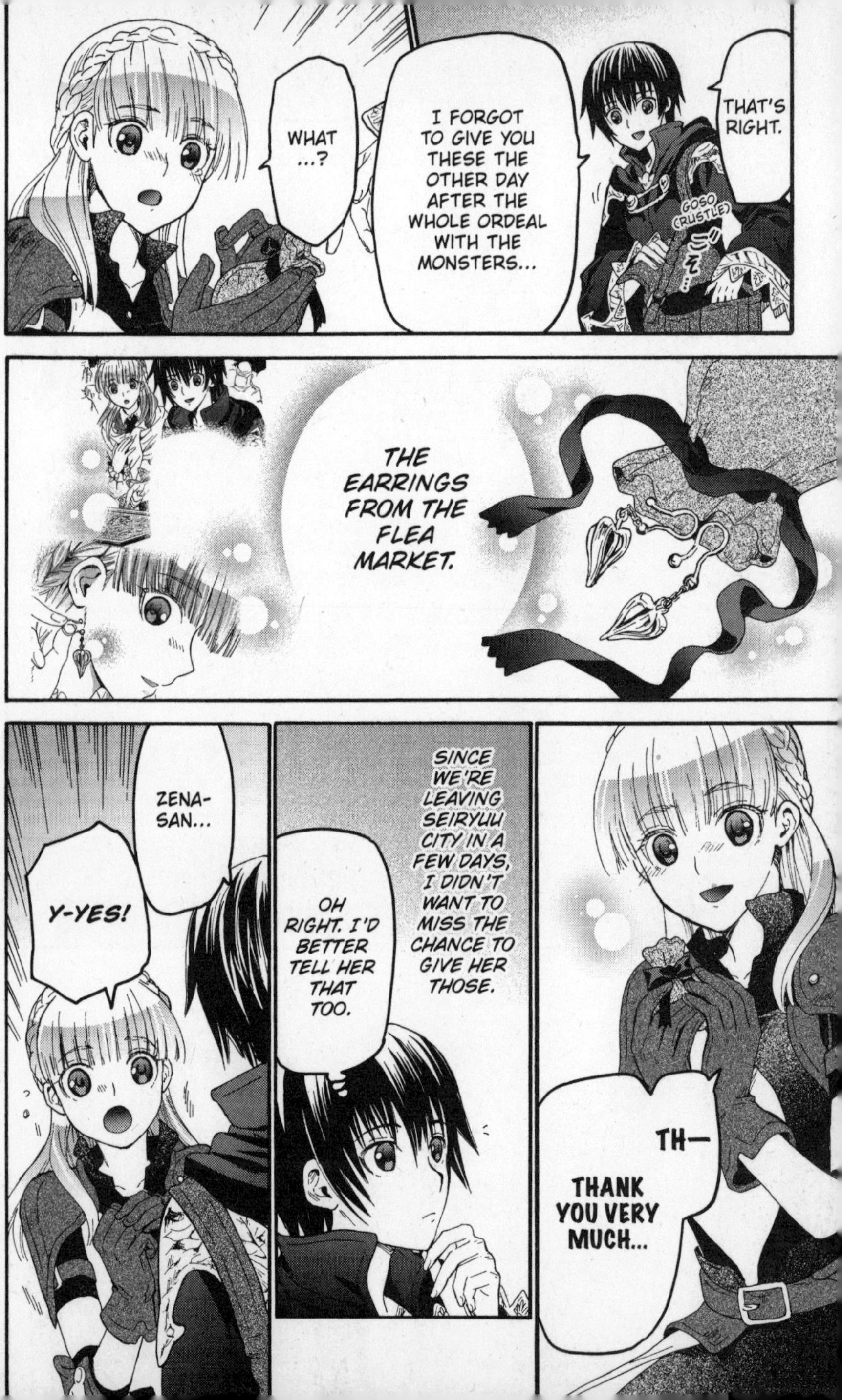
THAT'S RIGHT.
GOSO (RUSTLE)
I FORGOT TO GIVE YOU THESE THE OTHER DAY AFTER THE WHOLE ORDEAL WITH THE MONSTERS...
WHAT ...?
THE EARRINGS FROM THE FLEA MARKET.
TH—
THANK YOU VERY MUCH...
SINCE WE'RE LEAVING SEIRYUU CITY IN A FEW DAYS, I DIDN'T WANT TO MISS THE CHANCE TO GIVE HER THOSE.
OH RIGHT. I'D BETTER TELL HER THAT TOO.
ZENA-SAN...
Y-YES!

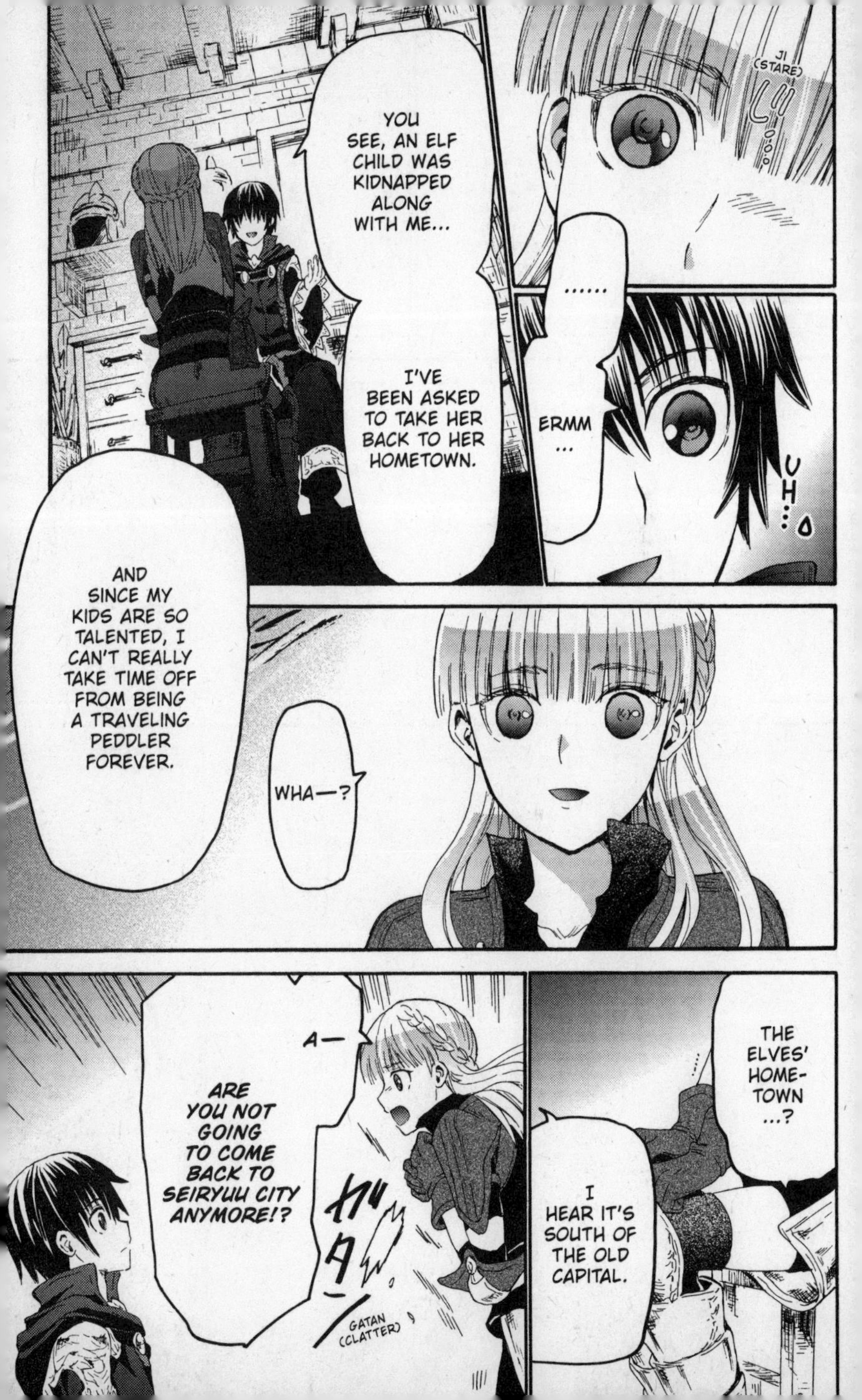
JI (STARE)
......
ERMM...
UH...
YOU SEE, AN ELF CHILD WAS KIDNAPPED ALONG WITH ME...
I'VE BEEN ASKED TO TAKE HER BACK TO HER HOMETOWN.
AND SINCE MY KIDS ARE SO TALENTED, I CAN'T REALLY TAKE TIME OFF FROM BEING A TRAVELING PEDDLER FOREVER.
WHA—?
THE ELVES' HOME-TOWN ...?
I HEAR IT'S SOUTH OF THE OLD CAPITAL.
A—
ARE YOU NOT GOING TO COME BACK TO SEIRYUU CITY ANYMORE!?
GATAN (CLATTER)

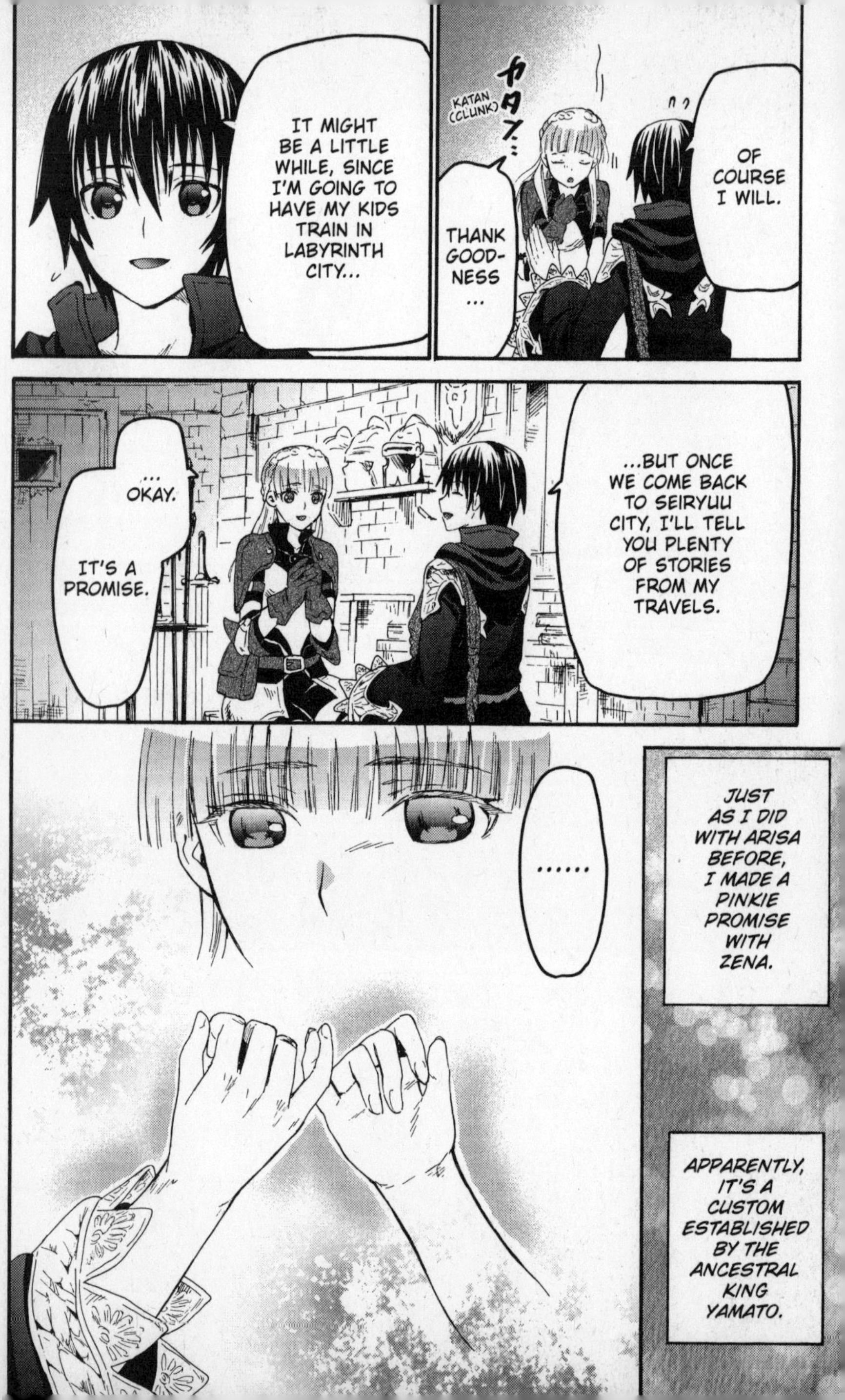
OF COURSE I WILL.
KATAN (CLUNK)
THANK GOODNESS...
IT MIGHT BE A LITTLE WHILE, SINCE I'M GOING TO HAVE MY KIDS TRAIN IN LABYRINTH CITY...
...BUT ONCE WE COME BACK TO SEIRYUU CITY, I'LL TELL YOU PLENTY OF STORIES FROM MY TRAVELS.
...OKAY.
IT'S A PROMISE.
JUST AS I DID WITH ARISA BEFORE, I MADE A PINKIE PROMISE WITH ZENA.
......
APPARENTLY, IT'S A CUSTOM ESTABLISHED BY THE ANCESTRAL KING YAMATO.

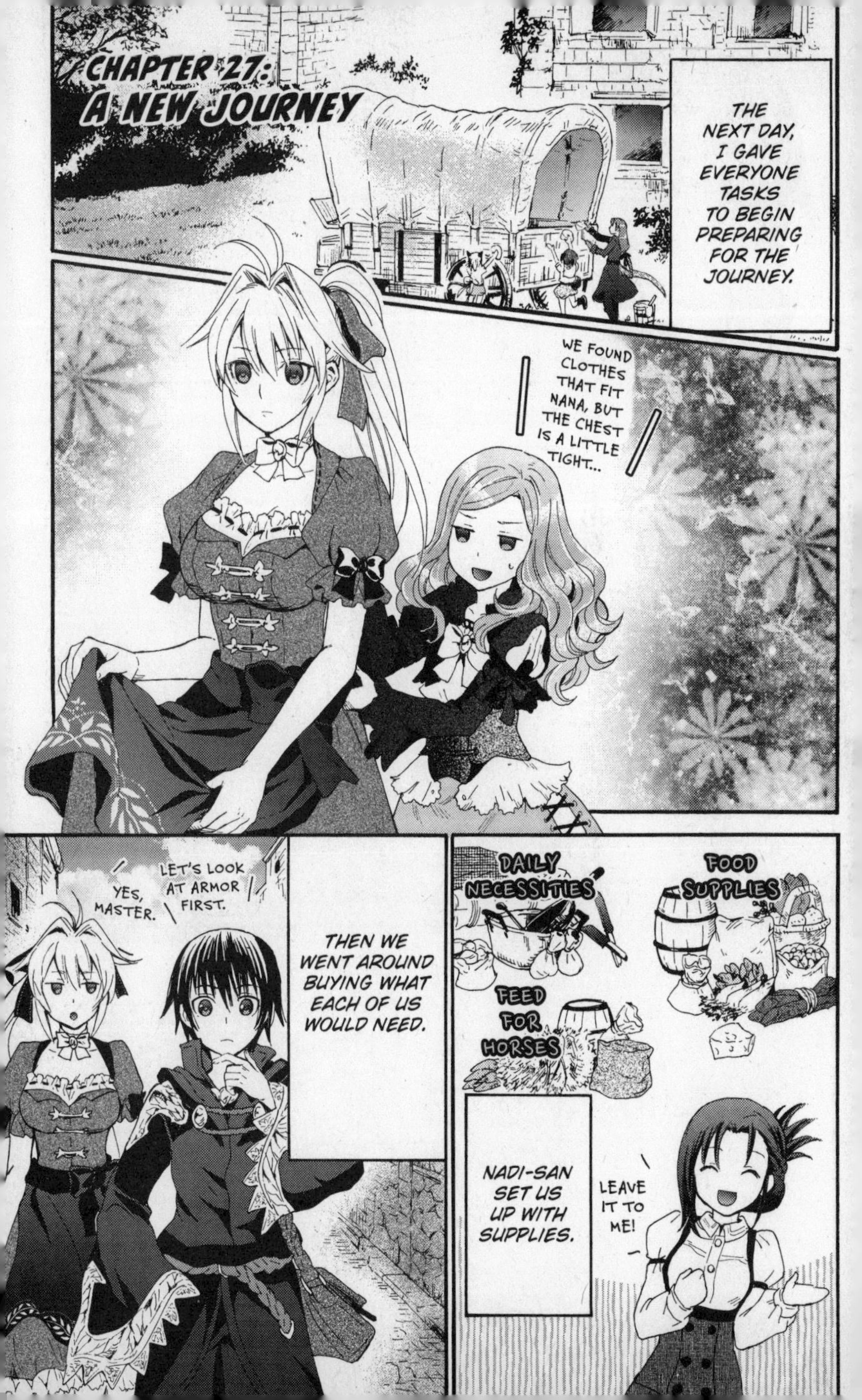
CHAPTER 27:
A NEW JOURNEY
THE NEXT DAY, I GAVE EVERYONE TASKS TO BEGIN PREPARING FOR THE JOURNEY.
WE FOUND CLOTHES THAT FIT NANA, BUT THE CHEST IS A LITTLE TIGHT...
DAILY NECESSITIES
FOOD SUPPLIES
FEED FOR HORSES
NADI-SAN SET US UP WITH SUPPLIES.
LEAVE IT TO ME!
THEN WE WENT AROUND BUYING WHAT EACH OF US WOULD NEED.
LET'S LOOK AT ARMOR FIRST.
YES, MASTER.

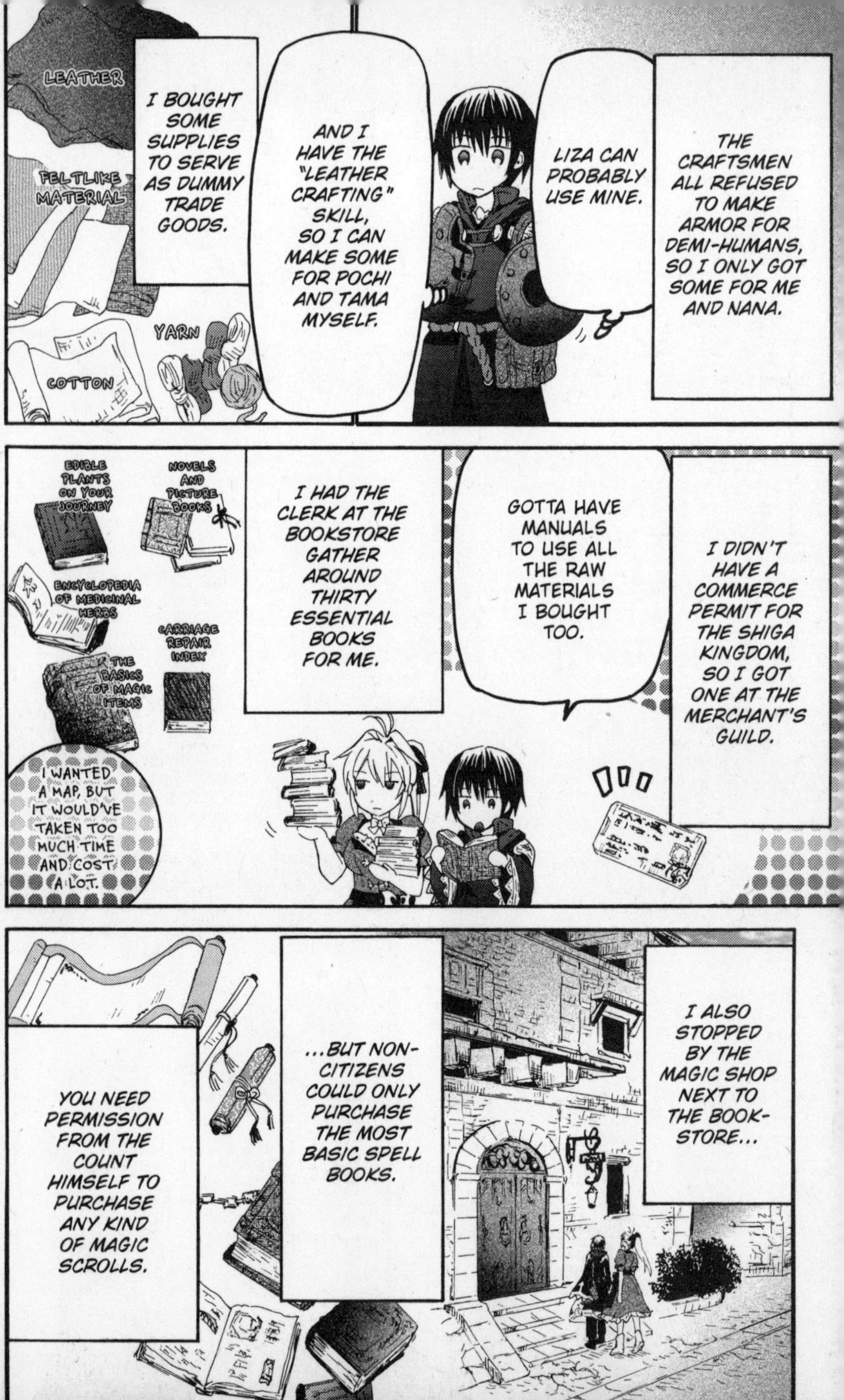
THE CRAFTSMEN ALL REFUSED TO MAKE ARMOR FOR DEMI-HUMANS, SO I ONLY GOT SOME FOR ME AND NANA.
LIZA CAN PROBABLY USE MINE.
AND I HAVE THE "LEATHER CRAFTING" SKILL, SO I CAN MAKE SOME FOR POCHI AND TAMA MYSELF.
I BOUGHT SOME SUPPLIES TO SERVE AS DUMMY TRADE GOODS.
LEATHER
FELTLIKE MATERIAL
YARN
COTTON
I DIDN'T HAVE A COMMERCE PERMIT FOR THE SHIGA KINGDOM, SO I GOT ONE AT THE MERCHANT'S GUILD.
GOTTA HAVE MANUALS TO USE ALL THE RAW MATERIALS I BOUGHT TOO.
I HAD THE CLERK AT THE BOOKSTORE GATHER AROUND THIRTY ESSENTIAL BOOKS FOR ME.
NOVELS AND PICTURE BOOKS
EDIBLE PLANTS ON YOUR JOURNEY
ENCYCLOPEDIA OF MEDICINAL HERBS
CARRIAGE REPAIR INDEX
THE BASICS OF MAGIC ITEMS
I WANTED A MAP, BUT IT WOULD'VE TAKEN TOO MUCH TIME AND COST A LOT.
I ALSO STOPPED BY THE MAGIC SHOP NEXT TO THE BOOK-STORE...
...BUT NON-CITIZENS COULD ONLY PURCHASE THE MOST BASIC SPELL BOOKS.
YOU NEED PERMISSION FROM THE COUNT HIMSELF TO PURCHASE ANY KIND OF MAGIC SCROLLS.

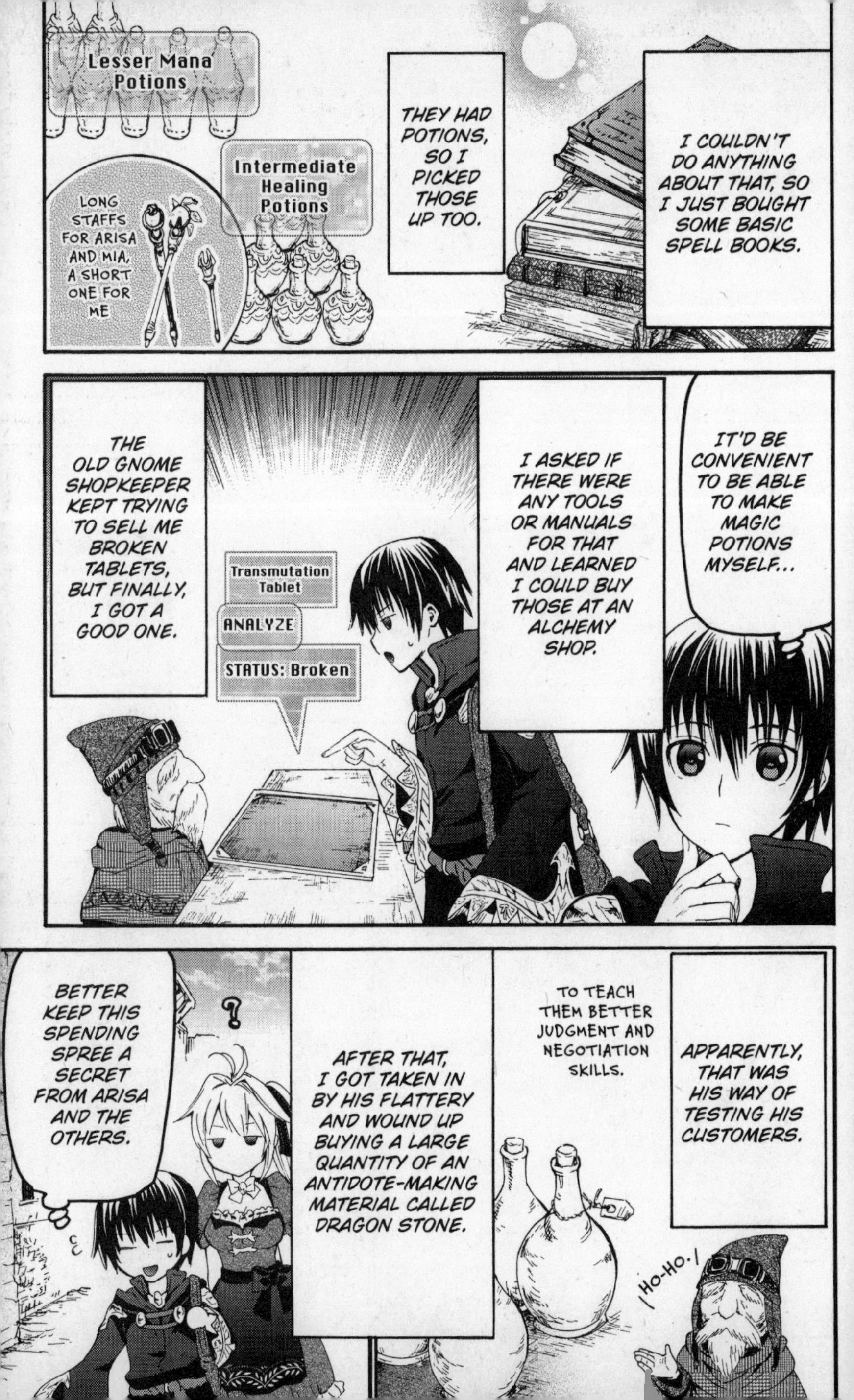
I COULDN'T DO ANYTHING ABOUT THAT, SO I JUST BOUGHT SOME BASIC SPELL BOOKS.
THEY HAD POTIONS, SO I PICKED THOSE UP TOO.
Lesser Mana Potions
Intermediate Healing Potions
LONG STAFFS FOR ARISA AND MIA, A SHORT ONE FOR ME
IT'D BE CONVENIENT TO BE ABLE TO MAKE MAGIC POTIONS MYSELF...
I ASKED IF THERE WERE ANY TOOLS OR MANUALS FOR THAT AND LEARNED I COULD BUY THOSE AT AN ALCHEMY SHOP.
Transmutation Tablet
ANALYZE
STATUS: Broken
THE OLD GNOME SHOPKEEPER KEPT TRYING TO SELL ME BROKEN TABLETS, BUT FINALLY, I GOT A GOOD ONE.
APPARENTLY, THAT WAS HIS WAY OF TESTING HIS CUSTOMERS.
HO-HO-!
TO TEACH THEM BETTER JUDGMENT AND NEGOTIATION SKILLS.
AFTER THAT, I GOT TAKEN IN BY HIS FLATTERY AND WOUND UP BUYING A LARGE QUANTITY OF AN ANTIDOTE-MAKING MATERIAL CALLED DRAGON STONE.
?
BETTER KEEP THIS SPENDING SPREE A SECRET FROM ARISA AND THE OTHERS.

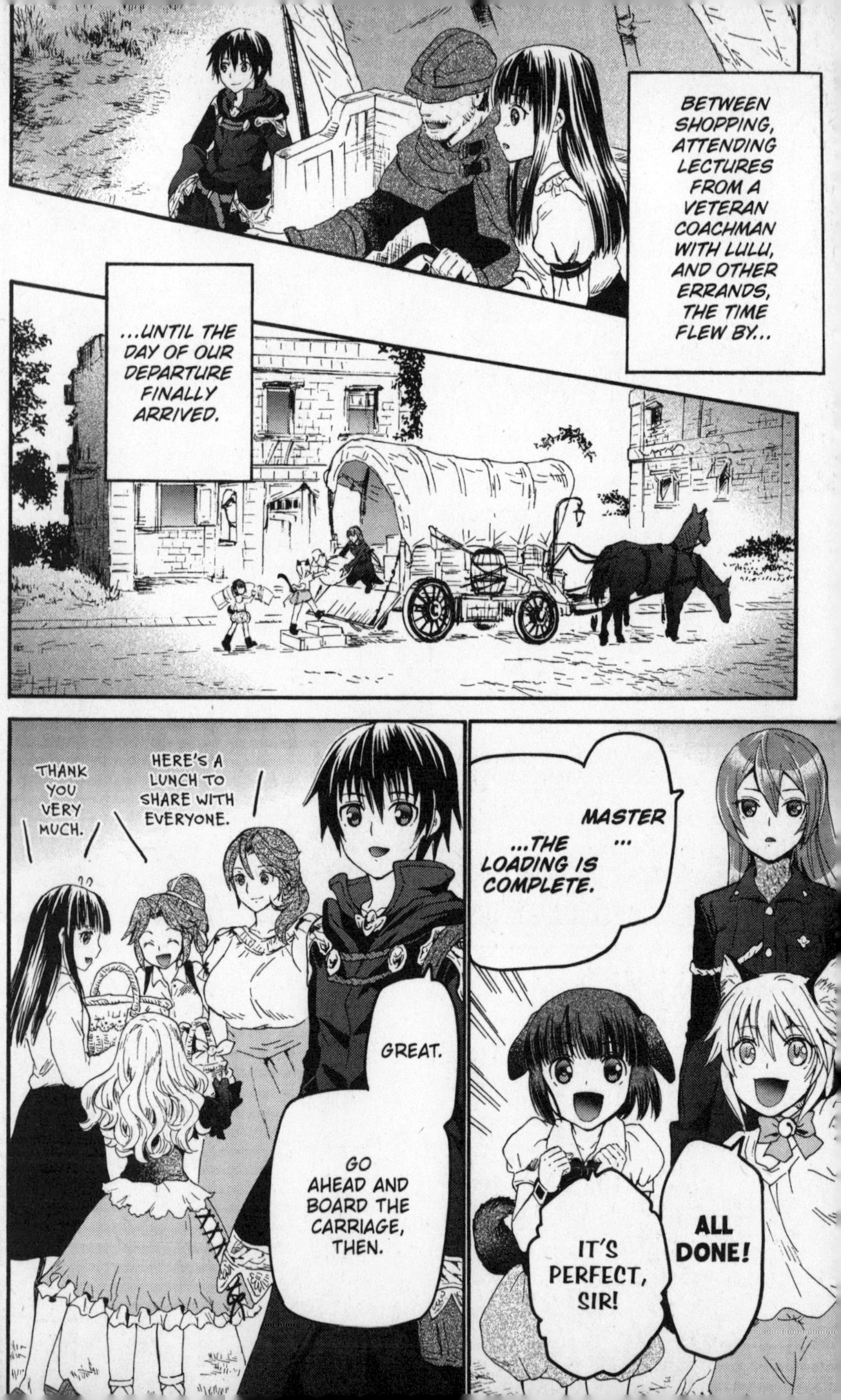
BETWEEN SHOPPING, ATTENDING LECTURES FROM A VETERAN COACHMAN WITH LULU, AND OTHER ERRANDS, THE TIME FLEW BY...
...UNTIL THE DAY OF OUR DEPARTURE FINALLY ARRIVED.
MASTER ...
...THE LOADING IS COMPLETE.
ALL DONE!
IT'S PERFECT, SIR!
HERE'S A LUNCH TO SHARE WITH EVERYONE.
THANK YOU VERY MUCH.
GREAT.
GO AHEAD AND BOARD THE CARRIAGE, THEN.

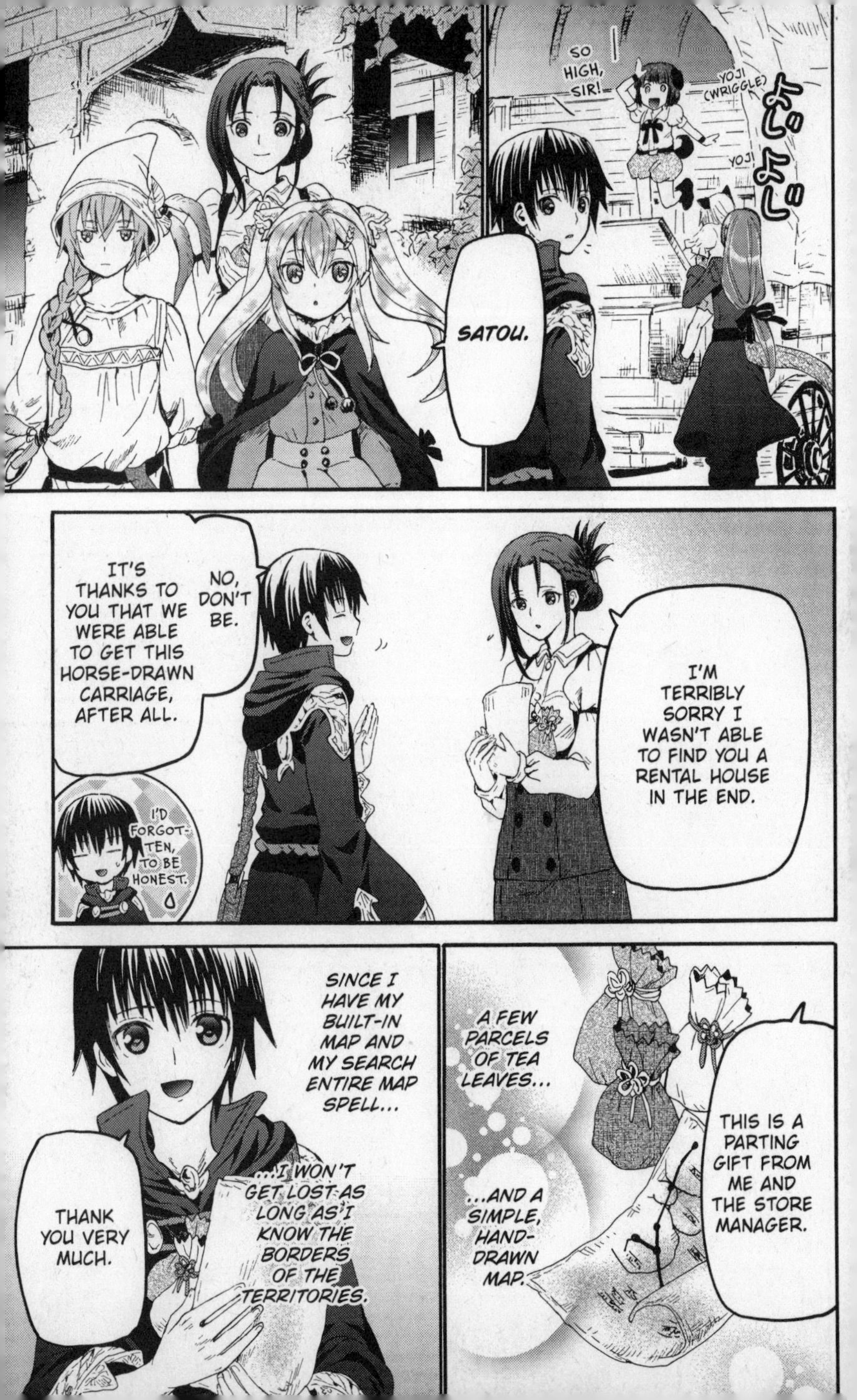
SO HIGH, SIR!
YOJI (WRIGGLE)
よじよじ
YOJI
SATOU.
I'M TERRIBLY SORRY I WASN'T ABLE TO FIND YOU A RENTAL HOUSE IN THE END.
NO, DON'T BE.
IT'S THANKS TO YOU THAT WE WERE ABLE TO GET THIS HORSE-DRAWN CARRIAGE, AFTER ALL.
I'D FORGOT-TEN, TO BE HONEST.
THIS IS A PARTING GIFT FROM ME AND THE STORE MANAGER.
A FEW PARCELS OF TEA LEAVES...
...AND A SIMPLE, HAND-DRAWN MAP.
SINCE I HAVE MY BUILT-IN MAP AND MY SEARCH ENTIRE MAP SPELL...
...I WON'T GET LOST AS LONG AS I KNOW THE BORDERS OF THE TERRITORIES.
THANK YOU VERY MUCH.

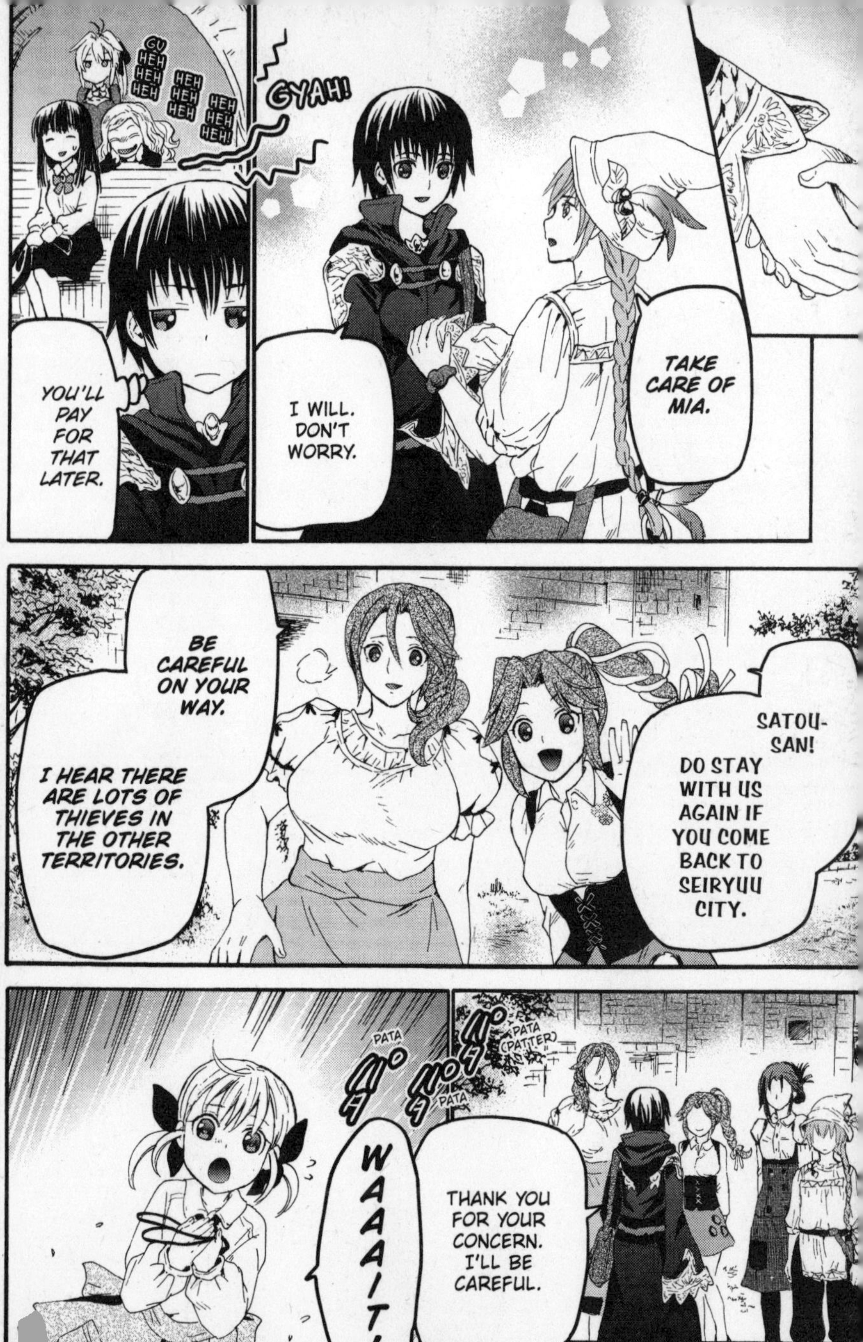
TAKE CARE OF MIA.
I WILL. DON'T WORRY.
GYAH!
GU HEH HEH HEH
HEH HEH HEH
HEH HEH HEH!
YOU'LL PAY FOR THAT LATER.
SATOU-SAN!
DO STAY WITH US AGAIN IF YOU COME BACK TO SEIRYUU CITY.
BE CAREFUL ON YOUR WAY.
I HEAR THERE ARE LOTS OF THIEVES IN THE OTHER TERRITORIES.
PATA
PATA (PATTER)
THANK YOU FOR YOUR CONCERN. I'LL BE CAREFUL.
PATA
PATA
WAAAIT!

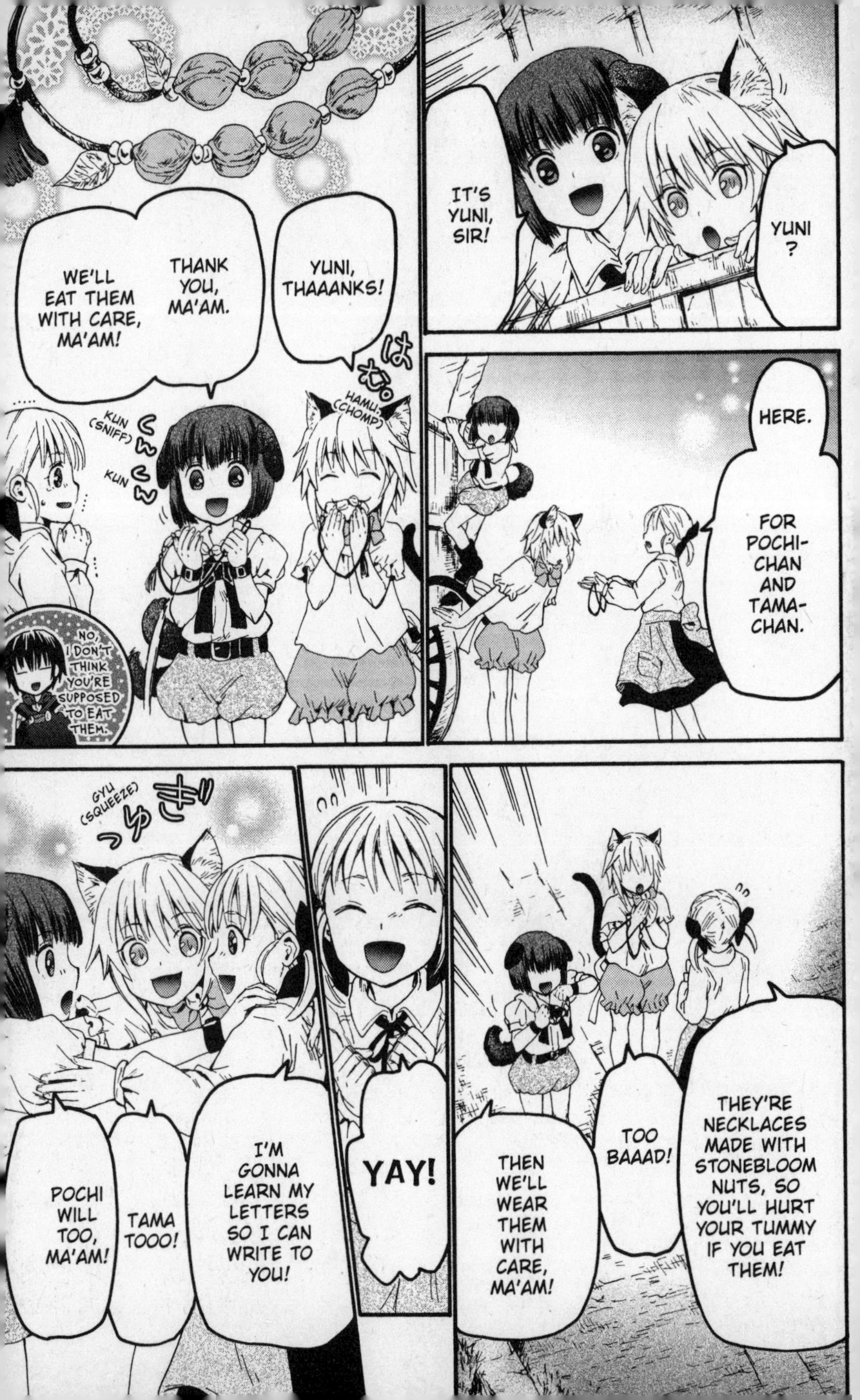
YUNI?
IT'S YUNI, SIR!
HERE.
FOR POCHI-CHAN AND TAMA-CHAN.
YUNI, THAAANKS!
はむ。
HAMU (CHOMP)
THANK YOU, MA'AM.
WE'LL EAT THEM WITH CARE, MA'AM!
くんくん
KUN KUN (SNIFF)
....
NO, I DON'T THINK YOU'RE SUPPOSED TO EAT THEM.
THEY'RE NECKLACES MADE WITH STONEBLOOM NUTS, SO YOU'LL HURT YOUR TUMMY IF YOU EAT THEM!
TOO BAAAD!
THEN WE'LL WEAR THEM WITH CARE, MA'AM!
YAY!
ぎゅっ
GYU (SQUEEZE)
I'M GONNA LEARN MY LETTERS SO I CAN WRITE TO YOU!
TAMA TOOO!
POCHI WILL TOO, MA'AM!

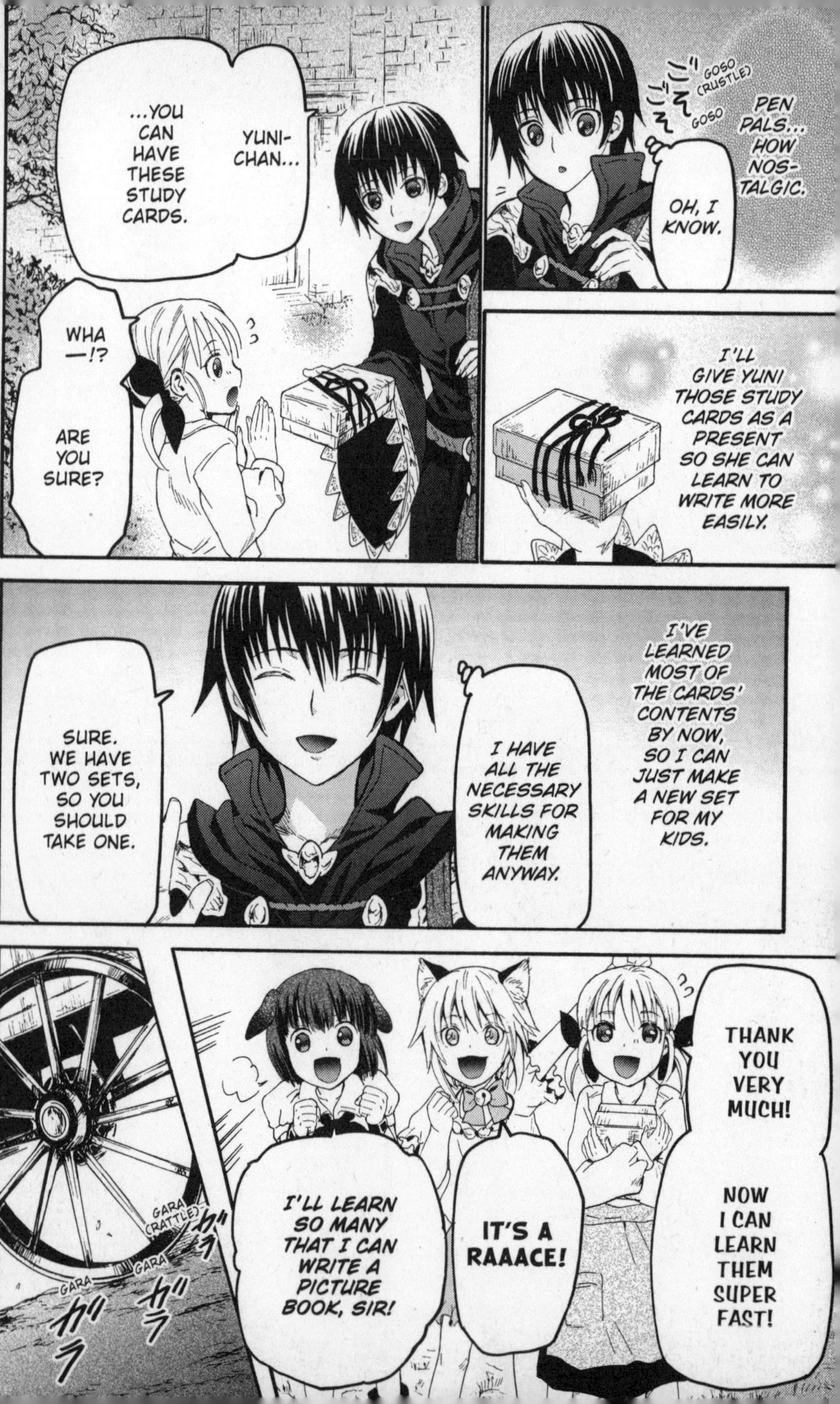

GOSO (RUSTLE)
GOSO
PEN PALS... HOW NOSTALGIC.
OH, I KNOW.
I'LL GIVE YUNI THOSE STUDY CARDS AS A PRESENT SO SHE CAN LEARN TO WRITE MORE EASILY.
YUNI-CHAN...
...YOU CAN HAVE THESE STUDY CARDS.
WHA—!?
ARE YOU SURE?
I'VE LEARNED MOST OF THE CARDS' CONTENTS BY NOW, SO I CAN JUST MAKE A NEW SET FOR MY KIDS.
I HAVE ALL THE NECESSARY SKILLS FOR MAKING THEM ANYWAY.
SURE. WE HAVE TWO SETS, SO YOU SHOULD TAKE ONE.
THANK YOU VERY MUCH!
NOW I CAN LEARN THEM SUPER FAST!
IT'S A RAAACE!
I'LL LEARN SO MANY THAT I CAN WRITE A PICTURE BOOK, SIR!
GARA (RATTLE)
GARA
GARA

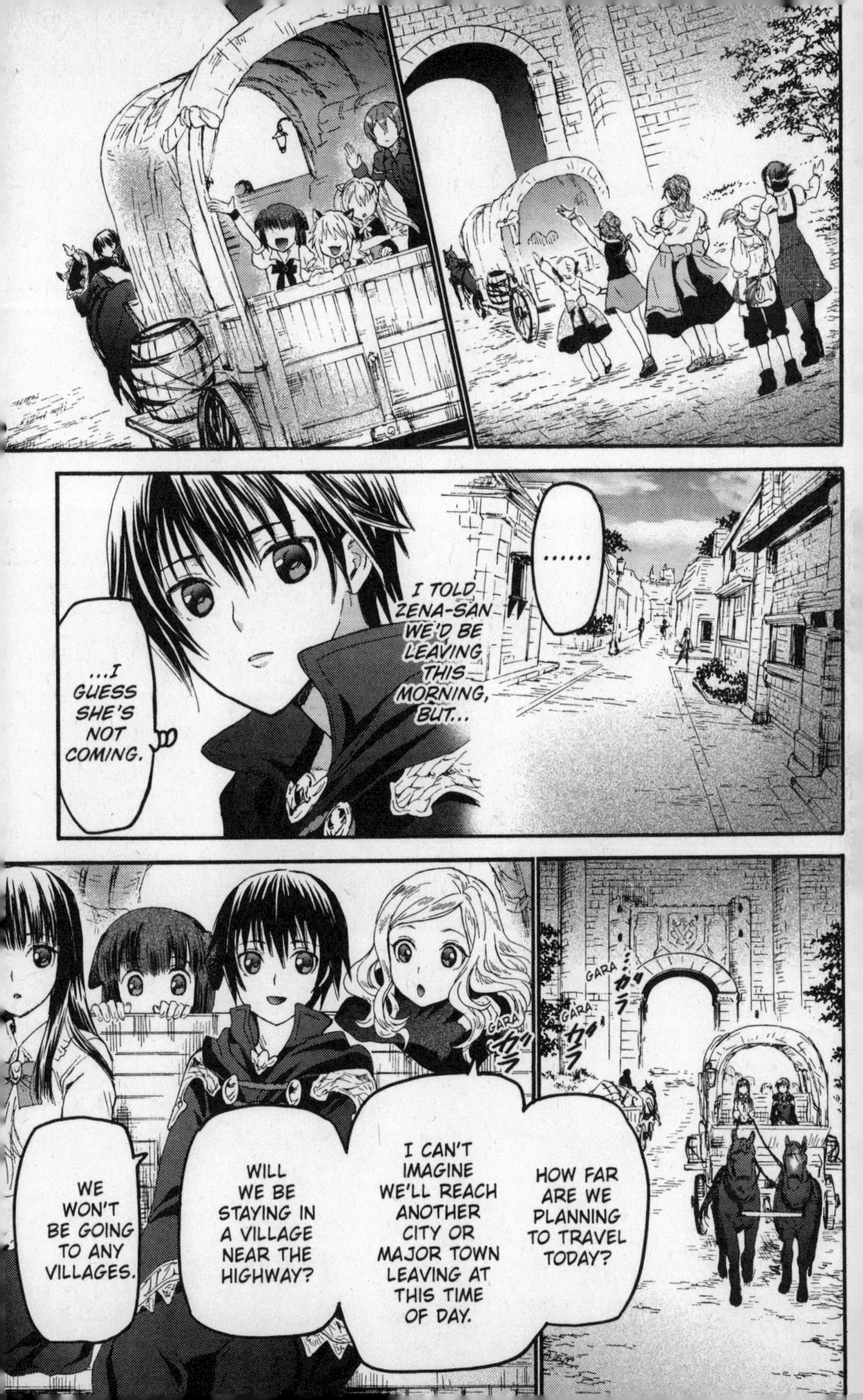
......
I TOLD ZENA-SAN WE'D BE LEAVING THIS MORNING, BUT...
...I GUESS SHE'S NOT COMING.
GARA
GARA
GARA
HOW FAR ARE WE PLANNING TO TRAVEL TODAY?
I CAN'T IMAGINE WE'LL REACH ANOTHER CITY OR MAJOR TOWN LEAVING AT THIS TIME OF DAY.
WILL WE BE STAYING IN A VILLAGE NEAR THE HIGHWAY?
WE WON'T BE GOING TO ANY VILLAGES.

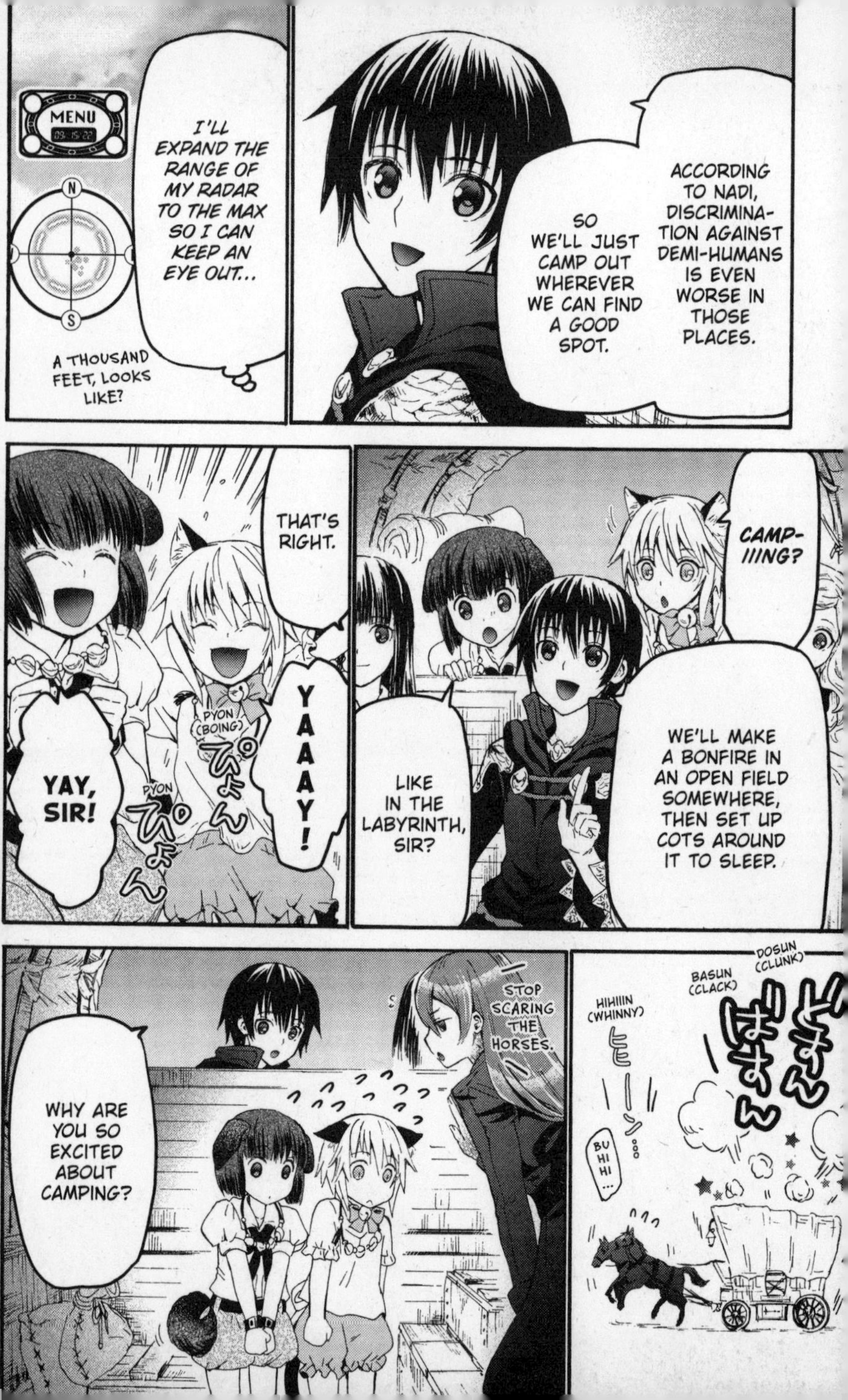
ACCORDING TO NADI, DISCRIMINATION AGAINST DEMI-HUMANS IS EVEN WORSE IN THOSE PLACES.
SO WE'LL JUST CAMP OUT WHEREVER WE CAN FIND A GOOD SPOT.
MENU
03:15:22
N
S
I'LL EXPAND THE RANGE OF MY RADAR TO THE MAX SO I CAN KEEP AN EYE OUT...
A THOUSAND FEET, LOOKS LIKE?
CAMP-IIING?
WE'LL MAKE A BONFIRE IN AN OPEN FIELD SOMEWHERE, THEN SET UP COTS AROUND IT TO SLEEP.
LIKE IN THE LABYRINTH, SIR?
THAT'S RIGHT.
YAAAAY!
PYON (BOING)
ぴょん
PYON
ぴょん
YAY, SIR!
DOSUN (CLUNK)
どすん
BASUN (CLACK)
ばすん
HIHIIIN (WHINNY)
ヒヒーン…
BU HI HI...
STOP SCARING THE HORSES.
WHY ARE YOU SO EXCITED ABOUT CAMPING?

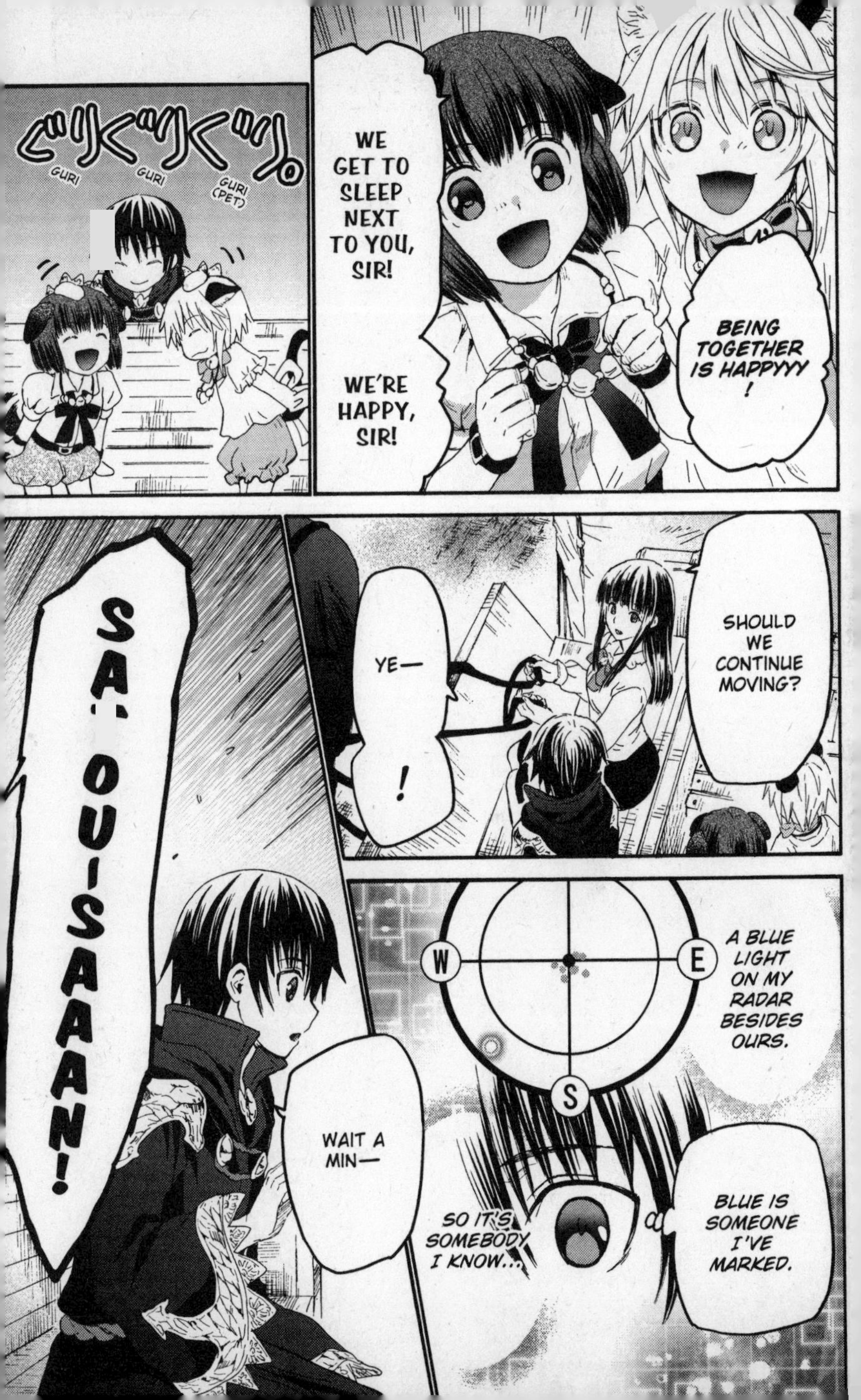
WE GET TO SLEEP NEXT TO YOU, SIR!
BEING TOGETHER IS HAPPYYY!
WE'RE HAPPY, SIR!
GURI
GURI
GURI (PET)
SHOULD WE CONTINUE MOVING?
YE— !
W
E
S
A BLUE LIGHT ON MY RADAR BESIDES OURS.
BLUE IS SOMEONE I'VE MARKED.
SO IT'S SOMEBODY I KNOW...
WAIT A MIN—
SA OUISAAAAN!

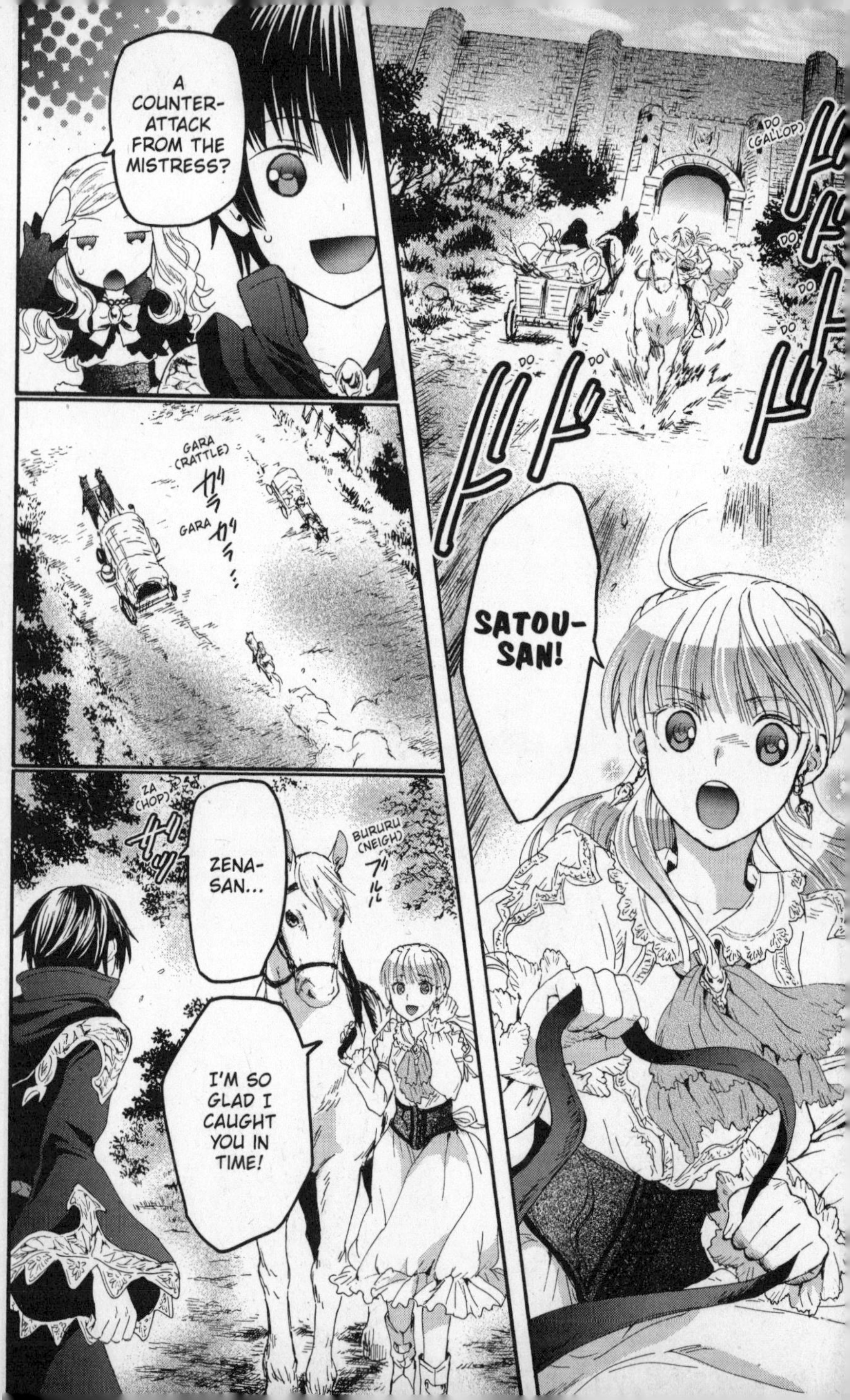
DO (GALLOP)
DO
DO
DO
DO
DO
SATOU-SAN!
A COUNTER-ATTACK FROM THE MISTRESS?
GARA (RATTLE)
GARA
BURURU (NEIGH)
ZENA-SAN...
ZA (HOP)
I'M SO GLAD I CAUGHT YOU IN TIME!

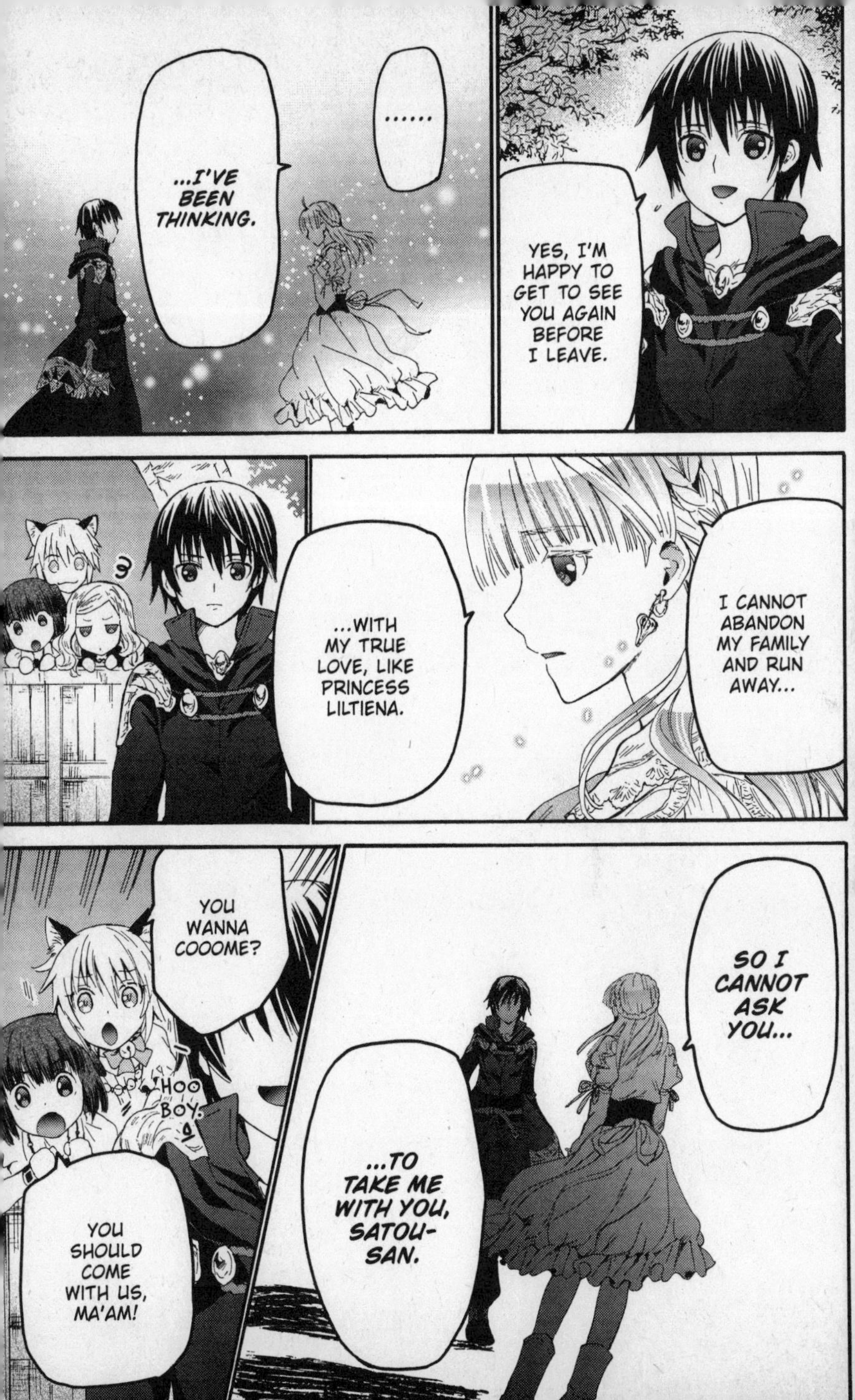
YES, I'M HAPPY TO GET TO SEE YOU AGAIN BEFORE I LEAVE.
......
...I'VE BEEN THINKING.
I CANNOT ABANDON MY FAMILY AND RUN AWAY...
...WITH MY TRUE LOVE, LIKE PRINCESS LILTIENA.
SO I CANNOT ASK YOU...
...TO TAKE ME WITH YOU, SATOU-SAN.
YOU WANNA COOOME?
HOO BOY.
YOU SHOULD COME WITH US, MA'AM!

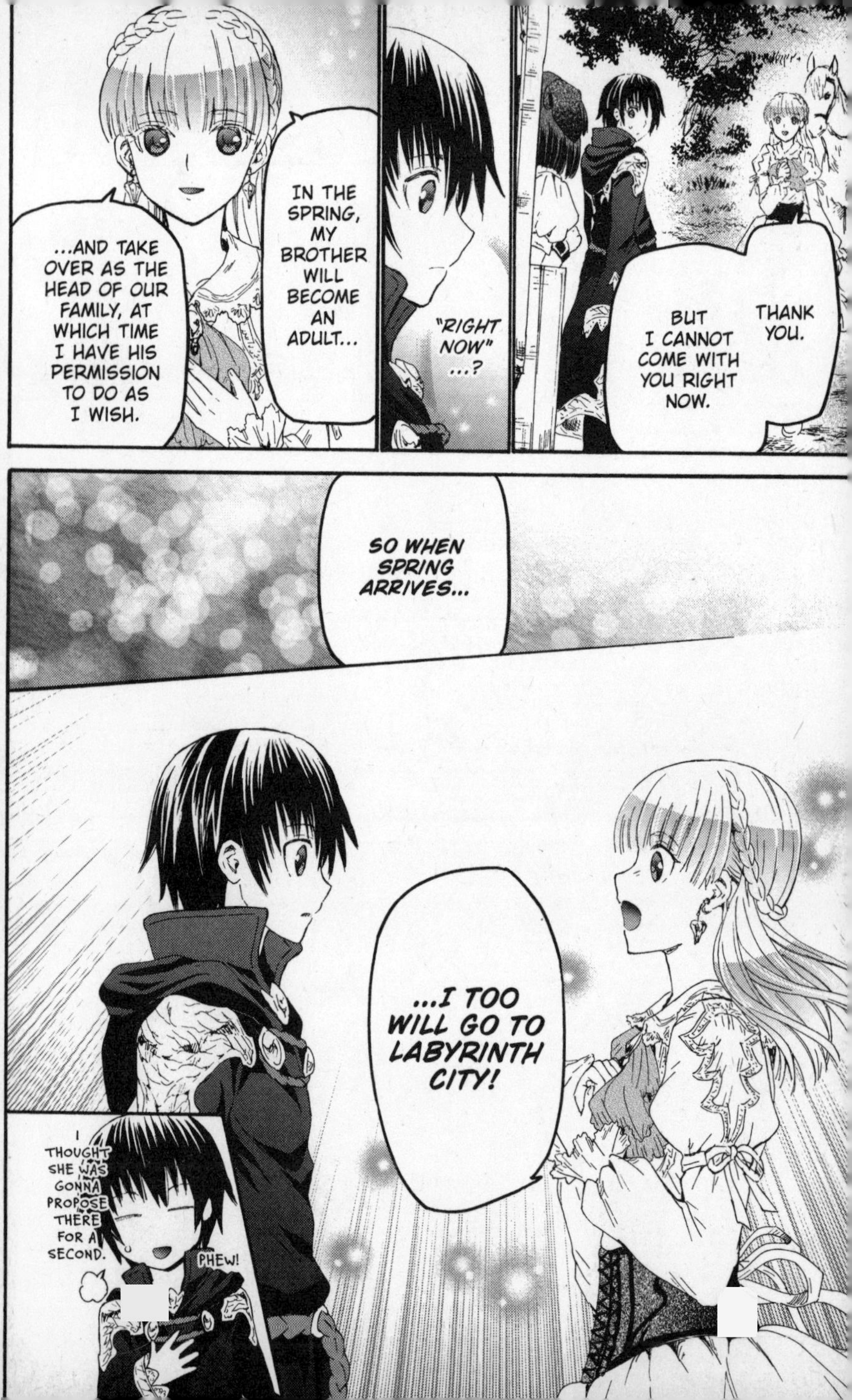
THANK YOU.
BUT I CANNOT COME WITH YOU RIGHT NOW.
"RIGHT NOW" ...?
IN THE SPRING, MY BROTHER WILL BECOME AN ADULT...
...AND TAKE OVER AS THE HEAD OF OUR FAMILY, AT WHICH TIME I HAVE HIS PERMISSION TO DO AS I WISH.
SO WHEN SPRING ARRIVES...
...I TOO WILL GO TO LABYRINTH CITY!
I THOUGHT SHE WAS GONNA PROPOSE THERE FOR A SECOND.
PHEW!

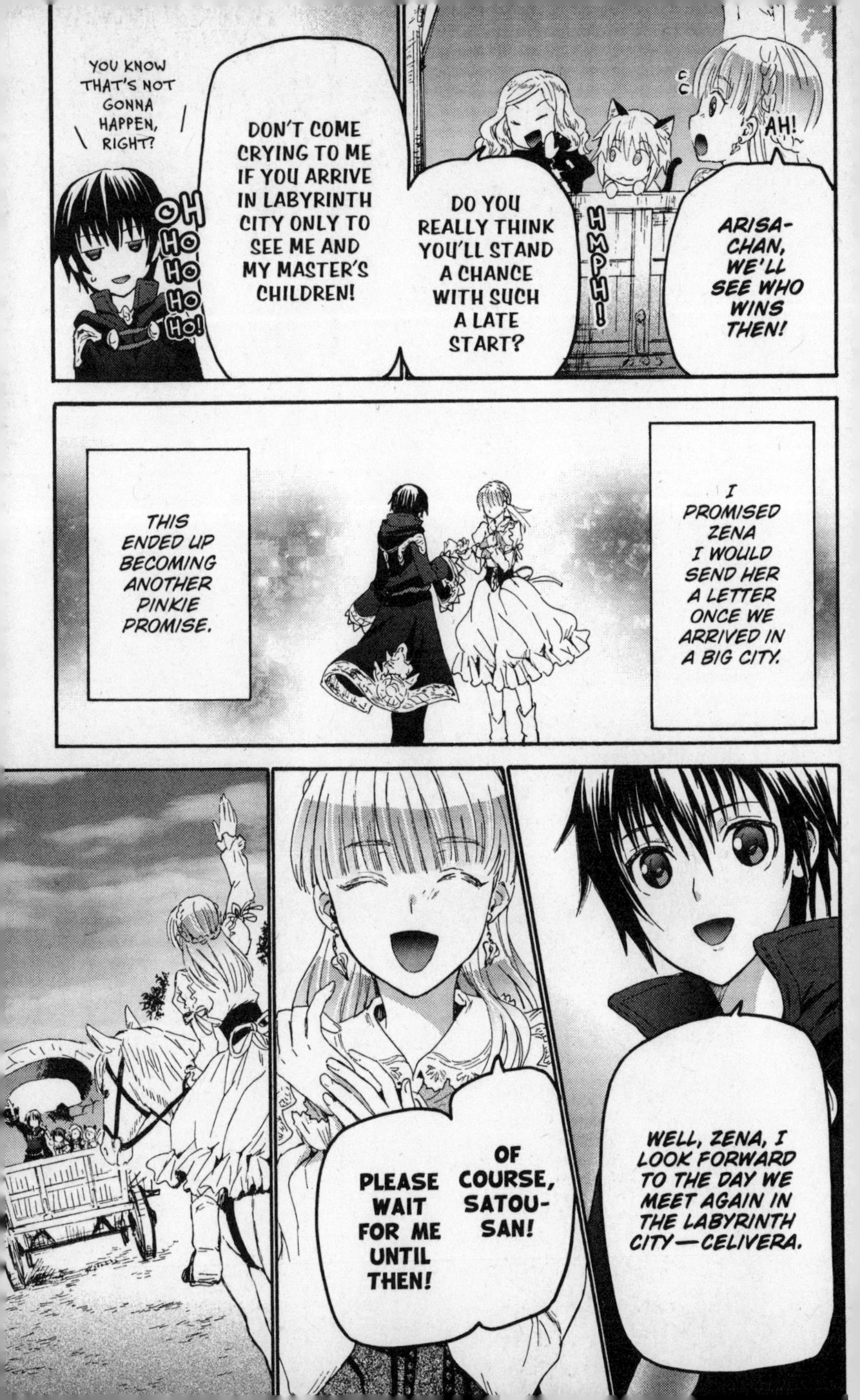
AH!
ARISA-CHAN, WE'LL SEE WHO WINS THEN!
HMPH!
DO YOU REALLY THINK YOU'LL STAND A CHANCE WITH SUCH A LATE START?
DON'T COME CRYING TO ME IF YOU ARRIVE IN LABYRINTH CITY ONLY TO SEE ME AND MY MASTER'S CHILDREN!
OH HO HO HO HO!
YOU KNOW THAT'S NOT GONNA HAPPEN, RIGHT?
I PROMISED ZENA I WOULD SEND HER A LETTER ONCE WE ARRIVED IN A BIG CITY.
THIS ENDED UP BECOMING ANOTHER PINKIE PROMISE.
WELL, ZENA, I LOOK FORWARD TO THE DAY WE MEET AGAIN IN THE LABYRINTH CITY—CELIVERA.
OF COURSE, SATOU-SAN!
PLEASE WAIT FOR ME UNTIL THEN!

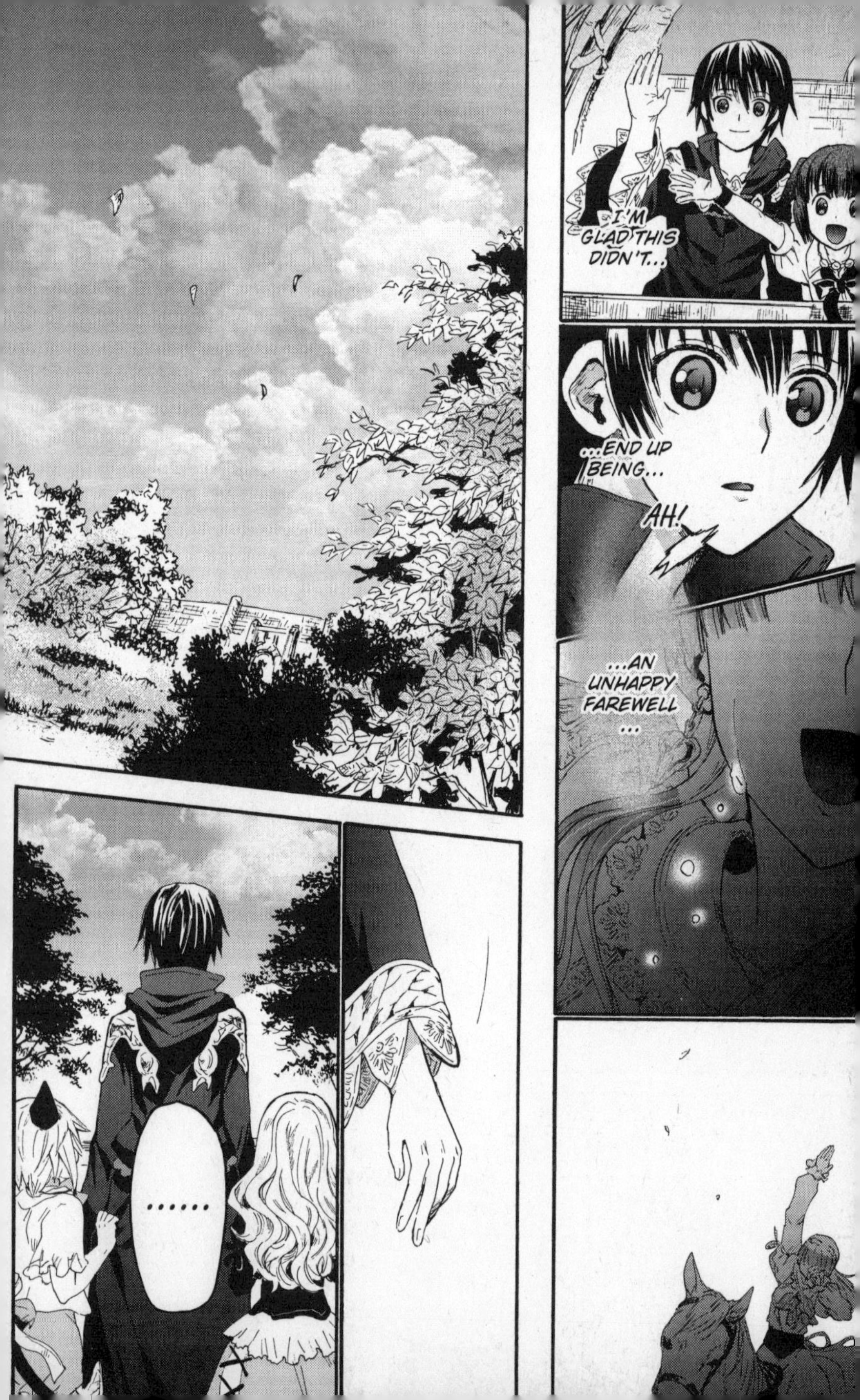
I'M GLAD THIS DIDN'T...
...END UP BEING...
AH!
...AN UNHAPPY FAREWELL ...
......

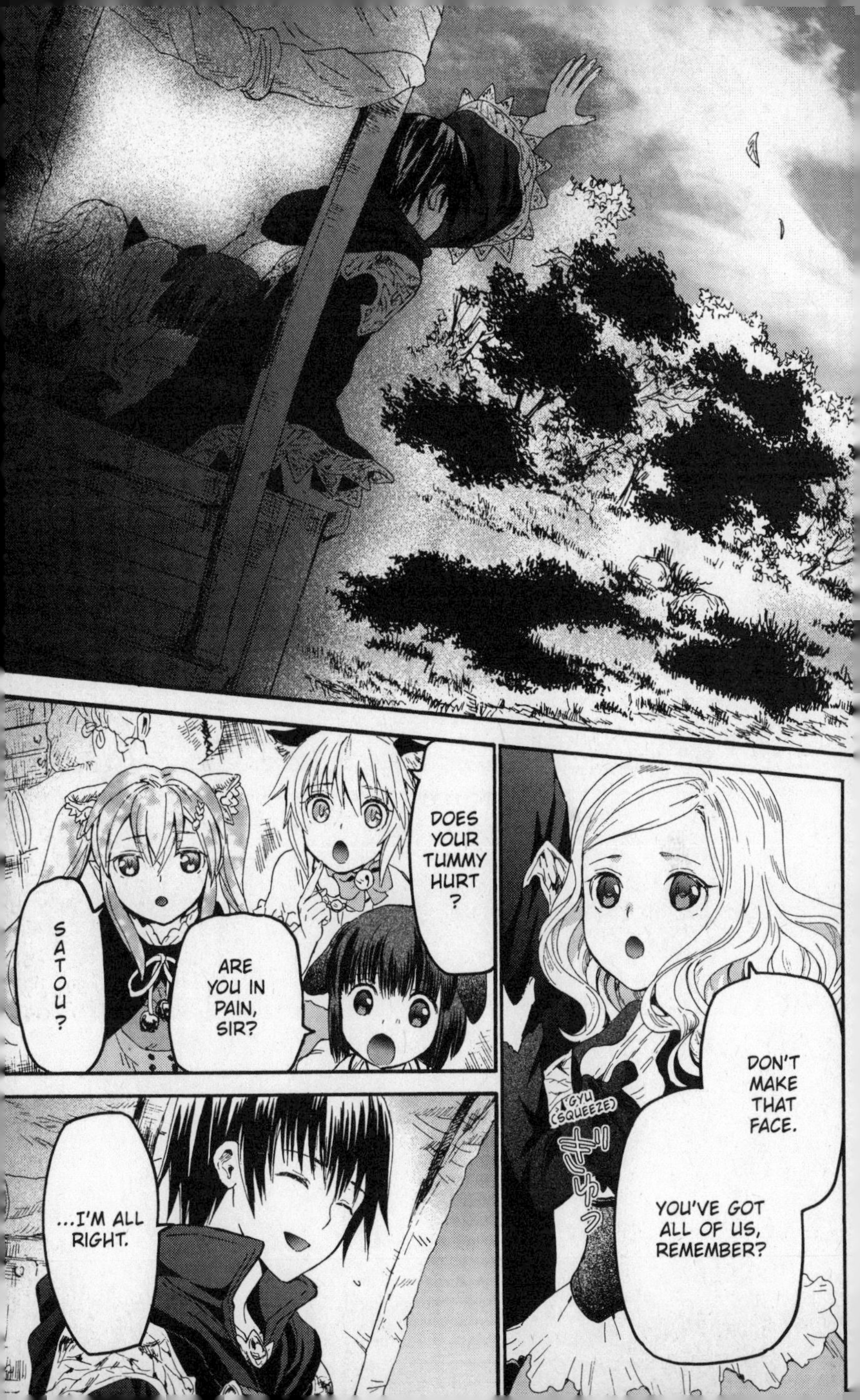

GYU (SQUEEZE)
DON'T MAKE THAT FACE.
YOU'VE GOT ALL OF US, REMEMBER?
DOES YOUR TUMMY HURT?
ARE YOU IN PAIN, SIR?
SATOU?
...I'M ALL RIGHT.

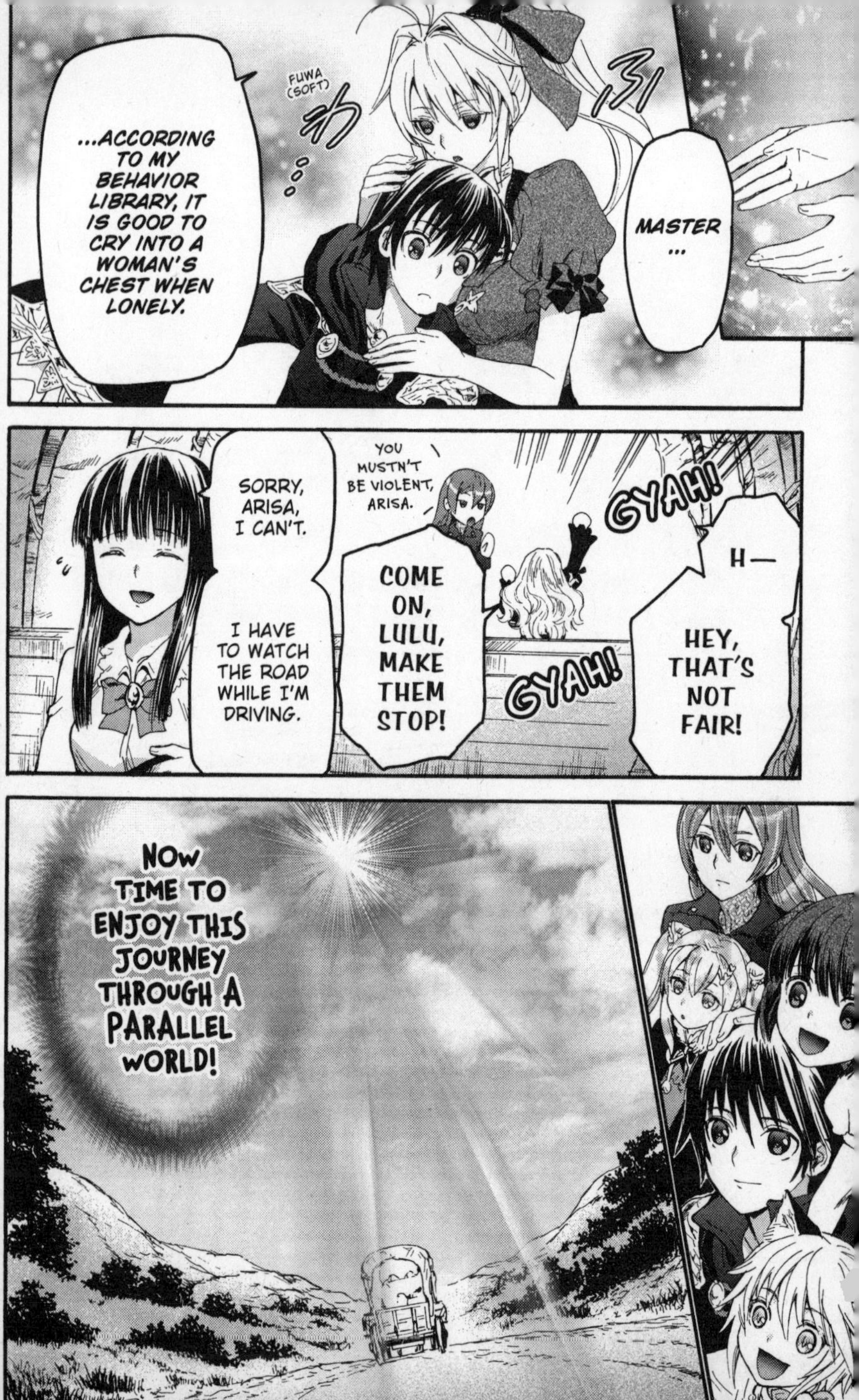
MASTER ...
FUWA (SOFT)
...ACCORDING TO MY BEHAVIOR LIBRARY, IT IS GOOD TO CRY INTO A WOMAN'S CHEST WHEN LONELY.
H—
HEY, THAT'S NOT FAIR!
GYAH!
GYAH!
YOU MUSTN'T BE VIOLENT, ARISA.
COME ON, LULU, MAKE THEM STOP!
SORRY, ARISA, I CAN'T.
I HAVE TO WATCH THE ROAD WHILE I'M DRIVING.
NOW TIME TO ENJOY THIS JOURNEY THROUGH A PARALLEL WORLD!

WINGED SHOES

Acquired in the
Valley of Dragons.
Very sturdy, with
an effect that helps
improve the user's
footing on rough
terrain.

STONEBLOOM NUT NECKLACES

Necklaces made
with the nuts of the
stonebloom fruit.

They are considered
good luck for journeys
and are given as a lucky
talisman to children who
are adopted from the
orphanage.

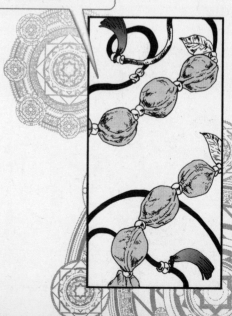

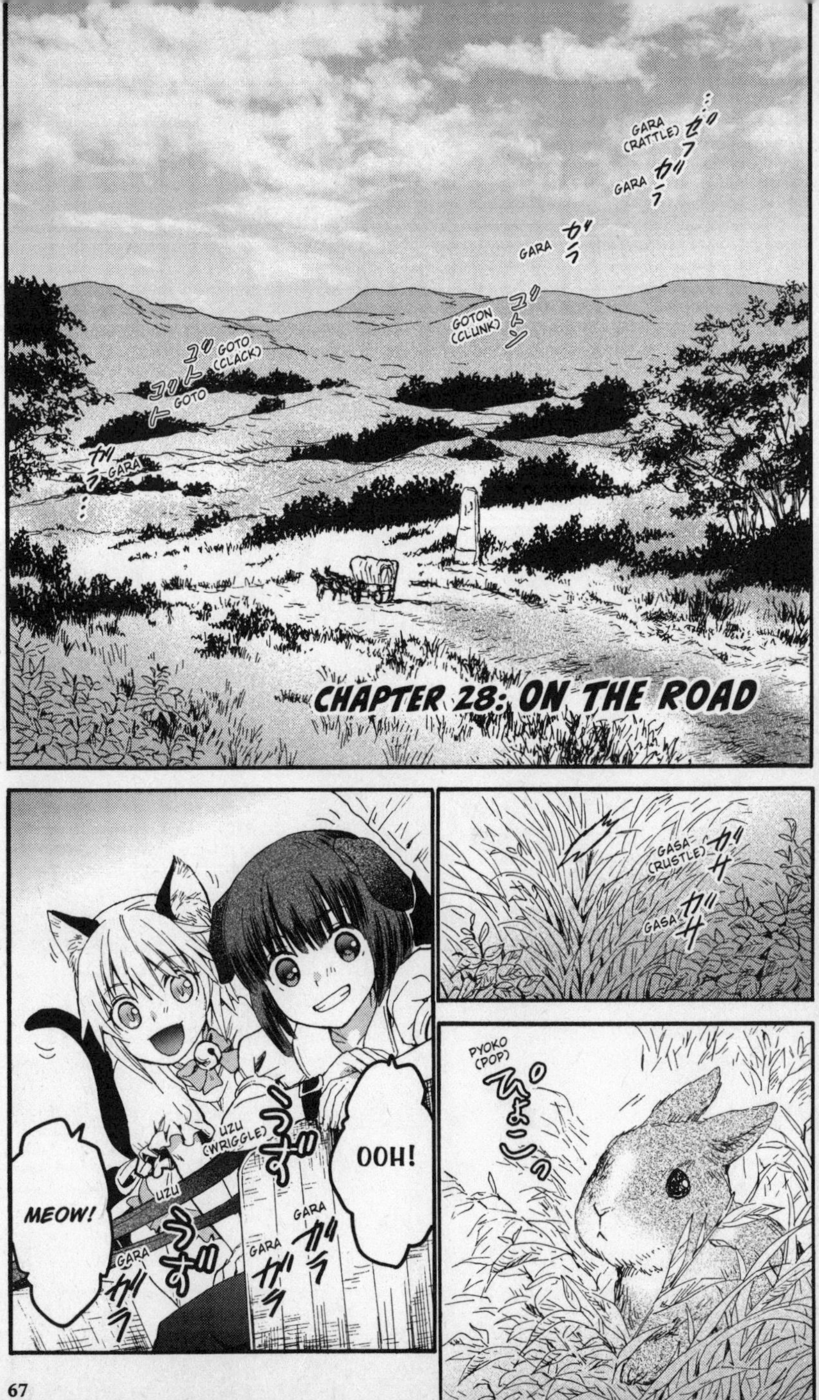
GARA (RATTLE)
GARA
GARA
GOTON (CLUNK)
GOTO (CLACK)
GOTO
GARA
CHAPTER 28: ON THE ROAD
GASA (RUSTLE)
GASA
PYOKO (POP)
OOH!
UZU (WRIGGLE)
GARA
UZU
MEOW!
GARA
GARA
GARA

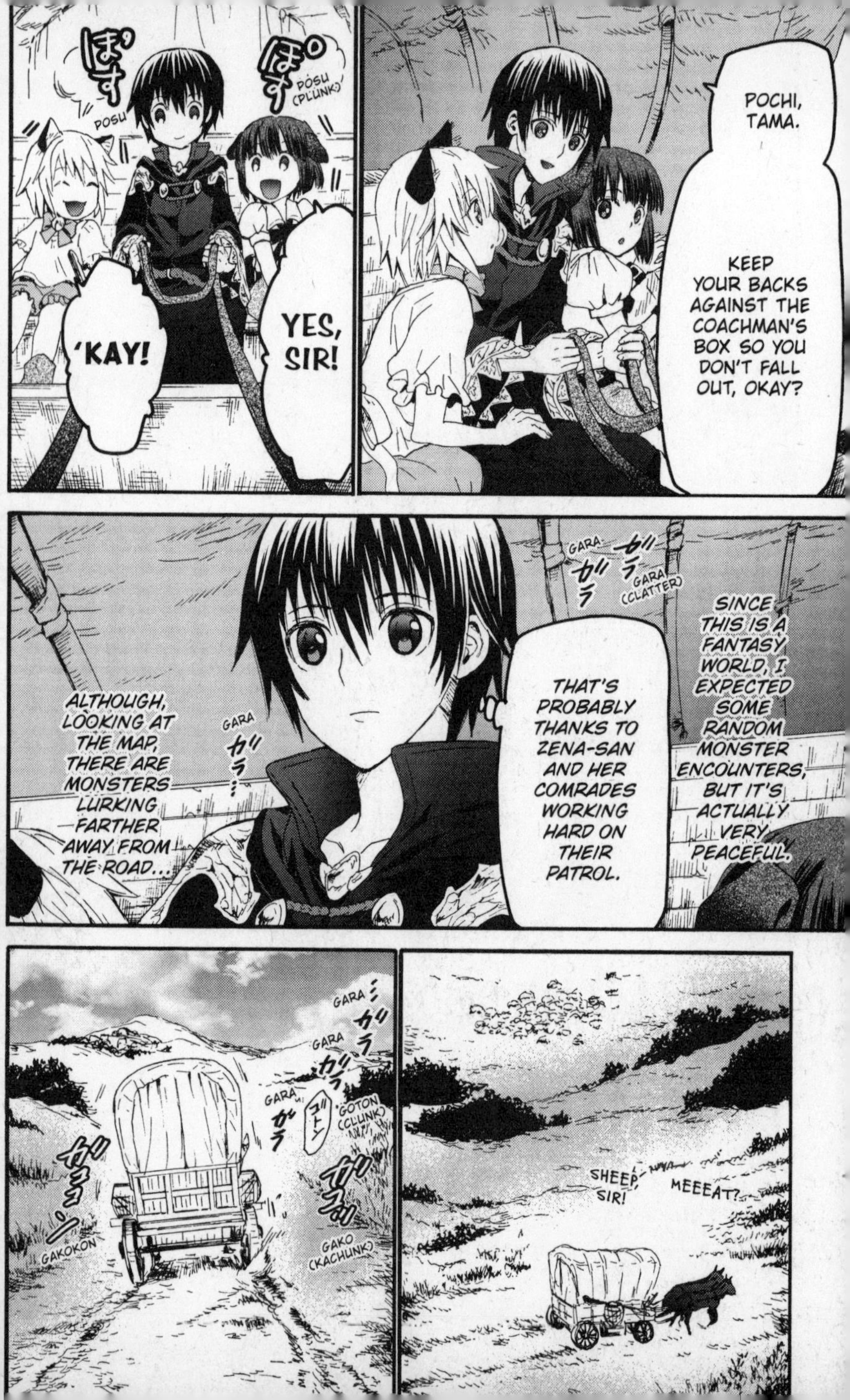
POCHI, TAMA.
KEEP YOUR BACKS AGAINST THE COACHMAN'S BOX SO YOU DON'T FALL OUT, OKAY?
ぽす
POSU (PLUNK)
ぽす
POSU
YES, SIR!
'KAY!
ガラ
GARA
ガラ
GARA (CLATTER)
SINCE THIS IS A FANTASY WORLD, I EXPECTED SOME RANDOM MONSTER ENCOUNTERS, BUT IT'S ACTUALLY VERY PEACEFUL.
THAT'S PROBABLY THANKS TO ZENA-SAN AND HER COMRADES WORKING HARD ON THEIR PATROL.
ガラ…
GARA
ALTHOUGH, LOOKING AT THE MAP, THERE ARE MONSTERS LURKING FARTHER AWAY FROM THE ROAD...
SHEEP, SIR!
MEEEAT?
ガラ
GARA
ガラ
GARA
ガラ
GARA
ゴトン
GOTON (CLUNK)
ガコ
GAKO (KACHUNK)
ガコン
GAKOKON

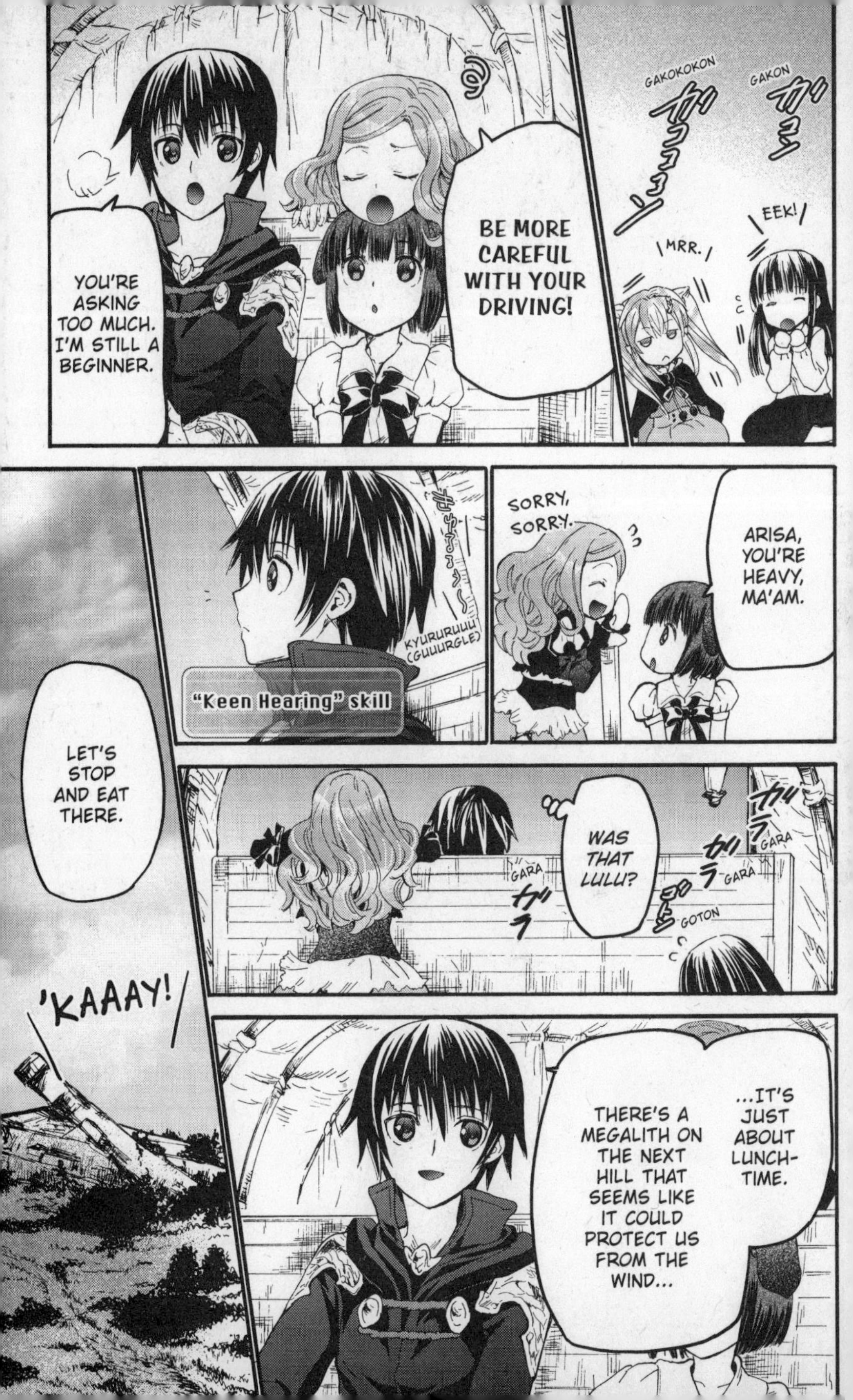
GAKON
GAKOKOKON
EEK!
MRR.
BE MORE CAREFUL WITH YOUR DRIVING!
YOU'RE ASKING TOO MUCH. I'M STILL A BEGINNER.
ARISA, YOU'RE HEAVY, MA'AM.
SORRY, SORRY.
KYURURUUU (GUUURGLE)
"Keen Hearing" skill
GARA
GARA
GARA
GOTON
WAS THAT LULU?
...IT'S JUST ABOUT LUNCH-TIME.
THERE'S A MEGALITH ON THE NEXT HILL THAT SEEMS LIKE IT COULD PROTECT US FROM THE WIND...
LET'S STOP AND EAT THERE.
'KAAAY!

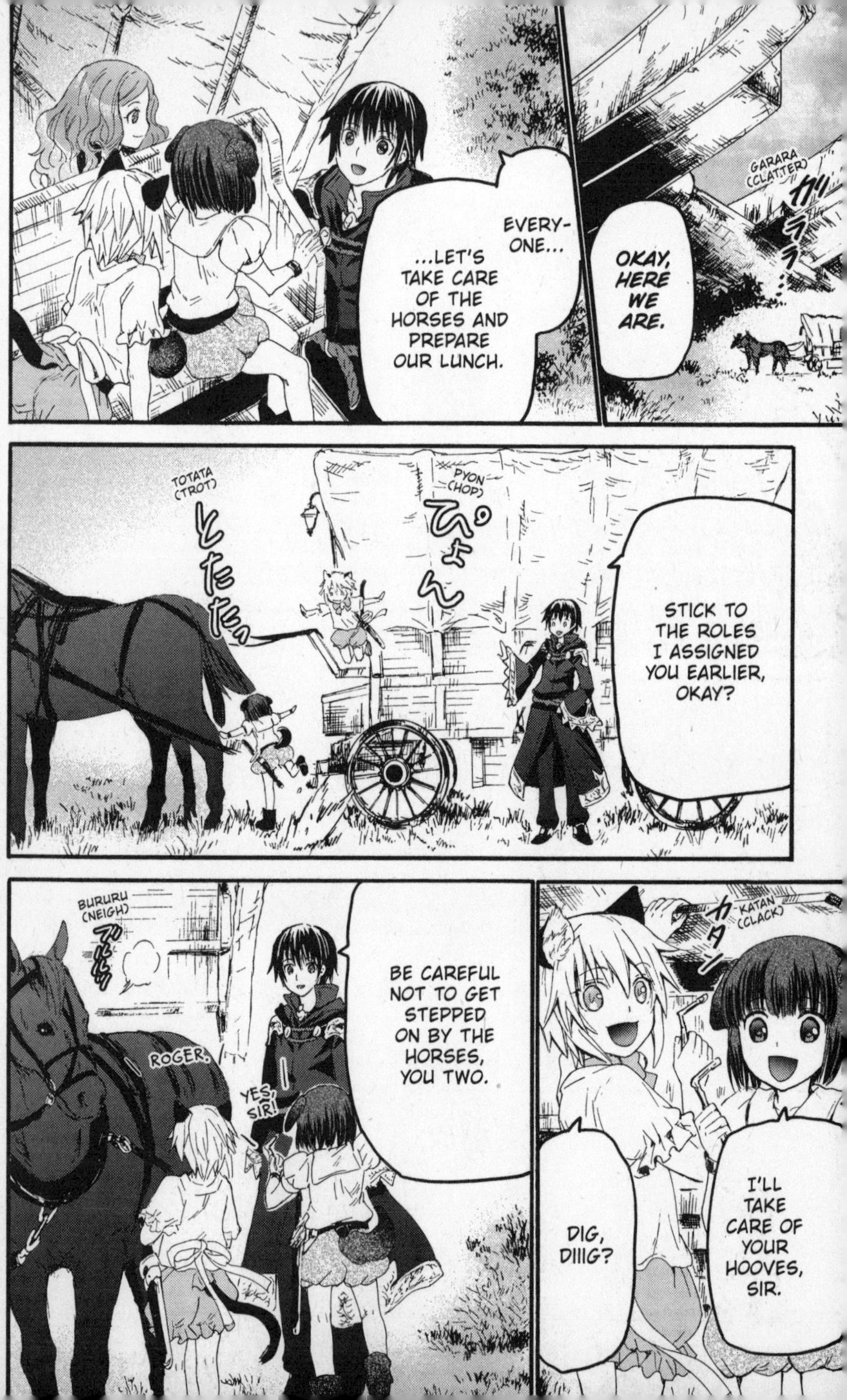
GARARA (CLATTER)
OKAY, HERE WE ARE.
EVERY-ONE...
...LET'S TAKE CARE OF THE HORSES AND PREPARE OUR LUNCH.
STICK TO THE ROLES I ASSIGNED YOU EARLIER, OKAY?
PYON (HOP)
TOTATA (TROT)
KATAN (CLACK)
I'LL TAKE CARE OF YOUR HOOVES, SIR.
DIG, DIIIG?
BE CAREFUL NOT TO GET STEPPED ON BY THE HORSES, YOU TWO.
YES, SIR!
ROGER.
BURURU (NEIGH)

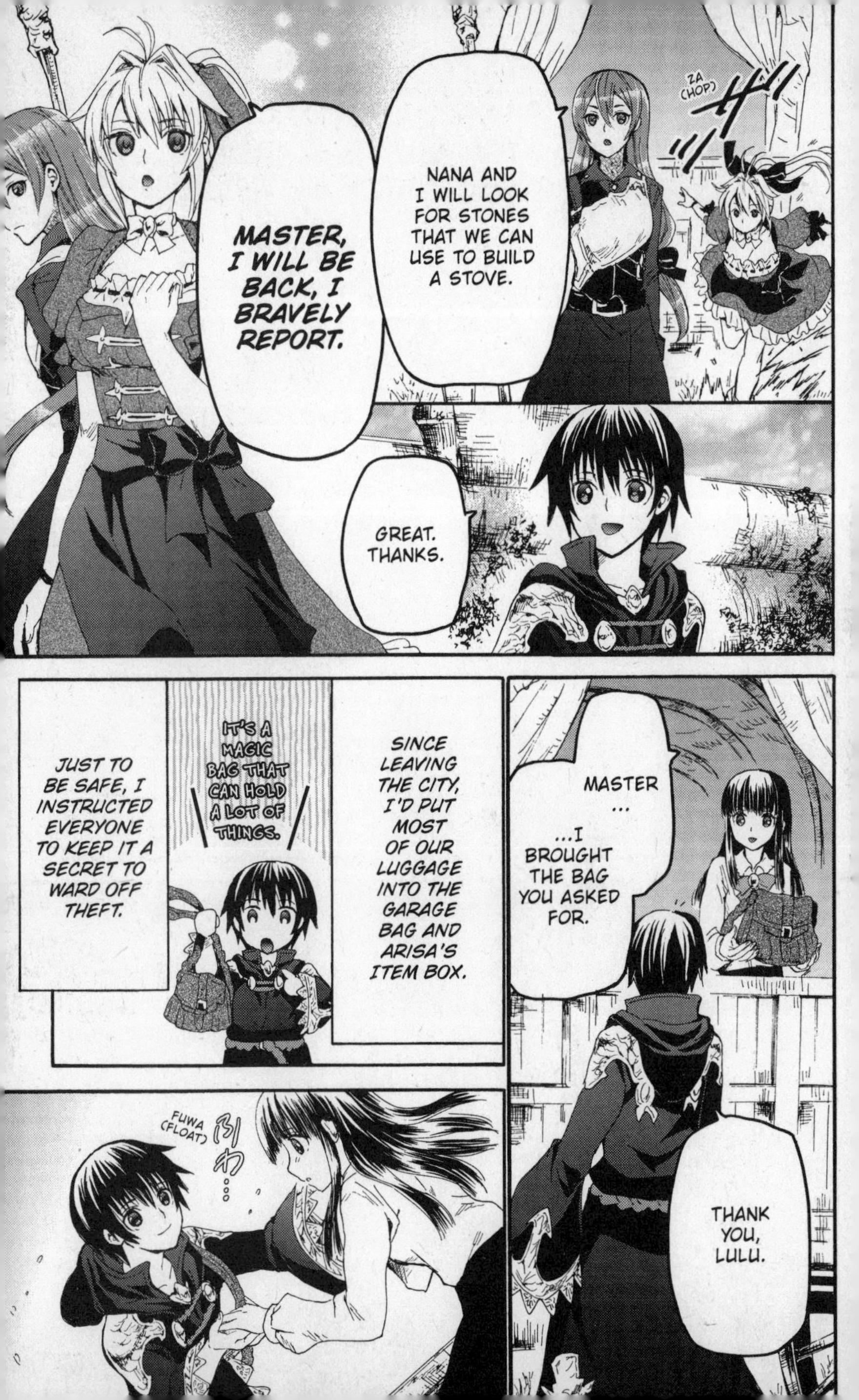
ZA (HOP)
NANA AND I WILL LOOK FOR STONES THAT WE CAN USE TO BUILD A STOVE.
MASTER, I WILL BE BACK, I BRAVELY REPORT.
GREAT. THANKS.
MASTER ...
...I BROUGHT THE BAG YOU ASKED FOR.
THANK YOU, LULU.
SINCE LEAVING THE CITY, I'D PUT MOST OF OUR LUGGAGE INTO THE GARAGE BAG AND ARISA'S ITEM BOX.
IT'S A MAGIC BAG THAT CAN HOLD A LOT OF THINGS.
JUST TO BE SAFE, I INSTRUCTED EVERYONE TO KEEP IT A SECRET TO WARD OFF THEFT.
FUWA (FLOAT)

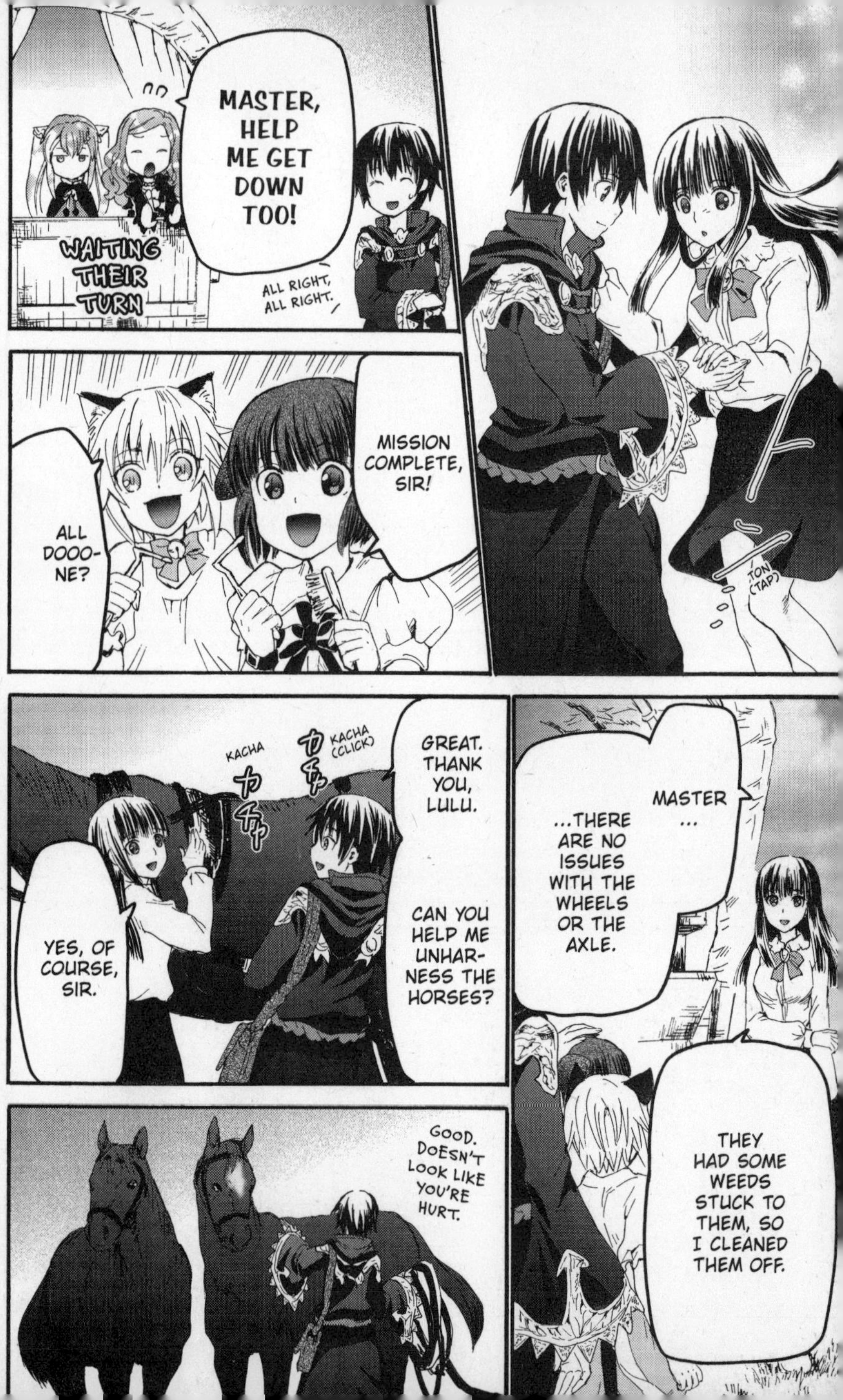
TON (TAP)
MASTER, HELP ME GET DOWN TOO!
WAITING THEIR TURN
ALL RIGHT, ALL RIGHT.
MISSION COMPLETE, SIR!
ALL DOOOO-NE?
MASTER ...
...THERE ARE NO ISSUES WITH THE WHEELS OR THE AXLE.
THEY HAD SOME WEEDS STUCK TO THEM, SO I CLEANED THEM OFF.
GREAT. THANK YOU, LULU.
KACHA (CLICK)
KACHA
CAN YOU HELP ME UNHARNESS THE HORSES?
YES, OF COURSE, SIR.
GOOD. DOESN'T LOOK LIKE YOU'RE HURT.

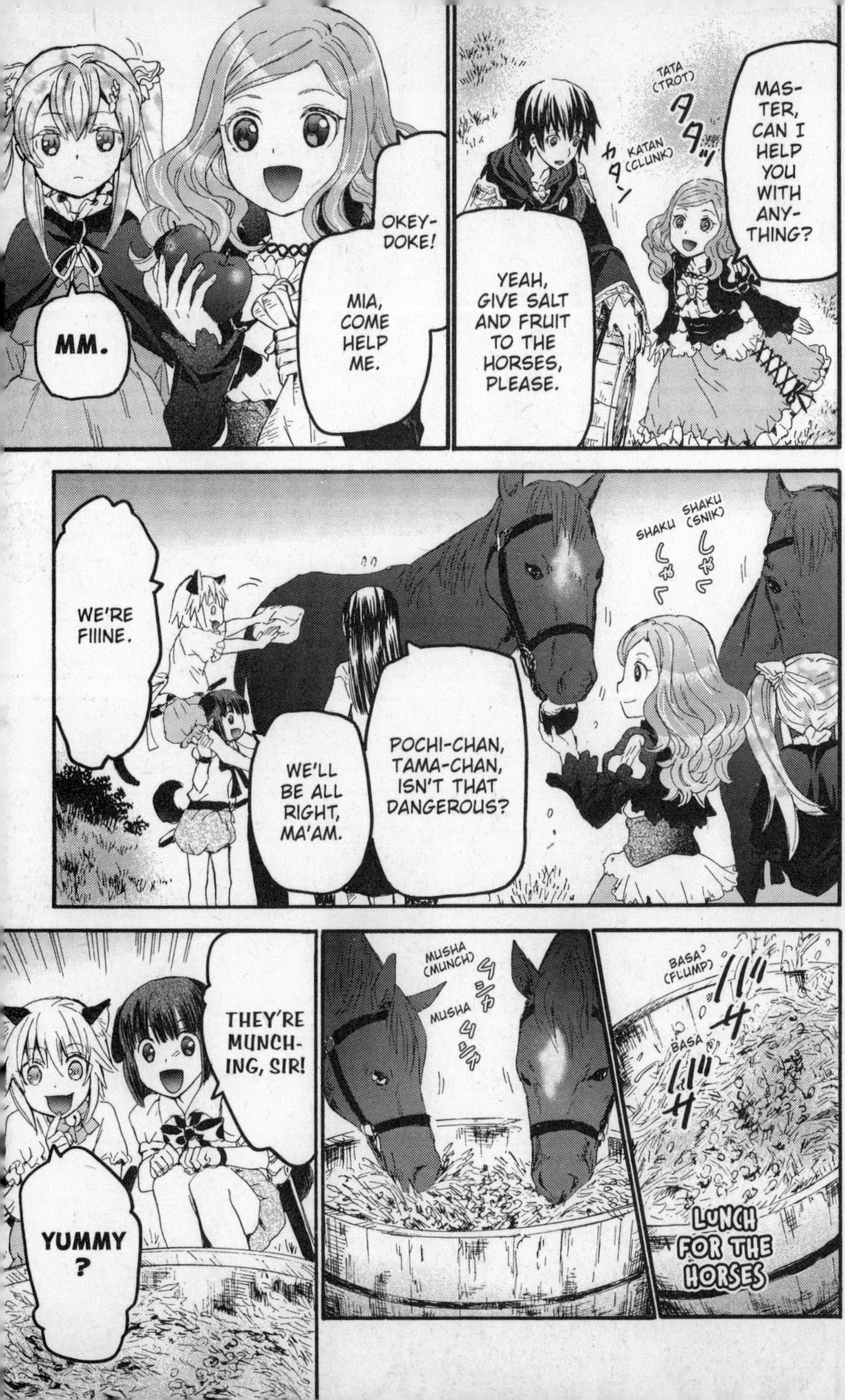
TATA (TROT)
KATAN (CLUNK)
MASTER, CAN I HELP YOU WITH ANYTHING?
YEAH, GIVE SALT AND FRUIT TO THE HORSES, PLEASE.
OKEY-DOKE!
MIA, COME HELP ME.
MM.
SHAKU SHAKU (SNIK)
POCHI-CHAN, TAMA-CHAN, ISN'T THAT DANGEROUS?
WE'LL BE ALL RIGHT, MA'AM.
WE'RE FIIINE.
BASA (FLUMP)
BASA
LUNCH FOR THE HORSES
MUSHA (MUNCH)
MUSHA
THEY'RE MUNCHING, SIR!
YUMMY?

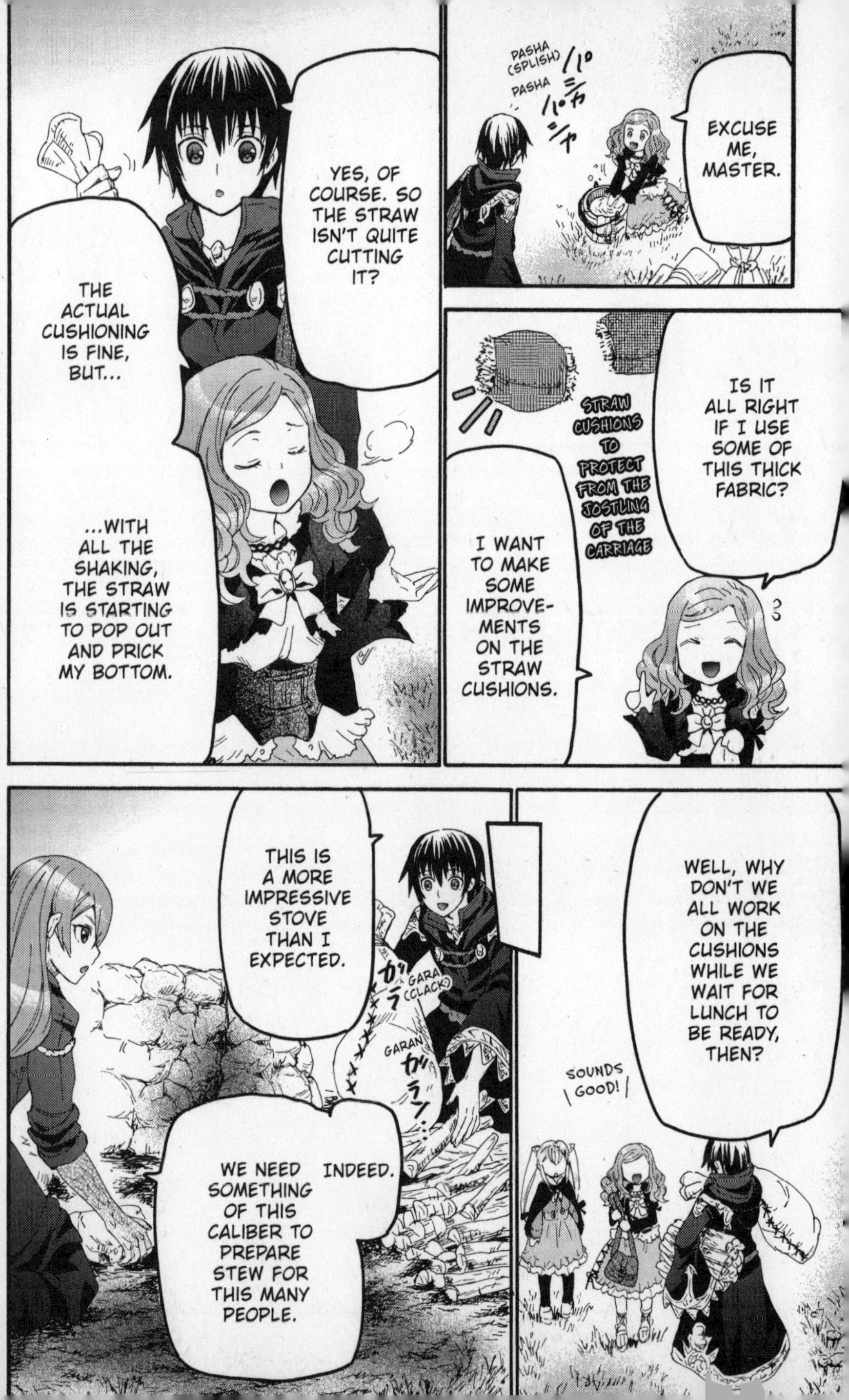
PASHA (SPLISH)
PASHA
EXCUSE ME, MASTER.
IS IT ALL RIGHT IF I USE SOME OF THIS THICK FABRIC?
STRAW CUSHIONS TO PROTECT FROM THE JOSTLING OF THE CARRIAGE
I WANT TO MAKE SOME IMPROVE-MENTS ON THE STRAW CUSHIONS.
YES, OF COURSE. SO THE STRAW ISN'T QUITE CUTTING IT?
THE ACTUAL CUSHIONING IS FINE, BUT...
...WITH ALL THE SHAKING, THE STRAW IS STARTING TO POP OUT AND PRICK MY BOTTOM.
WELL, WHY DON'T WE ALL WORK ON THE CUSHIONS WHILE WE WAIT FOR LUNCH TO BE READY, THEN?
SOUNDS GOOD!
THIS IS A MORE IMPRESSIVE STOVE THAN I EXPECTED.
GARA (CLACK)
GARAN
INDEED.
WE NEED SOMETHING OF THIS CALIBER TO PREPARE STEW FOR THIS MANY PEOPLE.

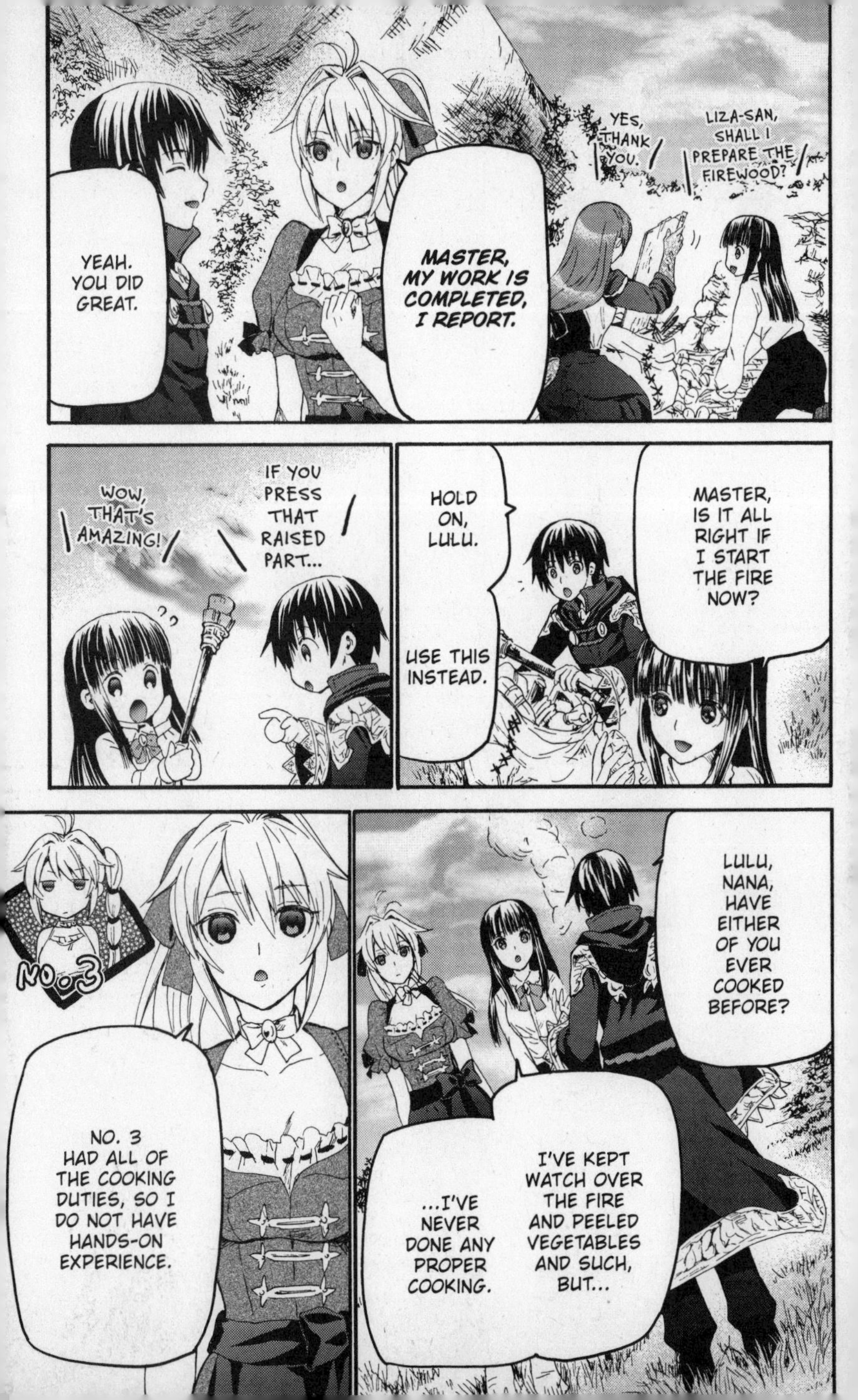
LIZA-SAN, SHALL I PREPARE THE FIREWOOD?
YES, THANK YOU.
MASTER, MY WORK IS COMPLETED, I REPORT.
YEAH. YOU DID GREAT.
MASTER, IS IT ALL RIGHT IF I START THE FIRE NOW?
HOLD ON, LULU.
USE THIS INSTEAD.
IF YOU PRESS THAT RAISED PART...
WOW, THAT's AMAZING!
LULU, NANA, HAVE EITHER OF YOU EVER COOKED BEFORE?
I'VE KEPT WATCH OVER THE FIRE AND PEELED VEGETABLES AND SUCH, BUT...
...I'VE NEVER DONE ANY PROPER COOKING.
NO. 3
NO. 3 HAD ALL OF THE COOKING DUTIES, SO I DO NOT HAVE HANDS-ON EXPERIENCE.

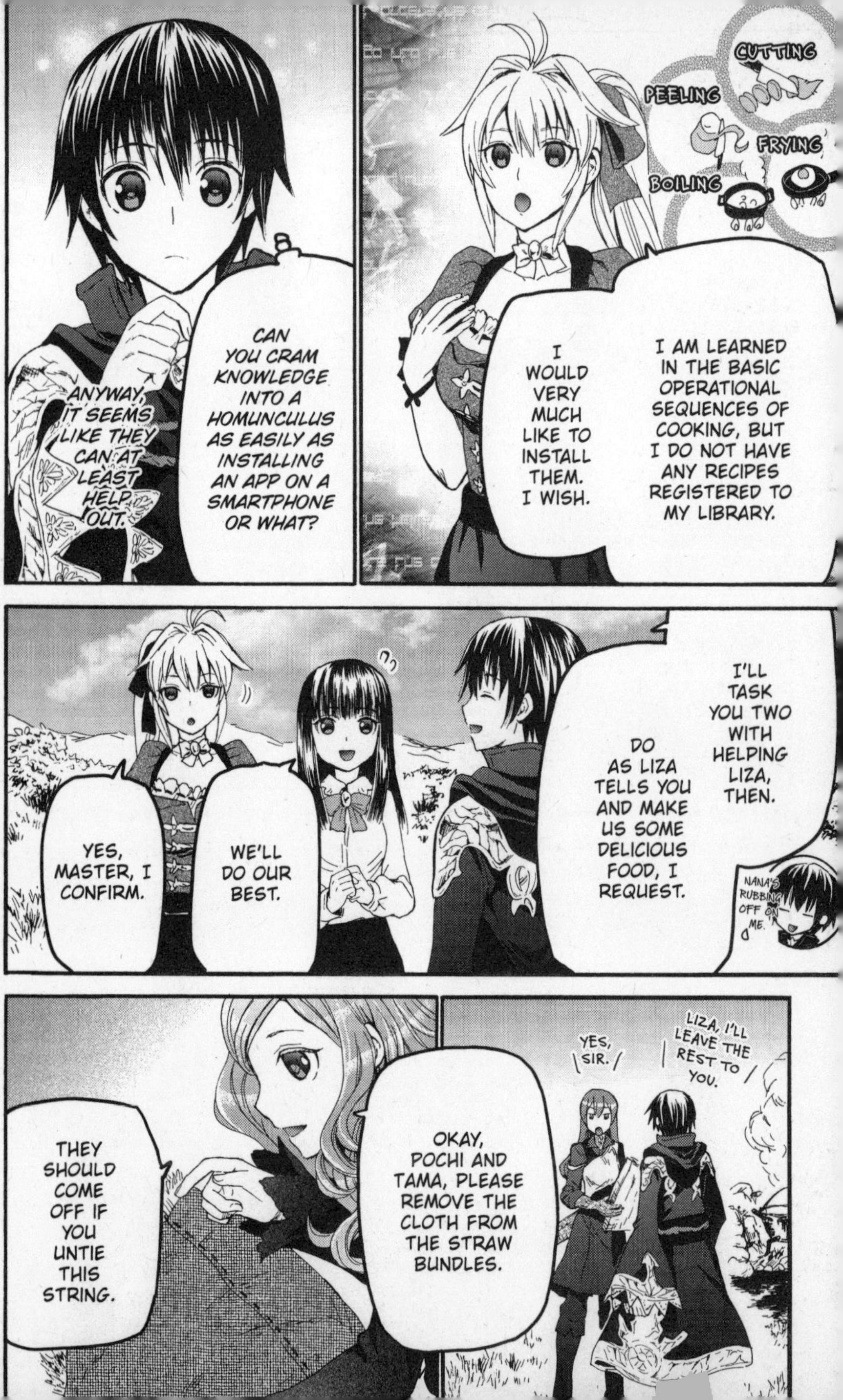
CUTTING
PEELING
FRYING
BOILING
I AM LEARNED IN THE BASIC OPERATIONAL SEQUENCES OF COOKING, BUT I DO NOT HAVE ANY RECIPES REGISTERED TO MY LIBRARY.
I WOULD VERY MUCH LIKE TO INSTALL THEM. I WISH.
CAN YOU CRAM KNOWLEDGE INTO A HOMUNCULUS AS EASILY AS INSTALLING AN APP ON A SMARTPHONE OR WHAT?
ANYWAY, IT SEEMS LIKE THEY CAN AT LEAST HELP OUT.
I'LL TASK YOU TWO WITH HELPING LIZA, THEN.
DO AS LIZA TELLS YOU AND MAKE US SOME DELICIOUS FOOD, I REQUEST.
NANA'S RUBBING OFF ON ME.
WE'LL DO OUR BEST.
YES, MASTER, I CONFIRM.
LIZA, I'LL LEAVE THE REST TO YOU.
YES, SIR.
OKAY, POCHI AND TAMA, PLEASE REMOVE THE CLOTH FROM THE STRAW BUNDLES.
THEY SHOULD COME OFF IF YOU UNTIE THIS STRING.

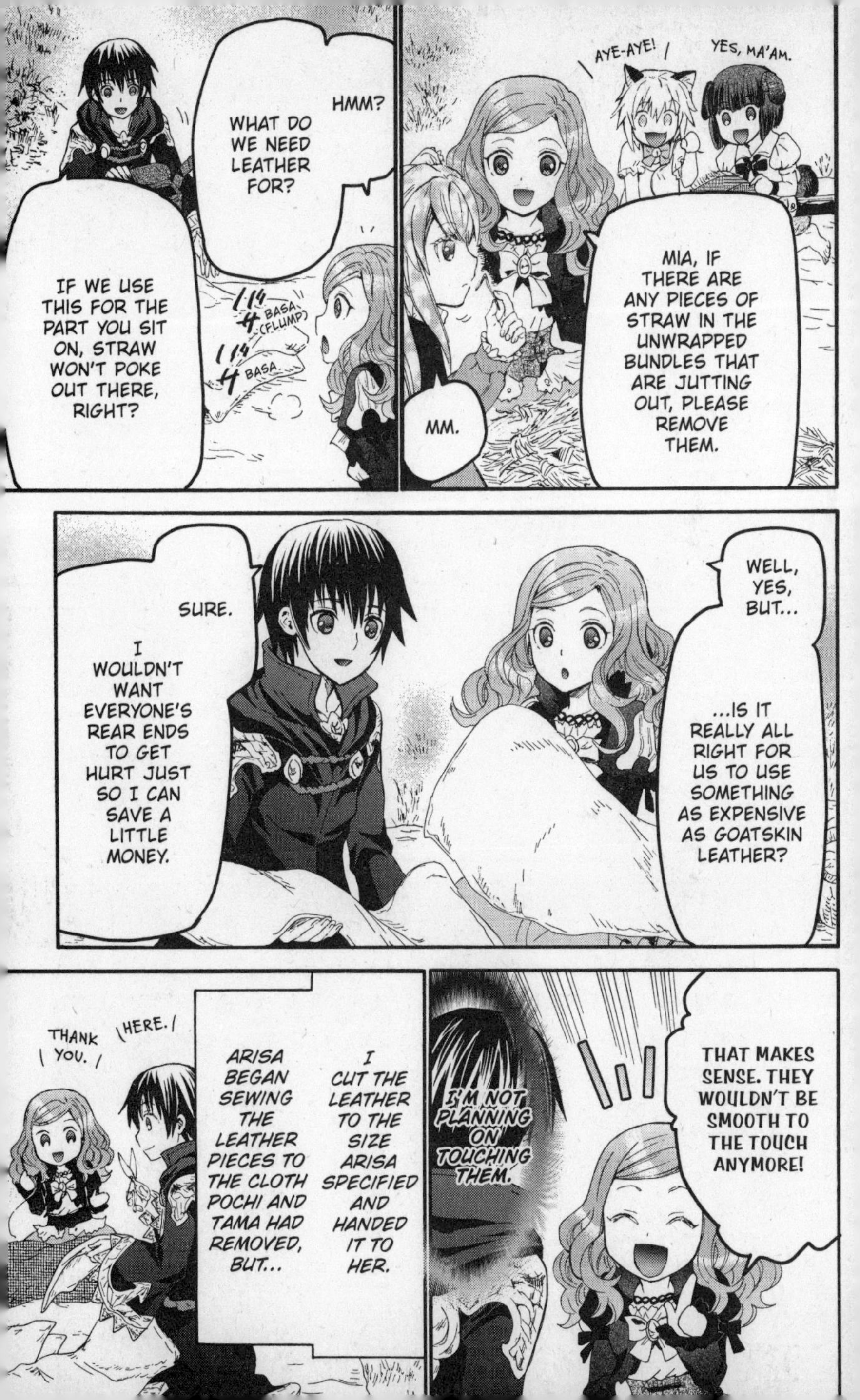
YES, MA'AM.
AYE-AYE!
MIA, IF THERE ARE ANY PIECES OF STRAW IN THE UNWRAPPED BUNDLES THAT ARE JUTTING OUT, PLEASE REMOVE THEM.
MM.
HMM?
WHAT DO WE NEED LEATHER FOR?
BASA (FLUMP)
BASA
IF WE USE THIS FOR THE PART YOU SIT ON, STRAW WON'T POKE OUT THERE, RIGHT?
WELL, YES, BUT...
...IS IT REALLY ALL RIGHT FOR US TO USE SOMETHING AS EXPENSIVE AS GOATSKIN LEATHER?
SURE.
I WOULDN'T WANT EVERYONE'S REAR ENDS TO GET HURT JUST SO I CAN SAVE A LITTLE MONEY.
THAT MAKES SENSE. THEY WOULDN'T BE SMOOTH TO THE TOUCH ANYMORE!
I'M NOT PLANNING ON TOUCHING THEM.
I CUT THE LEATHER TO THE SIZE ARISA SPECIFIED AND HANDED IT TO HER.
ARISA BEGAN SEWING THE LEATHER PIECES TO THE CLOTH POCHI AND TAMA HAD REMOVED, BUT...
HERE.
THANK YOU.

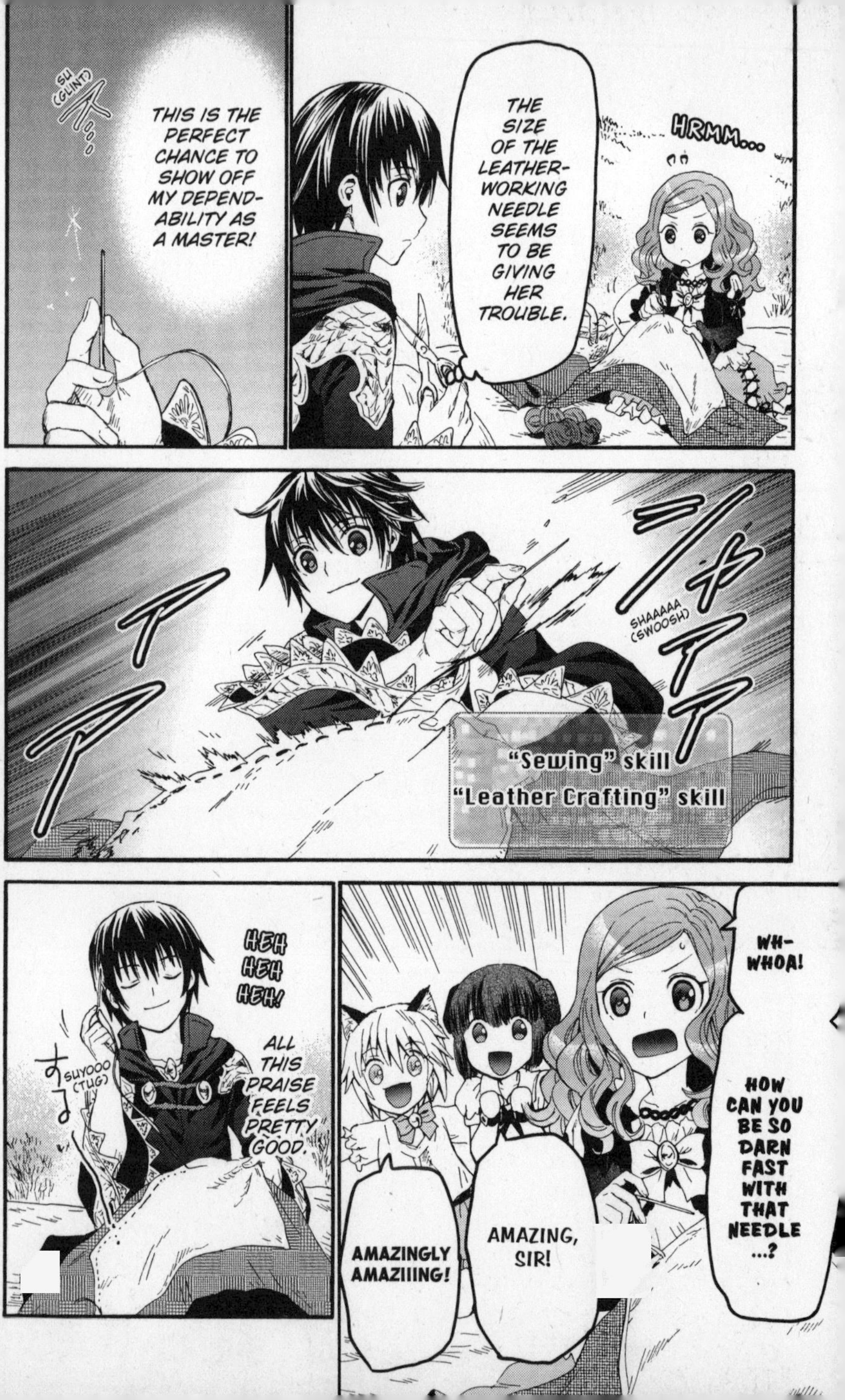
HRMM...
THE SIZE OF THE LEATHER-WORKING NEEDLE SEEMS TO BE GIVING HER TROUBLE.
SU (GLINT)
THIS IS THE PERFECT CHANCE TO SHOW OFF MY DEPEND-ABILITY AS A MASTER!
SHAAAAA (SWOOSH)
"Sewing" skill
"Leather Crafting" skill
WH-WHOA!
HOW CAN YOU BE SO DARN FAST WITH THAT NEEDLE...?
AMAZING, SIR!
AMAZINGLY AMAZIIING!
HEH HEH HEH!
ALL THIS PRAISE FEELS PRETTY GOOD.
SUYOOO (TUG)

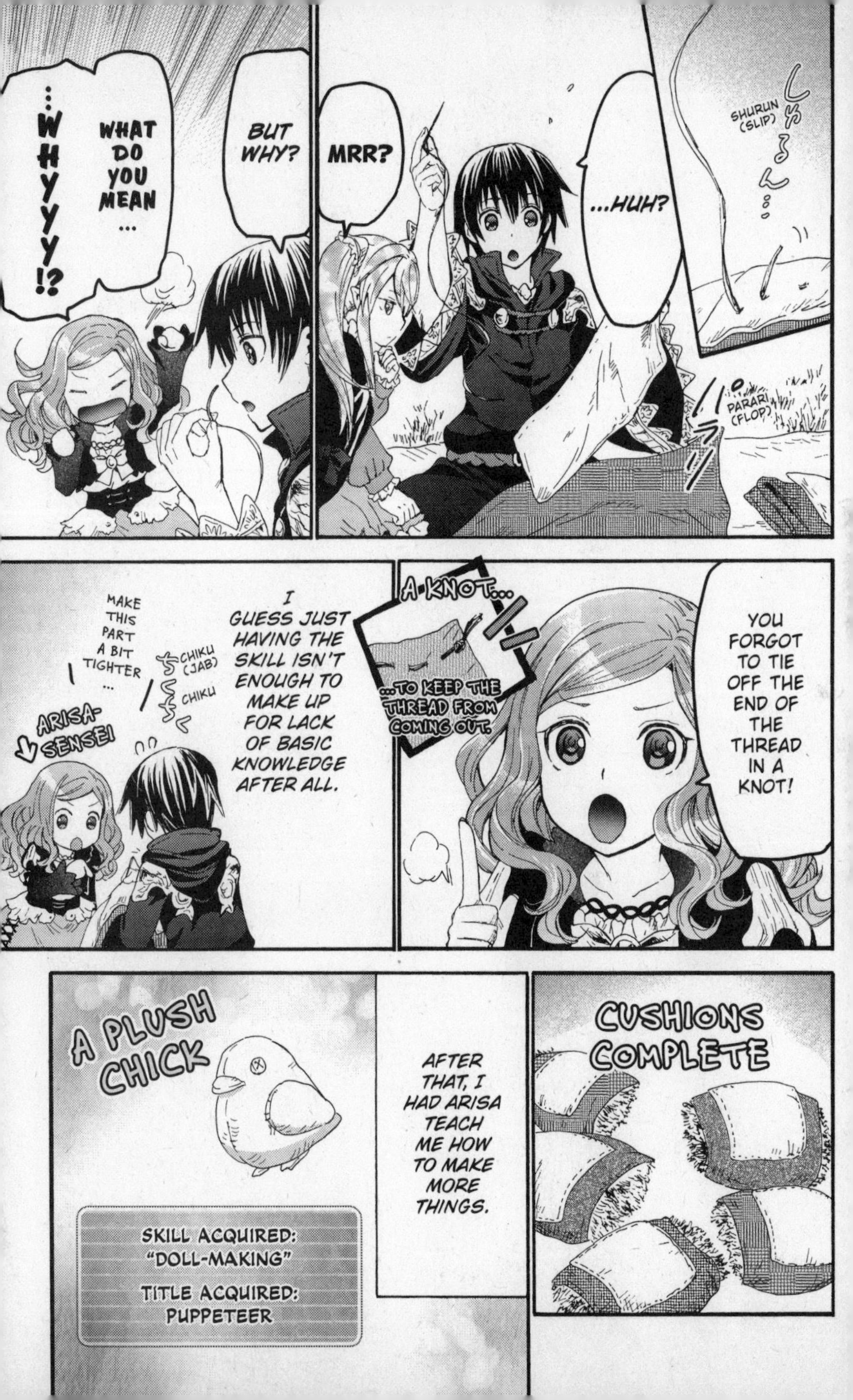
SHURUN (SLIP)
...HUH?
MRR?
PARARI (FLOP)
BUT WHY?
WHAT DO YOU MEAN...
...WHYYYY!?
YOU FORGOT TO TIE OFF THE END OF THE THREAD IN A KNOT!
A KNOT...
...TO KEEP THE THREAD FROM COMING OUT.
I GUESS JUST HAVING THE SKILL ISN'T ENOUGH TO MAKE UP FOR LACK OF BASIC KNOWLEDGE AFTER ALL.
MAKE THIS PART A BIT TIGHTER...
CHIKU (JAB)
CHIKU
ARISA-SENSEI
CUSHIONS COMPLETE
AFTER THAT, I HAD ARISA TEACH ME HOW TO MAKE MORE THINGS.
A PLUSH CHICK
SKILL ACQUIRED: "DOLL-MAKING"
TITLE ACQUIRED: PUPPETEER

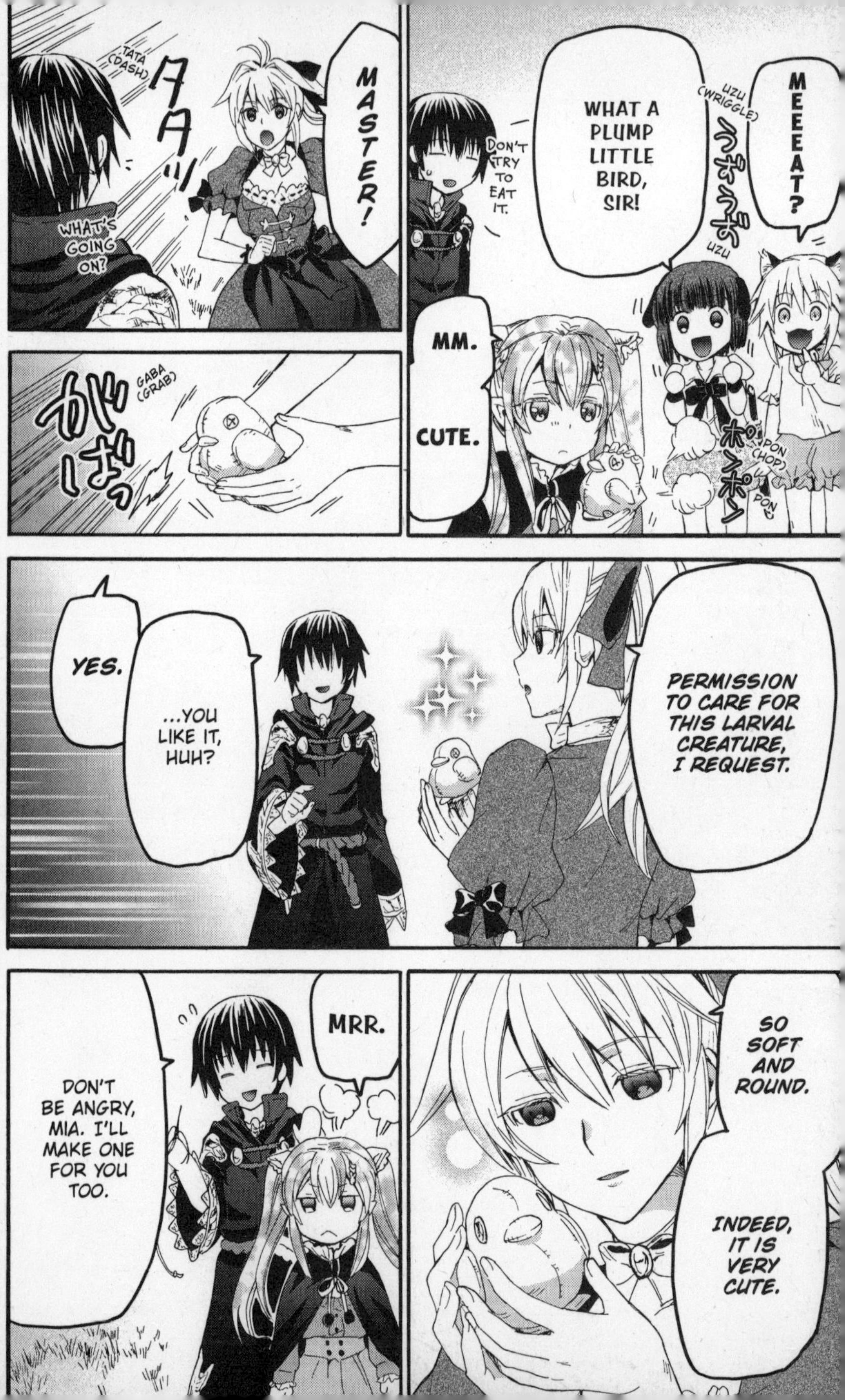
MEEEAT?
UZU (WRIGGLE)
うぞうぞ
UZU
WHAT A PLUMP LITTLE BIRD, SIR!
DON'T TRY TO EAT IT.
MM.
CUTE.
PON (HOP)
ポンポン
PON
MASTER!
TATA (DASH)
タタッ
WHAT'S GOING ON?
GABA (GRAB)
がばっ
PERMISSION TO CARE FOR THIS LARVAL CREATURE, I REQUEST.
...YOU LIKE IT, HUH?
YES.
SO SOFT AND ROUND.
INDEED, IT IS VERY CUTE.
MRR.
DON'T BE ANGRY, MIA. I'LL MAKE ONE FOR YOU TOO.

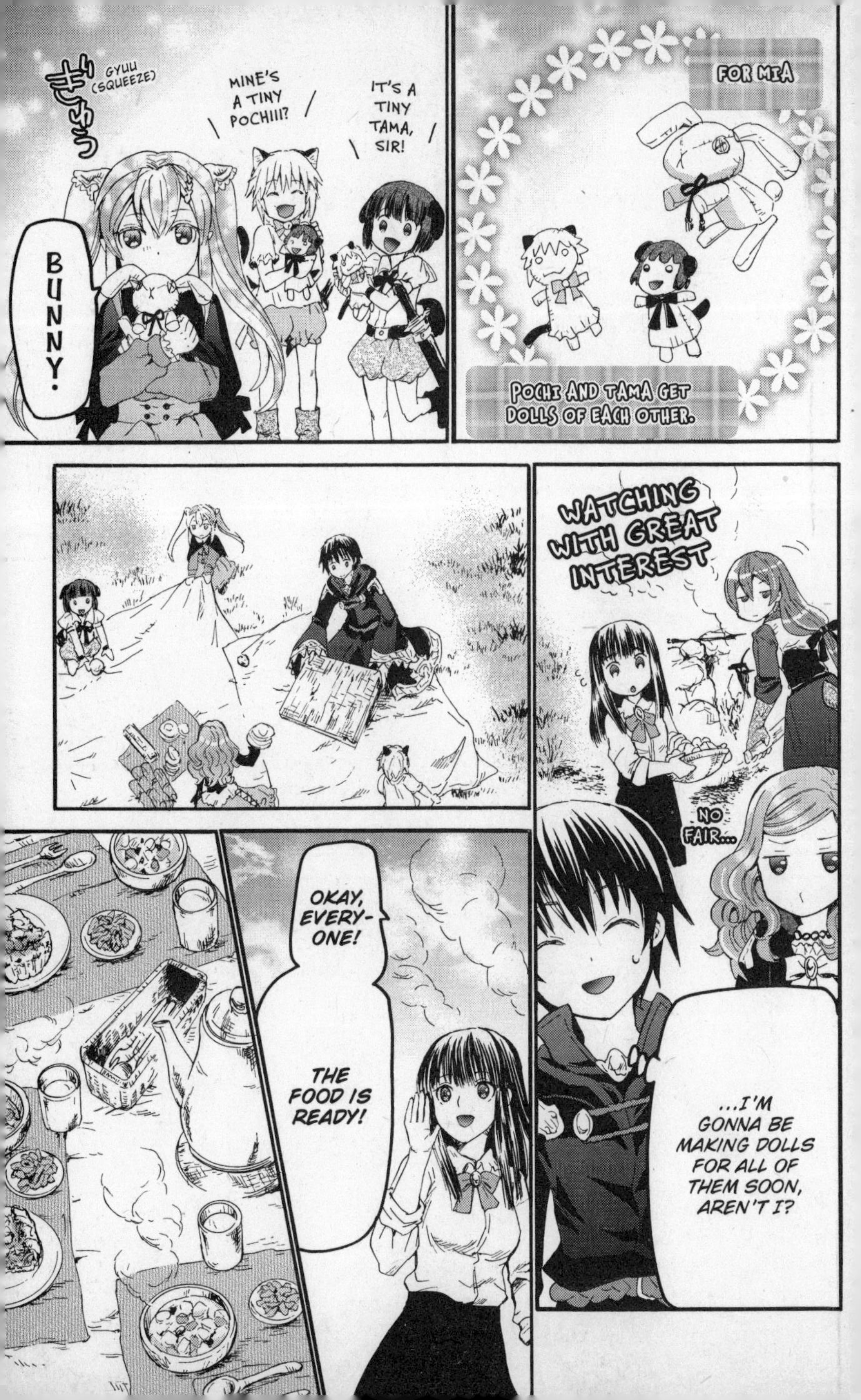
FOR MIA
POCHI AND TAMA GET DOLLS OF EACH OTHER.
IT'S A TINY TAMA, SIR!
MINE'S A TINY POCHIII?
ぎゅう
GYUU (SQUEEZE)
BUNNY.
WATCHING WITH GREAT INTEREST
NO FAIR...
...I'M GONNA BE MAKING DOLLS FOR ALL OF THEM SOON, AREN'T I?
OKAY, EVERY-ONE!
THE FOOD IS READY!

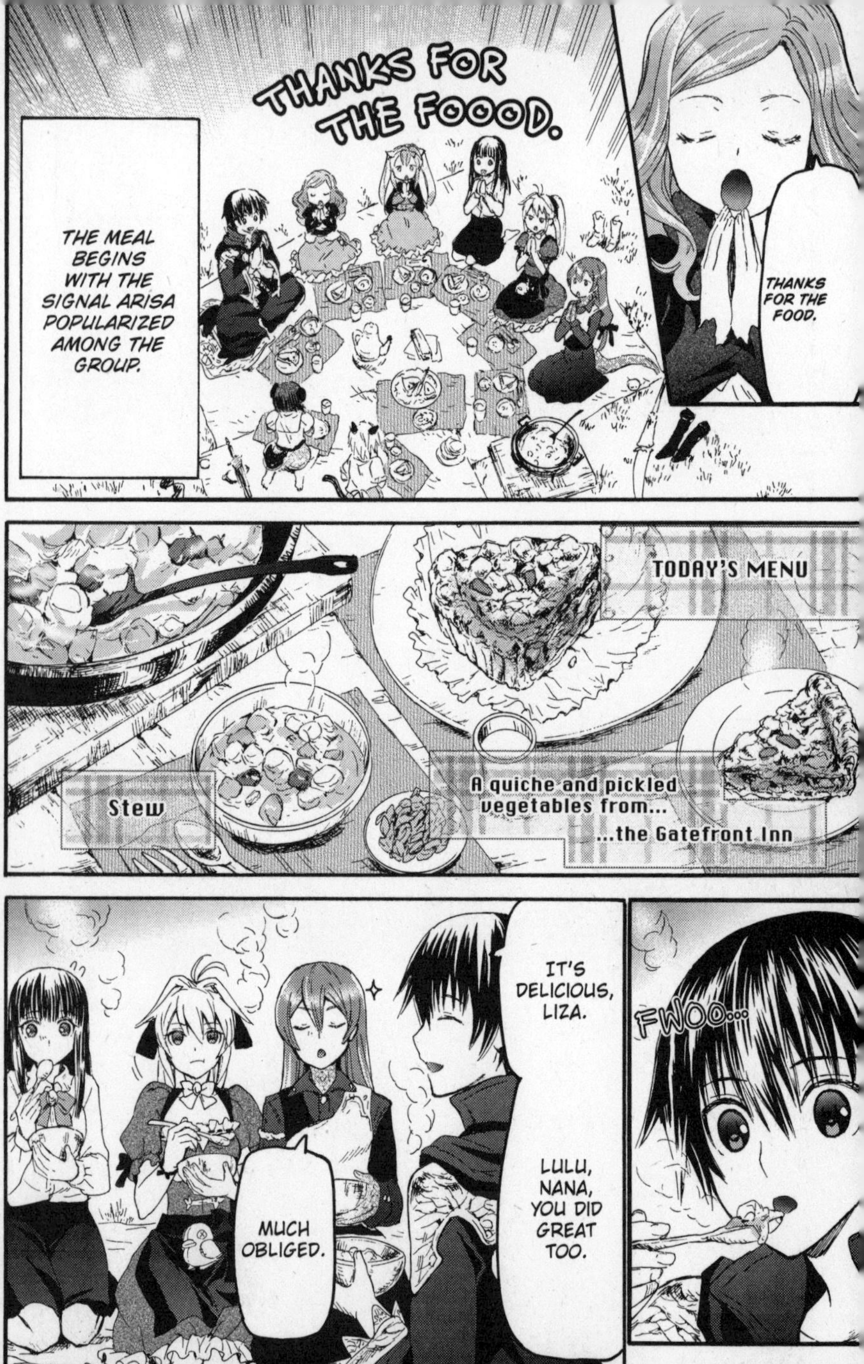
THANKS FOR THE FOOD.
THANKS FOR THE FOOOD.
THE MEAL BEGINS WITH THE SIGNAL ARISA POPULARIZED AMONG THE GROUP.
TODAY'S MENU
A quiche and pickled vegetables from...
...the Gatefront Inn
Stew
FWOO...
IT'S DELICIOUS, LIZA.
LULU, NANA, YOU DID GREAT TOO.
MUCH OBLIGED.

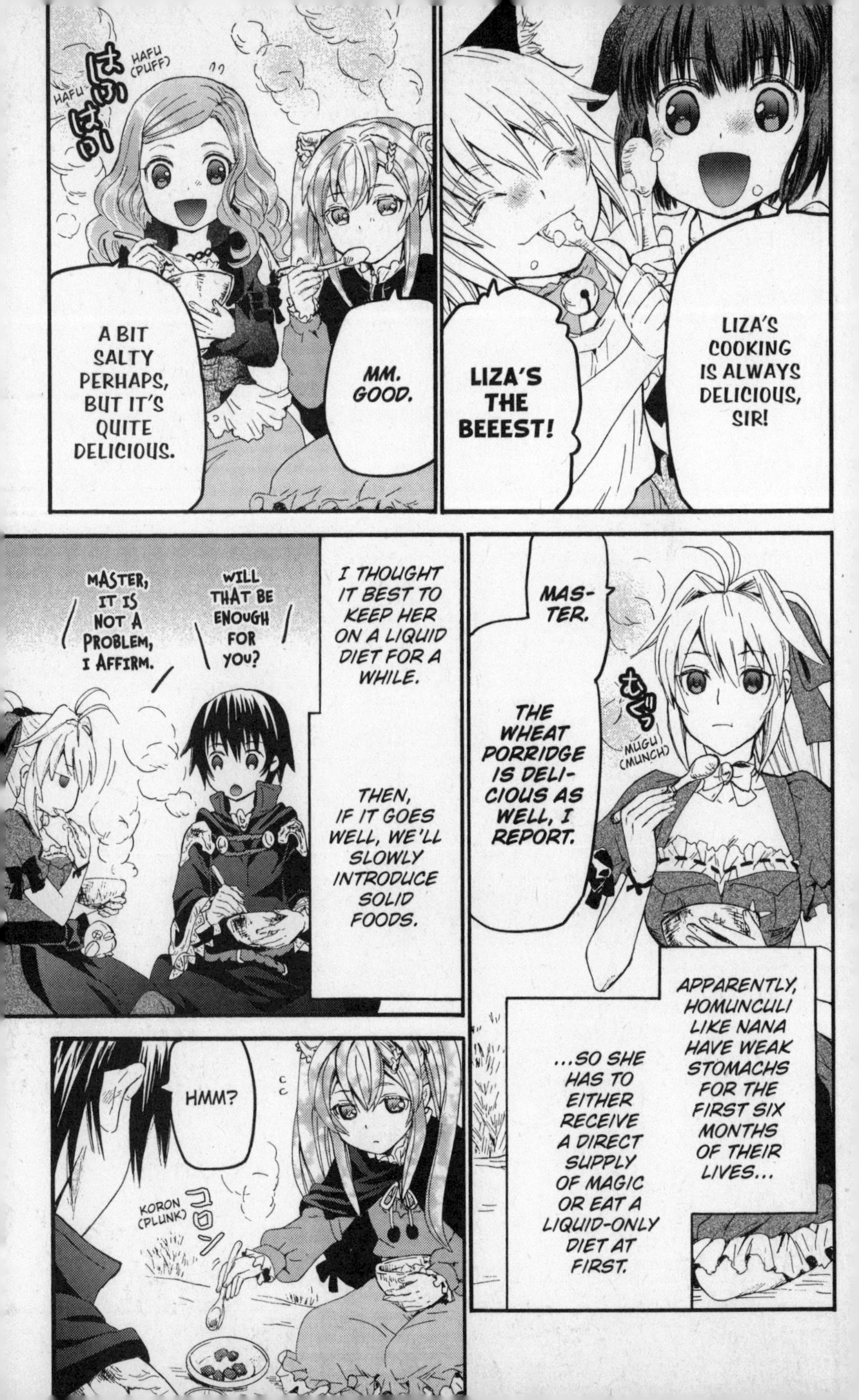
LIZA'S COOKING IS ALWAYS DELICIOUS, SIR!
LIZA'S THE BEEEST!
はふはふ
HAFU (PUFF)
HAFU
MM. GOOD.
A BIT SALTY PERHAPS, BUT IT'S QUITE DELICIOUS.
MASTER.
THE WHEAT PORRIDGE IS DELICIOUS AS WELL, I REPORT.
むぐっ
MUGU (MUNCH)
APPARENTLY, HOMUNCULI LIKE NANA HAVE WEAK STOMACHS FOR THE FIRST SIX MONTHS OF THEIR LIVES...
...SO SHE HAS TO EITHER RECEIVE A DIRECT SUPPLY OF MAGIC OR EAT A LIQUID-ONLY DIET AT FIRST.
I THOUGHT IT BEST TO KEEP HER ON A LIQUID DIET FOR A WHILE.
THEN, IF IT GOES WELL, WE'LL SLOWLY INTRODUCE SOLID FOODS.
WILL THAT BE ENOUGH FOR YOU?
MASTER, IT IS NOT A PROBLEM, I AFFIRM.
HMM?
コロン
KORON (PLUNK)

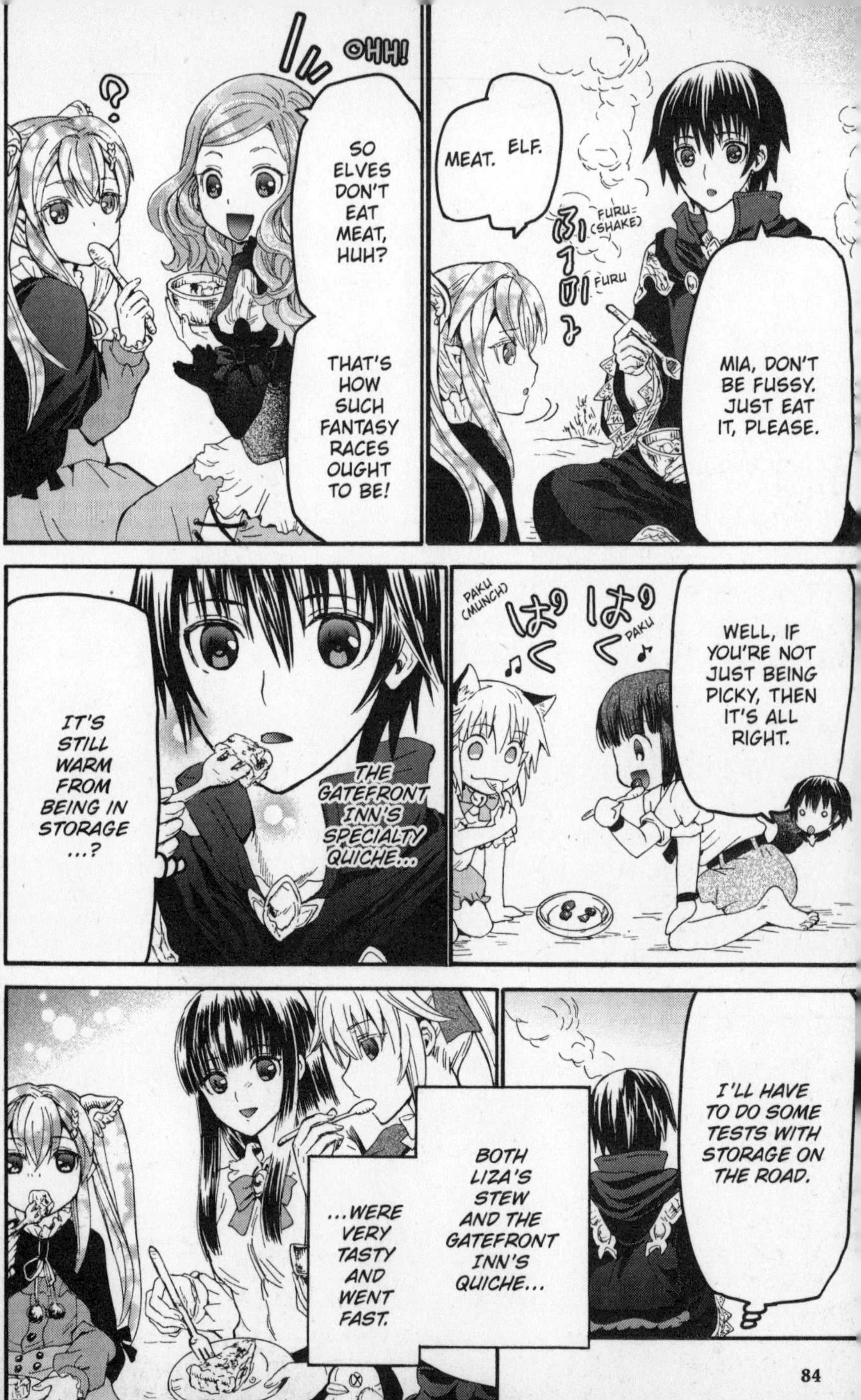
MEAT. ELF.
ふるふる
FURU (SHAKE)
FURU
MIA, DON'T BE FUSSY. JUST EAT IT, PLEASE.
OHH!
SO ELVES DON'T EAT MEAT, HUH?
THAT'S HOW SUCH FANTASY RACES OUGHT TO BE!
?
WELL, IF YOU'RE NOT JUST BEING PICKY, THEN IT'S ALL RIGHT.
はく はく
PAKU
PAKU (MUNCH)
THE GATEFRONT INN'S SPECIALTY QUICHE...
IT'S STILL WARM FROM BEING IN STORAGE ...?
I'LL HAVE TO DO SOME TESTS WITH STORAGE ON THE ROAD.
BOTH LIZA'S STEW AND THE GATEFRONT INN'S QUICHE...
...WERE VERY TASTY AND WENT FAST.

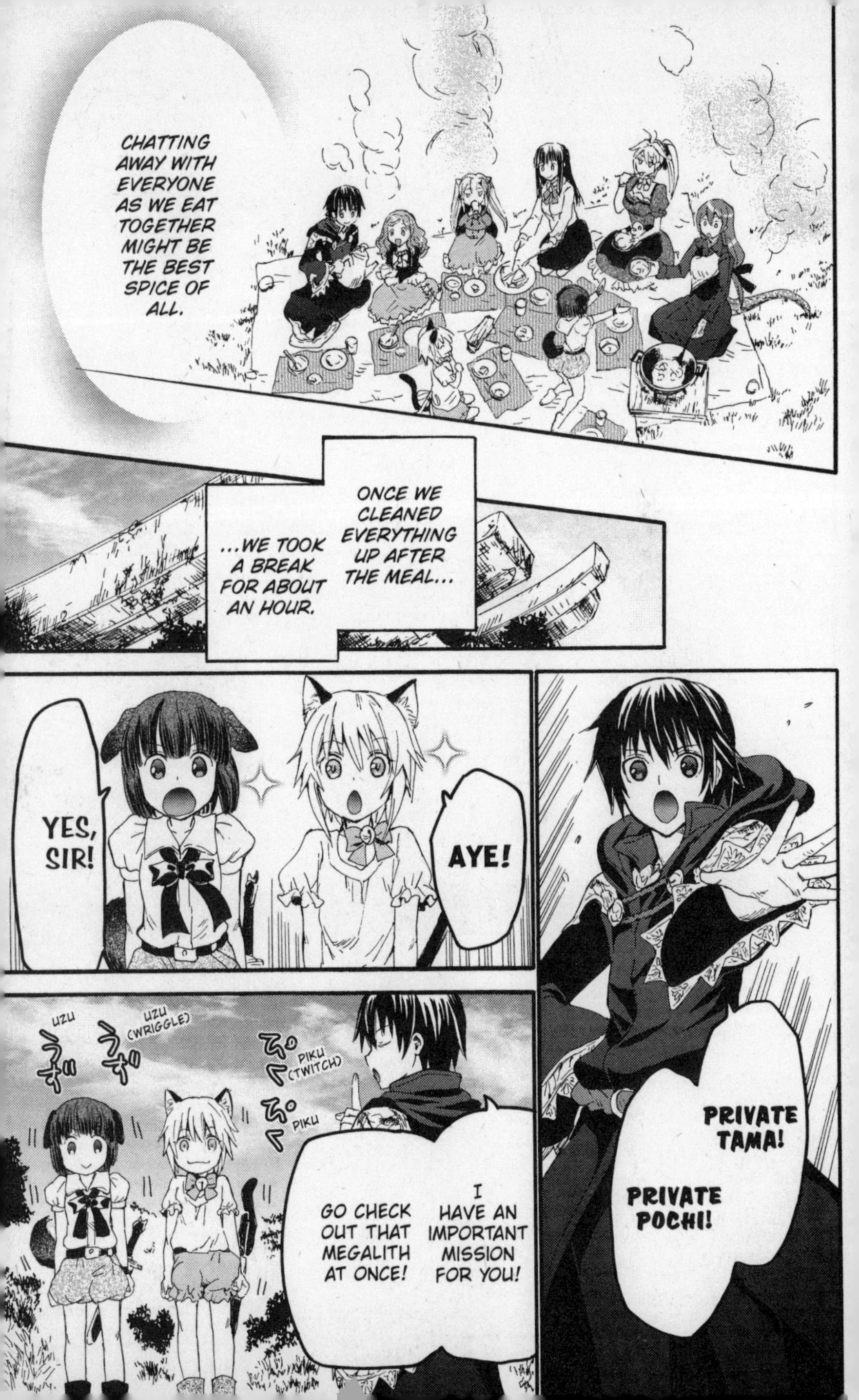
CHATTING AWAY WITH EVERYONE AS WE EAT TOGETHER MIGHT BE THE BEST SPICE OF ALL.
ONCE WE CLEANED EVERYTHING UP AFTER THE MEAL...
...WE TOOK A BREAK FOR ABOUT AN HOUR.
PRIVATE TAMA!
PRIVATE POCHI!
AYE!
YES, SIR!
I HAVE AN IMPORTANT MISSION FOR YOU!
GO CHECK OUT THAT MEGALITH AT ONCE!
PIKU (TWITCH)
PIKU
UZU (WRIGGLE)
UZU

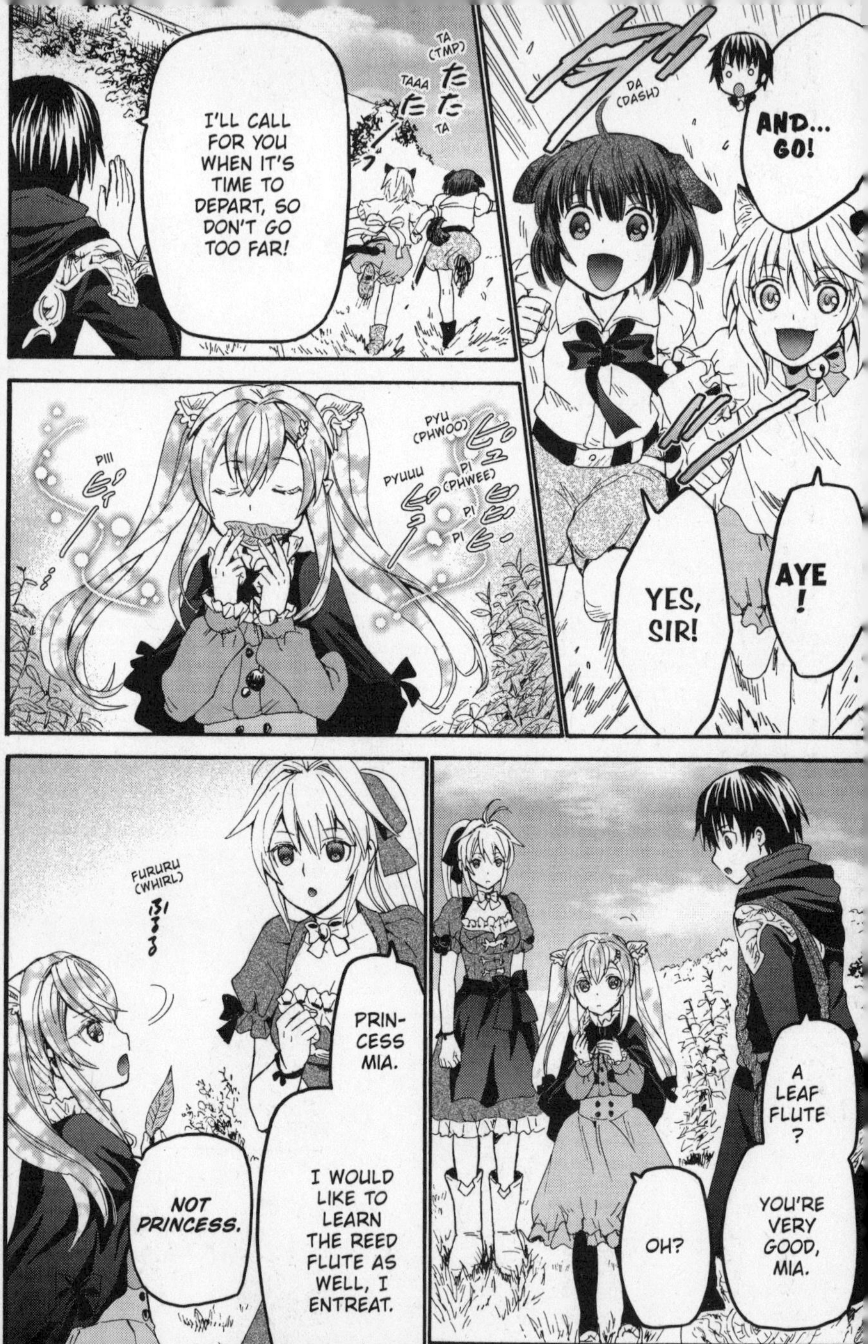

AND... GO!
DA (DASH)
AYE!
YES, SIR!
I'LL CALL FOR YOU WHEN IT'S TIME TO DEPART, SO DON'T GO TOO FAR!
TA (TMP)
TAAA
TA
PYU (PHWOO)
PI (PHWEE)
PI
PI
PYUUU
PIII
A LEAF FLUTE?
YOU'RE VERY GOOD, MIA.
OH?
FURURU (WHIRL)
PRIN-CESS MIA.
I WOULD LIKE TO LEARN THE REED FLUTE AS WELL, I ENTREAT.
NOT PRINCESS.

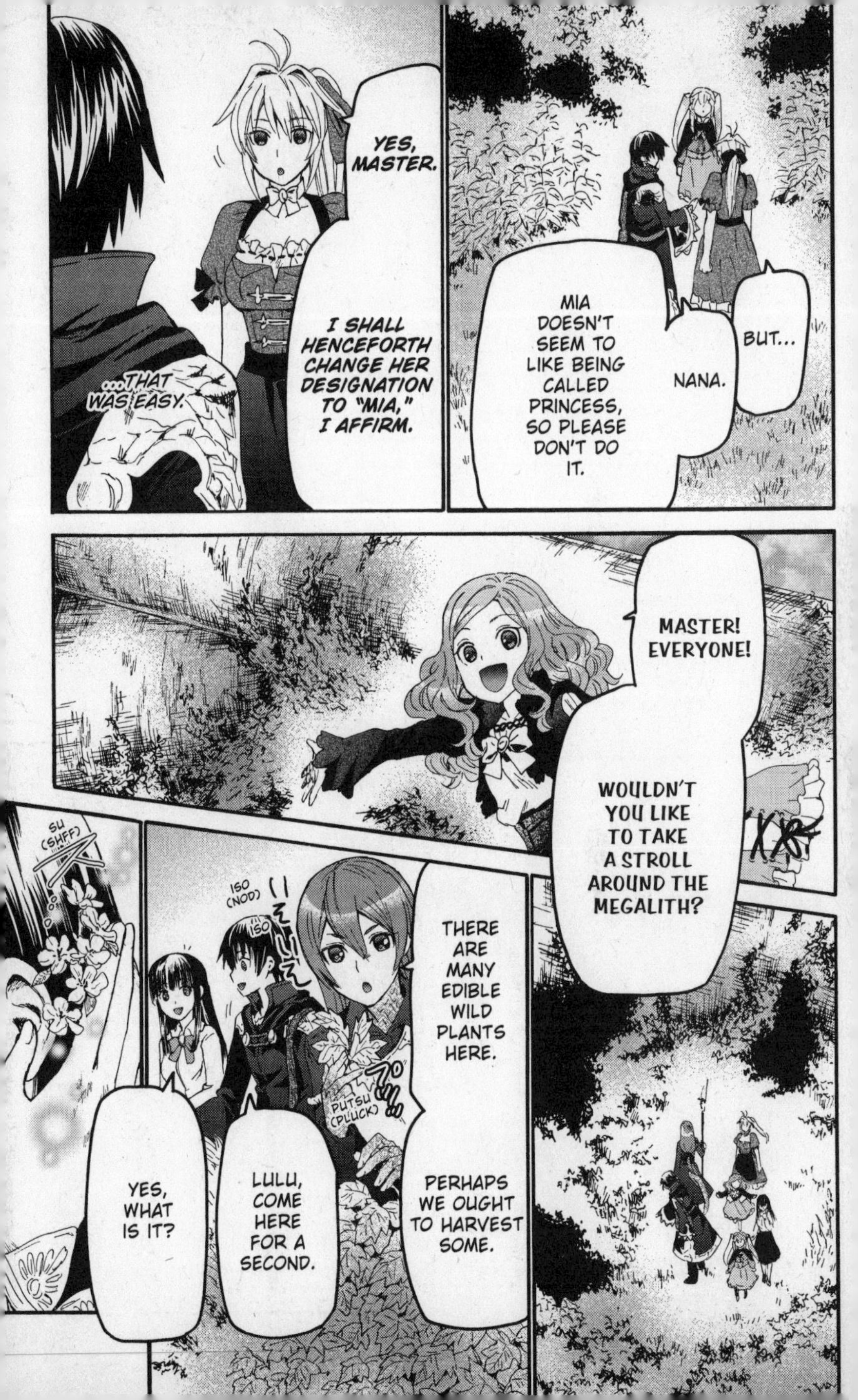
BUT...
NANA.
MIA DOESN'T SEEM TO LIKE BEING CALLED PRINCESS, SO PLEASE DON'T DO IT.
YES, MASTER.
I SHALL HENCEFORTH CHANGE HER DESIGNATION TO "MIA," I AFFIRM.
...THAT WAS EASY.
MASTER! EVERYONE!
WOULDN'T YOU LIKE TO TAKE A STROLL AROUND THE MEGALITH?
THERE ARE MANY EDIBLE WILD PLANTS HERE.
ISO (NOD) ISO
PUTSU (PLUCK)
PERHAPS WE OUGHT TO HARVEST SOME.
LULU, COME HERE FOR A SECOND.
SU (SHFF)
YES, WHAT IS IT?

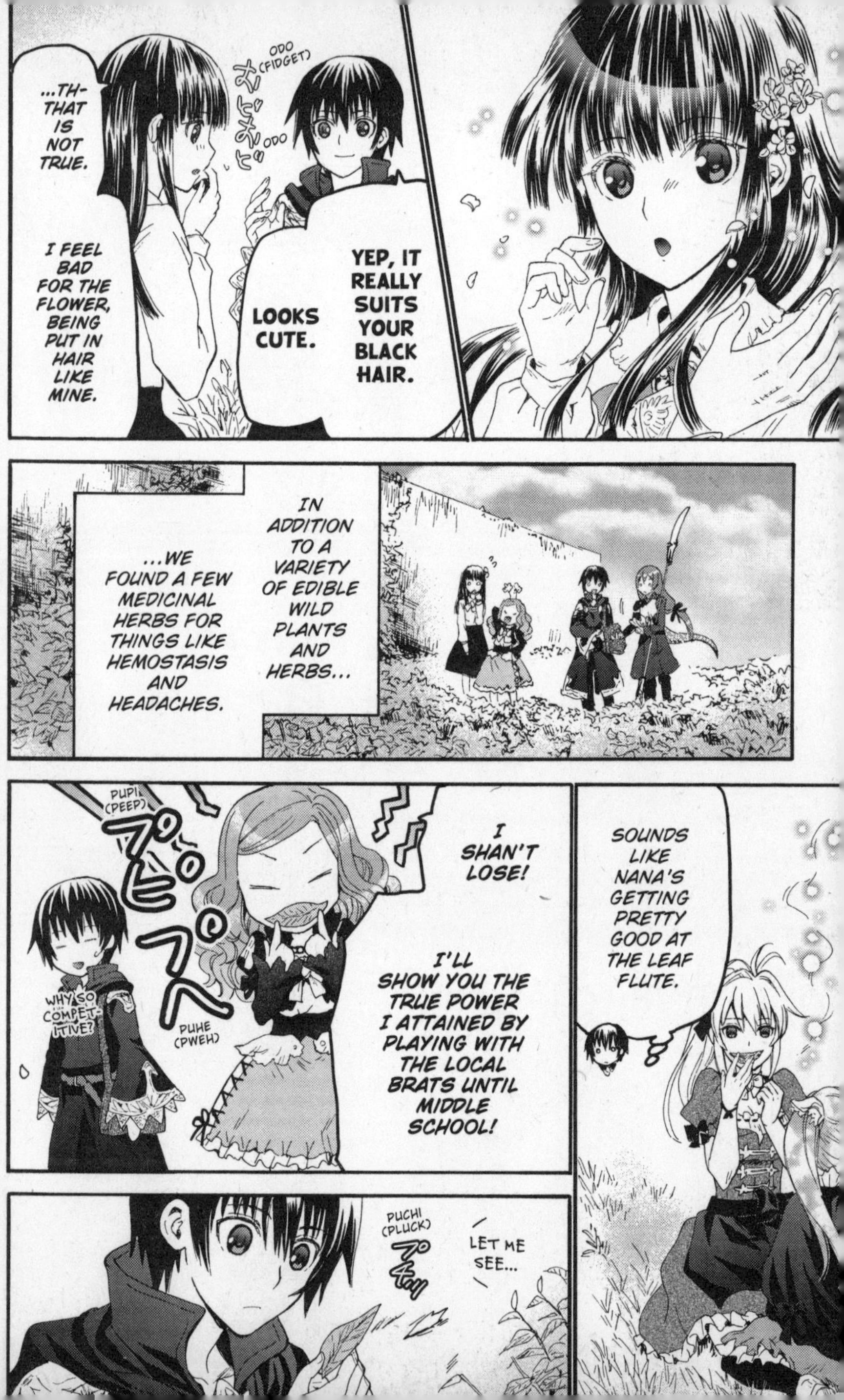
YEP, IT REALLY SUITS YOUR BLACK HAIR.
LOOKS CUTE.
ODO ODO (FIDGET)
...TH-THAT IS NOT TRUE.
I FEEL BAD FOR THE FLOWER, BEING PUT IN HAIR LIKE MINE.
IN ADDITION TO A VARIETY OF EDIBLE WILD PLANTS AND HERBS...
...WE FOUND A FEW MEDICINAL HERBS FOR THINGS LIKE HEMOSTASIS AND HEADACHES.
SOUNDS LIKE NANA'S GETTING PRETTY GOOD AT THE LEAF FLUTE.
I SHAN'T LOSE!
I'LL SHOW YOU THE TRUE POWER I ATTAINED BY PLAYING WITH THE LOCAL BRATS UNTIL MIDDLE SCHOOL!
PUPI (PEEP)
PUHE (PWEH)
WHY SO COMPET-ITIVE?
LET ME SEE...
PUCHI (PLUCK)

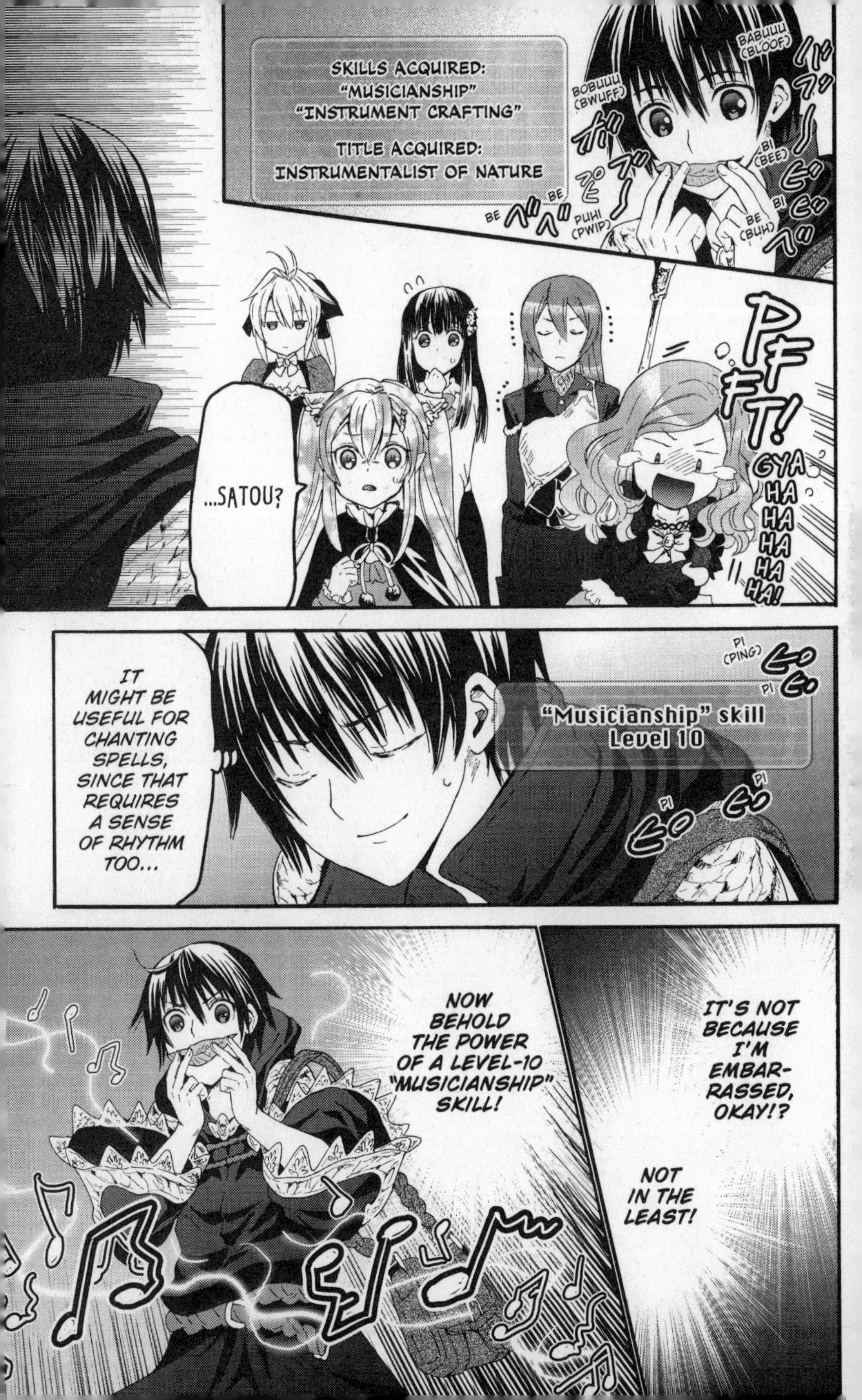
SKILLS ACQUIRED:
"MUSICIANSHIP"
"INSTRUMENT CRAFTING"
TITLE ACQUIRED:
INSTRUMENTALIST OF NATURE
BABUUU (BLOOF)
BI (BEE)
BI
BE (BUH)
BOBUUU (BWUFF)
PUHI (PWIP)
BE
BE
PFFT!
GYAHAHAHAHAHAHA!
...SATOU?
PI (PING)
PI
"Musicianship" skill
Level 10
IT MIGHT BE USEFUL FOR CHANTING SPELLS, SINCE THAT REQUIRES A SENSE OF RHYTHM TOO...
PI
PI
IT'S NOT BECAUSE I'M EMBARRASSED, OKAY!?
NOT IN THE LEAST!
NOW BEHOLD THE POWER OF A LEVEL-10 "MUSICIANSHIP" SKILL!

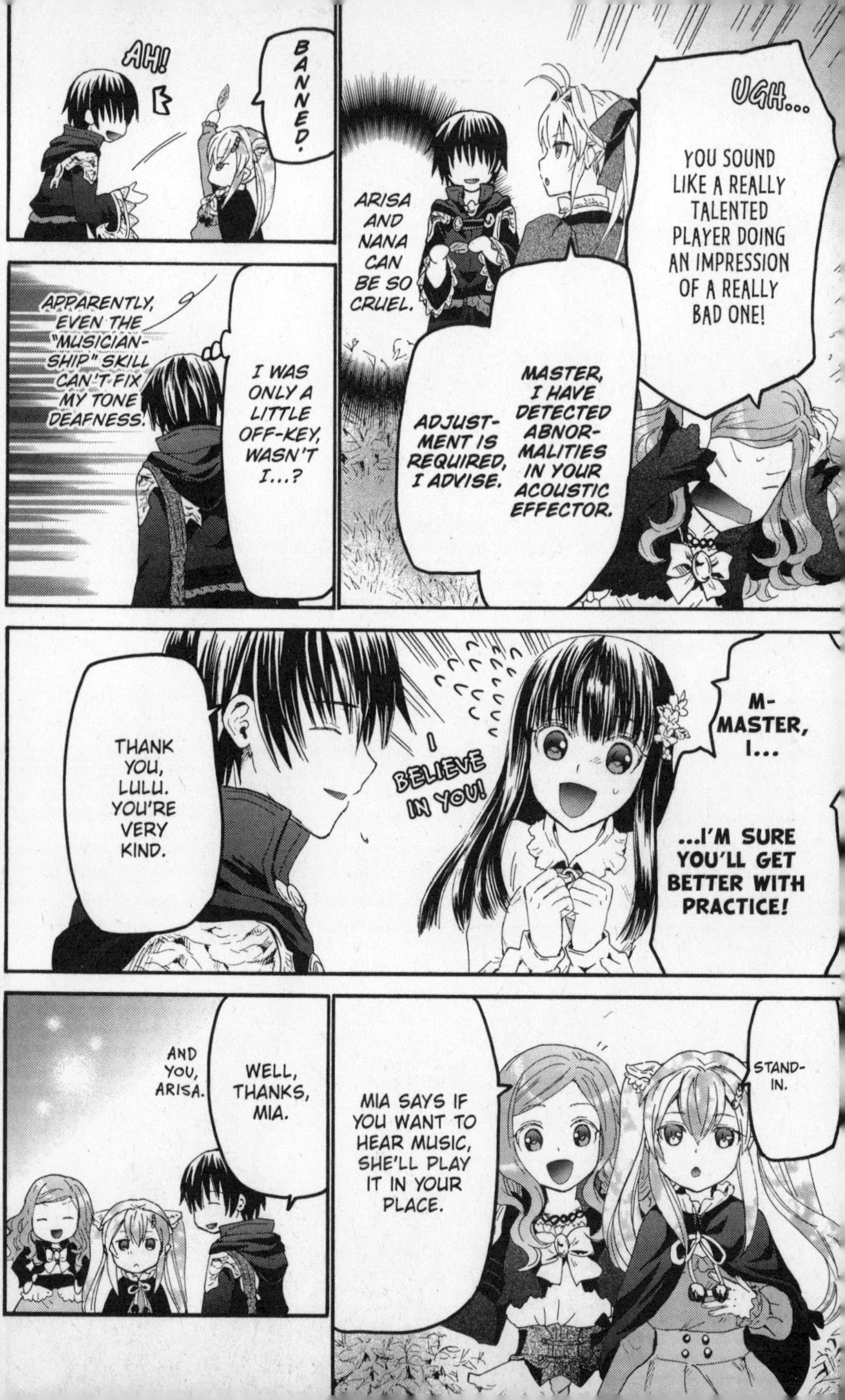
UGH...
YOU SOUND LIKE A REALLY TALENTED PLAYER DOING AN IMPRESSION OF A REALLY BAD ONE!
MASTER, I HAVE DETECTED ABNORMALITIES IN YOUR ACOUSTIC EFFECTOR.
ADJUSTMENT IS REQUIRED, I ADVISE.
ARISA AND NANA CAN BE SO CRUEL.
BANNED.
AH!
I WAS ONLY A LITTLE OFF-KEY, WASN'T I...?
APPARENTLY, EVEN THE "MUSICIANSHIP" SKILL CAN'T FIX MY TONE DEAFNESS.
M-MASTER, I...
...I'M SURE YOU'LL GET BETTER WITH PRACTICE!
I BELIEVE IN YOU!
THANK YOU, LULU. YOU'RE VERY KIND.
STAND-IN.
MIA SAYS IF YOU WANT TO HEAR MUSIC, SHE'LL PLAY IT IN YOUR PLACE.
WELL, THANKS, MIA.
AND YOU, ARISA.

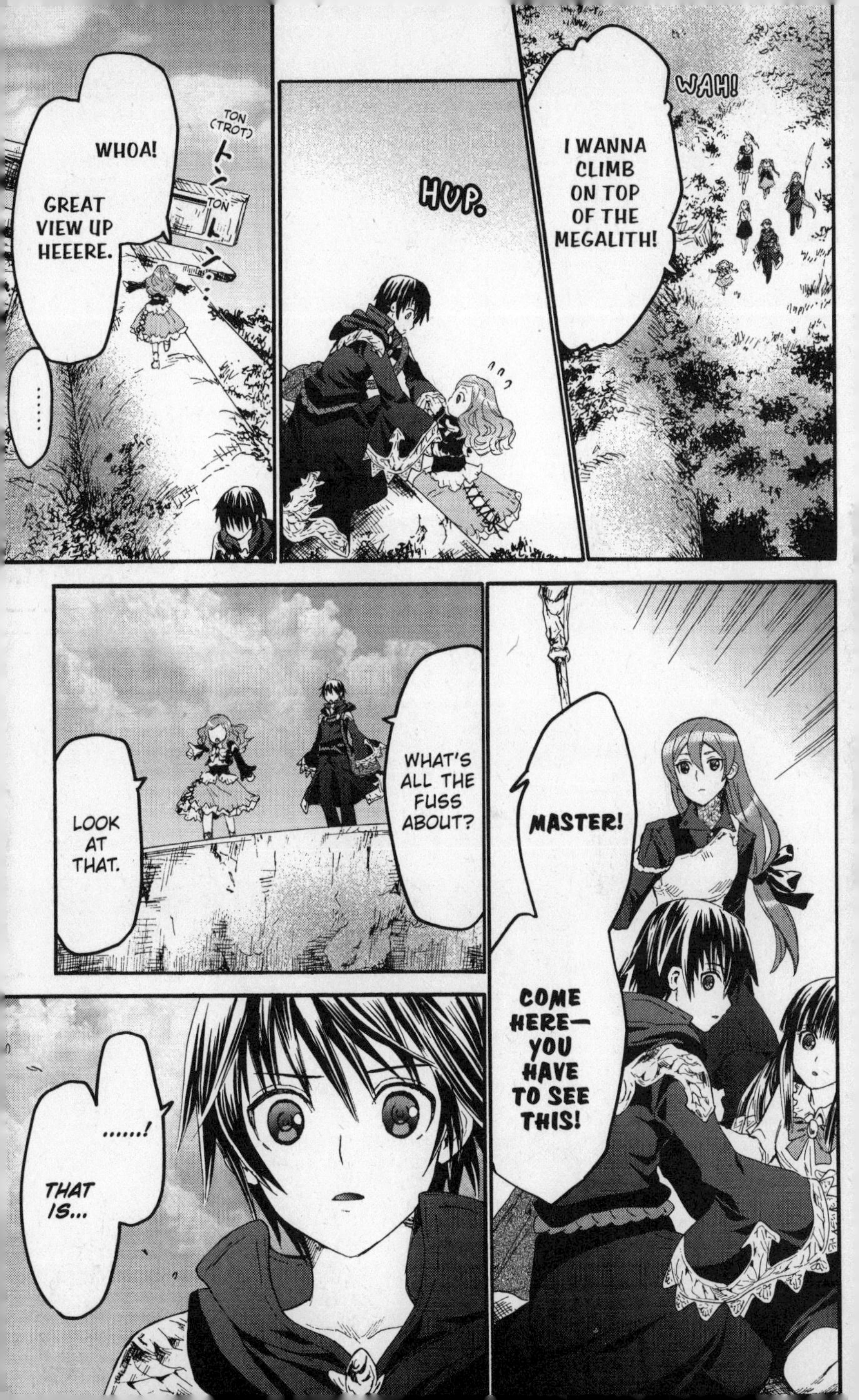
WAH!
I WANNA CLIMB ON TOP OF THE MEGALITH!
HUP.
TON (TROT)
TON
WHOA! GREAT VIEW UP HEEERE.
......
MASTER!
COME HERE—YOU HAVE TO SEE THIS!
WHAT'S ALL THE FUSS ABOUT?
LOOK AT THAT.
......!
THAT IS...

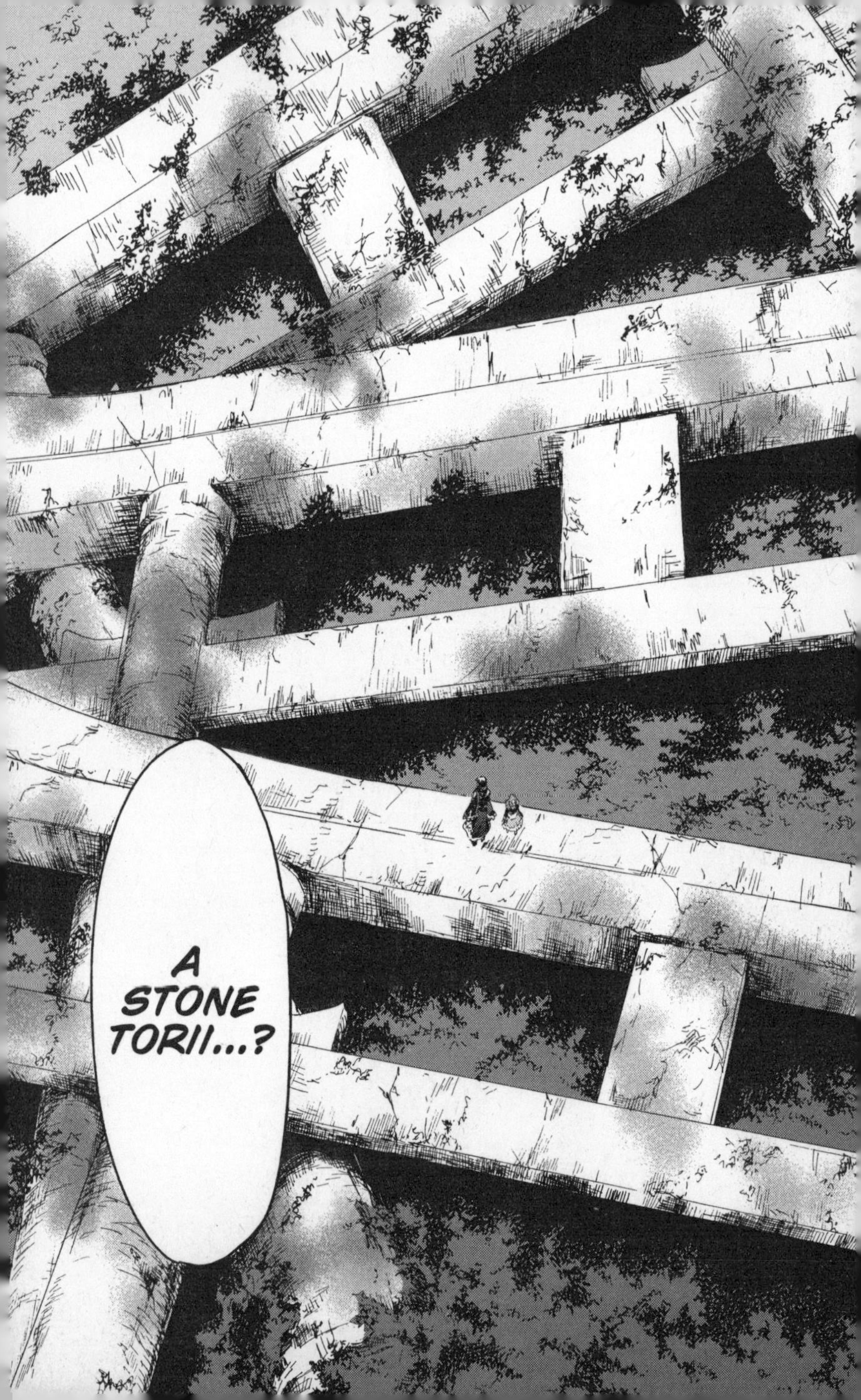
A STONE TORII...?

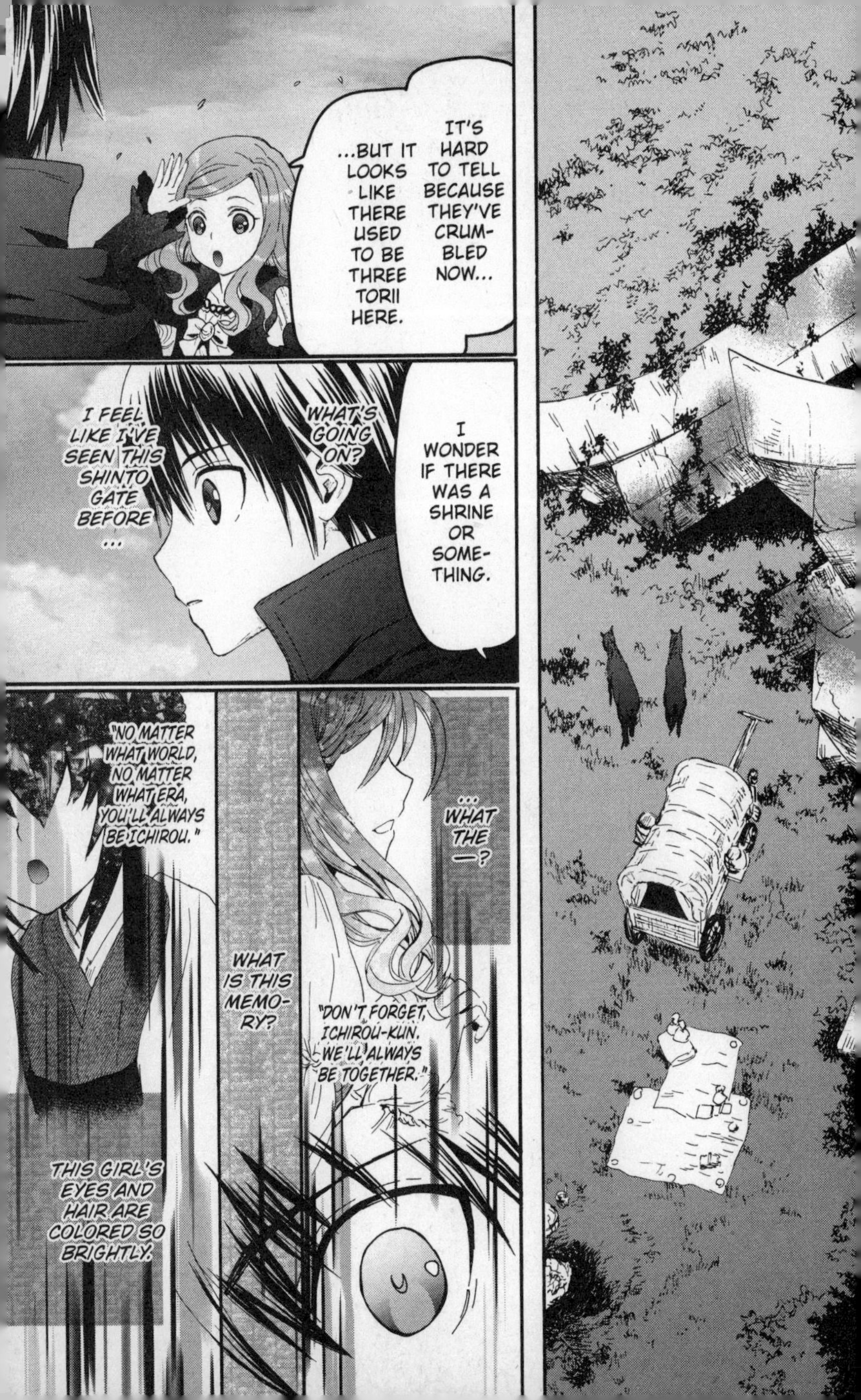
IT'S HARD TO TELL BECAUSE THEY'VE CRUMBLED NOW...
...BUT IT LOOKS LIKE THERE USED TO BE THREE TORII HERE.
I WONDER IF THERE WAS A SHRINE OR SOMETHING.
WHAT'S GOING ON?
I FEEL LIKE I'VE SEEN THIS SHINTO GATE BEFORE...
...WHAT THE—?
"DON'T FORGET, ICHIROU-KUN. WE'LL ALWAYS BE TOGETHER."
WHAT IS THIS MEMORY?
"NO MATTER WHAT WORLD, NO MATTER WHAT ERA, YOU'LL ALWAYS BE ICHIROU."
THIS GIRL'S EYES AND HAIR ARE COLORED SO BRIGHTLY.

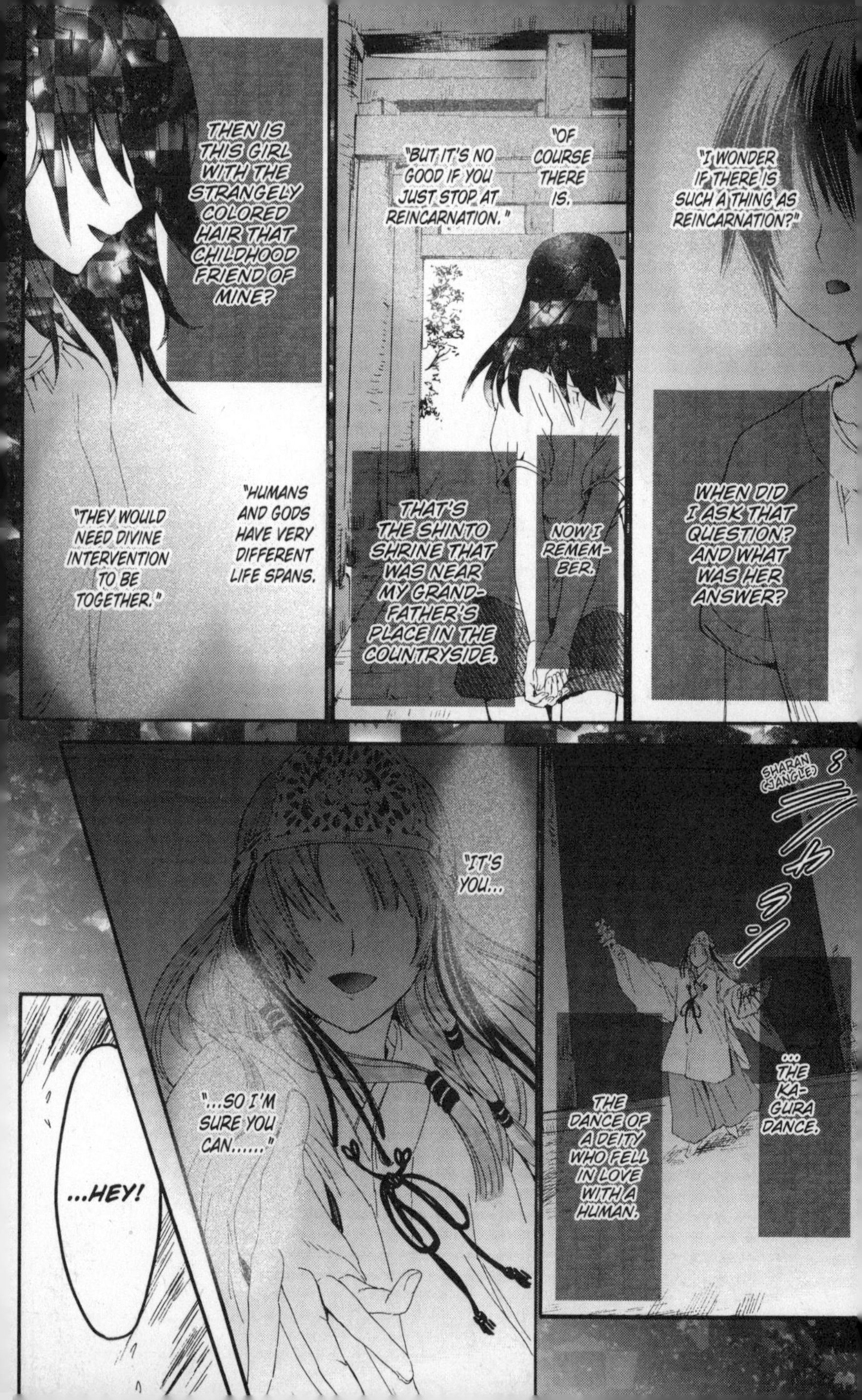

"I WONDER IF THERE IS SUCH A THING AS REINCARNATION?"
WHEN DID I ASK THAT QUESTION? AND WHAT WAS HER ANSWER?
"OF COURSE THERE IS.
"BUT IT'S NO GOOD IF YOU JUST STOP AT REINCARNATION."
NOW I REMEMBER.
THAT'S THE SHINTO SHRINE THAT WAS NEAR MY GRANDFATHER'S PLACE IN THE COUNTRYSIDE.
THEN IS THIS GIRL WITH THE STRANGELY COLORED HAIR THAT CHILDHOOD FRIEND OF MINE?
"HUMANS AND GODS HAVE VERY DIFFERENT LIFE SPANS.
"THEY WOULD NEED DIVINE INTERVENTION TO BE TOGETHER."
SHARAN (JANGLE)
...THE KAGURA DANCE.
THE DANCE OF A DEITY WHO FELL IN LOVE WITH A HUMAN.
"IT'S YOU...
"...SO I'M SURE YOU CAN......"
...HEY!

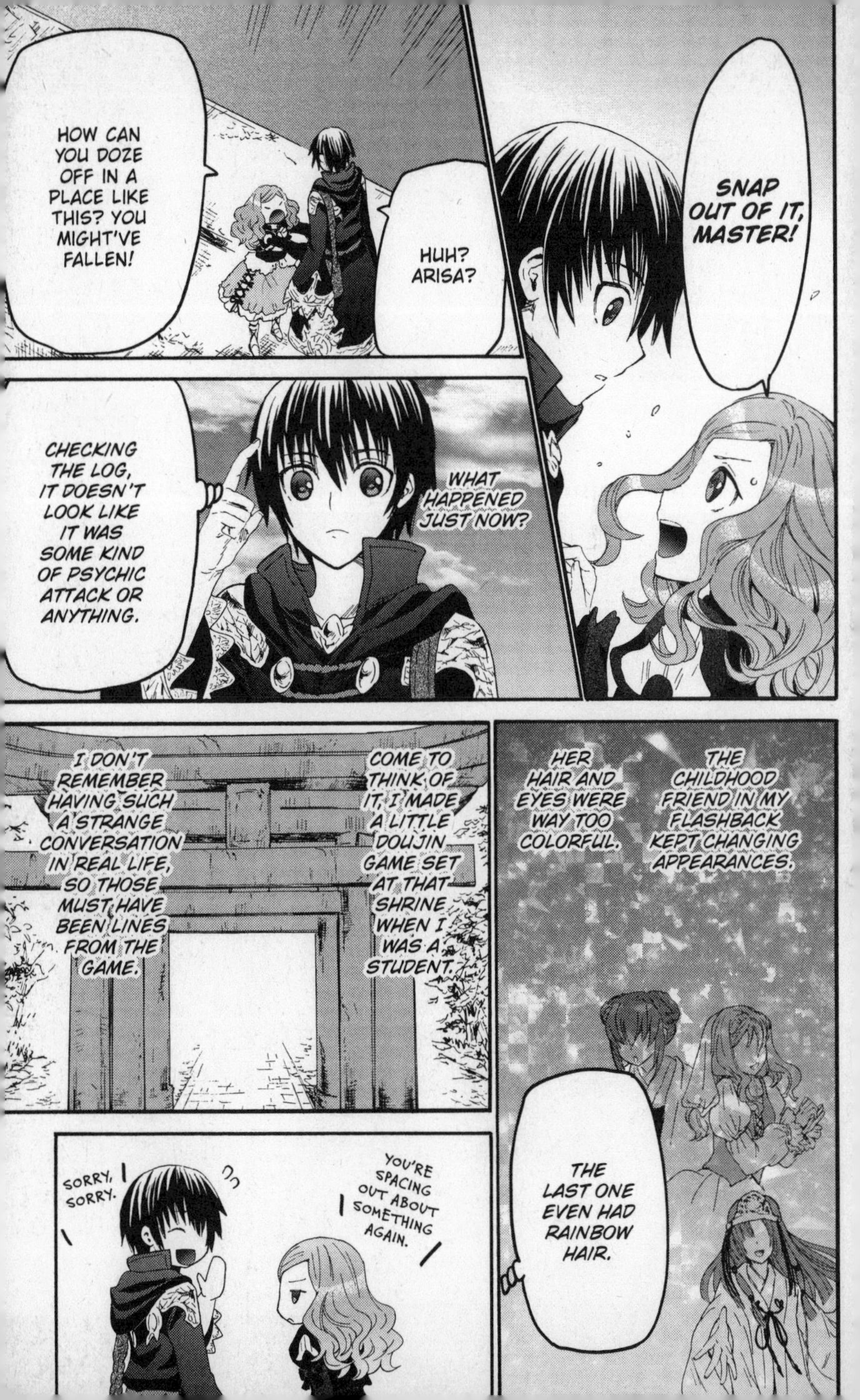
SNAP OUT OF IT, MASTER!
HUH? ARISA?
HOW CAN YOU DOZE OFF IN A PLACE LIKE THIS? YOU MIGHT'VE FALLEN!
WHAT HAPPENED JUST NOW?
CHECKING THE LOG, IT DOESN'T LOOK LIKE IT WAS SOME KIND OF PSYCHIC ATTACK OR ANYTHING.
THE CHILDHOOD FRIEND IN MY FLASHBACK KEPT CHANGING APPEARANCES.
HER HAIR AND EYES WERE WAY TOO COLORFUL.
THE LAST ONE EVEN HAD RAINBOW HAIR.
COME TO THINK OF IT, I MADE A LITTLE DOUJIN GAME SET AT THAT SHRINE WHEN I WAS A STUDENT.
I DON'T REMEMBER HAVING SUCH A STRANGE CONVERSATION IN REAL LIFE, SO THOSE MUST HAVE BEEN LINES FROM THE GAME.
YOU'RE SPACING OUT ABOUT SOMETHING AGAIN.
SORRY, SORRY.

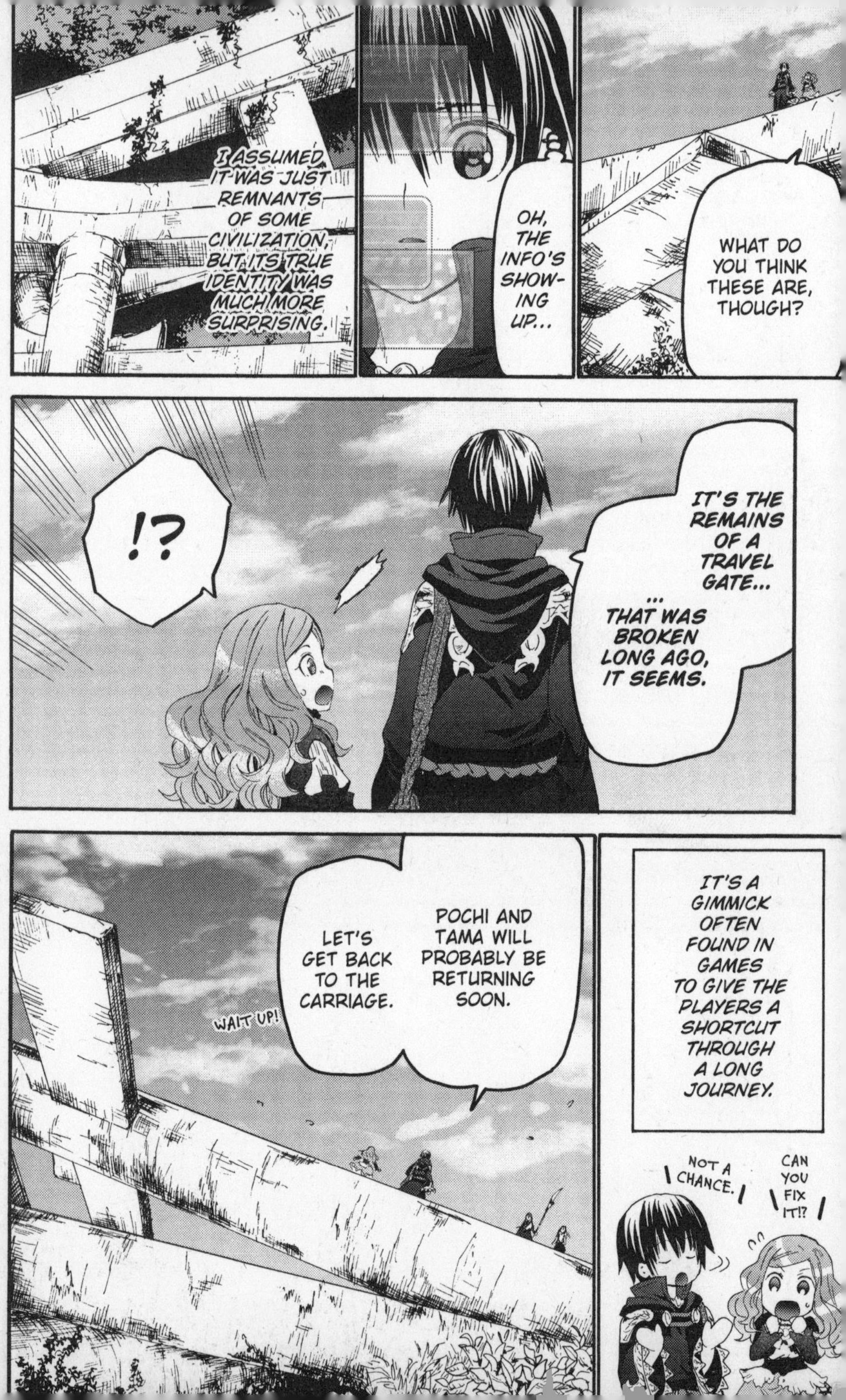
WHAT DO YOU THINK THESE ARE, THOUGH?
OH, THE INFO'S SHOWING-UP...
I ASSUMED IT WAS JUST REMNANTS OF SOME CIVILIZATION, BUT ITS TRUE IDENTITY WAS MUCH MORE SURPRISING.
IT'S THE REMAINS OF A TRAVEL GATE...
...THAT WAS BROKEN LONG AGO, IT SEEMS.
!?
IT'S A GIMMICK OFTEN FOUND IN GAMES TO GIVE THE PLAYERS A SHORTCUT THROUGH A LONG JOURNEY.
CAN YOU FIX IT!?
NOT A CHANCE.
POCHI AND TAMA WILL PROBABLY BE RETURNING SOON.
LET'S GET BACK TO THE CARRIAGE.
WAIT UP!

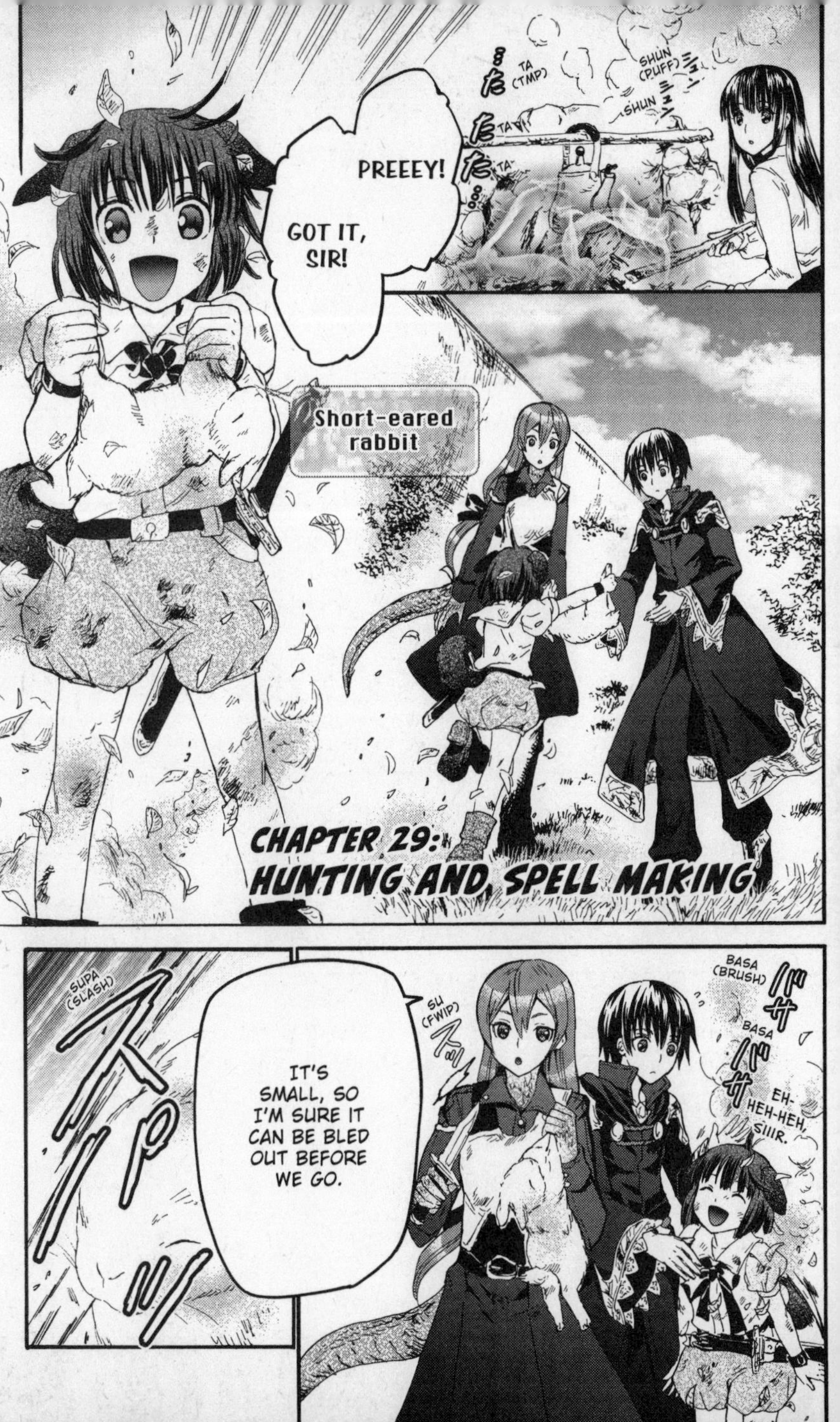

TA (TMP)
TA
TA
SHUN (PUFF)
SHUN
CHAPTER 29:
HUNTING AND SPELL MAKING
PREEEY!
GOT IT, SIR!
Short-eared rabbit
BASA (BRUSH)
BASA
SU (FWIP)
IT'S SMALL, SO I'M SURE IT CAN BE BLED OUT BEFORE WE GO.
EH-HEH-HEH, SIIIR.
SUPA (SLASH)

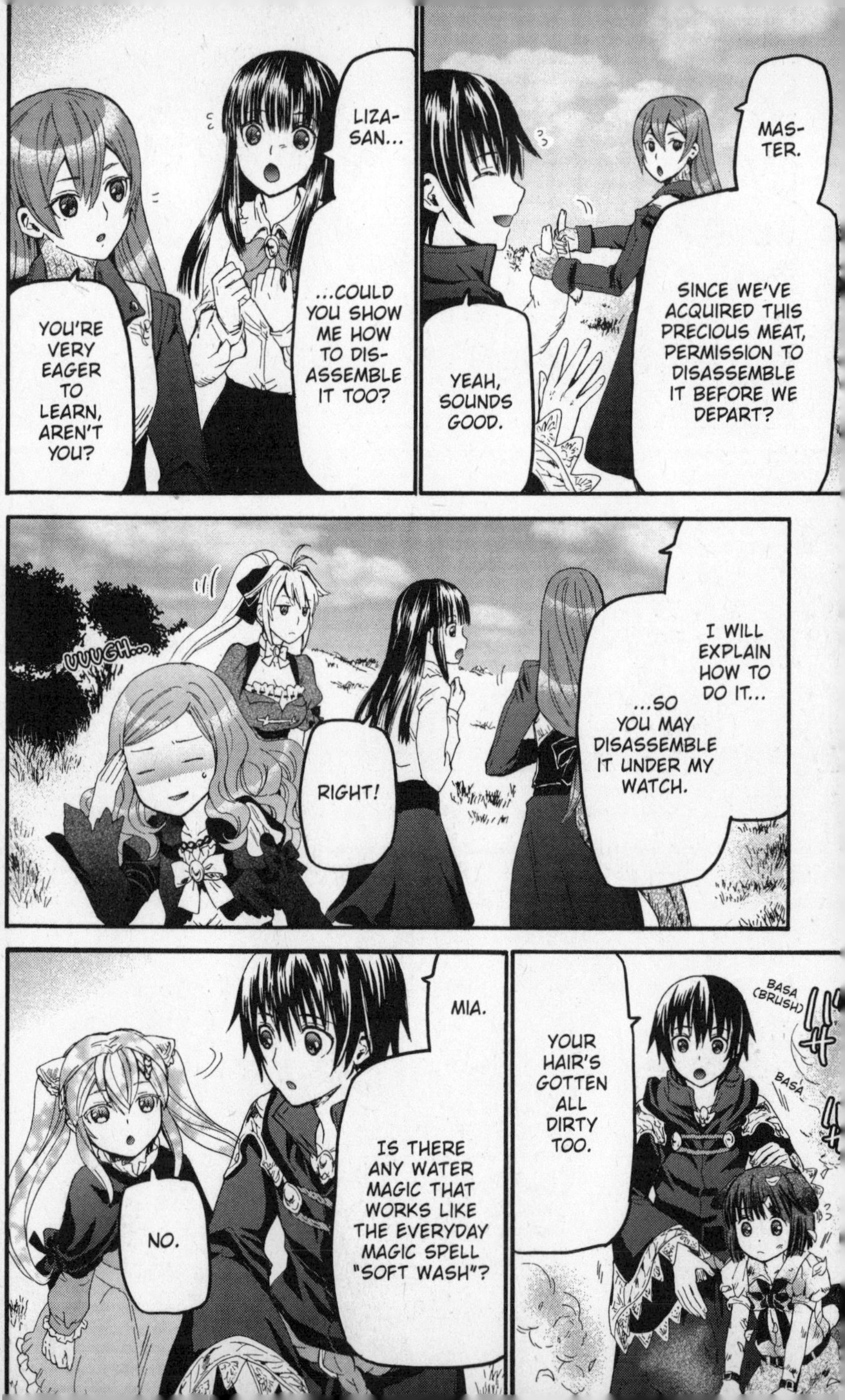
MAS-TER.
SINCE WE'VE ACQUIRED THIS PRECIOUS MEAT, PERMISSION TO DISASSEMBLE IT BEFORE WE DEPART?
YEAH, SOUNDS GOOD.
LIZA-SAN...
...COULD YOU SHOW ME HOW TO DIS-ASSEMBLE IT TOO?
YOU'RE VERY EAGER TO LEARN, AREN'T YOU?
I WILL EXPLAIN HOW TO DO IT...
...SO YOU MAY DISASSEMBLE IT UNDER MY WATCH.
RIGHT!
UUUGH...
BASA (BRUSH)
BASA
YOUR HAIR'S GOTTEN ALL DIRTY TOO.
MIA.
IS THERE ANY WATER MAGIC THAT WORKS LIKE THE EVERYDAY MAGIC SPELL "SOFT WASH"?
NO.

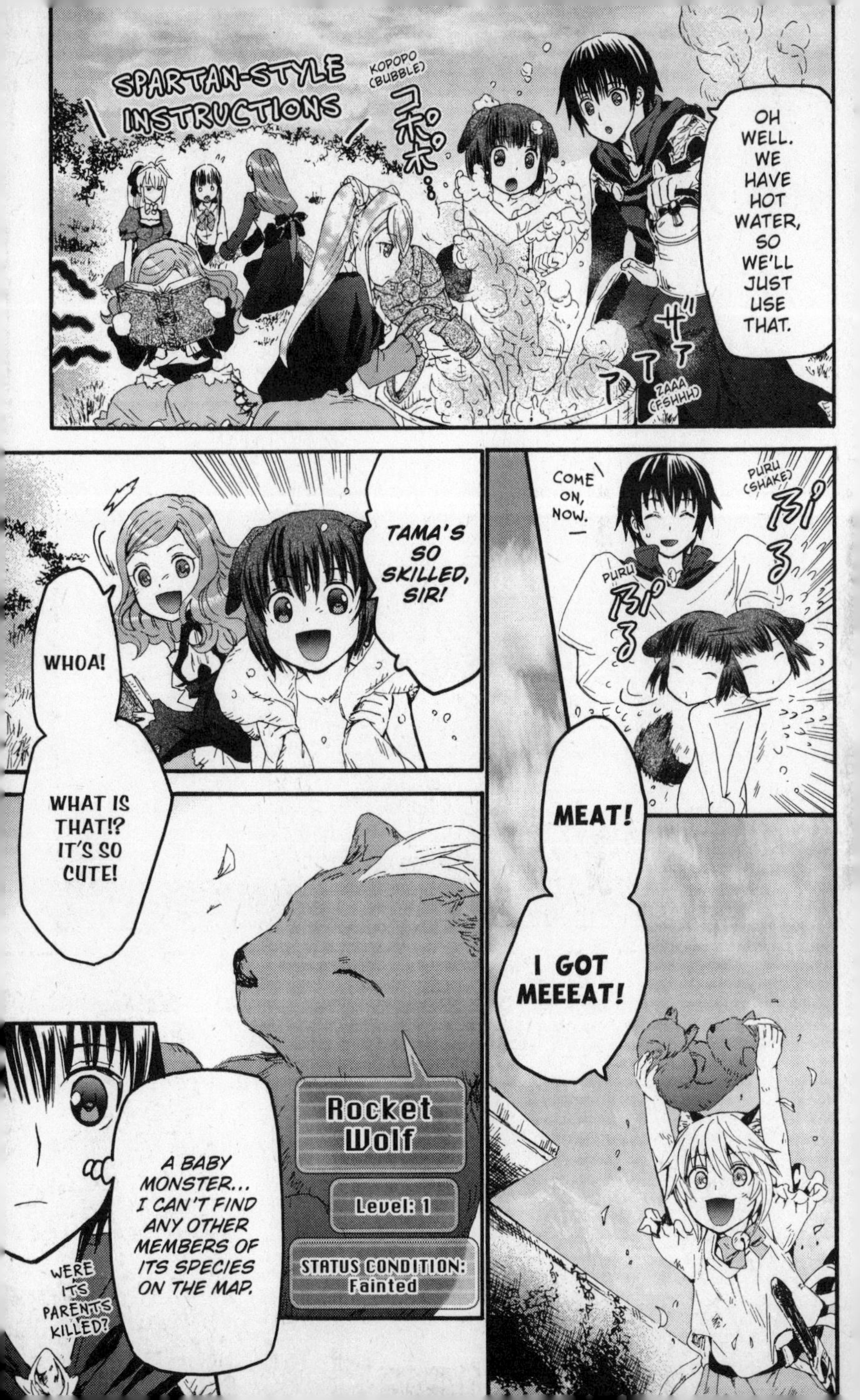
OH WELL. WE HAVE HOT WATER, SO WE'LL JUST USE THAT.
ZAAA (FSHHH)
KOPOPO (BUBBLE)
SPARTAN-STYLE INSTRUCTIONS
PURU (SHAKE)
COME ON, NOW.
PURU
MEAT!
I GOT MEEEAT!
TAMA'S SO SKILLED, SIR!
WHOA!
WHAT IS THAT!? IT'S SO CUTE!
Rocket Wolf
Level: 1
STATUS CONDITION: Fainted
A BABY MONSTER... I CAN'T FIND ANY OTHER MEMBERS OF ITS SPECIES ON THE MAP.
WERE ITS PARENTS KILLED?

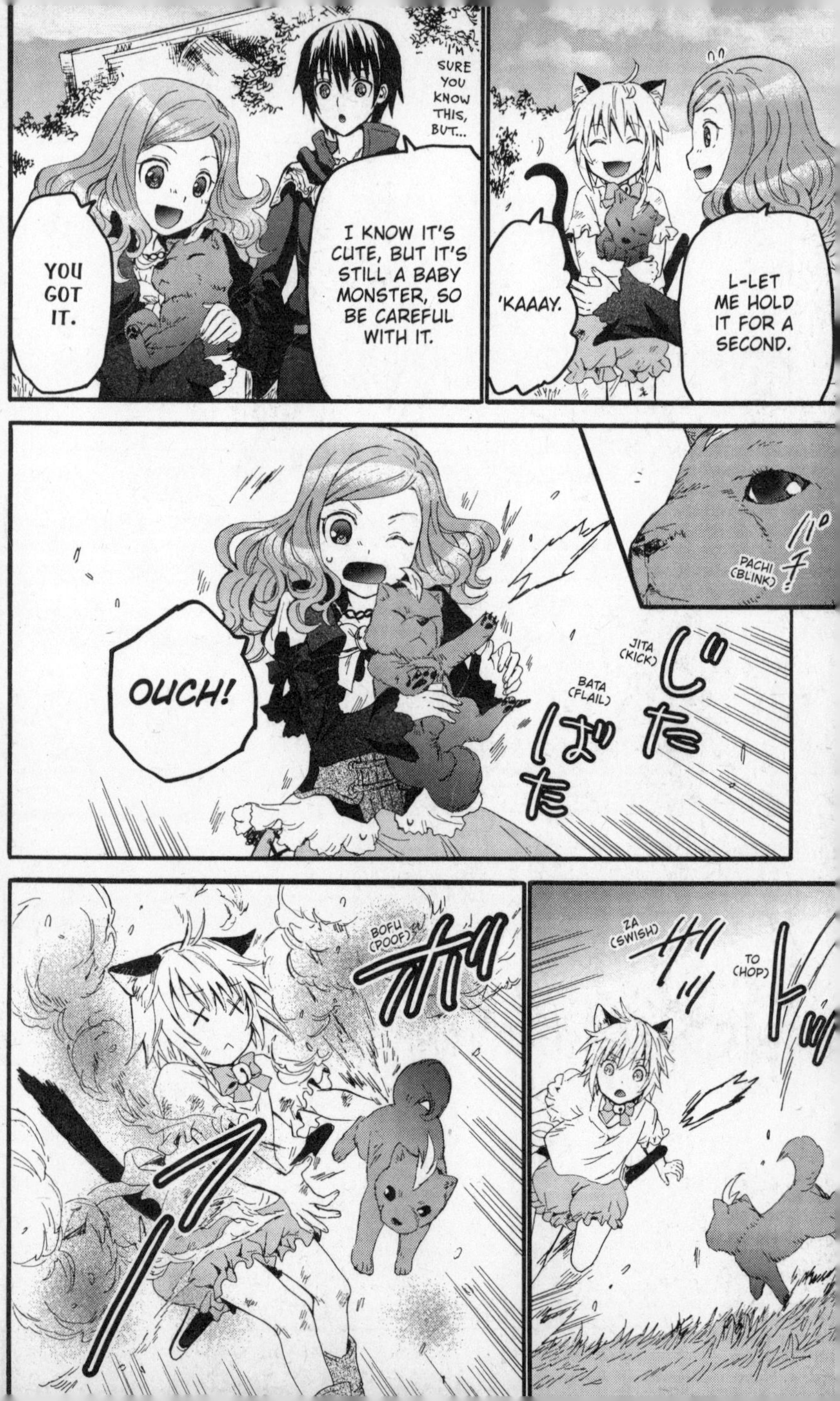

L-LET ME HOLD IT FOR A SECOND.
'KAAAY.
I'M SURE YOU KNOW THIS, BUT...
I KNOW IT'S CUTE, BUT IT'S STILL A BABY MONSTER, SO BE CAREFUL WITH IT.
YOU GOT IT.
パチ
PACHI (BLINK)
じた
JITA (KICK)
ばた
BATA (FLAIL)
OUCH!
ザッ
ZA (SWISH)
トッ
TO (HOP)
ボフ
BOFU (POOF)

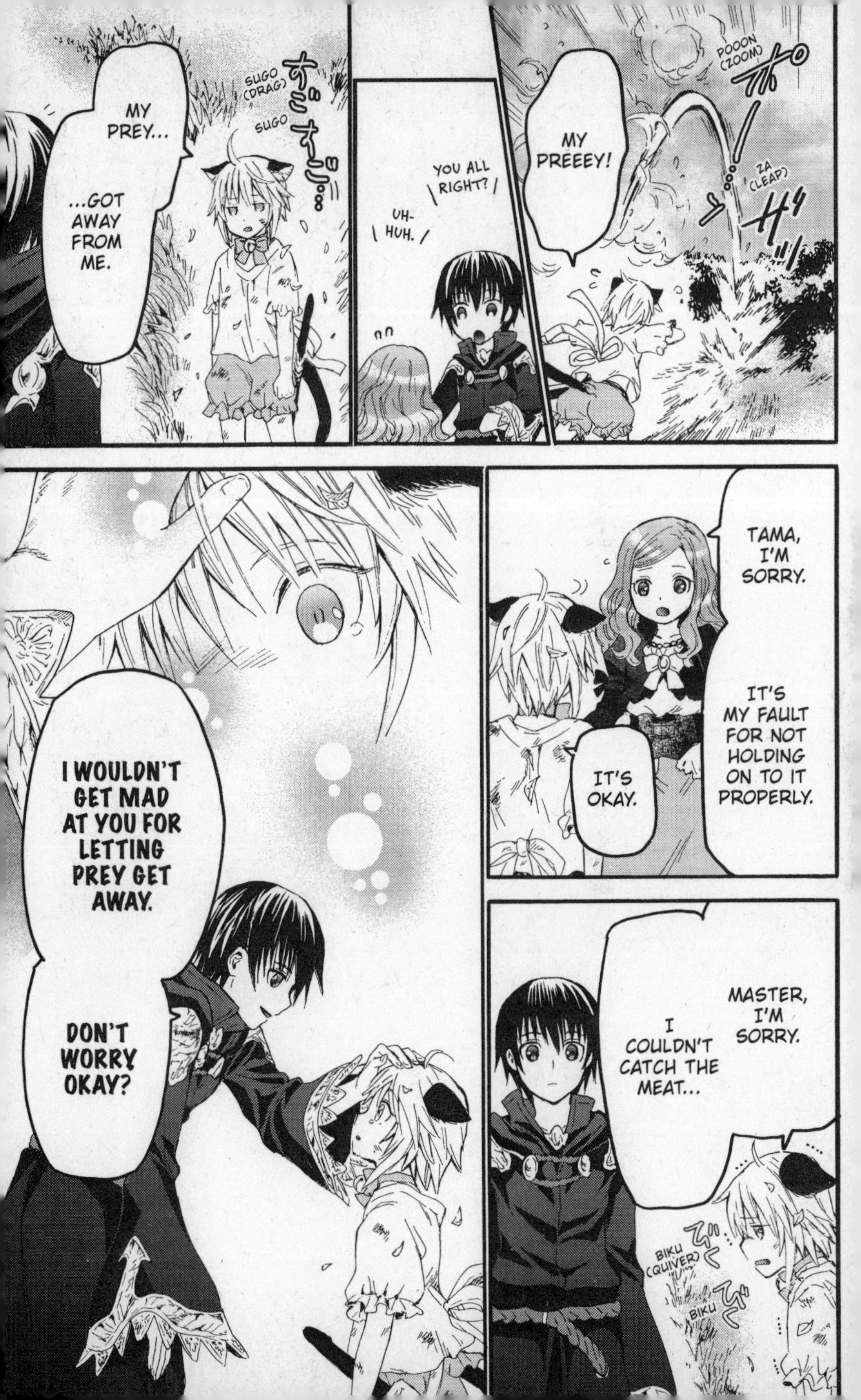
POOON (ZOOM)
ZA (LEAP)
MY PREEEY!
YOU ALL RIGHT?
UH-HUH.
SUGO (DRAG) SUGO
MY PREY...
...GOT AWAY FROM ME.
TAMA, I'M SORRY.
IT'S MY FAULT FOR NOT HOLDING ON TO IT PROPERLY.
IT'S OKAY.
MASTER, I'M SORRY.
I COULDN'T CATCH THE MEAT...
BIKU (QUIVER) BIKU
I WOULDN'T GET MAD AT YOU FOR LETTING PREY GET AWAY.
DON'T WORRY, OKAY?

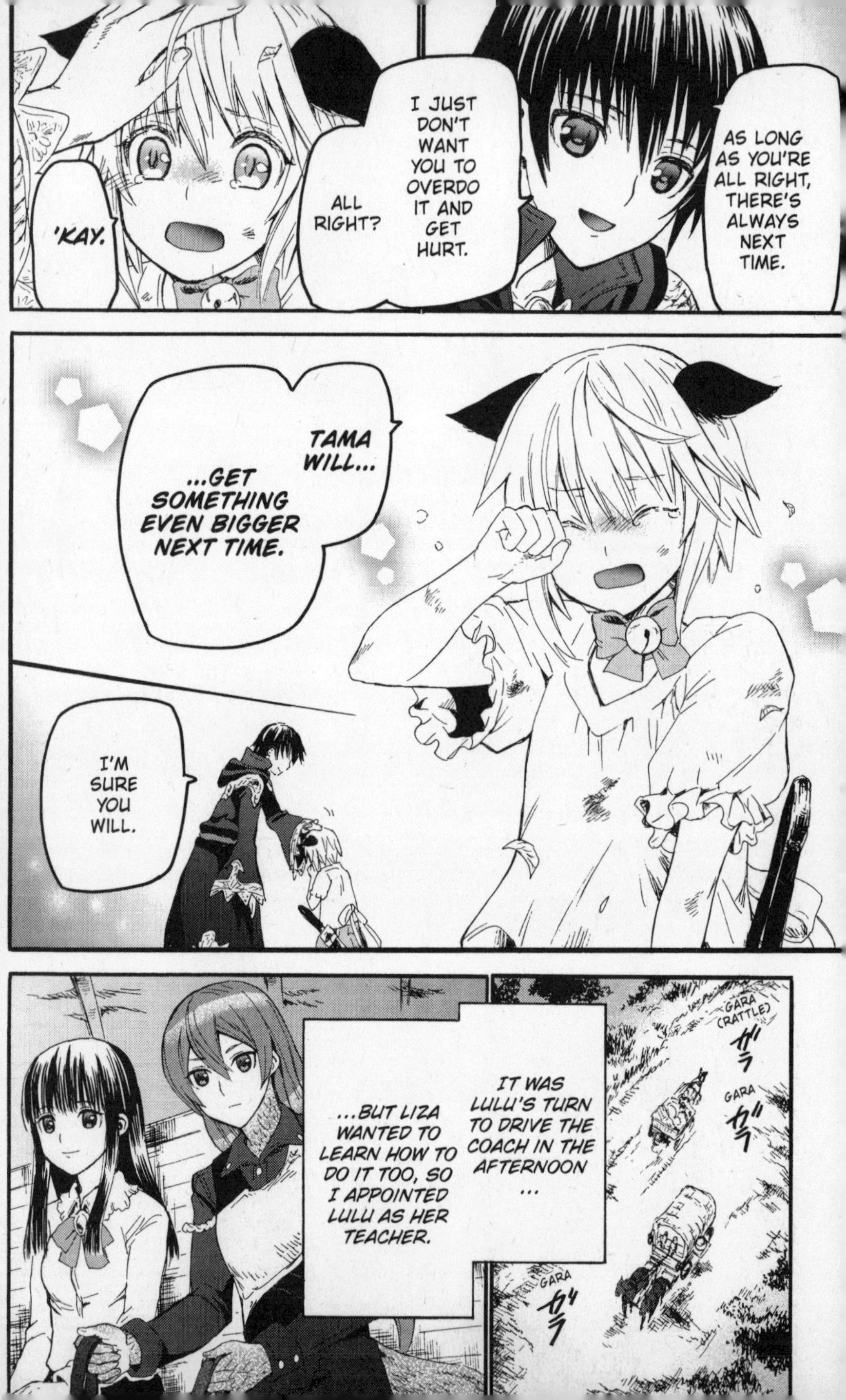
AS LONG AS YOU'RE ALL RIGHT, THERE'S ALWAYS NEXT TIME.
I JUST DON'T WANT YOU TO OVERDO IT AND GET HURT.
ALL RIGHT?
'KAY.
TAMA WILL...
...GET SOMETHING EVEN BIGGER NEXT TIME.
I'M SURE YOU WILL.
GARA (RATTLE)
ガラ
GARA
ガラ
GARA
ガラ
IT WAS LULU'S TURN TO DRIVE THE COACH IN THE AFTERNOON...
...BUT LIZA WANTED TO LEARN HOW TO DO IT TOO, SO I APPOINTED LULU AS HER TEACHER.

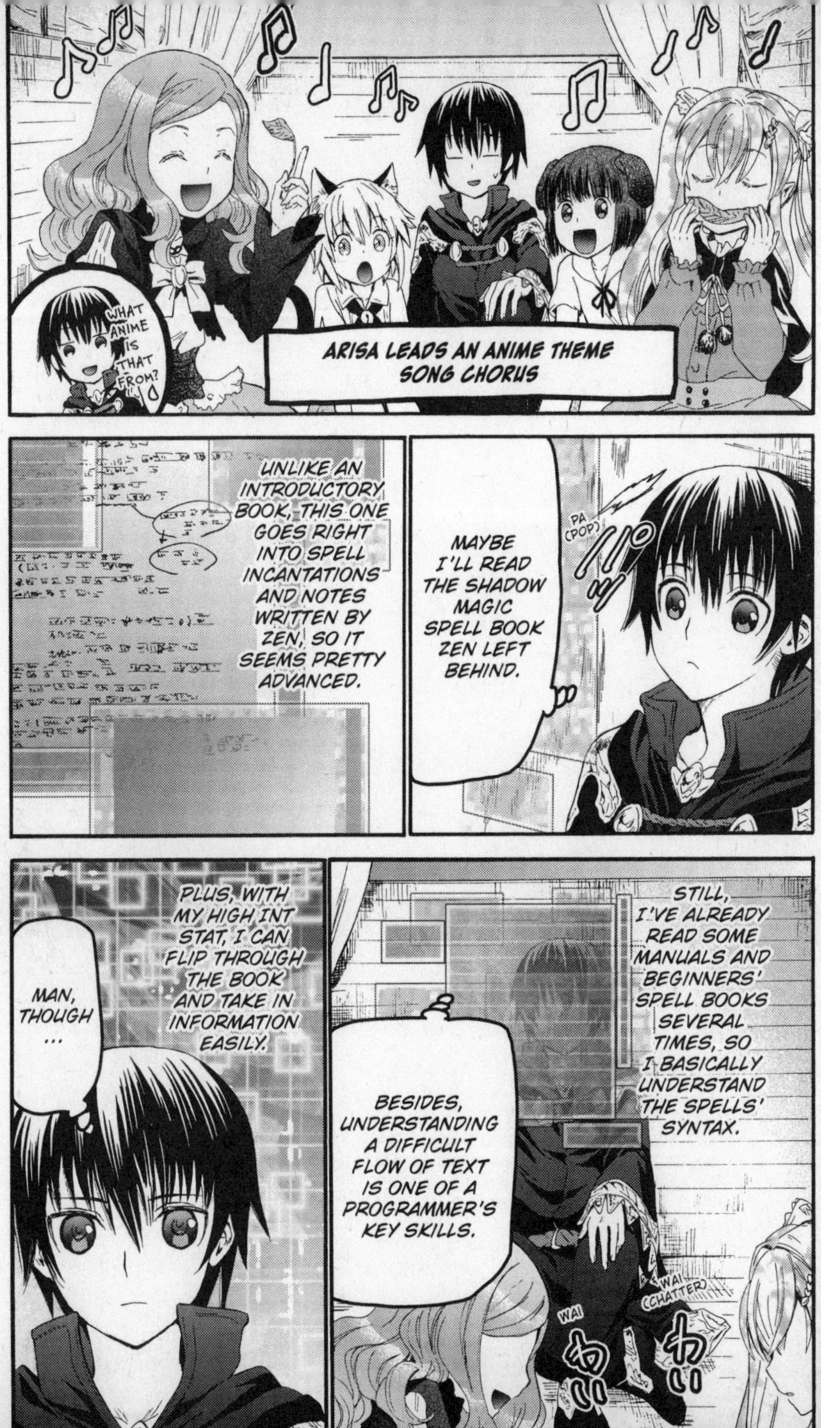
ARISA LEADS AN ANIME THEME SONG CHORUS
WHAT ANIME IS THAT FROM?
PA (POP)
MAYBE I'LL READ THE SHADOW MAGIC SPELL BOOK ZEN LEFT BEHIND.
UNLIKE AN INTRODUCTORY BOOK, THIS ONE GOES RIGHT INTO SPELL INCANTATIONS AND NOTES WRITTEN BY ZEN, SO IT SEEMS PRETTY ADVANCED.
STILL, I'VE ALREADY READ SOME MANUALS AND BEGINNERS' SPELL BOOKS SEVERAL TIMES, SO I BASICALLY UNDERSTAND THE SPELLS' SYNTAX.
BESIDES, UNDERSTANDING A DIFFICULT FLOW OF TEXT IS ONE OF A PROGRAMMER'S KEY SKILLS.
WAI (CHATTER)
WAI
PLUS, WITH MY HIGH INT STAT, I CAN FLIP THROUGH THE BOOK AND TAKE IN INFORMATION EASILY.
MAN, THOUGH...

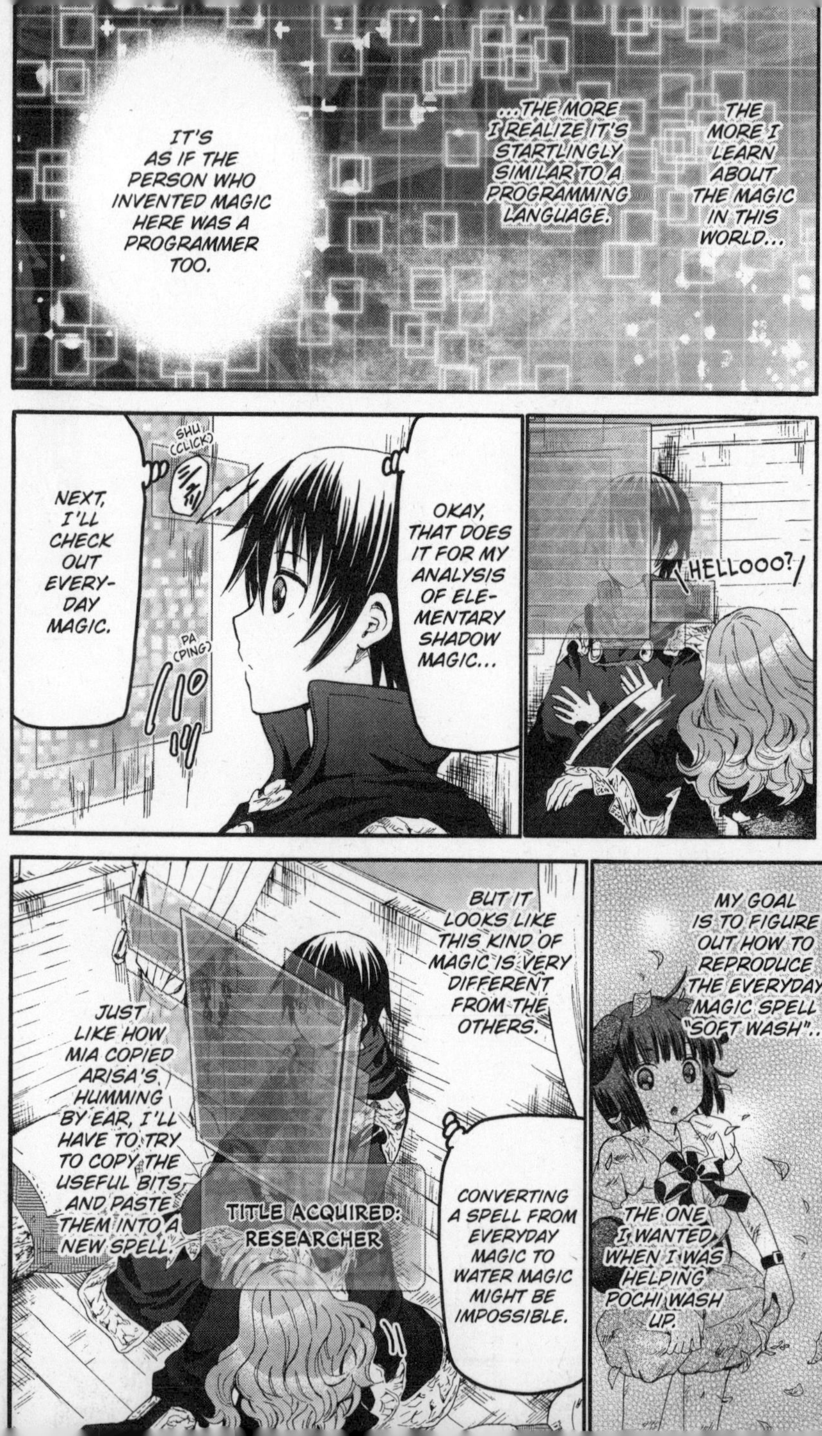
THE MORE I LEARN ABOUT THE MAGIC IN THIS WORLD...
...THE MORE I REALIZE IT'S STARTLINGLY SIMILAR TO A PROGRAMMING LANGUAGE.
IT'S AS IF THE PERSON WHO INVENTED MAGIC HERE WAS A PROGRAMMER TOO.
HELLOOO?
OKAY, THAT DOES IT FOR MY ANALYSIS OF ELE-MENTARY SHADOW MAGIC...
SHU (CLICK)
PA (PING)
NEXT, I'LL CHECK OUT EVERY-DAY MAGIC.
MY GOAL IS TO FIGURE OUT HOW TO REPRODUCE THE EVERYDAY MAGIC SPELL "SOFT WASH"...
THE ONE I WANTED WHEN I WAS HELPING POCHI WASH UP.
BUT IT LOOKS LIKE THIS KIND OF MAGIC IS VERY DIFFERENT FROM THE OTHERS.
CONVERTING A SPELL FROM EVERYDAY MAGIC TO WATER MAGIC MIGHT BE IMPOSSIBLE.
JUST LIKE HOW MIA COPIED ARISA'S HUMMING BY EAR, I'LL HAVE TO TRY TO COPY THE USEFUL BITS AND PASTE THEM INTO A NEW SPELL.
TITLE ACQUIRED: RESEARCHER

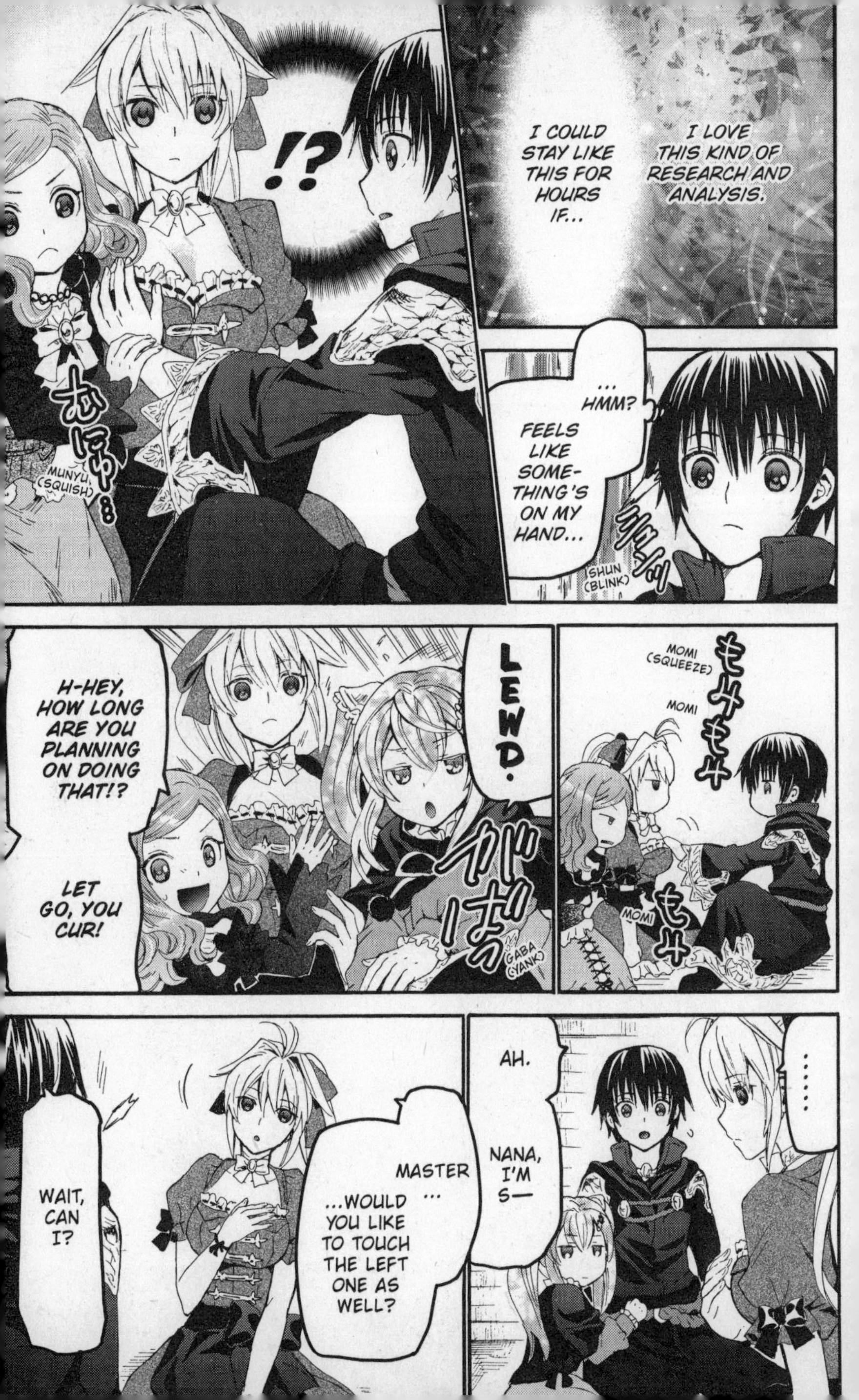
I LOVE THIS KIND OF RESEARCH AND ANALYSIS.
I COULD STAY LIKE THIS FOR HOURS IF...
...HMM?
FEELS LIKE SOME-THING'S ON MY HAND...
SHUN (BLINK)
!?
MUNYU (SQUISH)
MOMI (SQUEEZE)
MOMI
MOMI
LEWD.
GABA (YANK)
H-HEY, HOW LONG ARE YOU PLANNING ON DOING THAT!?
LET GO, YOU CUR!
......
AH.
NANA, I'M S—
MASTER...
...WOULD YOU LIKE TO TOUCH THE LEFT ONE AS WELL?
WAIT, CAN I?

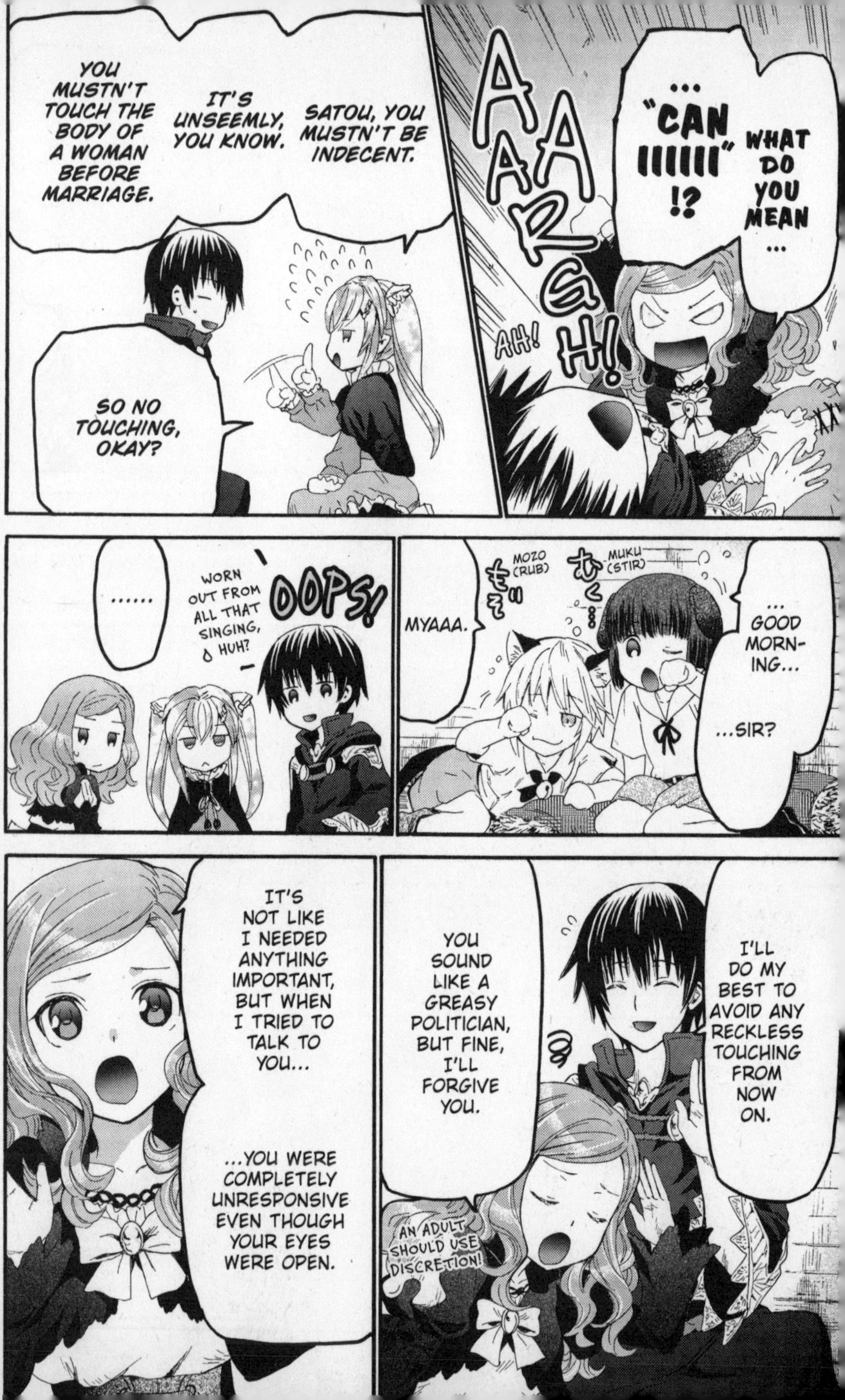

... "CAN IIIIII" !?
WHAT DO YOU MEAN ...
AAARGH!
AH!
SATOU, YOU MUSTN'T BE INDECENT.
IT'S UNSEEMLY, YOU KNOW.
YOU MUSTN'T TOUCH THE BODY OF A WOMAN BEFORE MARRIAGE.
SO NO TOUCHING, OKAY?
... GOOD MORNING...
...SIR?
MUKU (STIR)
MOZO (RUB)
MYAAA.
OOPS!
WORN OUT FROM ALL THAT SINGING, HUH?
......
I'LL DO MY BEST TO AVOID ANY RECKLESS TOUCHING FROM NOW ON.
YOU SOUND LIKE A GREASY POLITICIAN, BUT FINE, I'LL FORGIVE YOU.
AN ADULT SHOULD USE DISCRETION!
IT'S NOT LIKE I NEEDED ANYTHING IMPORTANT, BUT WHEN I TRIED TO TALK TO YOU...
...YOU WERE COMPLETELY UNRESPONSIVE EVEN THOUGH YOUR EYES WERE OPEN.

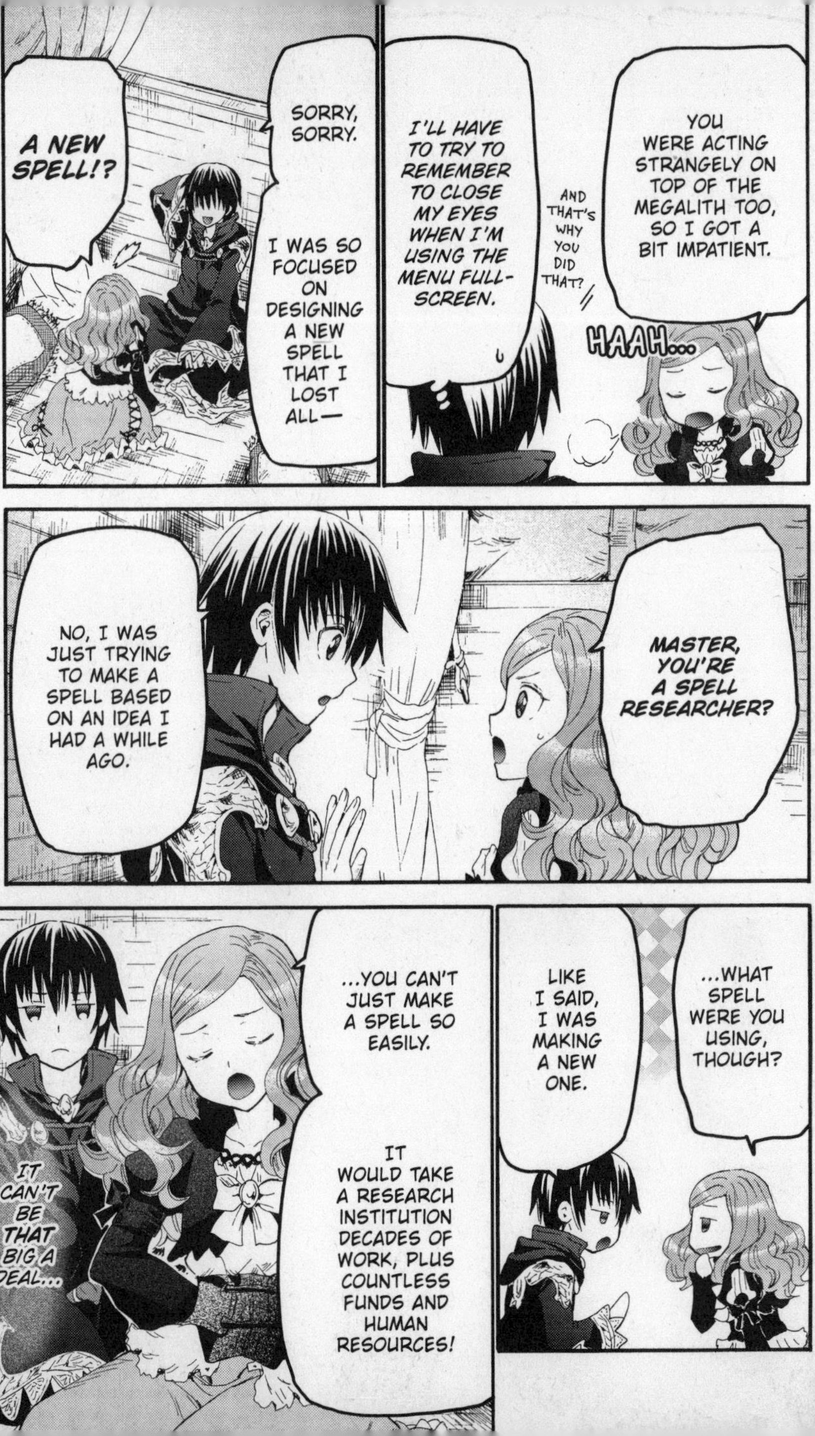
YOU WERE ACTING STRANGELY ON TOP OF THE MEGALITH TOO, SO I GOT A BIT IMPATIENT.
HAAH...
AND THAT'S WHY YOU DID THAT?
I'LL HAVE TO TRY TO REMEMBER TO CLOSE MY EYES WHEN I'M USING THE MENU FULL-SCREEN.
SORRY, SORRY.
I WAS SO FOCUSED ON DESIGNING A NEW SPELL THAT I LOST ALL—
A NEW SPELL!?
MASTER, YOU'RE A SPELL RESEARCHER?
NO, I WAS JUST TRYING TO MAKE A SPELL BASED ON AN IDEA I HAD A WHILE AGO.
...WHAT SPELL WERE YOU USING, THOUGH?
LIKE I SAID, I WAS MAKING A NEW ONE.
...YOU CAN'T JUST MAKE A SPELL SO EASILY.
IT WOULD TAKE A RESEARCH INSTITUTION DECADES OF WORK, PLUS COUNTLESS FUNDS AND HUMAN RESOURCES!
IT CAN'T BE THAT BIG A DEAL...

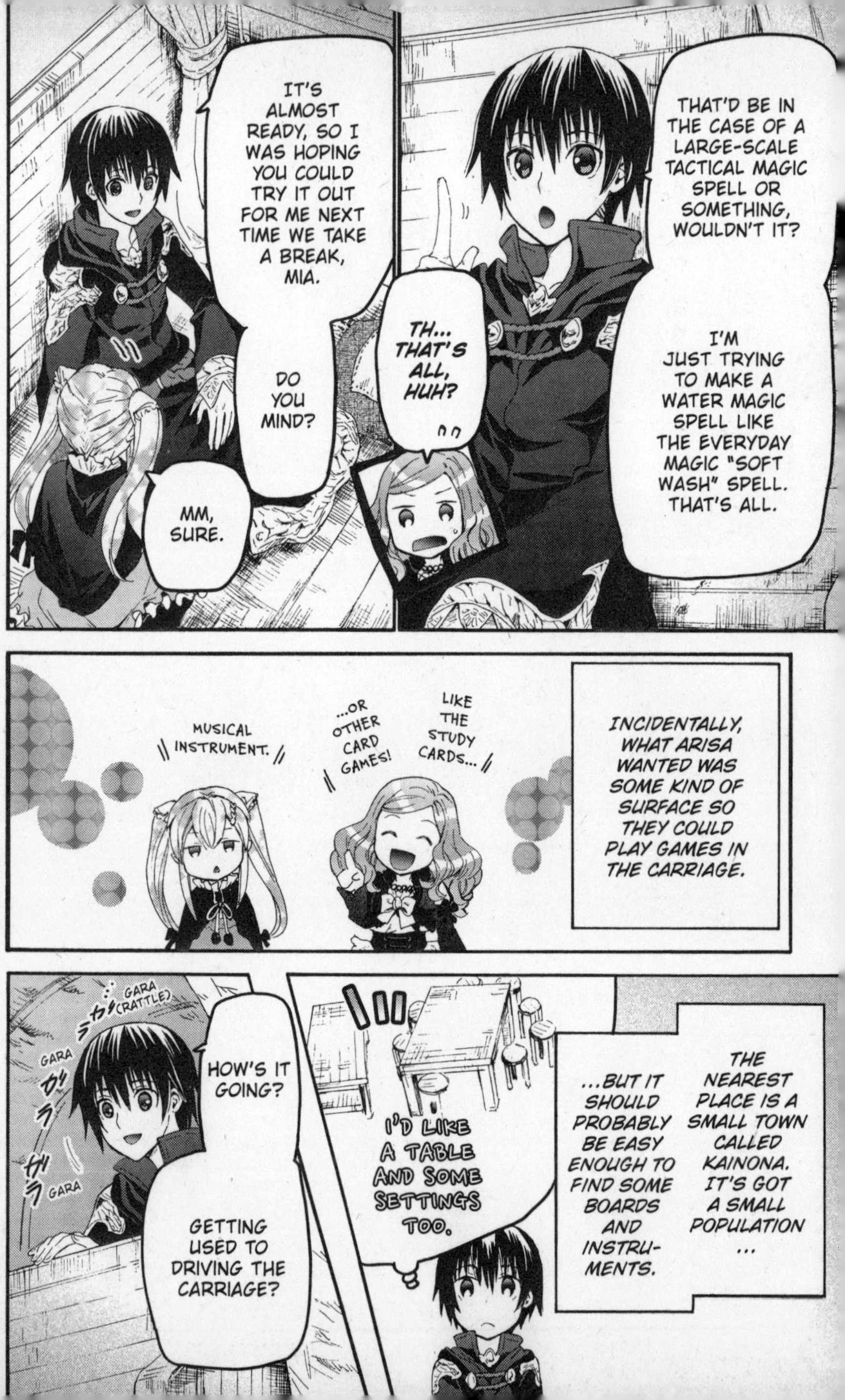
THAT'D BE IN THE CASE OF A LARGE-SCALE TACTICAL MAGIC SPELL OR SOMETHING, WOULDN'T IT?
I'M JUST TRYING TO MAKE A WATER MAGIC SPELL LIKE THE EVERYDAY MAGIC "SOFT WASH" SPELL. THAT'S ALL.
TH... THAT'S ALL, HUH?
IT'S ALMOST READY, SO I WAS HOPING YOU COULD TRY IT OUT FOR ME NEXT TIME WE TAKE A BREAK, MIA.
DO YOU MIND?
MM, SURE.
INCIDENTALLY, WHAT ARISA WANTED WAS SOME KIND OF SURFACE SO THEY COULD PLAY GAMES IN THE CARRIAGE.
LIKE THE STUDY CARDS...
...OR OTHER CARD GAMES!
MUSICAL INSTRUMENT.
THE NEAREST PLACE IS A SMALL TOWN CALLED KAINONA. IT'S GOT A SMALL POPULATION...
...BUT IT SHOULD PROBABLY BE EASY ENOUGH TO FIND SOME BOARDS AND INSTRU-MENTS.
I'D LIKE A TABLE AND SOME SETTINGS TOO.
GARA (RATTLE)
HOW'S IT GOING?
GETTING USED TO DRIVING THE CARRIAGE?
GARA
GARA

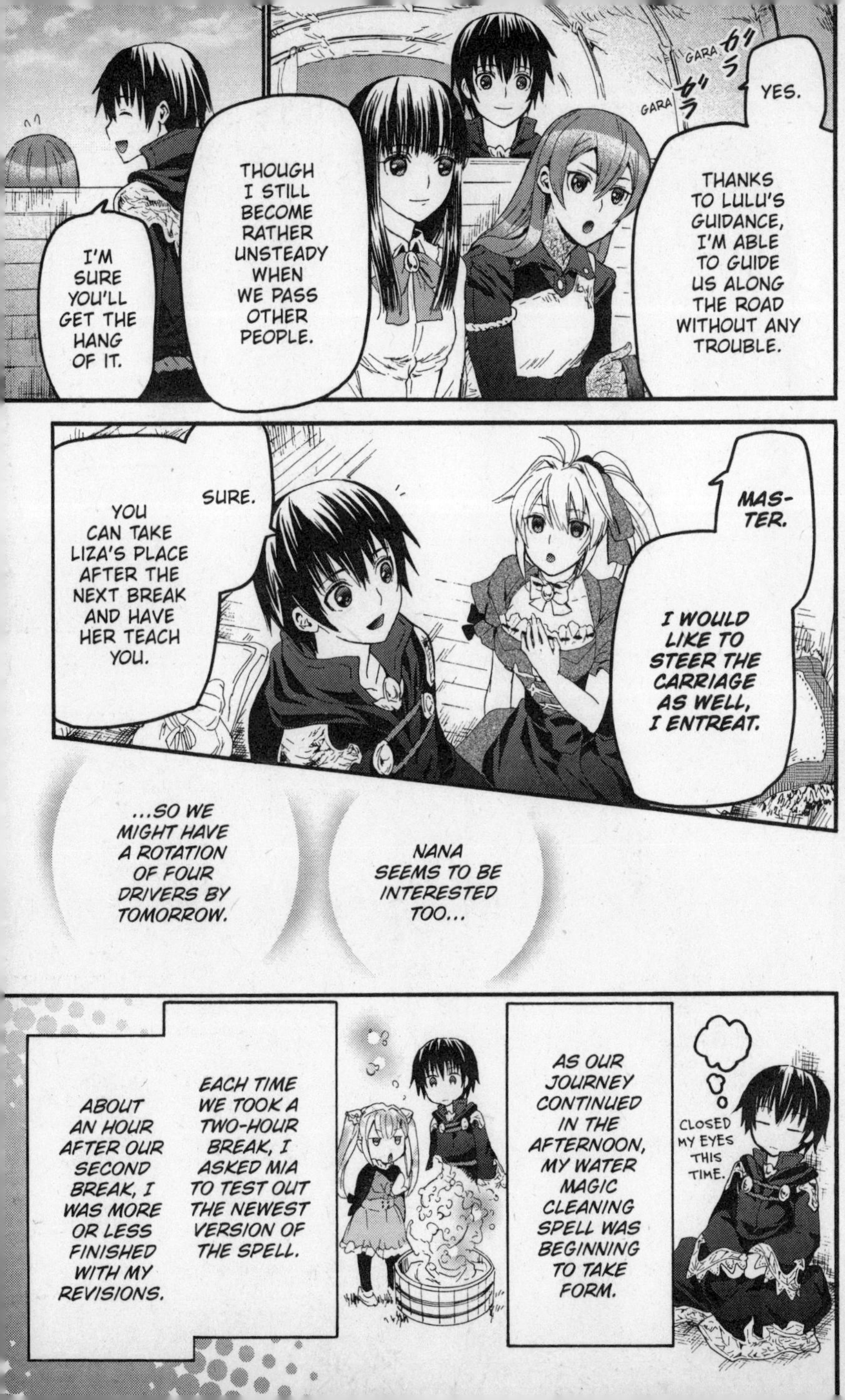

GARA
GARA
YES.
THANKS TO LULU'S GUIDANCE, I'M ABLE TO GUIDE US ALONG THE ROAD WITHOUT ANY TROUBLE.
THOUGH I STILL BECOME RATHER UNSTEADY WHEN WE PASS OTHER PEOPLE.
I'M SURE YOU'LL GET THE HANG OF IT.
MAS-TER.
I WOULD LIKE TO STEER THE CARRIAGE AS WELL, I ENTREAT.
SURE.
YOU CAN TAKE LIZA'S PLACE AFTER THE NEXT BREAK AND HAVE HER TEACH YOU.
NANA SEEMS TO BE INTERESTED TOO...
...SO WE MIGHT HAVE A ROTATION OF FOUR DRIVERS BY TOMORROW.
AS OUR JOURNEY CONTINUED IN THE AFTERNOON, MY WATER MAGIC CLEANING SPELL WAS BEGINNING TO TAKE FORM.
CLOSED MY EYES THIS TIME.
EACH TIME WE TOOK A TWO-HOUR BREAK, I ASKED MIA TO TEST OUT THE NEWEST VERSION OF THE SPELL.
ABOUT AN HOUR AFTER OUR SECOND BREAK, I WAS MORE OR LESS FINISHED WITH MY REVISIONS.

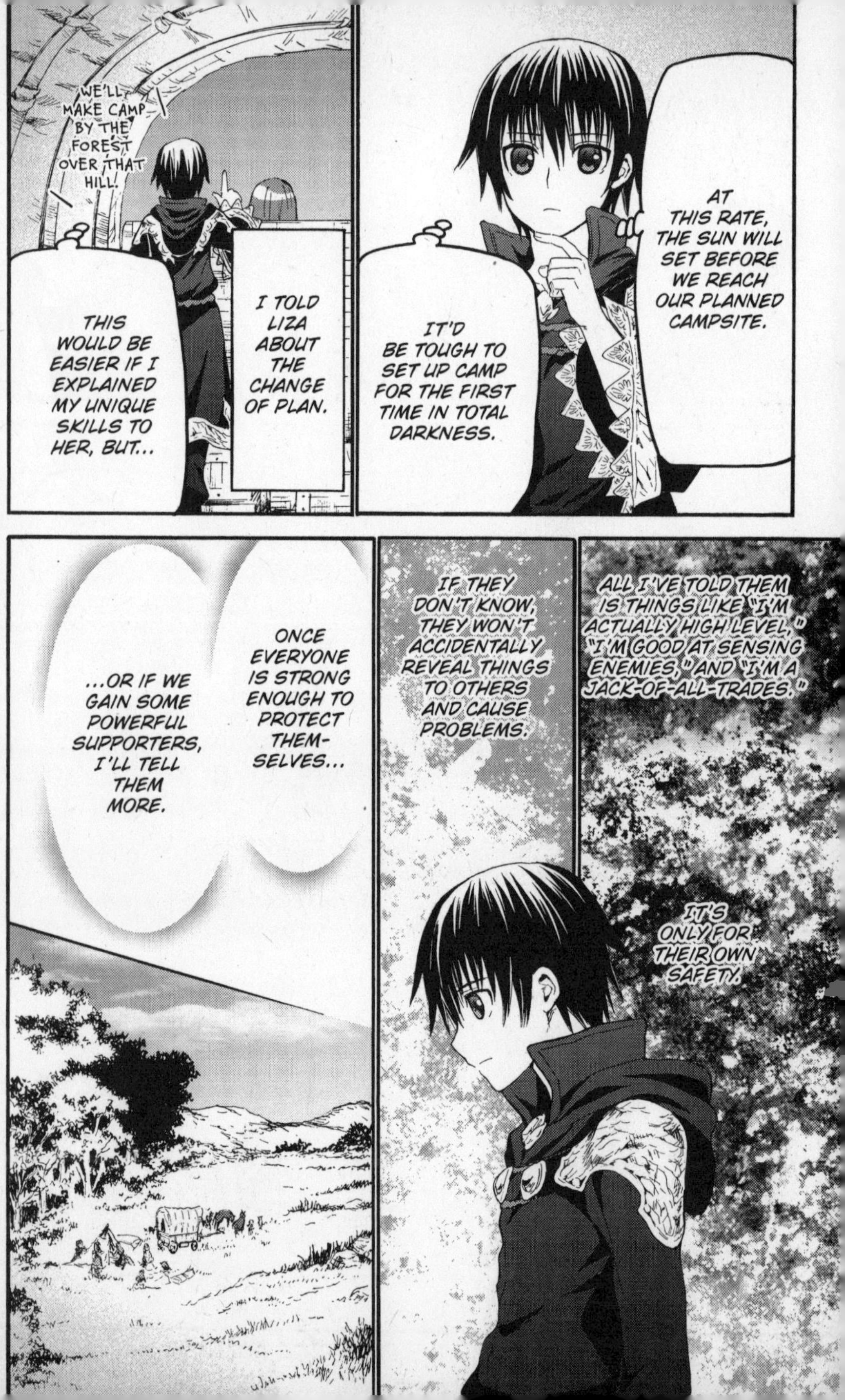
AT THIS RATE, THE SUN WILL SET BEFORE WE REACH OUR PLANNED CAMPSITE.
IT'D BE TOUGH TO SET UP CAMP FOR THE FIRST TIME IN TOTAL DARKNESS.
WE'LL MAKE CAMP BY THE FOREST OVER THAT HILL!
I TOLD LIZA ABOUT THE CHANGE OF PLAN.
THIS WOULD BE EASIER IF I EXPLAINED MY UNIQUE SKILLS TO HER, BUT...
ALL I'VE TOLD THEM IS THINGS LIKE "I'M ACTUALLY HIGH LEVEL," "I'M GOOD AT SENSING ENEMIES," AND "I'M A JACK-OF-ALL-TRADES."
IF THEY DON'T KNOW, THEY WON'T ACCIDENTALLY REVEAL THINGS TO OTHERS AND CAUSE PROBLEMS.
IT'S ONLY FOR THEIR OWN SAFETY.
ONCE EVERYONE IS STRONG ENOUGH TO PROTECT THEMSELVES...
...OR IF WE GAIN SOME POWERFUL SUPPORTERS, I'LL TELL THEM MORE.

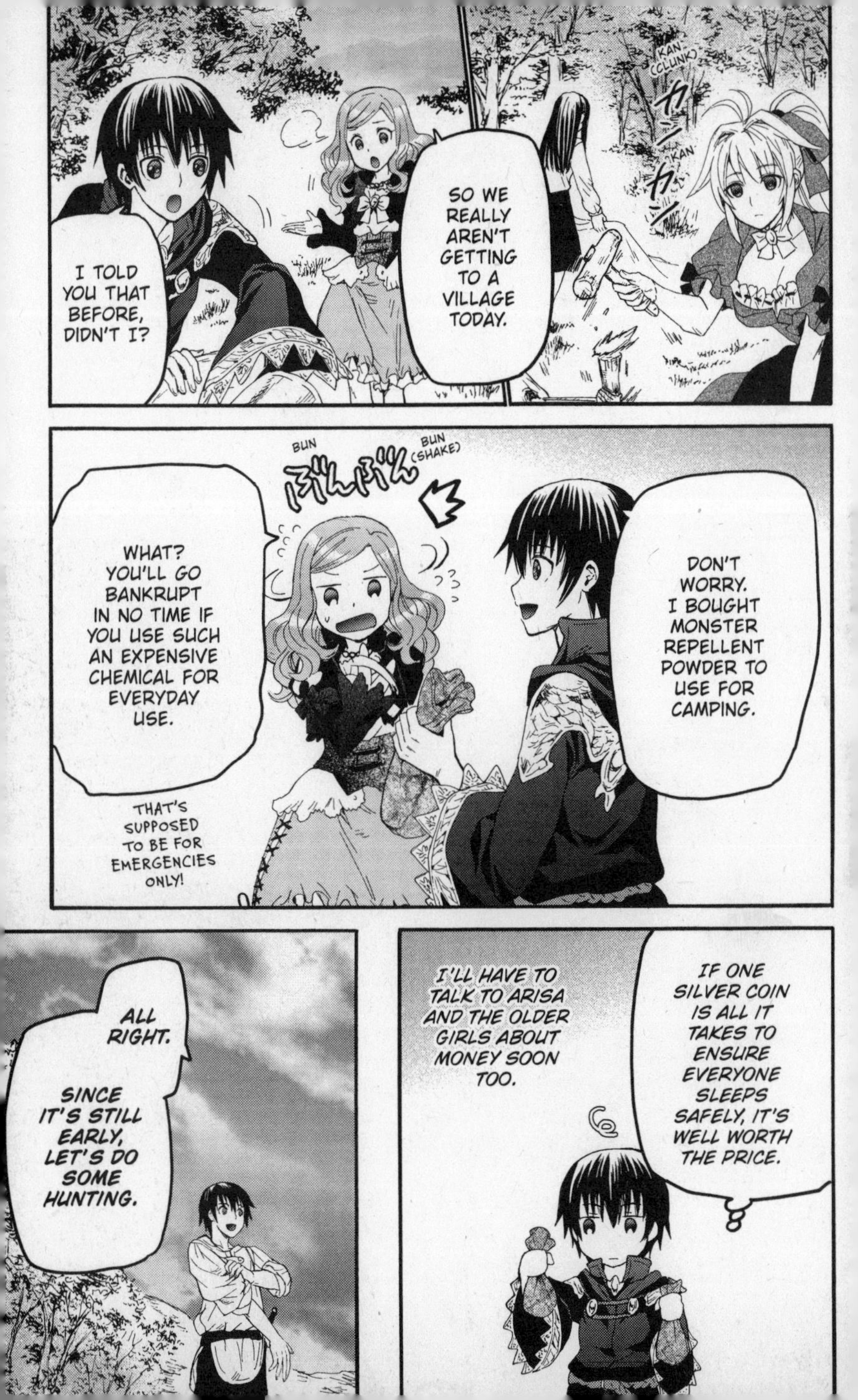
KAN (CLUNK)
KAN
SO WE REALLY AREN'T GETTING TO A VILLAGE TODAY.
I TOLD YOU THAT BEFORE, DIDN'T I?
DON'T WORRY. I BOUGHT MONSTER REPELLENT POWDER TO USE FOR CAMPING.
BUN BUN (SHAKE)
WHAT? YOU'LL GO BANKRUPT IN NO TIME IF YOU USE SUCH AN EXPENSIVE CHEMICAL FOR EVERYDAY USE.
THAT'S SUPPOSED TO BE FOR EMERGENCIES ONLY!
IF ONE SILVER COIN IS ALL IT TAKES TO ENSURE EVERYONE SLEEPS SAFELY, IT'S WELL WORTH THE PRICE.
I'LL HAVE TO TALK TO ARISA AND THE OLDER GIRLS ABOUT MONEY SOON TOO.
ALL RIGHT.
SINCE IT'S STILL EARLY, LET'S DO SOME HUNTING.

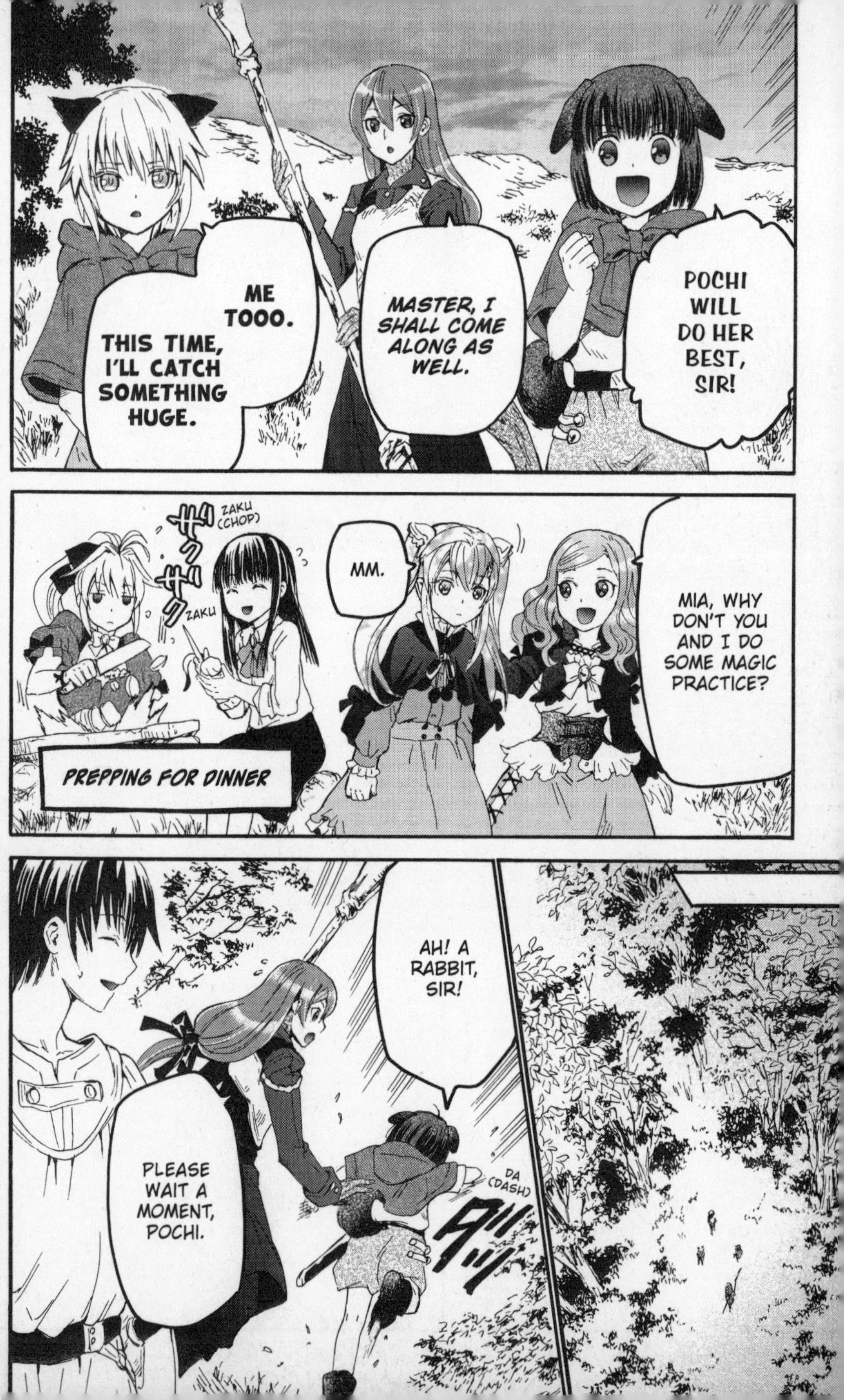
POCHI WILL DO HER BEST, SIR!
MASTER, I SHALL COME ALONG AS WELL.
ME TOOO.
THIS TIME, I'LL CATCH SOMETHING HUGE.
MIA, WHY DON'T YOU AND I DO SOME MAGIC PRACTICE?
MM.
ZAKU (CHOP)
ZAKU
PREPPING FOR DINNER
AH! A RABBIT, SIR!
DA (DASH)
PLEASE WAIT A MOMENT, POCHI.

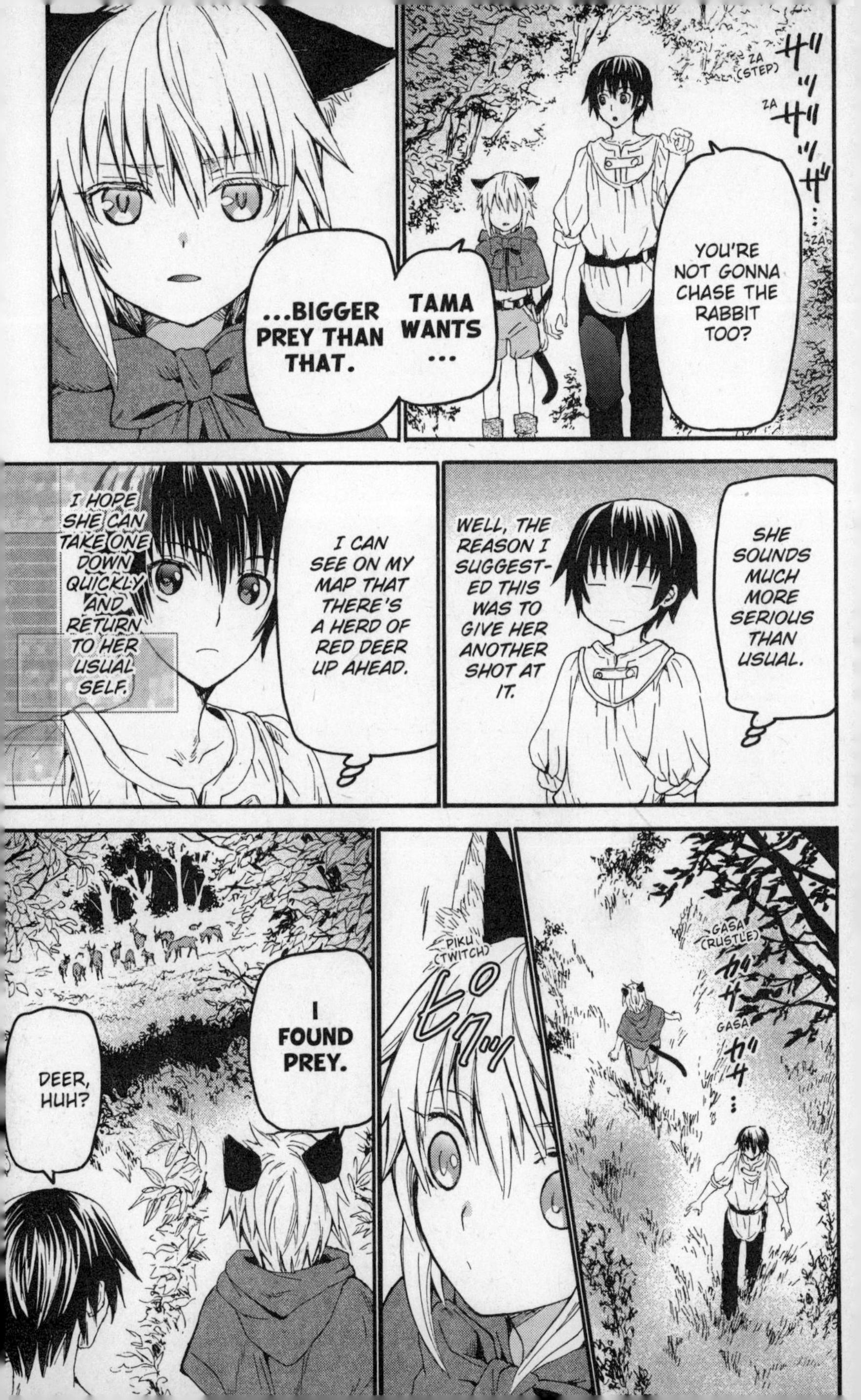

ZA (STEP)
ZA
ZA
YOU'RE NOT GONNA CHASE THE RABBIT TOO?
TAMA WANTS...
...BIGGER PREY THAN THAT.
SHE SOUNDS MUCH MORE SERIOUS THAN USUAL.
WELL, THE REASON I SUGGEST-ED THIS WAS TO GIVE HER ANOTHER SHOT AT IT.
I CAN SEE ON MY MAP THAT THERE'S A HERD OF RED DEER UP AHEAD.
I HOPE SHE CAN TAKE ONE DOWN QUICKLY AND RETURN TO HER USUAL SELF.
GASA (RUSTLE)
GASA
PIKU (TWITCH)
I FOUND PREY.
DEER, HUH?

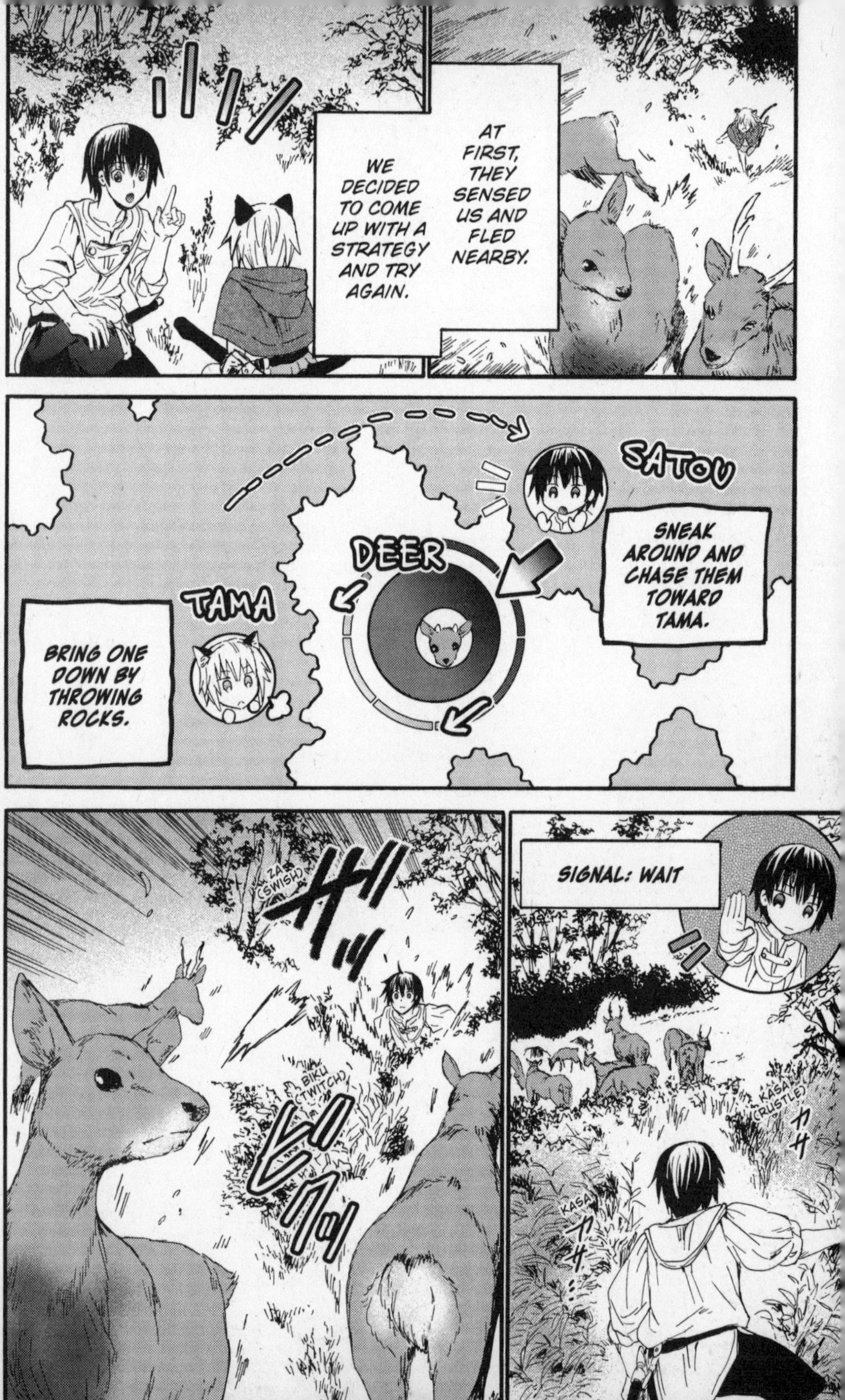
AT FIRST, THEY SENSED US AND FLED NEARBY.
WE DECIDED TO COME UP WITH A STRATEGY AND TRY AGAIN.
SATOU
SNEAK AROUND AND CHASE THEM TOWARD TAMA.
DEER
TAMA
BRING ONE DOWN BY THROWING ROCKS.
SIGNAL: WAIT
KASA (RUSTLE)
KASA
ZA (SWISH)
BIKU (TWITCH)

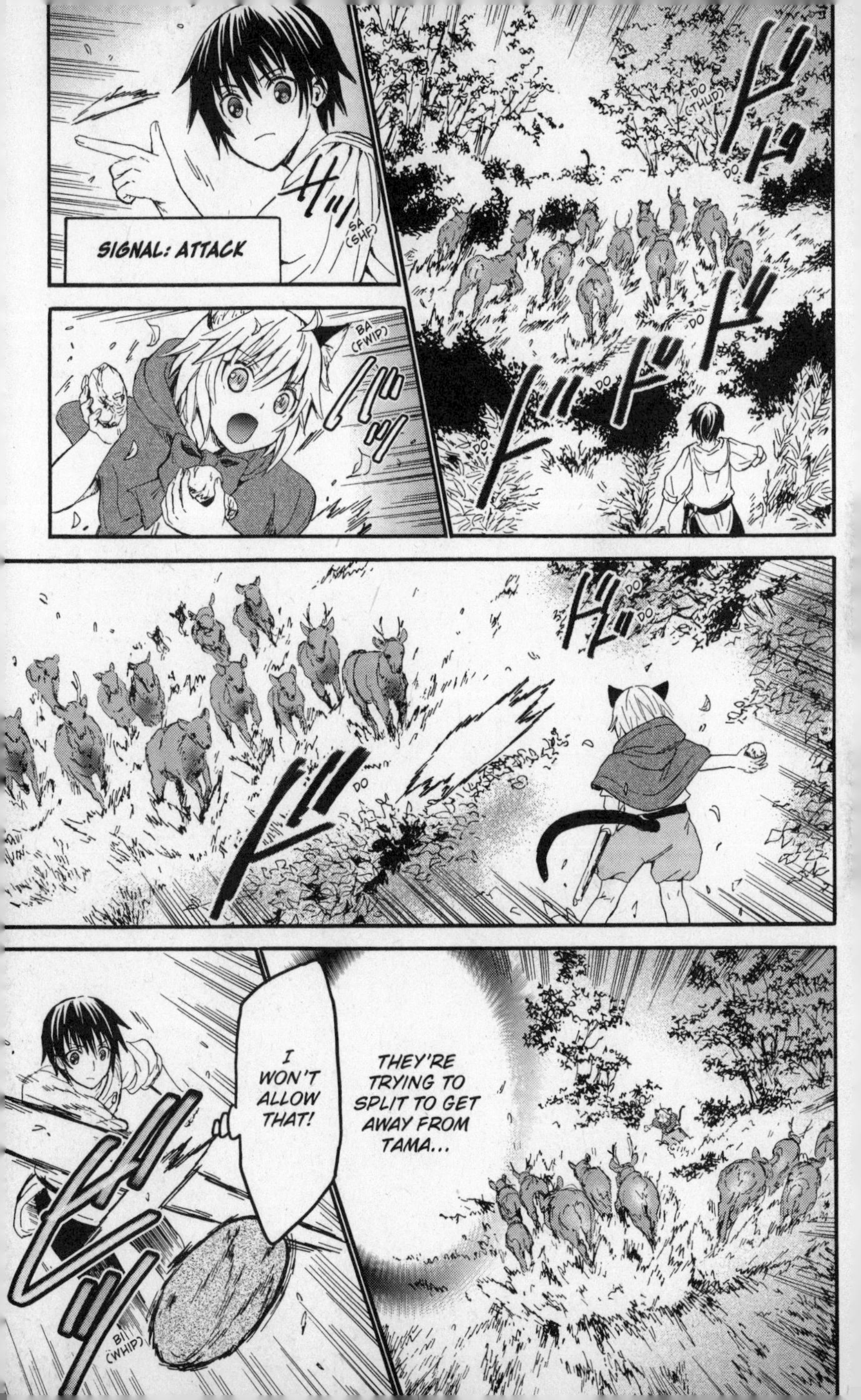
DO (THUD)
DO
DO
DO
DO
SA (SHF)
SIGNAL: ATTACK
BA (FWIP)
DO
DO
DO
THEY'RE TRYING TO SPLIT TO GET AWAY FROM TAMA...
I WON'T ALLOW THAT!
BI (WHIP)

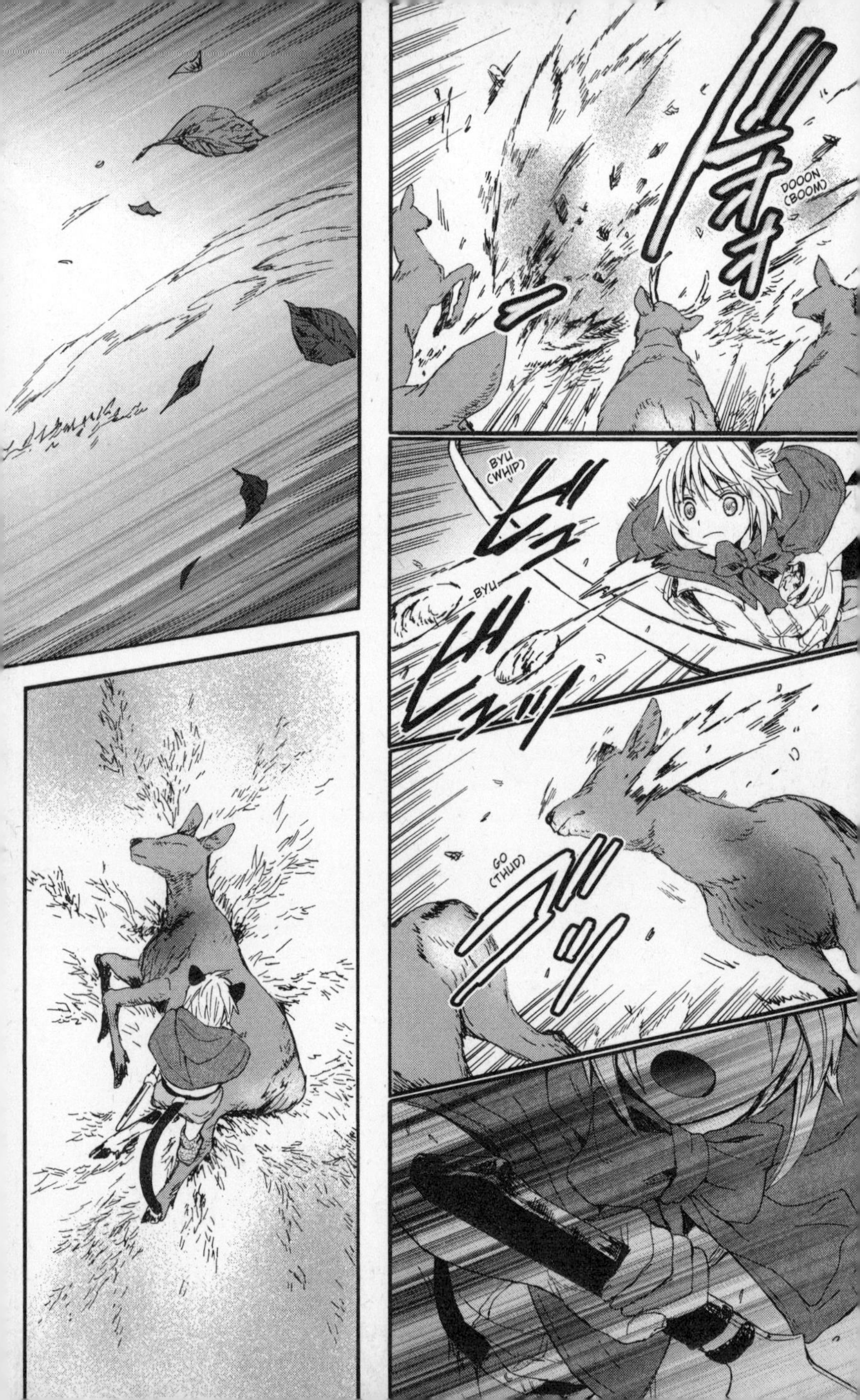
DOOON (BOOM)
BYU (WHIP)
BYU
GO (THUD)

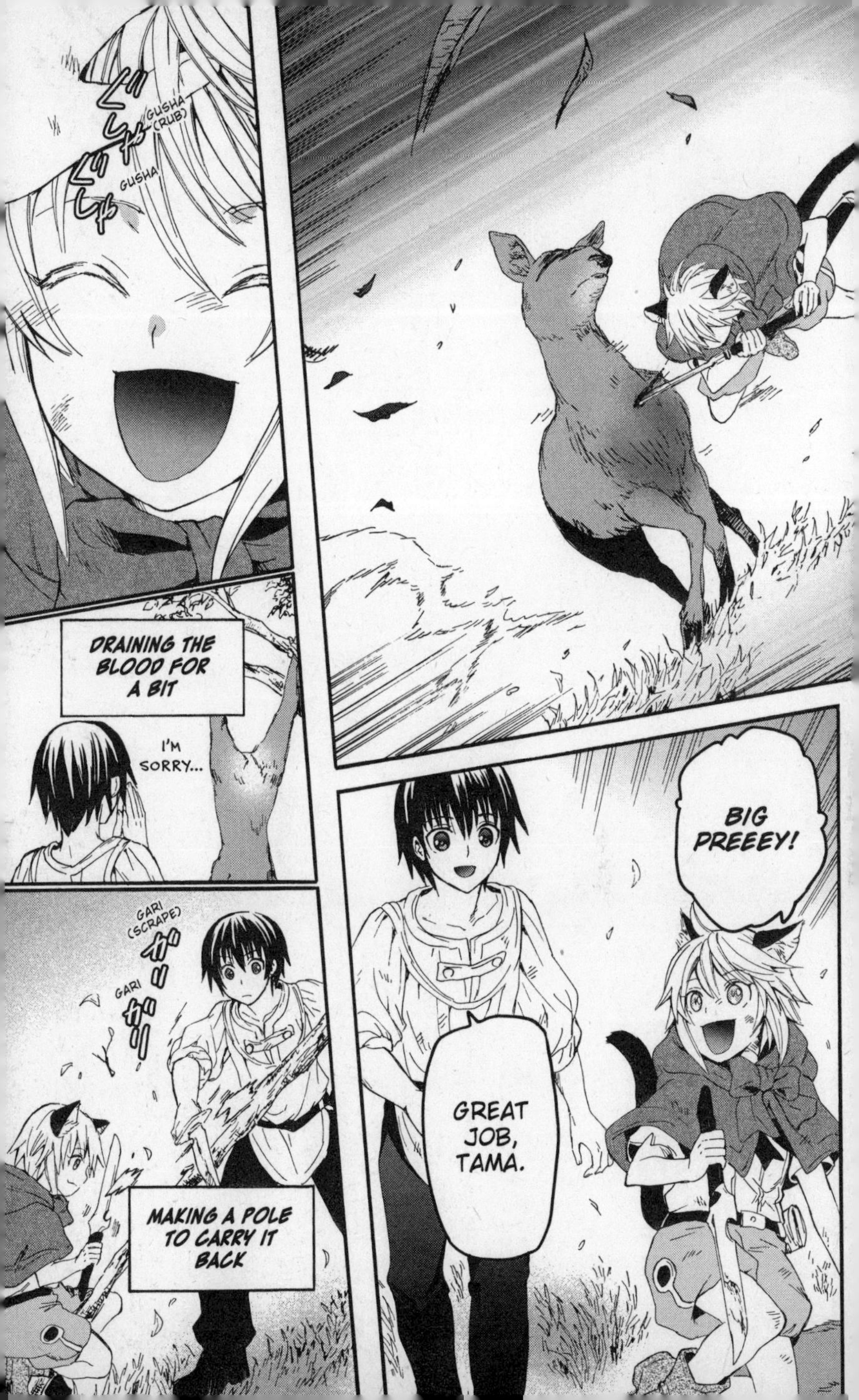
BIG PREEEY!
GREAT JOB, TAMA.
GUSHA (RUB)
GUSHA
DRAINING THE BLOOD FOR A BIT
I'M SORRY...
GARI (SCRAPE)
GARI
MAKING A POLE TO CARRY IT BACK

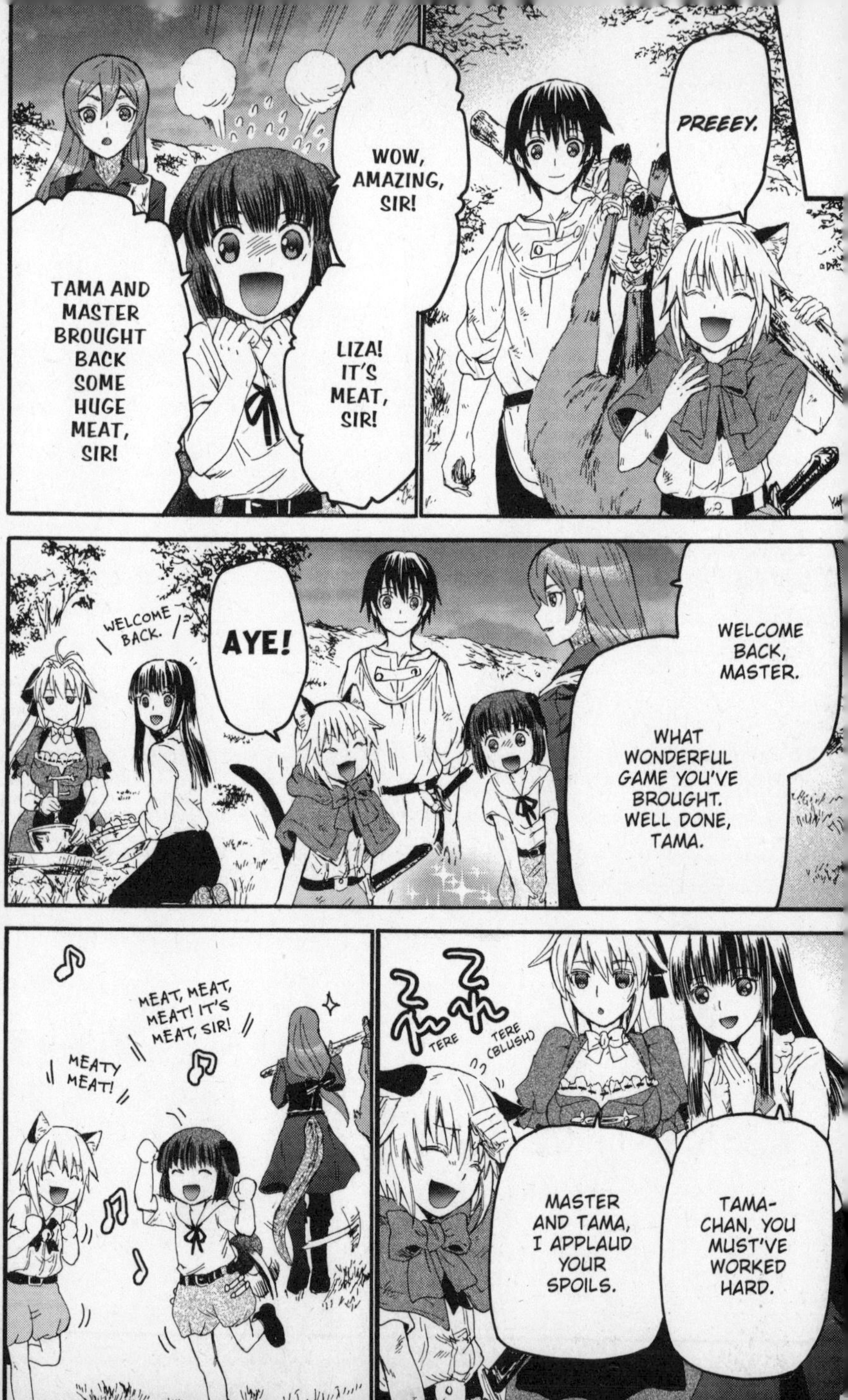
PREEEY.
WOW, AMAZING, SIR!
LIZA! IT'S MEAT, SIR!
TAMA AND MASTER BROUGHT BACK SOME HUGE MEAT, SIR!
WELCOME BACK, MASTER.
WHAT WONDERFUL GAME YOU'VE BROUGHT. WELL DONE, TAMA.
AYE!
WELCOME BACK.
TAMA-CHAN, YOU MUST'VE WORKED HARD.
MASTER AND TAMA, I APPLAUD YOUR SPOILS.
TERE TERE (BLUSH)
MEAT, MEAT, MEAT! IT'S MEAT, SIR!
MEATY MEAT!

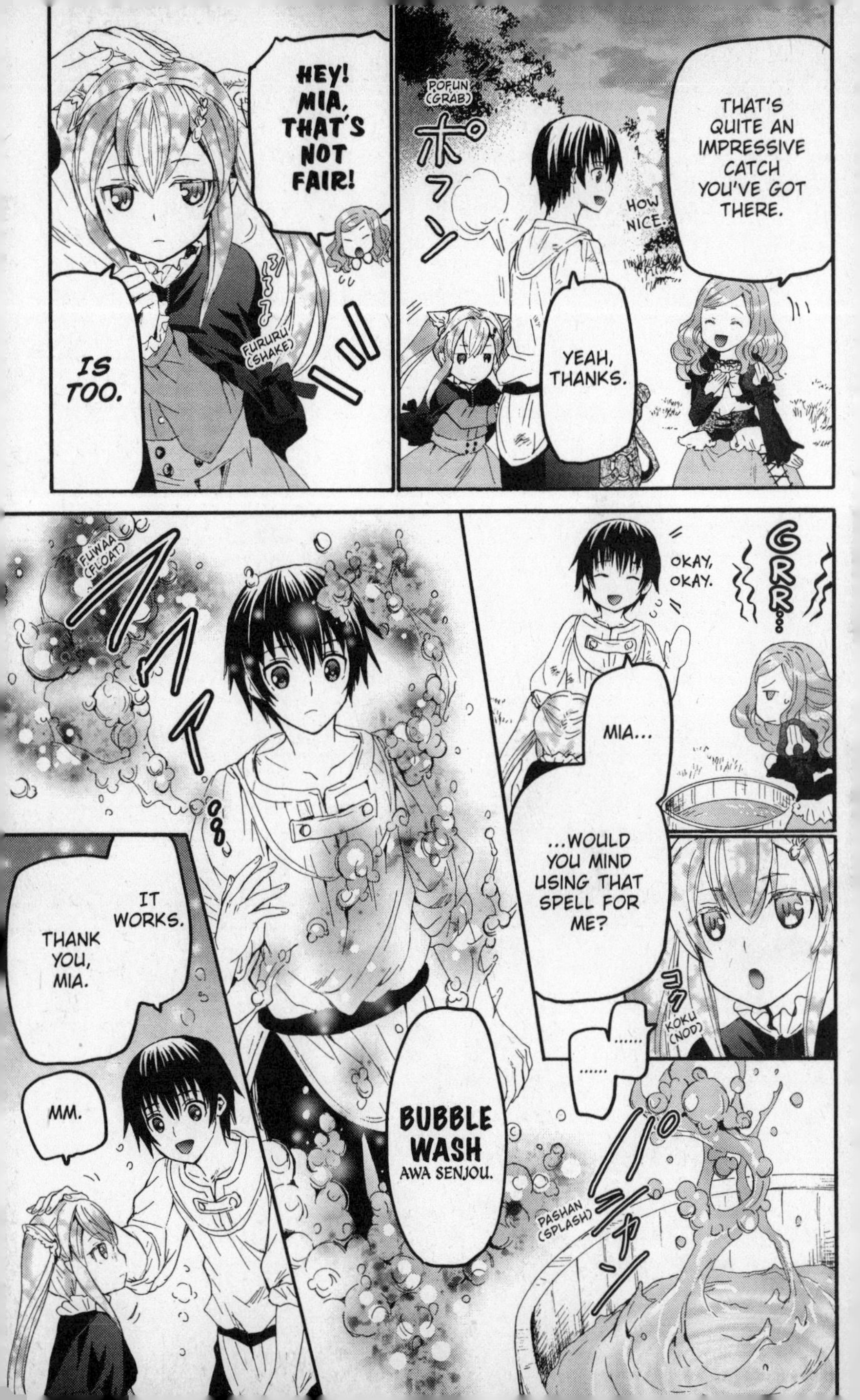
THAT'S QUITE AN IMPRESSIVE CATCH YOU'VE GOT THERE.
HOW NICE.
POFUN (GRAB)
YEAH, THANKS.
HEY! MIA, THAT'S NOT FAIR!
FURURU (SHAKE)
IS TOO.
GRR...
OKAY, OKAY.
MIA...
...WOULD YOU MIND USING THAT SPELL FOR ME?
KOKU (NOD)
......
......
BUBBLE WASH
AWA SENJOU.
PASHAN (SPLASH)
FUWAA (FLOAT)
IT WORKS.
THANK YOU, MIA.
MM.

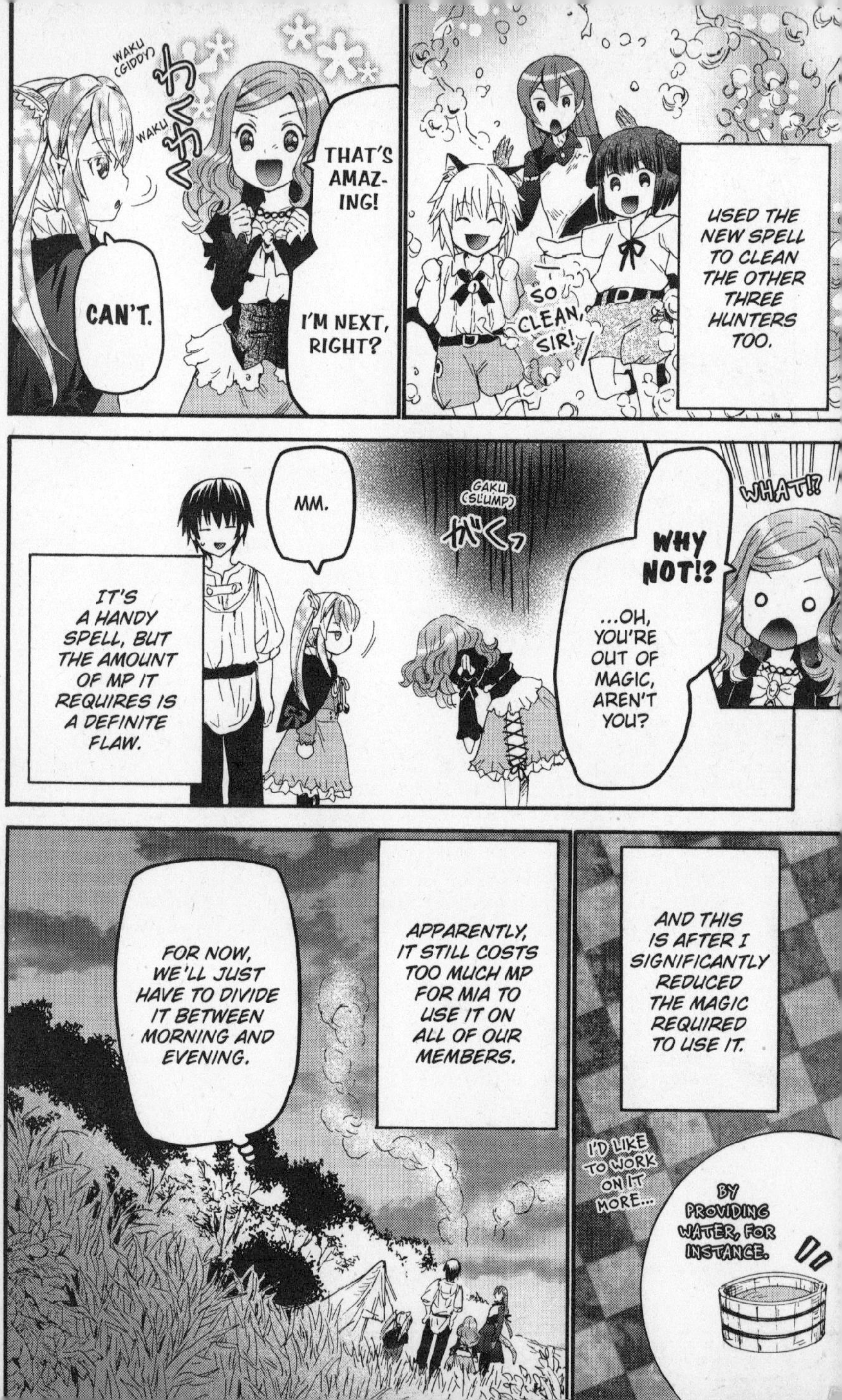
USED THE NEW SPELL TO CLEAN THE OTHER THREE HUNTERS TOO.
SO CLEAN, SIR!
WAKU (GIDDY) WAKU
THAT'S AMAZ-ING!
I'M NEXT, RIGHT?
CAN'T.
WHAT!?
WHY NOT!?
...OH, YOU'RE OUT OF MAGIC, AREN'T YOU?
GAKU (SLUMP)
MM.
IT'S A HANDY SPELL, BUT THE AMOUNT OF MP IT REQUIRES IS A DEFINITE FLAW.
AND THIS IS AFTER I SIGNIFICANTLY REDUCED THE MAGIC REQUIRED TO USE IT.
I'D LIKE TO WORK ON IT MORE...
BY PROVIDING WATER, FOR INSTANCE.
APPARENTLY, IT STILL COSTS TOO MUCH MP FOR MIA TO USE IT ON ALL OF OUR MEMBERS.
FOR NOW, WE'LL JUST HAVE TO DIVIDE IT BETWEEN MORNING AND EVENING.

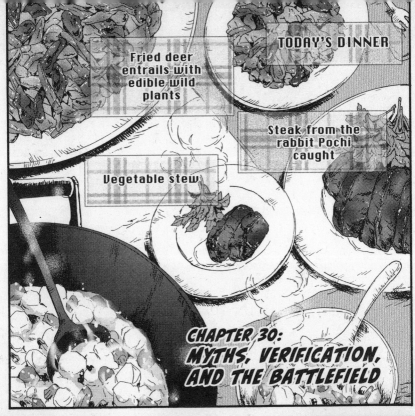

TODAY'S DINNER

Fried deer entrails with edible wild plants

Steak from the rabbit Pochi caught

Vegetable stew

CHAPTER 30:
MYTHS, VERIFICATION, AND THE BATTLEFIELD

MUGU
むぐ

MUGU (MUNCH)
むぐ!!

|MEAT...|

...

I HAVE TO COME UP WITH SOME VEGETARIAN AND LIQUID-BASED VARIATIONS FOR THEIR MEALS.

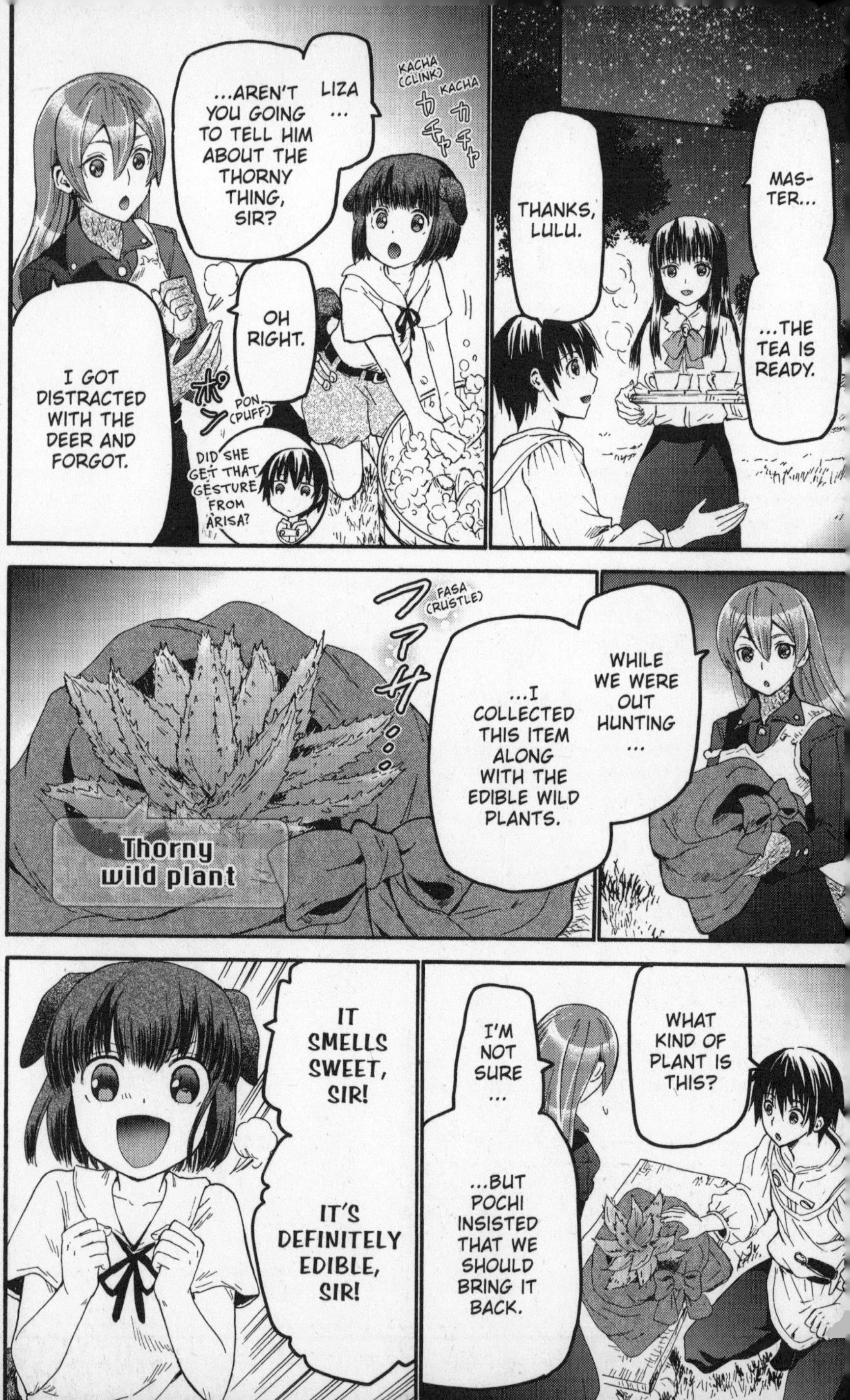
MASTER...
...THE TEA IS READY.
THANKS, LULU.
LIZA ...
...AREN'T YOU GOING TO TELL HIM ABOUT THE THORNY THING, SIR?
KACHA (CLINK) KACHA
OH RIGHT.
I GOT DISTRACTED WITH THE DEER AND FORGOT.
PON (PUFF)
DID SHE GET THAT GESTURE FROM ARISA?
WHILE WE WERE OUT HUNTING ...
...I COLLECTED THIS ITEM ALONG WITH THE EDIBLE WILD PLANTS.
FASA (RUSTLE)
Thorny wild plant
WHAT KIND OF PLANT IS THIS?
I'M NOT SURE ...
...BUT POCHI INSISTED THAT WE SHOULD BRING IT BACK.
IT SMELLS SWEET, SIR!
IT'S DEFINITELY EDIBLE, SIR!

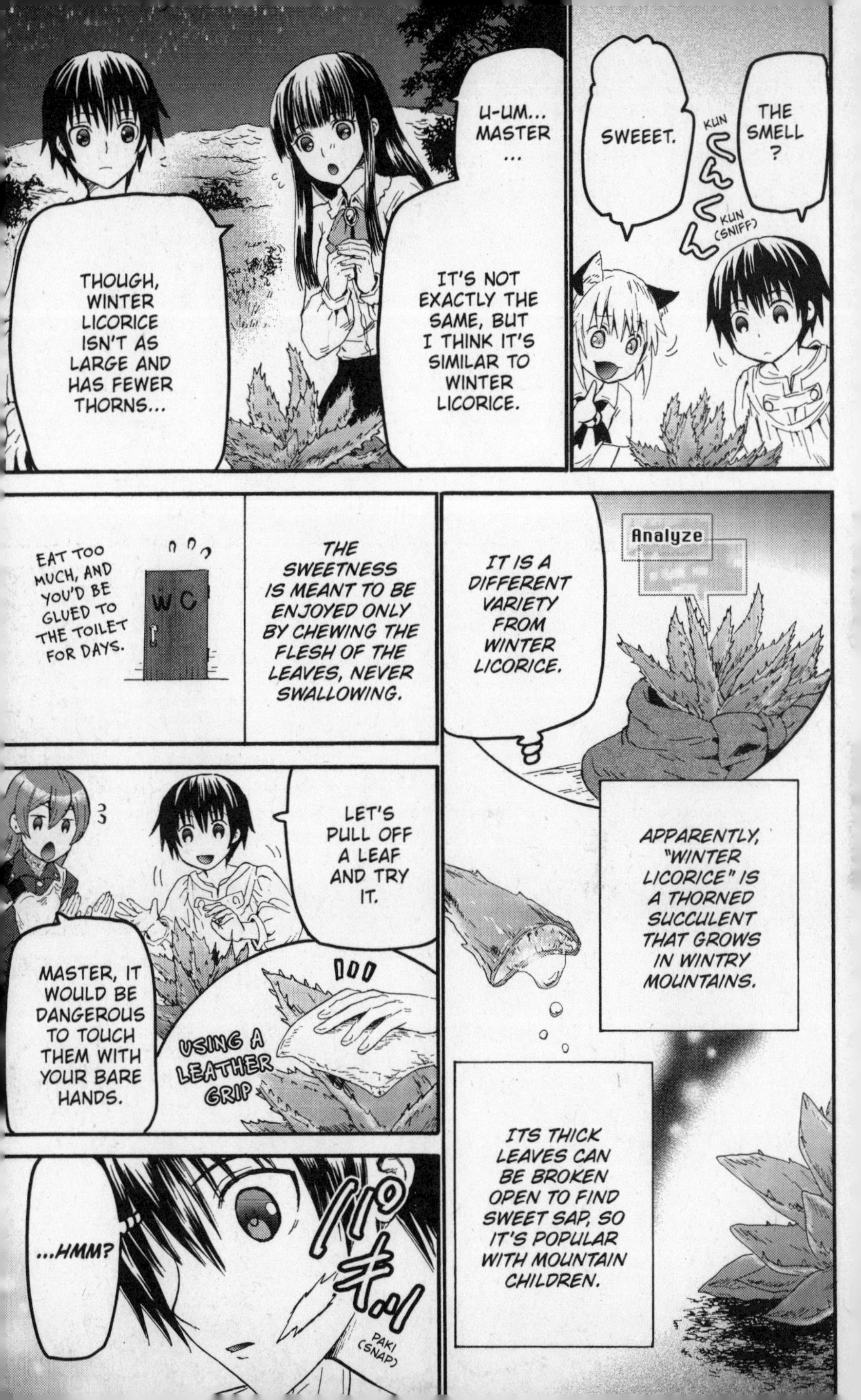
THE SMELL ?
KUN KUN (SNIFF)
SWEEET.
U-UM... MASTER ...
IT'S NOT EXACTLY THE SAME, BUT I THINK IT'S SIMILAR TO WINTER LICORICE.
THOUGH, WINTER LICORICE ISN'T AS LARGE AND HAS FEWER THORNS...
Analyze
IT IS A DIFFERENT VARIETY FROM WINTER LICORICE.
APPARENTLY, "WINTER LICORICE" IS A THORNED SUCCULENT THAT GROWS IN WINTRY MOUNTAINS.
ITS THICK LEAVES CAN BE BROKEN OPEN TO FIND SWEET SAP, SO IT'S POPULAR WITH MOUNTAIN CHILDREN.
THE SWEETNESS IS MEANT TO BE ENJOYED ONLY BY CHEWING THE FLESH OF THE LEAVES, NEVER SWALLOWING.
WC
EAT TOO MUCH, AND YOU'D BE GLUED TO THE TOILET FOR DAYS.
LET'S PULL OFF A LEAF AND TRY IT.
MASTER, IT WOULD BE DANGEROUS TO TOUCH THEM WITH YOUR BARE HANDS.
USING A LEATHER GRIP
PAKI (SNAP)
...HMM?

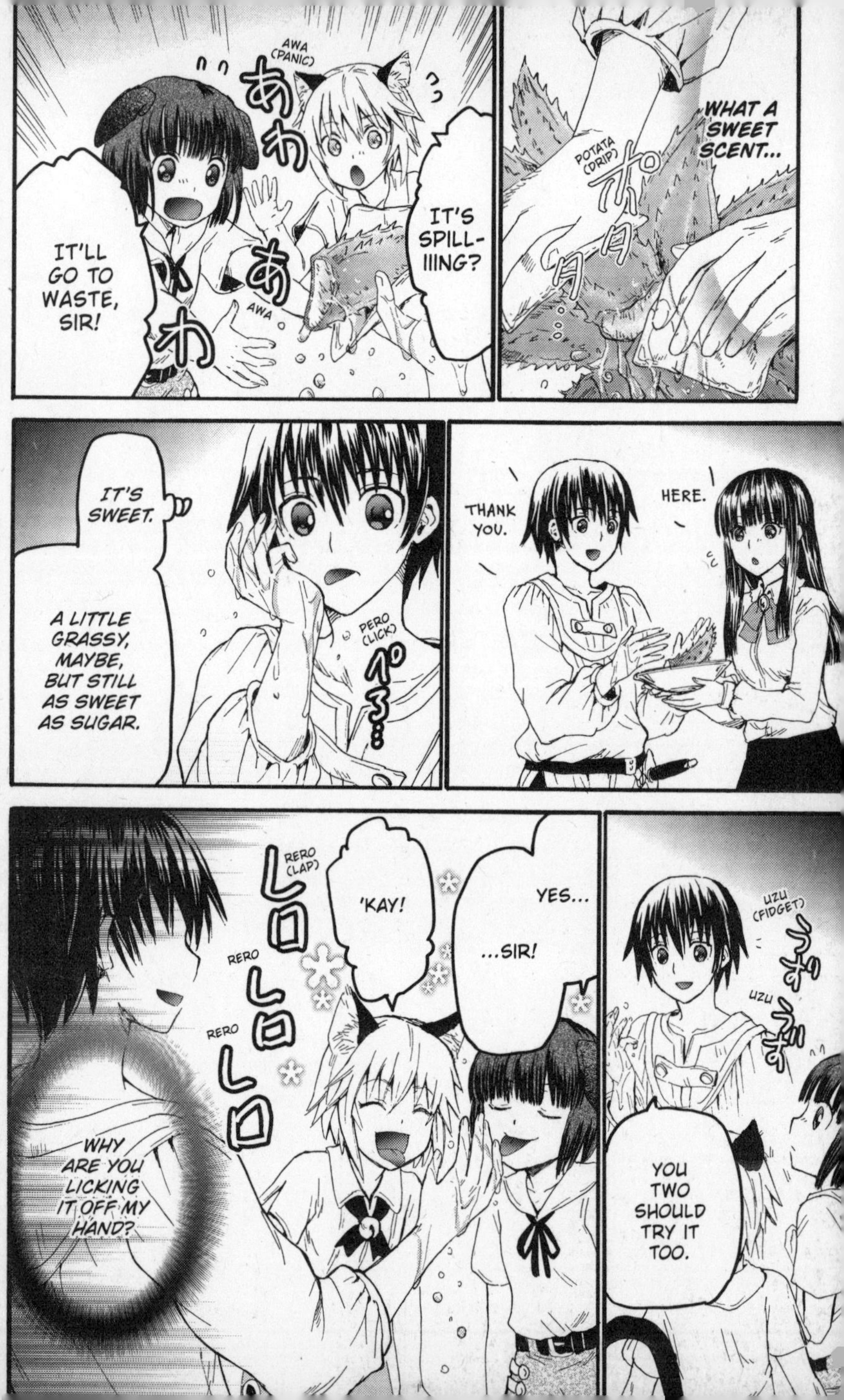
WHAT A SWEET SCENT...
POTATA (DRIP)
AWA (PANIC)
IT'S SPILL-IIING?
IT'LL GO TO WASTE, SIR!
AWA
HERE.
THANK YOU.
IT'S SWEET.
PERO (LICK)
A LITTLE GRASSY, MAYBE, BUT STILL AS SWEET AS SUGAR.
UZU (FIDGET)
UZU
YOU TWO SHOULD TRY IT TOO.
YES... ...SIR!
'KAY!
RERO (LAP)
RERO
RERO
WHY ARE YOU LICKING IT OFF MY HAND?

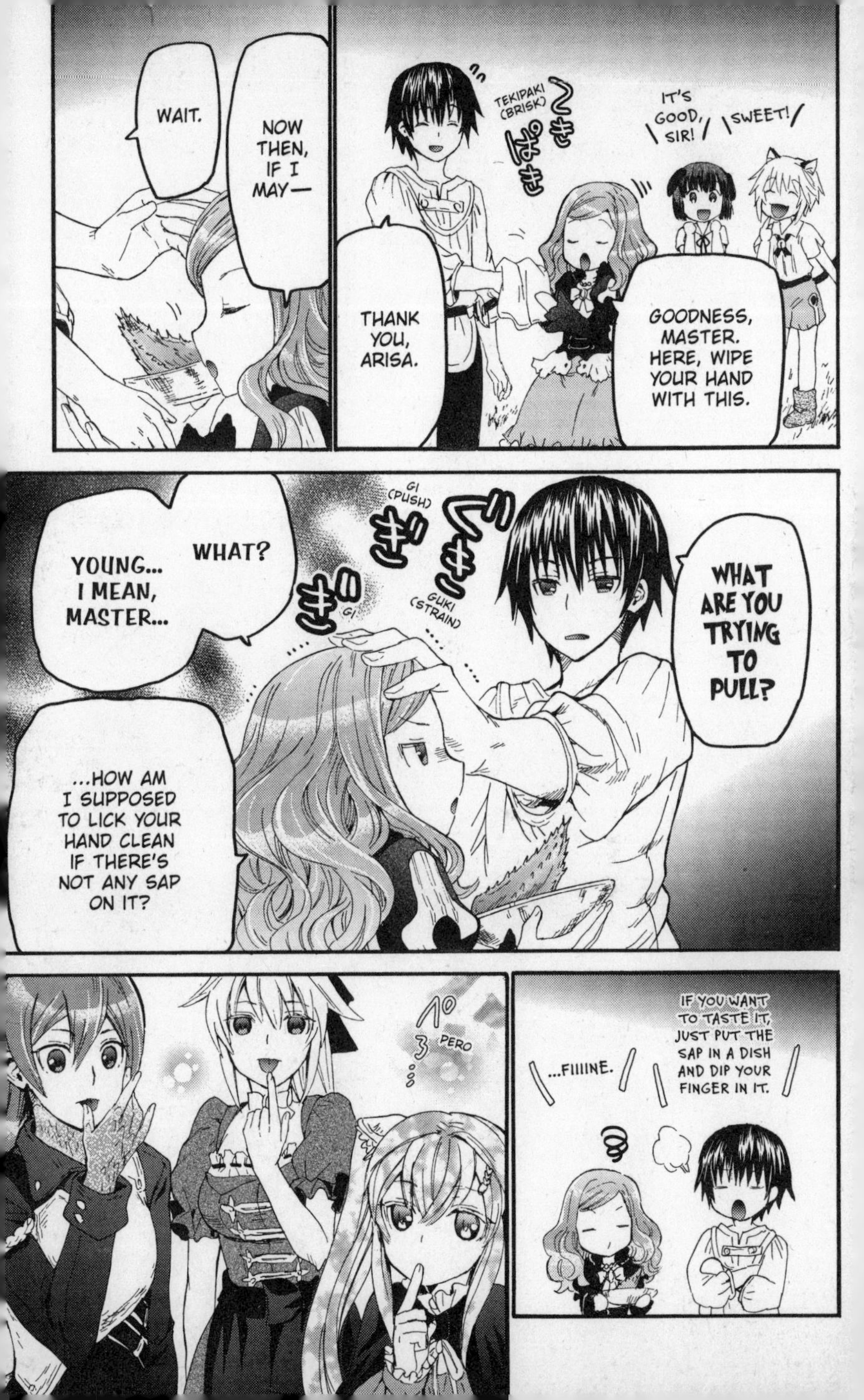
TEKIPAKI (BRISK)
IT'S GOOD, SIR!
SWEET!
GOODNESS, MASTER. HERE, WIPE YOUR HAND WITH THIS.
THANK YOU, ARISA.
NOW THEN, IF I MAY—
WAIT.
WHAT ARE YOU TRYING TO PULL?
GI (PUSH)
GUKI (STRAIN)
GI
WHAT?
YOUNG... I MEAN, MASTER...
...HOW AM I SUPPOSED TO LICK YOUR HAND CLEAN IF THERE'S NOT ANY SAP ON IT?
IF YOU WANT TO TASTE IT, JUST PUT THE SAP IN A DISH AND DIP YOUR FINGER IN IT.
...FIIIINE.
PERO

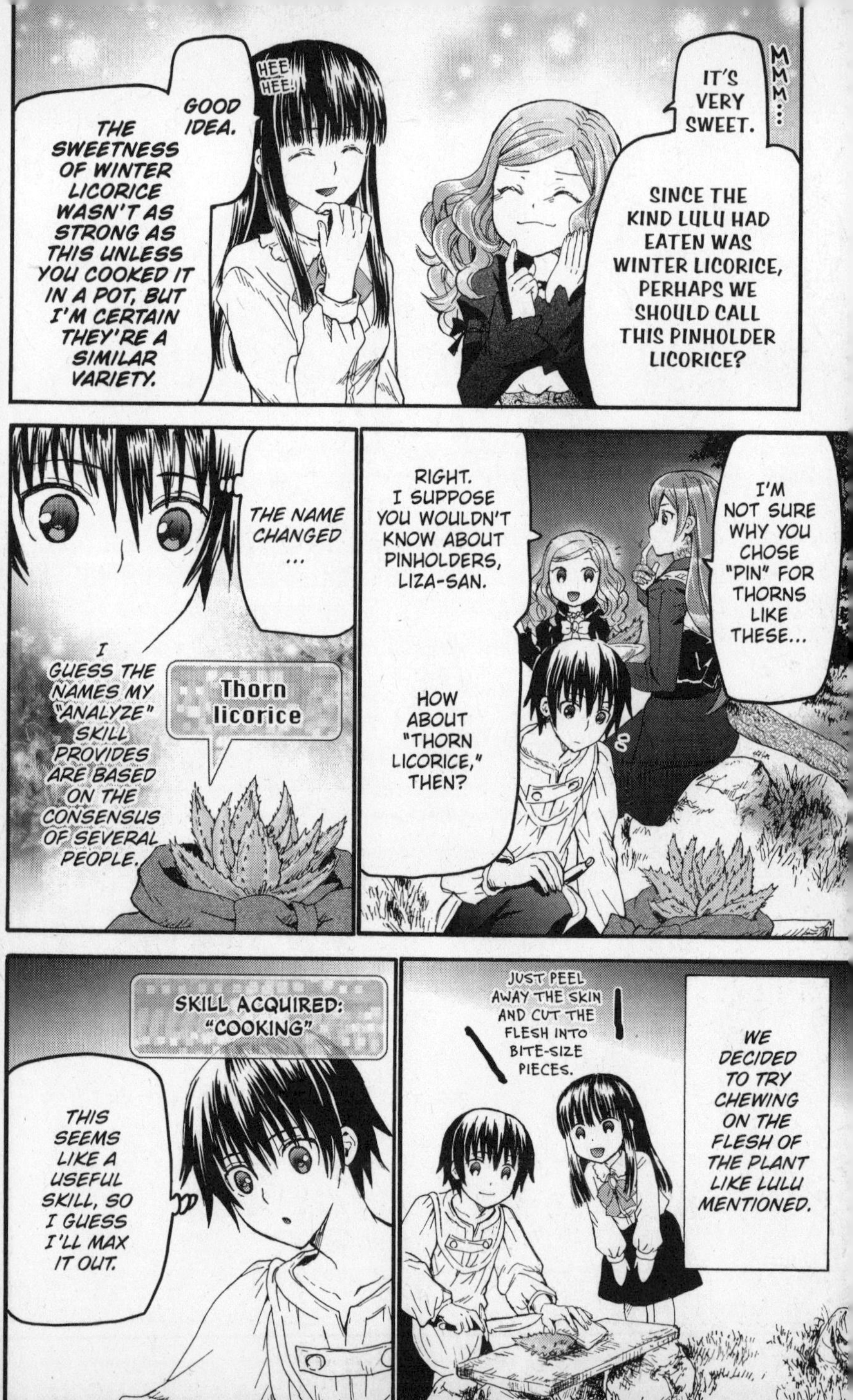
MMM...
IT'S VERY SWEET.
SINCE THE KIND LULU HAD EATEN WAS WINTER LICORICE, PERHAPS WE SHOULD CALL THIS PINHOLDER LICORICE?
HEE HEE.
GOOD IDEA.
THE SWEETNESS OF WINTER LICORICE WASN'T AS STRONG AS THIS UNLESS YOU COOKED IT IN A POT, BUT I'M CERTAIN THEY'RE A SIMILAR VARIETY.
I'M NOT SURE WHY YOU CHOSE "PIN" FOR THORNS LIKE THESE...
RIGHT. I SUPPOSE YOU WOULDN'T KNOW ABOUT PINHOLDERS, LIZA-SAN.
HOW ABOUT "THORN LICORICE," THEN?
THE NAME CHANGED ...
Thorn licorice
I GUESS THE NAMES MY "ANALYZE" SKILL PROVIDES ARE BASED ON THE CONSENSUS OF SEVERAL PEOPLE.
WE DECIDED TO TRY CHEWING ON THE FLESH OF THE PLANT LIKE LULU MENTIONED.
JUST PEEL AWAY THE SKIN AND CUT THE FLESH INTO BITE-SIZE PIECES.
SKILL ACQUIRED: "COOKING"
THIS SEEMS LIKE A USEFUL SKILL, SO I GUESS I'LL MAX IT OUT.

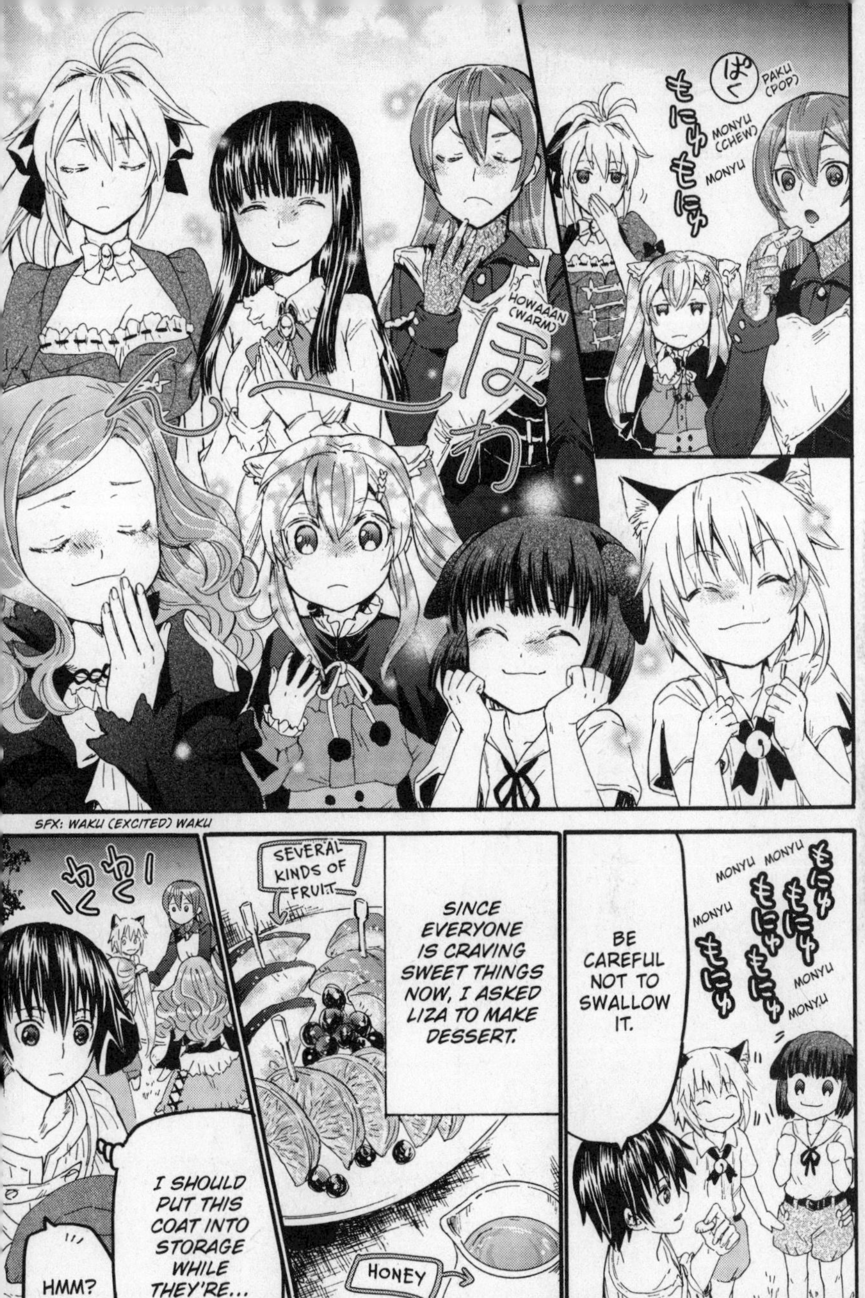
PAKU (POP)
MONYU (CHEW)
MONYU
HOWAAAN (WARM)
SFX: WAKU (EXCITED) WAKU
MONYU MONYU
MONYU
MONYU
MONYU
BE CAREFUL NOT TO SWALLOW IT.
SINCE EVERYONE IS CRAVING SWEET THINGS NOW, I ASKED LIZA TO MAKE DESSERT.
SEVERAL KINDS OF FRUIT
HONEY
I SHOULD PUT THIS COAT INTO STORAGE WHILE THEY'RE...
HMM?

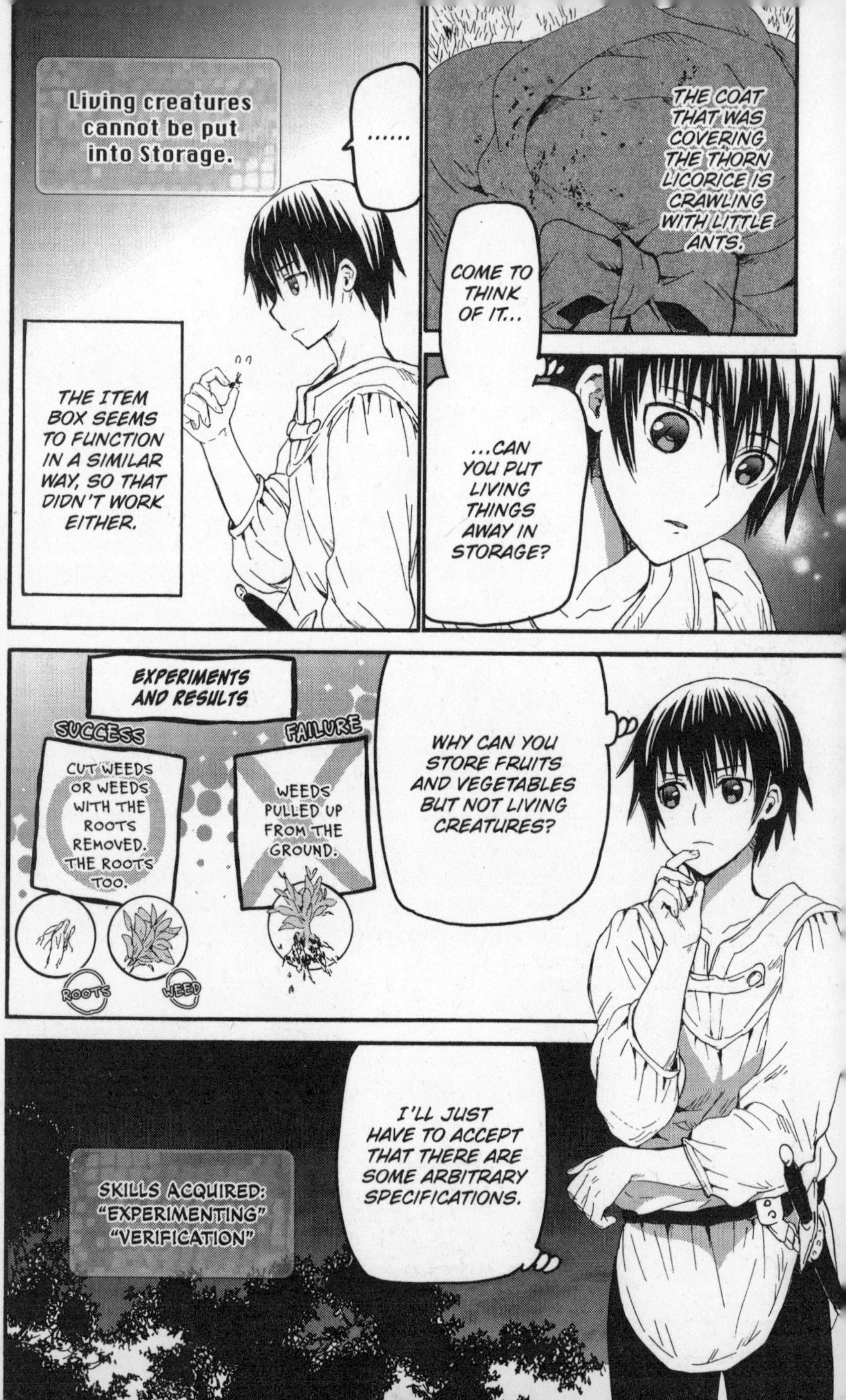
THE COAT THAT WAS COVERING THE THORN LICORICE IS CRAWLING WITH LITTLE ANTS.
COME TO THINK OF IT...
...CAN YOU PUT LIVING THINGS AWAY IN STORAGE?
......
Living creatures cannot be put into Storage.
THE ITEM BOX SEEMS TO FUNCTION IN A SIMILAR WAY, SO THAT DIDN'T WORK EITHER.
WHY CAN YOU STORE FRUITS AND VEGETABLES BUT NOT LIVING CREATURES?
EXPERIMENTS AND RESULTS
FAILURE
WEEDS PULLED UP FROM THE GROUND.
SUCCESS
CUT WEEDS OR WEEDS WITH THE ROOTS REMOVED. THE ROOTS TOO.
WEED
ROOTS
I'LL JUST HAVE TO ACCEPT THAT THERE ARE SOME ARBITRARY SPECIFICATIONS.
SKILLS ACQUIRED: "EXPERIMENTING" "VERIFICATION"

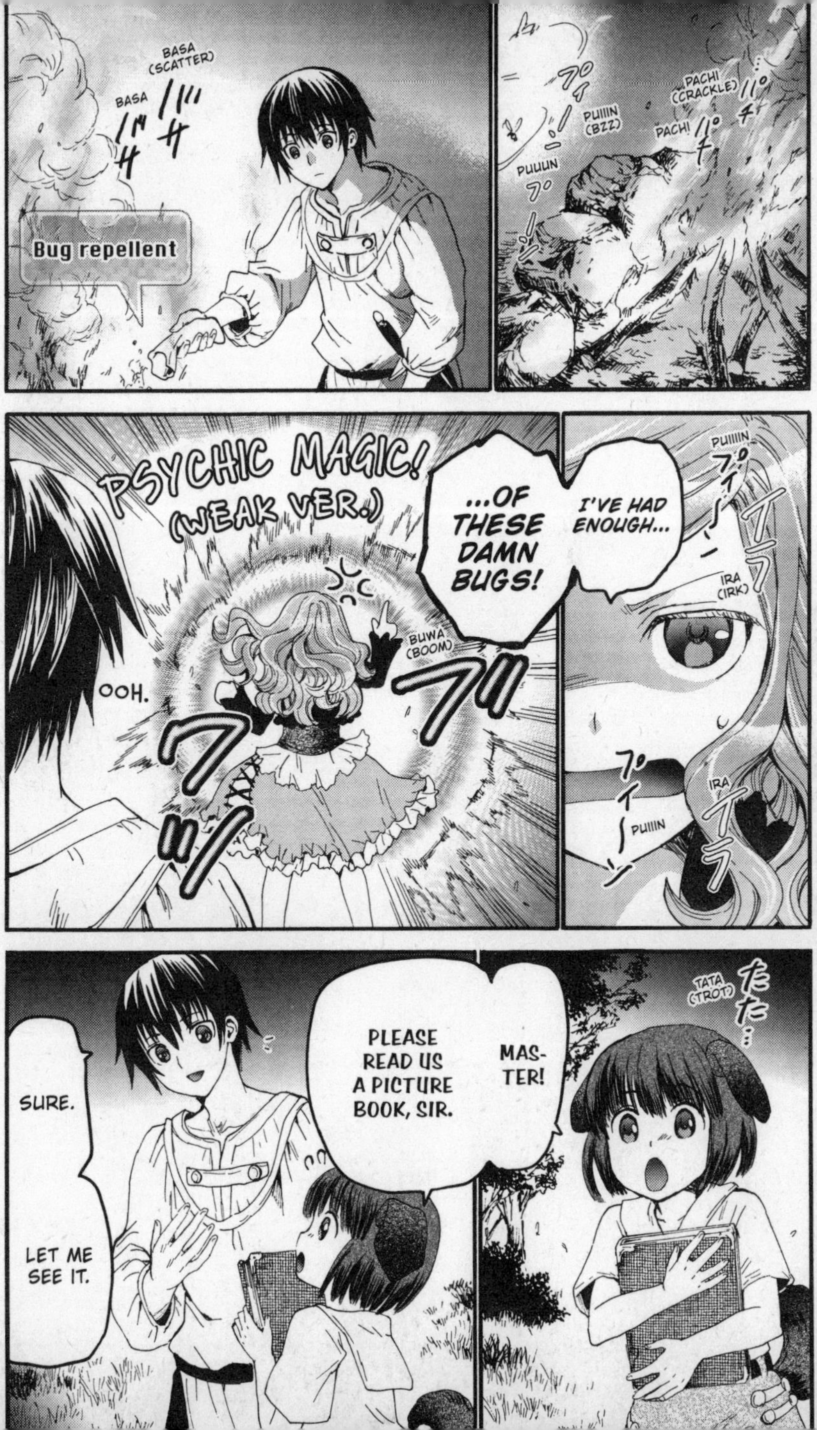
PACHI (CRACKLE)
PACHI!
PUIIIN (BZZ)
PUUUN
BASA (SCATTER)
BASA
Bug repellent
PUIIIN
I'VE HAD ENOUGH...
IRA (IRK)
IRA
PUIIIN
...OF THESE DAMN BUGS!
PSYCHIC MAGIC! (WEAK VER.)
BUWA (BOOM)
OOH.
TATA (TROT)
MAS-TER!
PLEASE READ US A PICTURE BOOK, SIR.
SURE.
LET ME SEE IT.

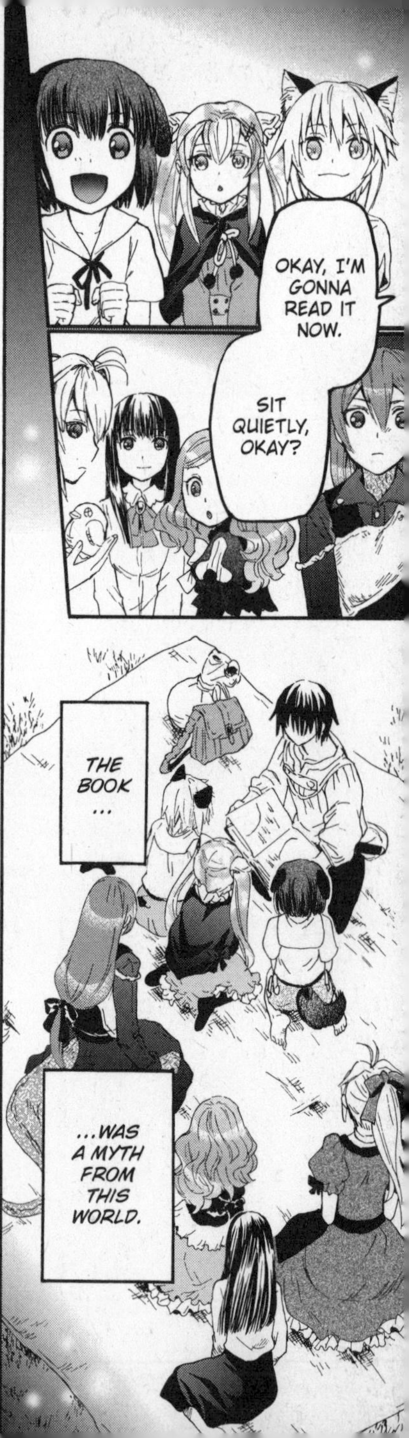
OKAY, I'M GONNA READ IT NOW.
SIT QUIETLY, OKAY?
THE BOOK...
...WAS A MYTH FROM THIS WORLD.

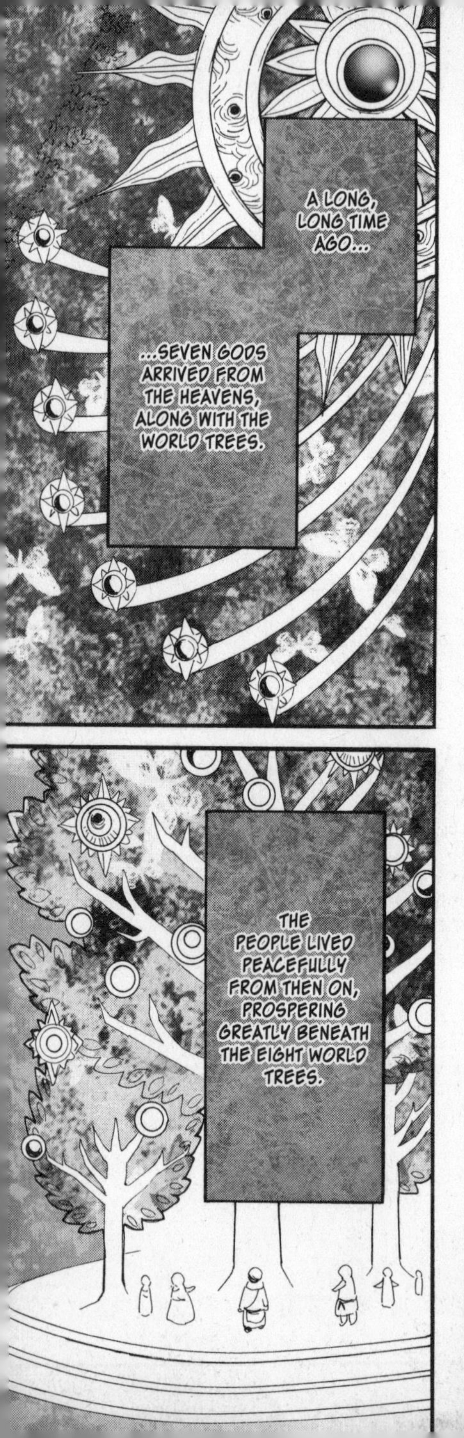
A LONG, LONG TIME AGO...
...SEVEN GODS ARRIVED FROM THE HEAVENS, ALONG WITH THE WORLD TREES.
THE PEOPLE LIVED PEACEFULLY FROM THEN ON, PROSPERING GREATLY BENEATH THE EIGHT WORLD TREES.

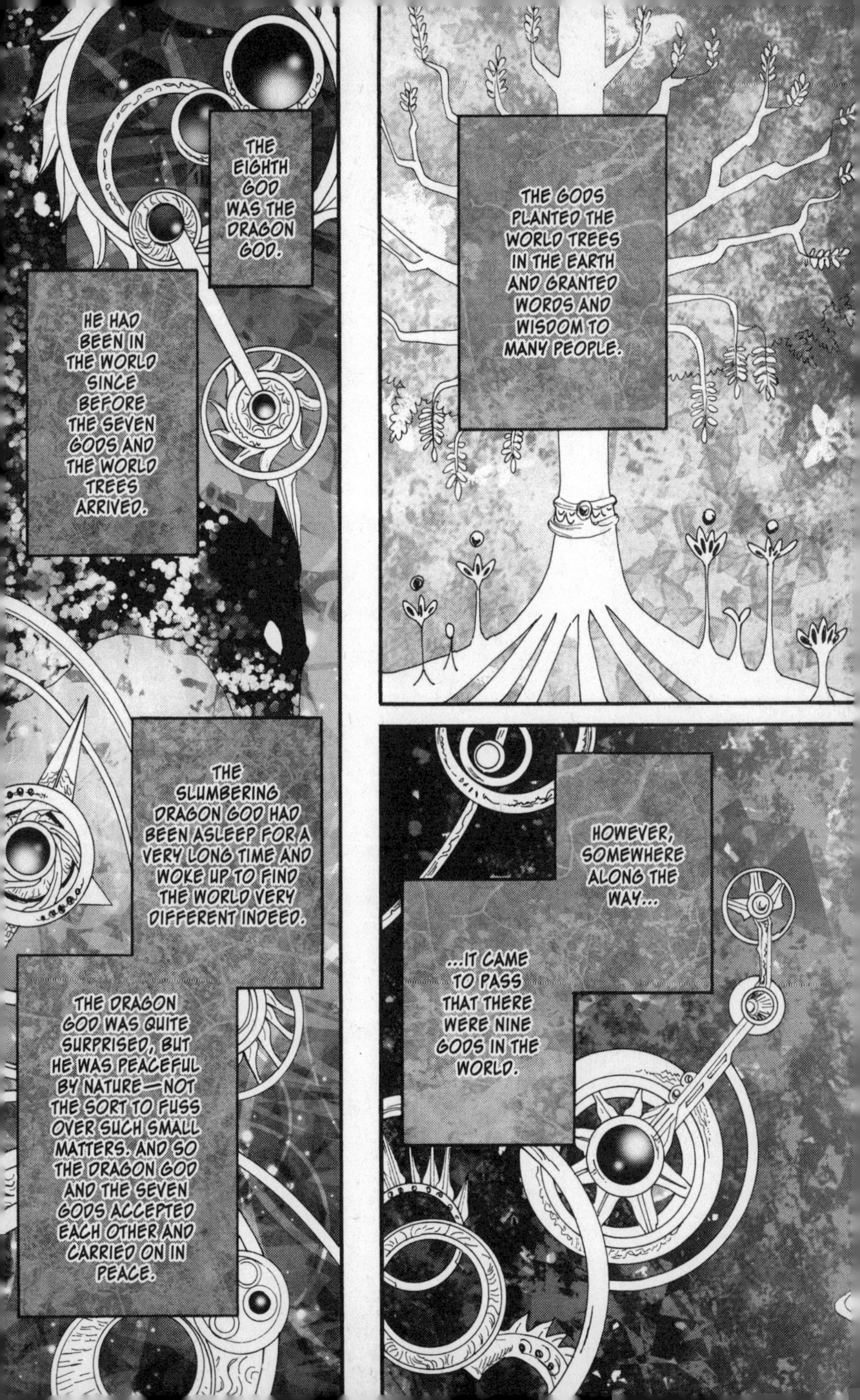
THE GODS PLANTED THE WORLD TREES IN THE EARTH AND GRANTED WORDS AND WISDOM TO MANY PEOPLE.
THE EIGHTH GOD WAS THE DRAGON GOD.
HE HAD BEEN IN THE WORLD SINCE BEFORE THE SEVEN GODS AND THE WORLD TREES ARRIVED.
THE SLUMBERING DRAGON GOD HAD BEEN ASLEEP FOR A VERY LONG TIME AND WOKE UP TO FIND THE WORLD VERY DIFFERENT INDEED.
THE DRAGON GOD WAS QUITE SURPRISED, BUT HE WAS PEACEFUL BY NATURE—NOT THE SORT TO FUSS OVER SUCH SMALL MATTERS. AND SO THE DRAGON GOD AND THE SEVEN GODS ACCEPTED EACH OTHER AND CARRIED ON IN PEACE.
HOWEVER, SOMEWHERE ALONG THE WAY...
...IT CAME TO PASS THAT THERE WERE NINE GODS IN THE WORLD.

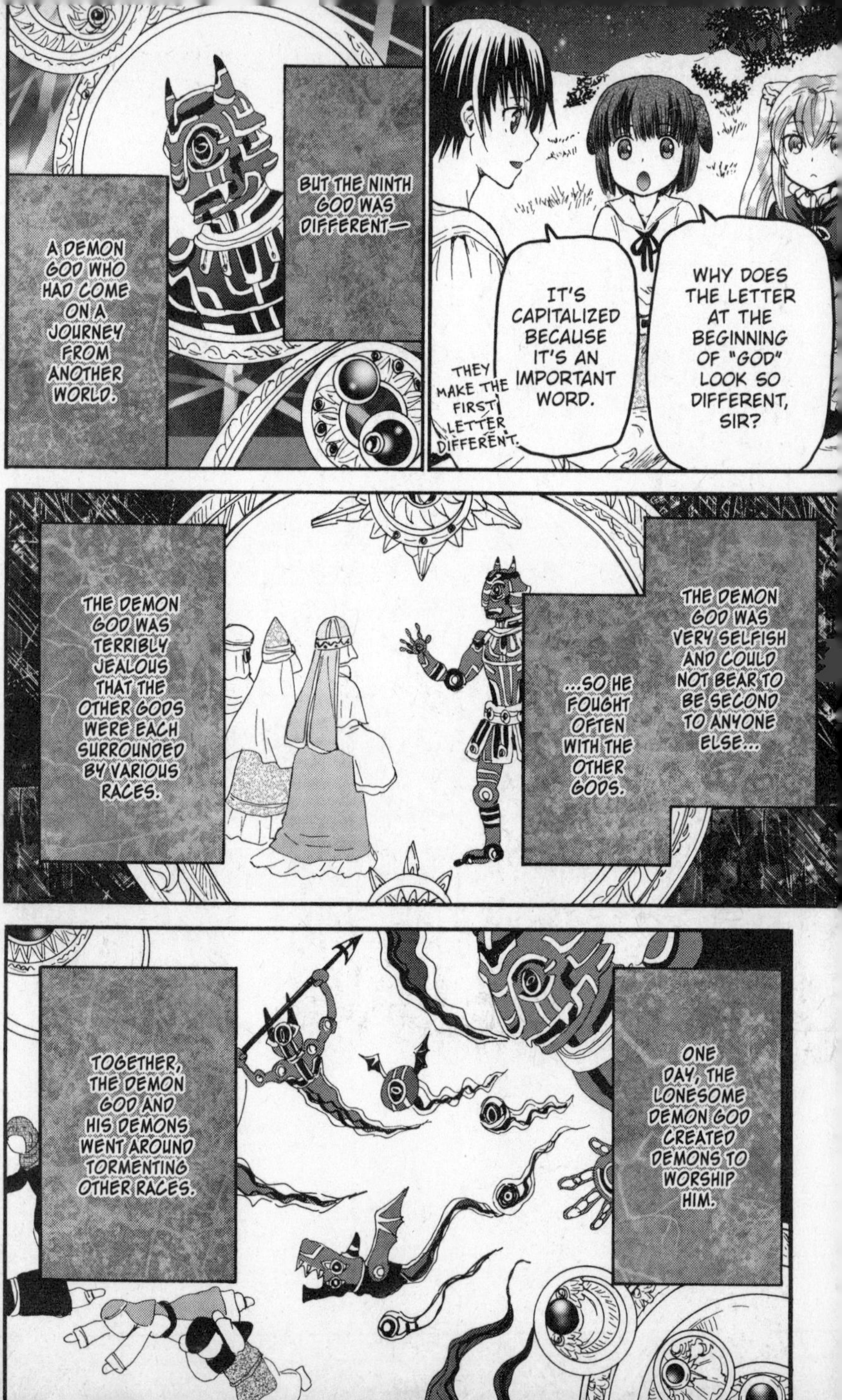

WHY DOES THE LETTER AT THE BEGINNING OF "GOD" LOOK SO DIFFERENT, SIR?
IT'S CAPITALIZED BECAUSE IT'S AN IMPORTANT WORD.
THEY MAKE THE FIRST LETTER DIFFERENT.
BUT THE NINTH GOD WAS DIFFERENT—
A DEMON GOD WHO HAD COME ON A JOURNEY FROM ANOTHER WORLD.
THE DEMON GOD WAS VERY SELFISH AND COULD NOT BEAR TO BE SECOND TO ANYONE ELSE...
...SO HE FOUGHT OFTEN WITH THE OTHER GODS.
THE DEMON GOD WAS TERRIBLY JEALOUS THAT THE OTHER GODS WERE EACH SURROUNDED BY VARIOUS RACES.
ONE DAY, THE LONESOME DEMON GOD CREATED DEMONS TO WORSHIP HIM.
TOGETHER, THE DEMON GOD AND HIS DEMONS WENT AROUND TORMENTING OTHER RACES.

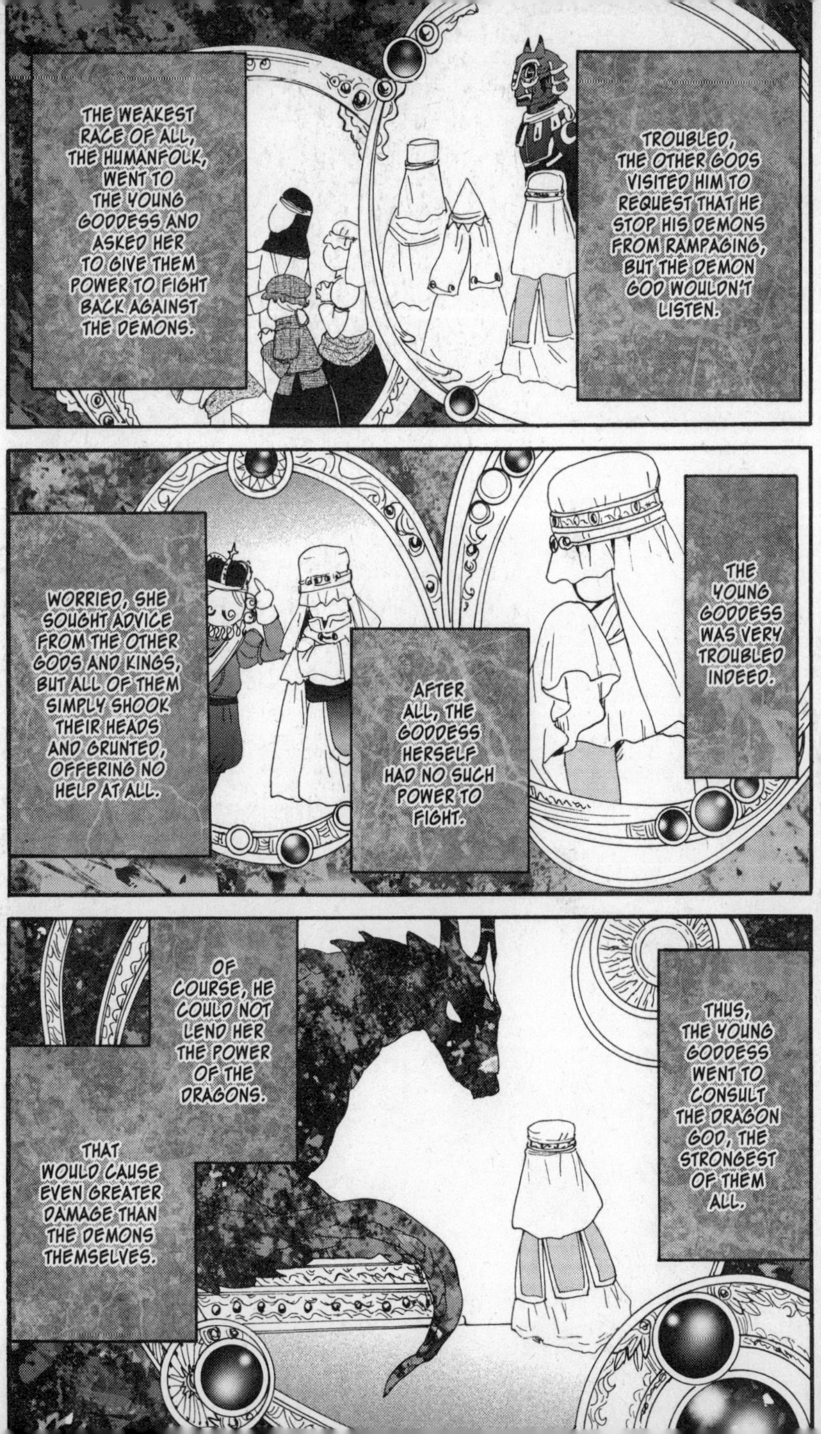
TROUBLED, THE OTHER GODS VISITED HIM TO REQUEST THAT HE STOP HIS DEMONS FROM RAMPAGING, BUT THE DEMON GOD WOULDN'T LISTEN.
THE WEAKEST RACE OF ALL, THE HUMANFOLK, WENT TO THE YOUNG GODDESS AND ASKED HER TO GIVE THEM POWER TO FIGHT BACK AGAINST THE DEMONS.
THE YOUNG GODDESS WAS VERY TROUBLED INDEED.
AFTER ALL, THE GODDESS HERSELF HAD NO SUCH POWER TO FIGHT.
WORRIED, SHE SOUGHT ADVICE FROM THE OTHER GODS AND KINGS, BUT ALL OF THEM SIMPLY SHOOK THEIR HEADS AND GRUNTED, OFFERING NO HELP AT ALL.
THUS, THE YOUNG GODDESS WENT TO CONSULT THE DRAGON GOD, THE STRONGEST OF THEM ALL.
OF COURSE, HE COULD NOT LEND HER THE POWER OF THE DRAGONS.
THAT WOULD CAUSE EVEN GREATER DAMAGE THAN THE DEMONS THEMSELVES.

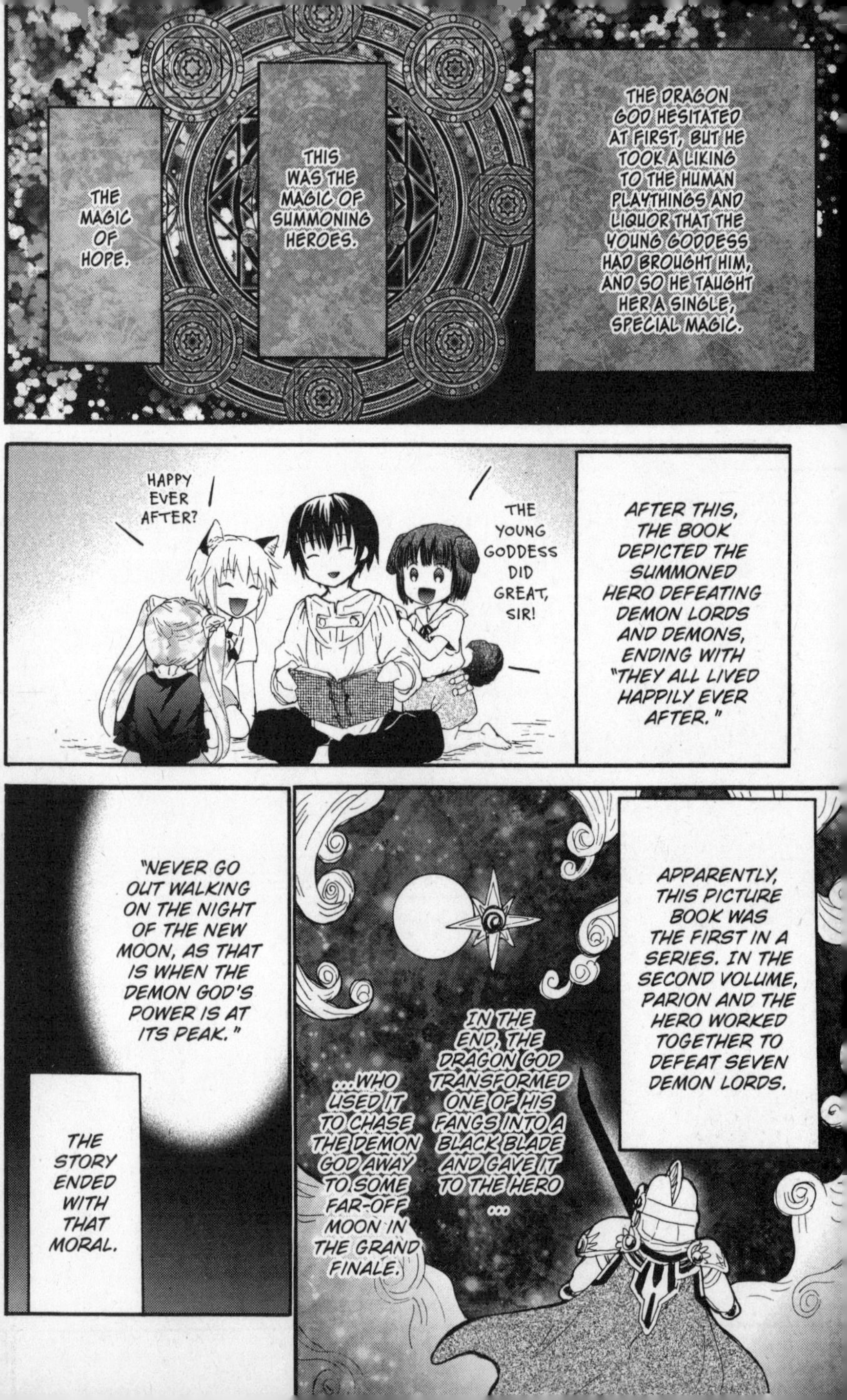
THE DRAGON GOD HESITATED AT FIRST, BUT HE TOOK A LIKING TO THE HUMAN PLAYTHINGS AND LIQUOR THAT THE YOUNG GODDESS HAD BROUGHT HIM, AND SO HE TAUGHT HER A SINGLE, SPECIAL MAGIC.
THIS WAS THE MAGIC OF SUMMONING HEROES.
THE MAGIC OF HOPE.
AFTER THIS, THE BOOK DEPICTED THE SUMMONED HERO DEFEATING DEMON LORDS AND DEMONS, ENDING WITH "THEY ALL LIVED HAPPILY EVER AFTER."
THE YOUNG GODDESS DID GREAT, SIR!
HAPPY EVER AFTER?
APPARENTLY, THIS PICTURE BOOK WAS THE FIRST IN A SERIES. IN THE SECOND VOLUME, PARION AND THE HERO WORKED TOGETHER TO DEFEAT SEVEN DEMON LORDS.
IN THE END, THE DRAGON GOD TRANSFORMED ONE OF HIS FANGS INTO A BLACK BLADE AND GAVE IT TO THE HERO...
...WHO USED IT TO CHASE THE DEMON GOD AWAY TO SOME FAR-OFF MOON IN THE GRAND FINALE.
"NEVER GO OUT WALKING ON THE NIGHT OF THE NEW MOON, AS THAT IS WHEN THE DEMON GOD'S POWER IS AT ITS PEAK."
THE STORY ENDED WITH THAT MORAL.

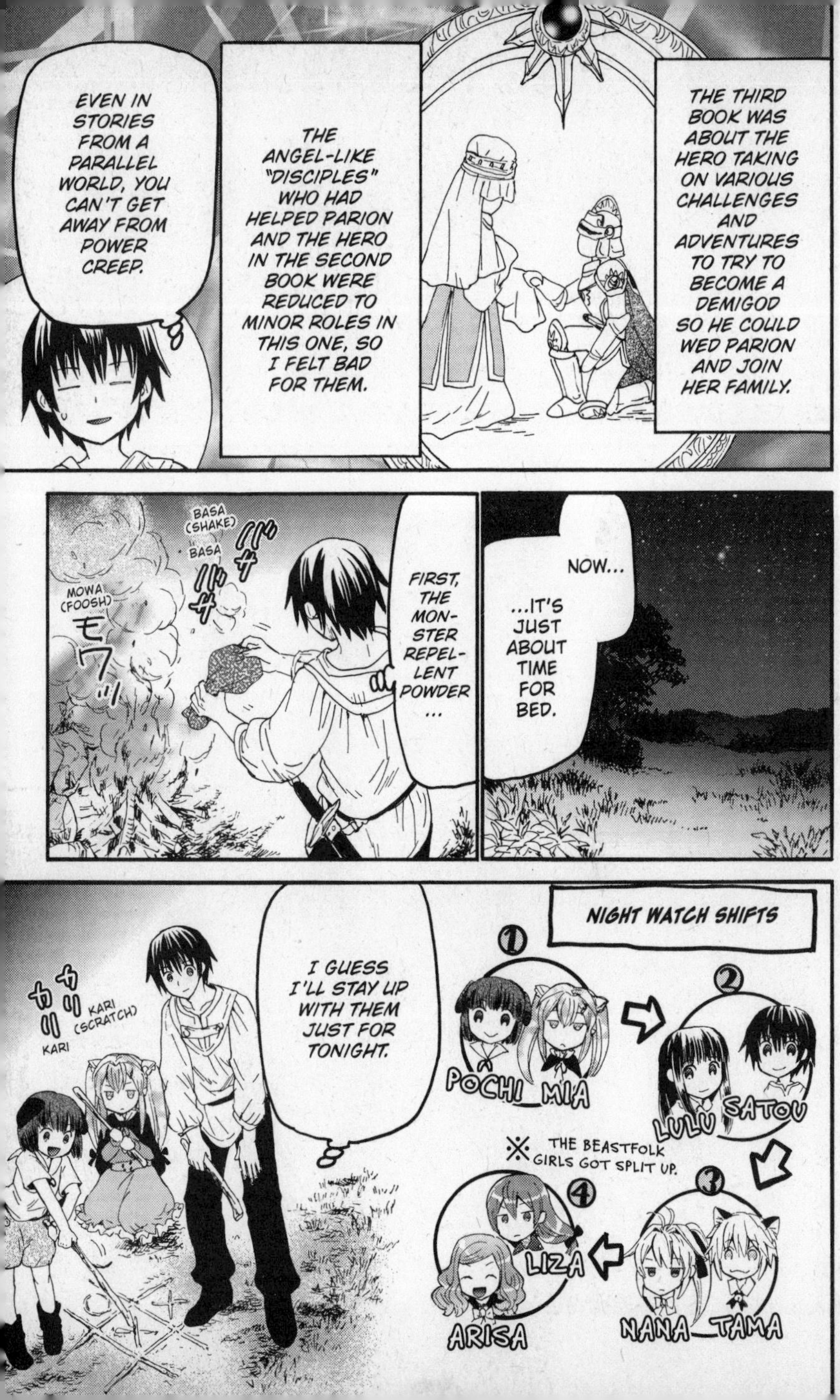
THE THIRD BOOK WAS ABOUT THE HERO TAKING ON VARIOUS CHALLENGES AND ADVENTURES TO TRY TO BECOME A DEMIGOD SO HE COULD WED PARION AND JOIN HER FAMILY.
THE ANGEL-LIKE "DISCIPLES" WHO HAD HELPED PARION AND THE HERO IN THE SECOND BOOK WERE REDUCED TO MINOR ROLES IN THIS ONE, SO I FELT BAD FOR THEM.
EVEN IN STORIES FROM A PARALLEL WORLD, YOU CAN'T GET AWAY FROM POWER CREEP.
NOW...
...IT'S JUST ABOUT TIME FOR BED.
FIRST, THE MONSTER REPELLENT POWDER...
BASA (SHAKE)
BASA
MOWA (FOOSH)
NIGHT WATCH SHIFTS
①
POCHI
MIA
②
LULU
SATOU
③
NANA
TAMA
④
LIZA
ARISA
※ THE BEASTFOLK GIRLS GOT SPLIT UP.
I GUESS I'LL STAY UP WITH THEM JUST FOR TONIGHT.
KARI (SCRATCH)
KARI

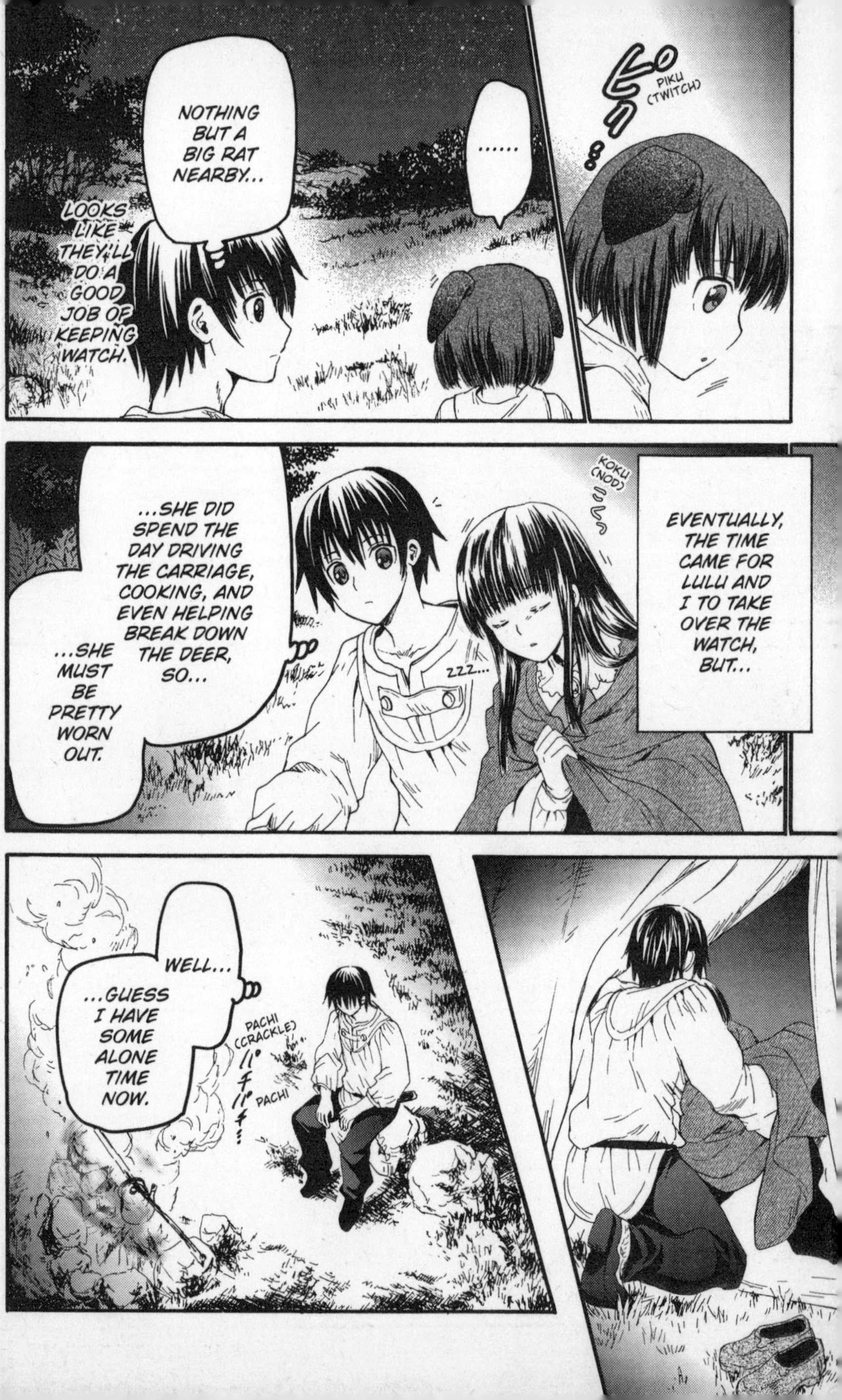
PIKU (TWITCH)
......
NOTHING BUT A BIG RAT NEARBY...
LOOKS LIKE THEY'LL DO A GOOD JOB OF KEEPING WATCH.
EVENTUALLY, THE TIME CAME FOR LULU AND I TO TAKE OVER THE WATCH, BUT...
KOKU (NOD)
ZZZ...
...SHE DID SPEND THE DAY DRIVING THE CARRIAGE, COOKING, AND EVEN HELPING BREAK DOWN THE DEER, SO...
...SHE MUST BE PRETTY WORN OUT.
WELL...
...GUESS I HAVE SOME ALONE TIME NOW.
PACHI (CRACKLE)
PACHI

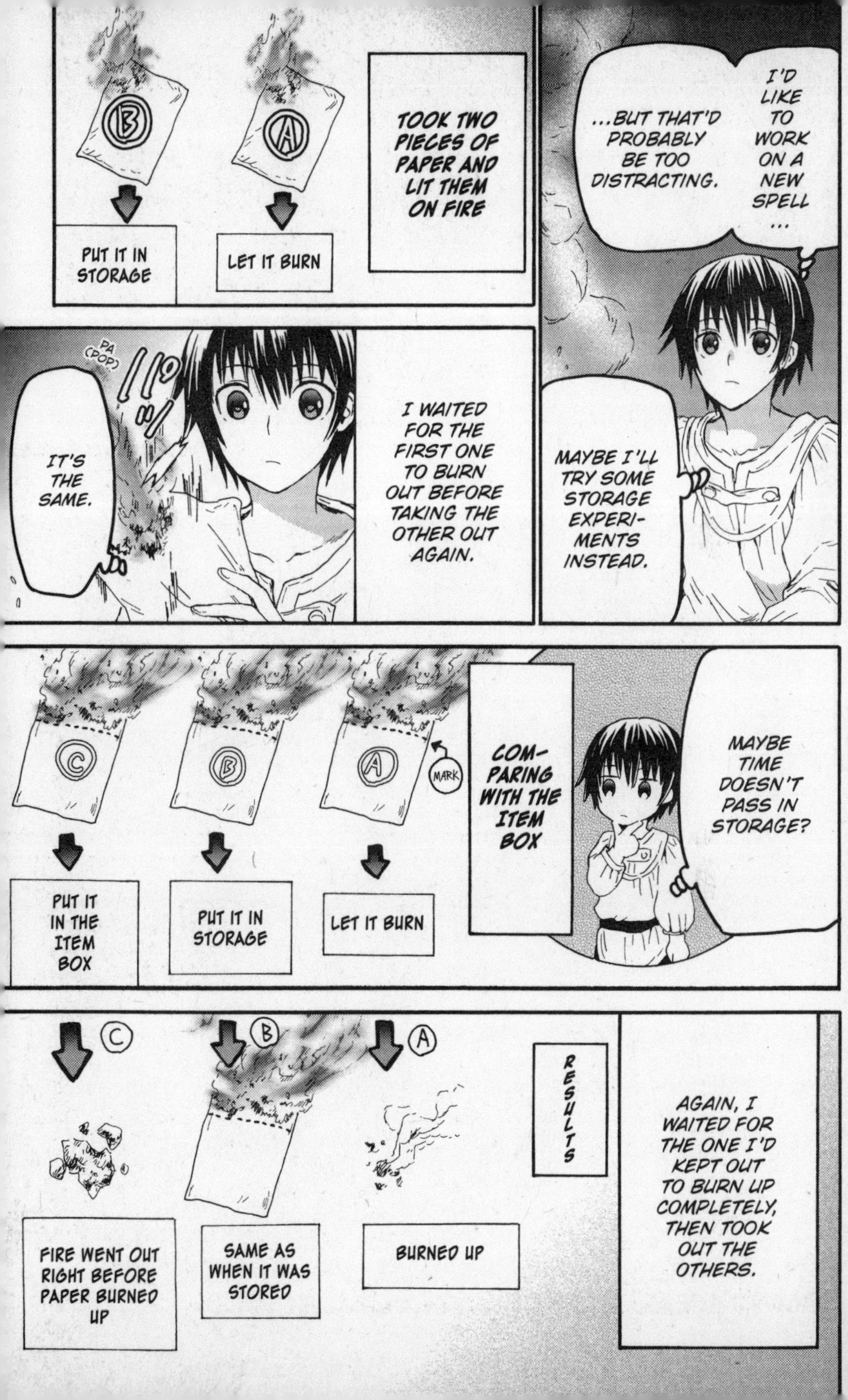
I'D LIKE TO WORK ON A NEW SPELL...
...BUT THAT'D PROBABLY BE TOO DISTRACTING.
MAYBE I'LL TRY SOME STORAGE EXPERI-MENTS INSTEAD.
TOOK TWO PIECES OF PAPER AND LIT THEM ON FIRE
LET IT BURN
PUT IT IN STORAGE
I WAITED FOR THE FIRST ONE TO BURN OUT BEFORE TAKING THE OTHER OUT AGAIN.
PA (POP)
IT'S THE SAME.
MAYBE TIME DOESN'T PASS IN STORAGE?
COM-PARING WITH THE ITEM BOX
MARK
LET IT BURN
PUT IT IN STORAGE
PUT IT IN THE ITEM BOX
AGAIN, I WAITED FOR THE ONE I'D KEPT OUT TO BURN UP COMPLETELY, THEN TOOK OUT THE OTHERS.
RESULTS
BURNED UP
SAME AS WHEN IT WAS STORED
FIRE WENT OUT RIGHT BEFORE PAPER BURNED UP

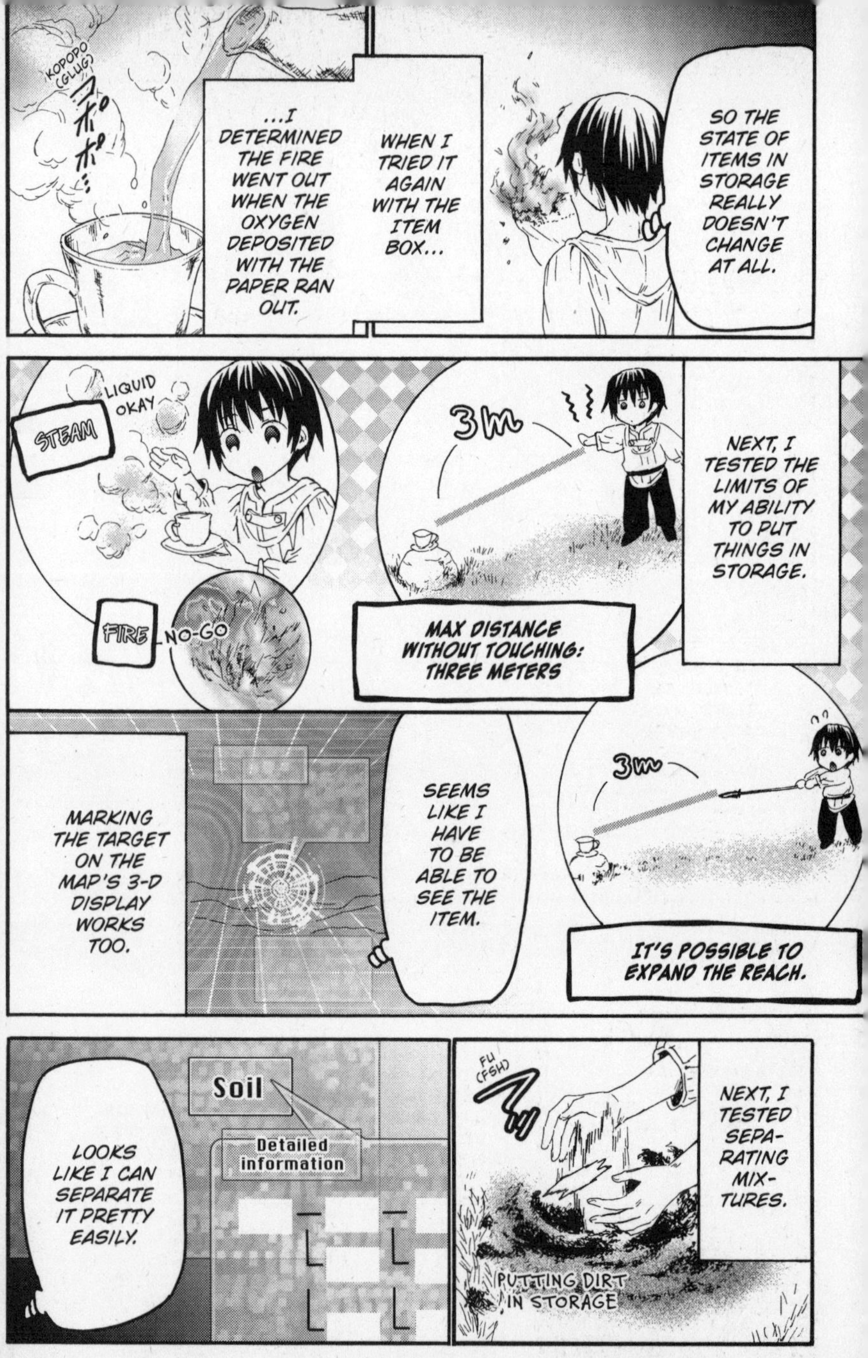
SO THE STATE OF ITEMS IN STORAGE REALLY DOESN'T CHANGE AT ALL.
WHEN I TRIED IT AGAIN WITH THE ITEM BOX...
...I DETERMINED THE FIRE WENT OUT WHEN THE OXYGEN DEPOSITED WITH THE PAPER RAN OUT.
KOPOPO (GLUG)
NEXT, I TESTED THE LIMITS OF MY ABILITY TO PUT THINGS IN STORAGE.
3m
MAX DISTANCE WITHOUT TOUCHING: THREE METERS
LIQUID OKAY
STEAM
FIRE
NO-GO
3m
IT'S POSSIBLE TO EXPAND THE REACH.
SEEMS LIKE I HAVE TO BE ABLE TO SEE THE ITEM.
MARKING THE TARGET ON THE MAP'S 3-D DISPLAY WORKS TOO.
NEXT, I TESTED SEPA-RATING MIX-TURES.
FU (FSH)
PUTTING DIRT IN STORAGE
Soil
Detailed information
LOOKS LIKE I CAN SEPARATE IT PRETTY EASILY.

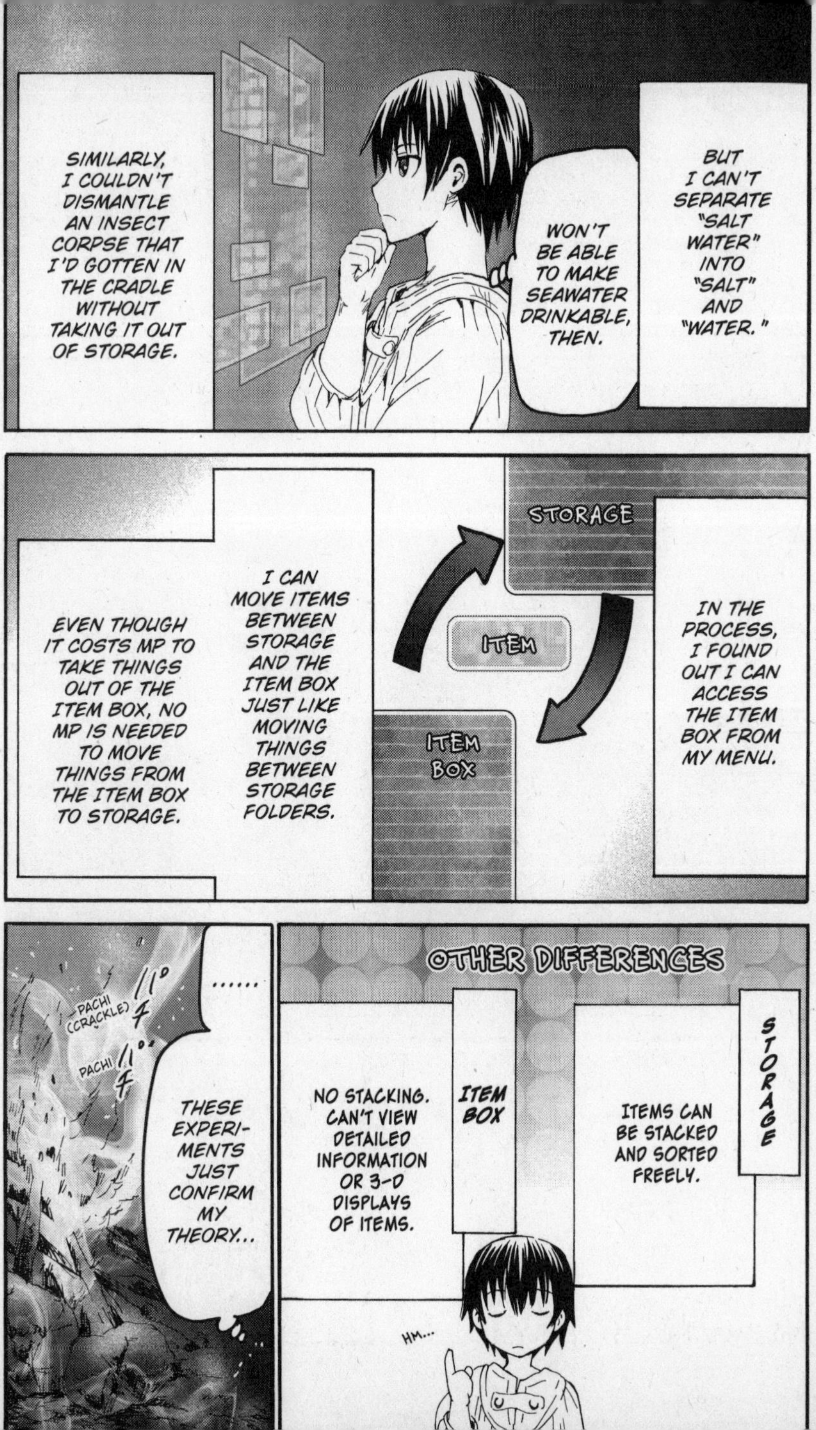
BUT I CAN'T SEPARATE "SALT WATER" INTO "SALT" AND "WATER."
WON'T BE ABLE TO MAKE SEAWATER DRINKABLE, THEN.
SIMILARLY, I COULDN'T DISMANTLE AN INSECT CORPSE THAT I'D GOTTEN IN THE CRADLE WITHOUT TAKING IT OUT OF STORAGE.
IN THE PROCESS, I FOUND OUT I CAN ACCESS THE ITEM BOX FROM MY MENU.
STORAGE
ITEM
ITEM BOX
I CAN MOVE ITEMS BETWEEN STORAGE AND THE ITEM BOX JUST LIKE MOVING THINGS BETWEEN STORAGE FOLDERS.
EVEN THOUGH IT COSTS MP TO TAKE THINGS OUT OF THE ITEM BOX, NO MP IS NEEDED TO MOVE THINGS FROM THE ITEM BOX TO STORAGE.
OTHER DIFFERENCES
STORAGE
ITEMS CAN BE STACKED AND SORTED FREELY.
ITEM BOX
NO STACKING. CAN'T VIEW DETAILED INFORMATION OR 3-D DISPLAYS OF ITEMS.
HM...
......
THESE EXPERIMENTS JUST CONFIRM MY THEORY...
PACHI (CRACKLE)
PACHI

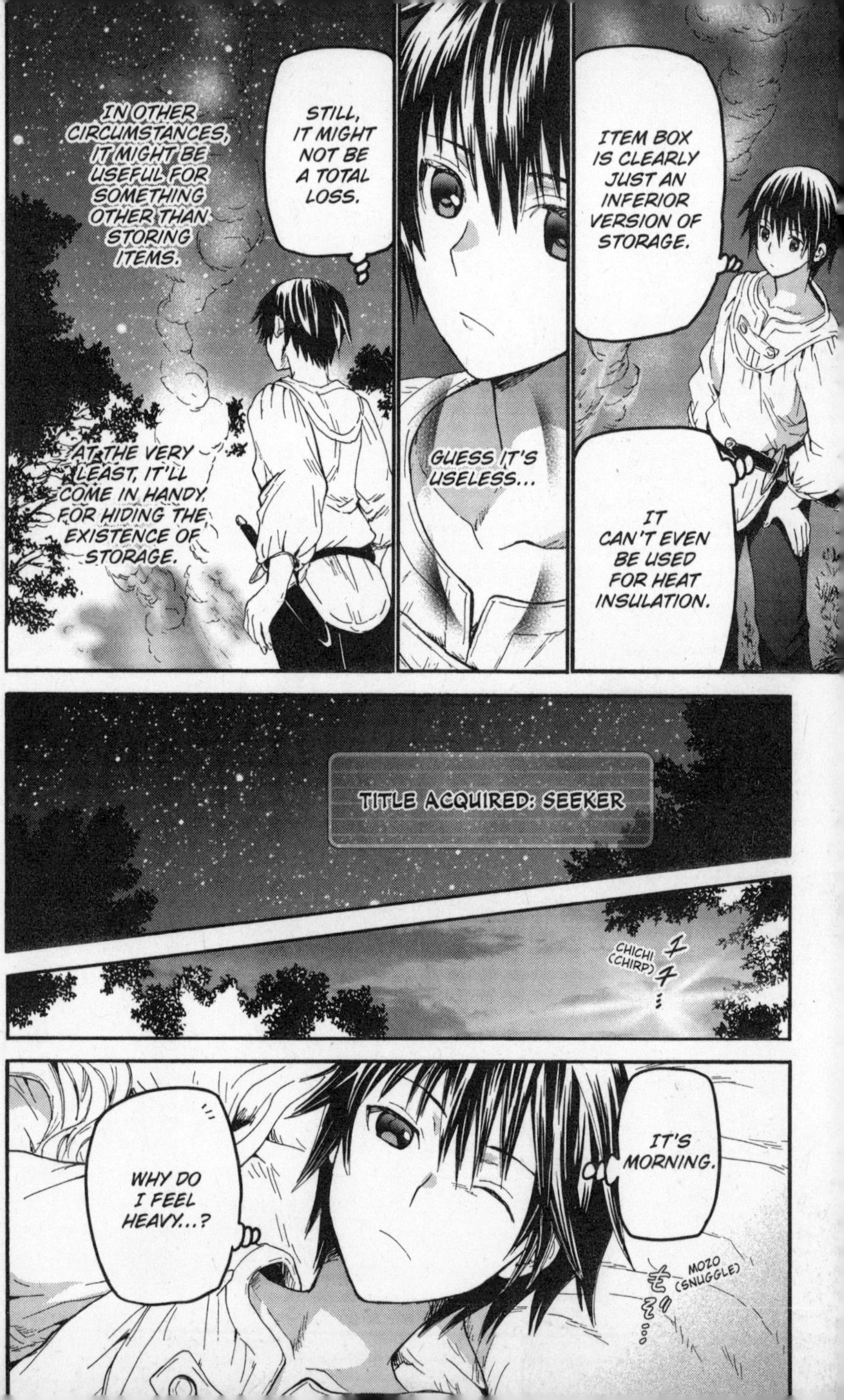
ITEM BOX IS CLEARLY JUST AN INFERIOR VERSION OF STORAGE.
IT CAN'T EVEN BE USED FOR HEAT INSULATION.
GUESS IT'S USELESS...
STILL, IT MIGHT NOT BE A TOTAL LOSS.
IN OTHER CIRCUMSTANCES, IT MIGHT BE USEFUL FOR SOMETHING OTHER THAN STORING ITEMS.
AT THE VERY LEAST, IT'LL COME IN HANDY FOR HIDING THE EXISTENCE OF STORAGE.
TITLE ACQUIRED: SEEKER
CHICHI (CHIRP)
IT'S MORNING.
WHY DO I FEEL HEAVY...?
MOZO (SNUGGLE)

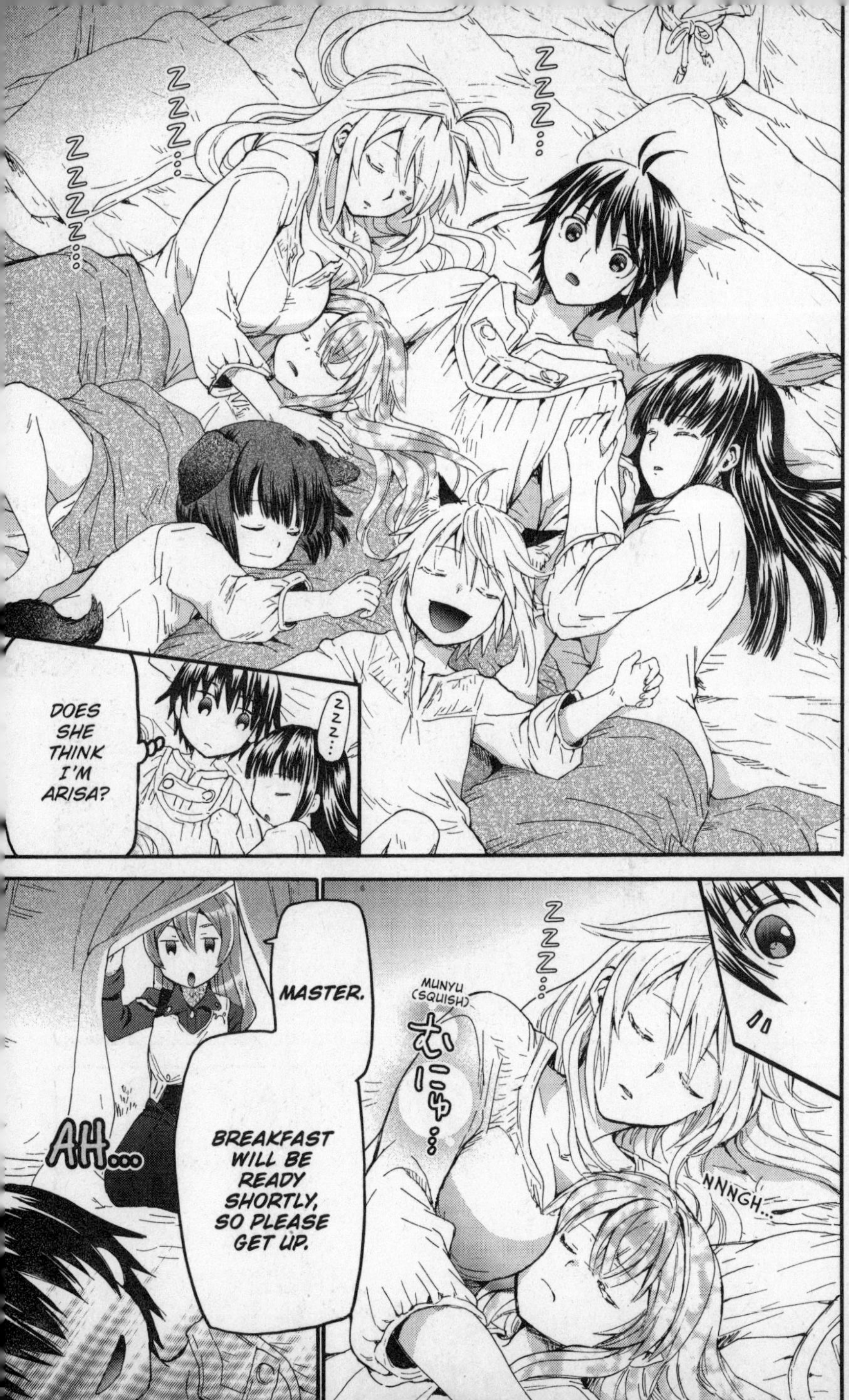
ZZZ...
ZZZ...
ZZZZ...
DOES SHE THINK I'M ARISA?
ZZZ...
ZZZ...
MUNYU (SQUISH)
むにゅ…
NNNGH...
MASTER.
BREAKFAST WILL BE READY SHORTLY, SO PLEASE GET UP.
AH...

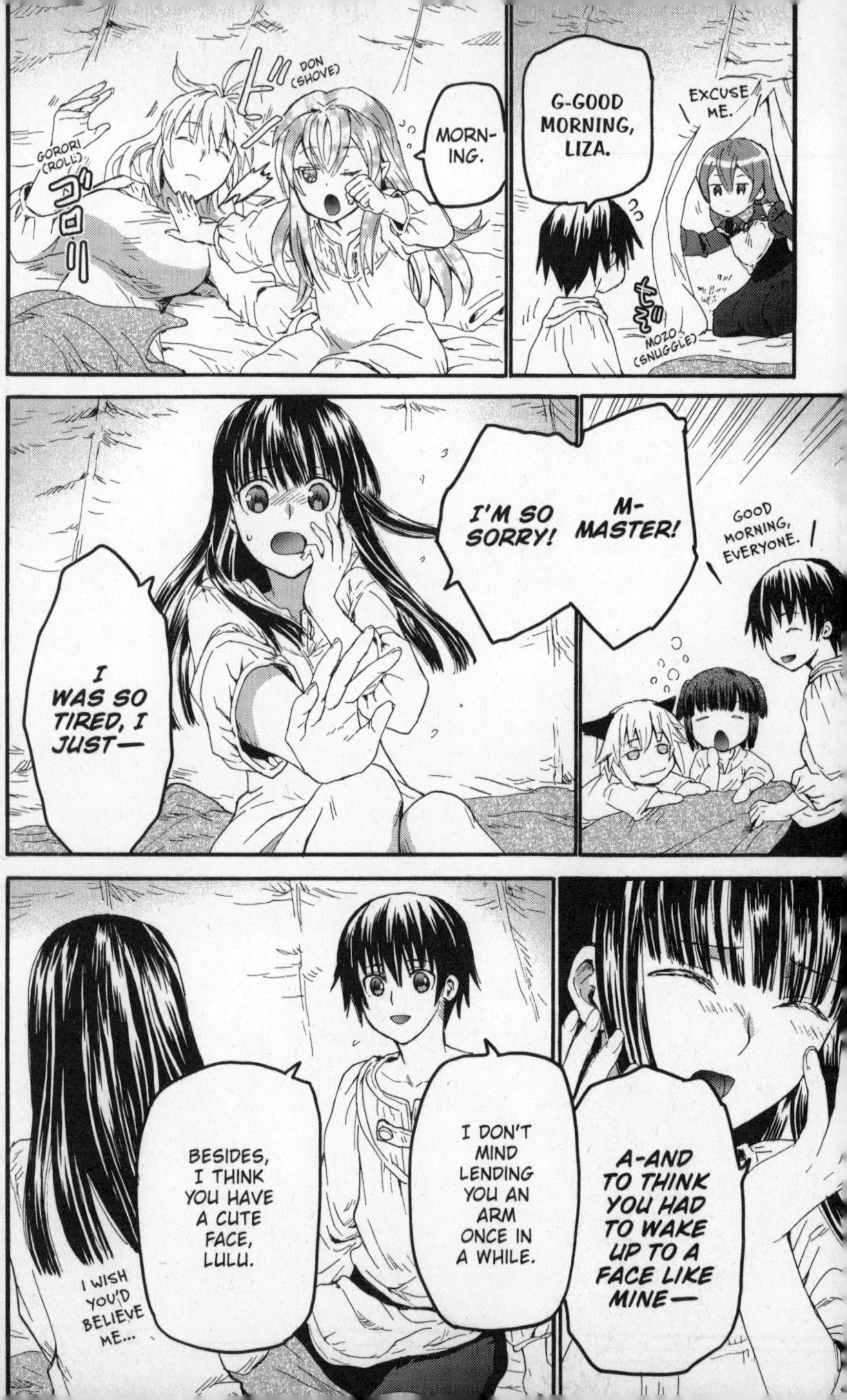
EXCUSE ME.
G-GOOD MORNING, LIZA.
MOZO (SNUGGLE)
MORN-ING.
DON (SHOVE)
GORORI (ROLL)
GOOD MORNING, EVERYONE.
M-MASTER!
I'M SO SORRY!
I WAS SO TIRED, I JUST—
A-AND TO THINK YOU HAD TO WAKE UP TO A FACE LIKE MINE—
I DON'T MIND LENDING YOU AN ARM ONCE IN A WHILE.
BESIDES, I THINK YOU HAVE A CUTE FACE, LULU.
I WISH YOU'D BELIEVE ME...

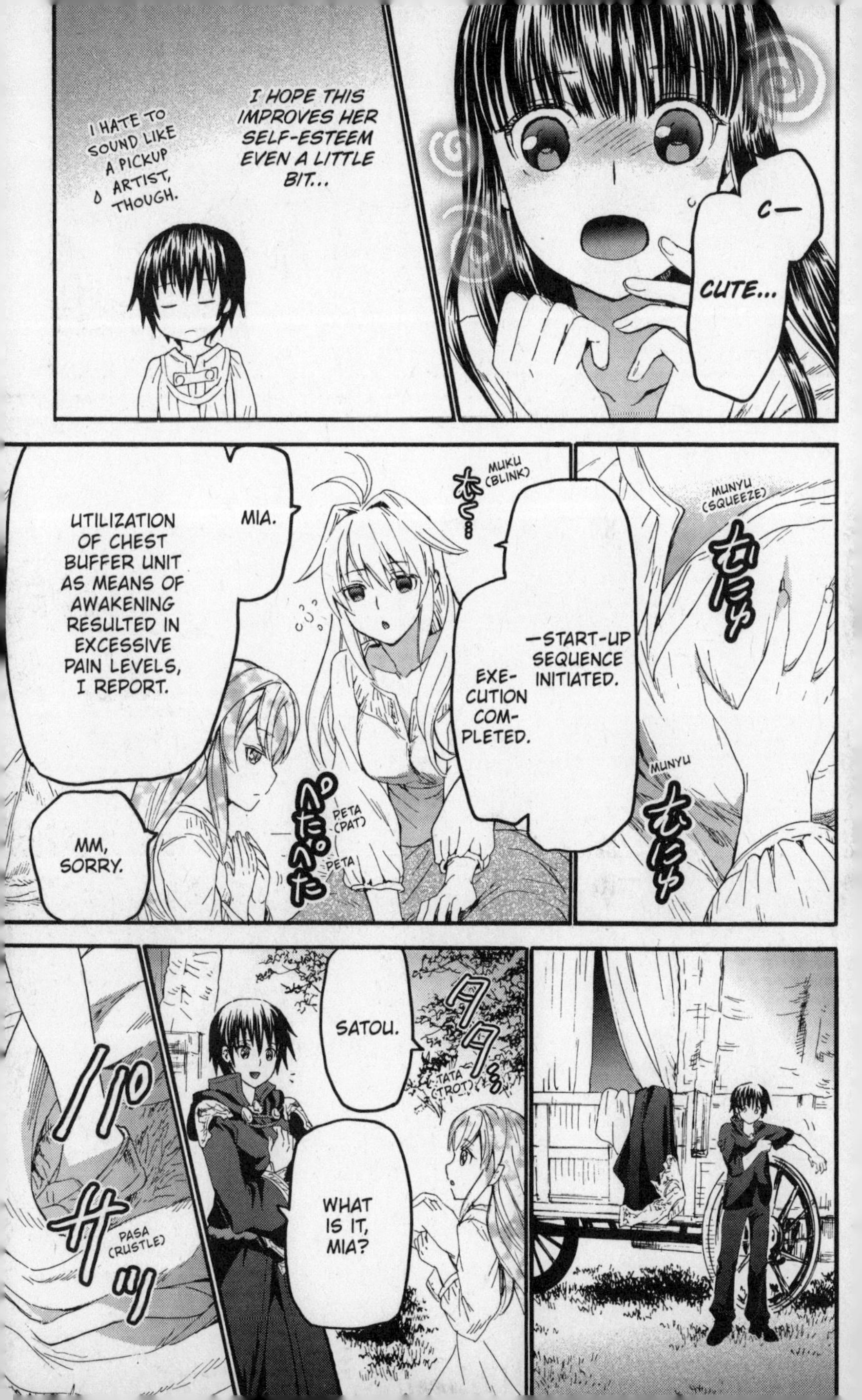
C—
CUTE...
I HOPE THIS IMPROVES HER SELF-ESTEEM EVEN A LITTLE BIT...
I HATE TO SOUND LIKE A PICKUP ARTIST, THOUGH.
MUNYU (SQUEEZE)
MUNYU
MUKU (BLINK)
—START-UP SEQUENCE INITIATED.
EXE-CUTION COM-PLETED.
MIA.
UTILIZATION OF CHEST BUFFER UNIT AS MEANS OF AWAKENING RESULTED IN EXCESSIVE PAIN LEVELS, I REPORT.
PETA (PAT)
PETA
MM, SORRY.
SATOU.
TATA (TROT)
WHAT IS IT, MIA?
PASA (RUSTLE)

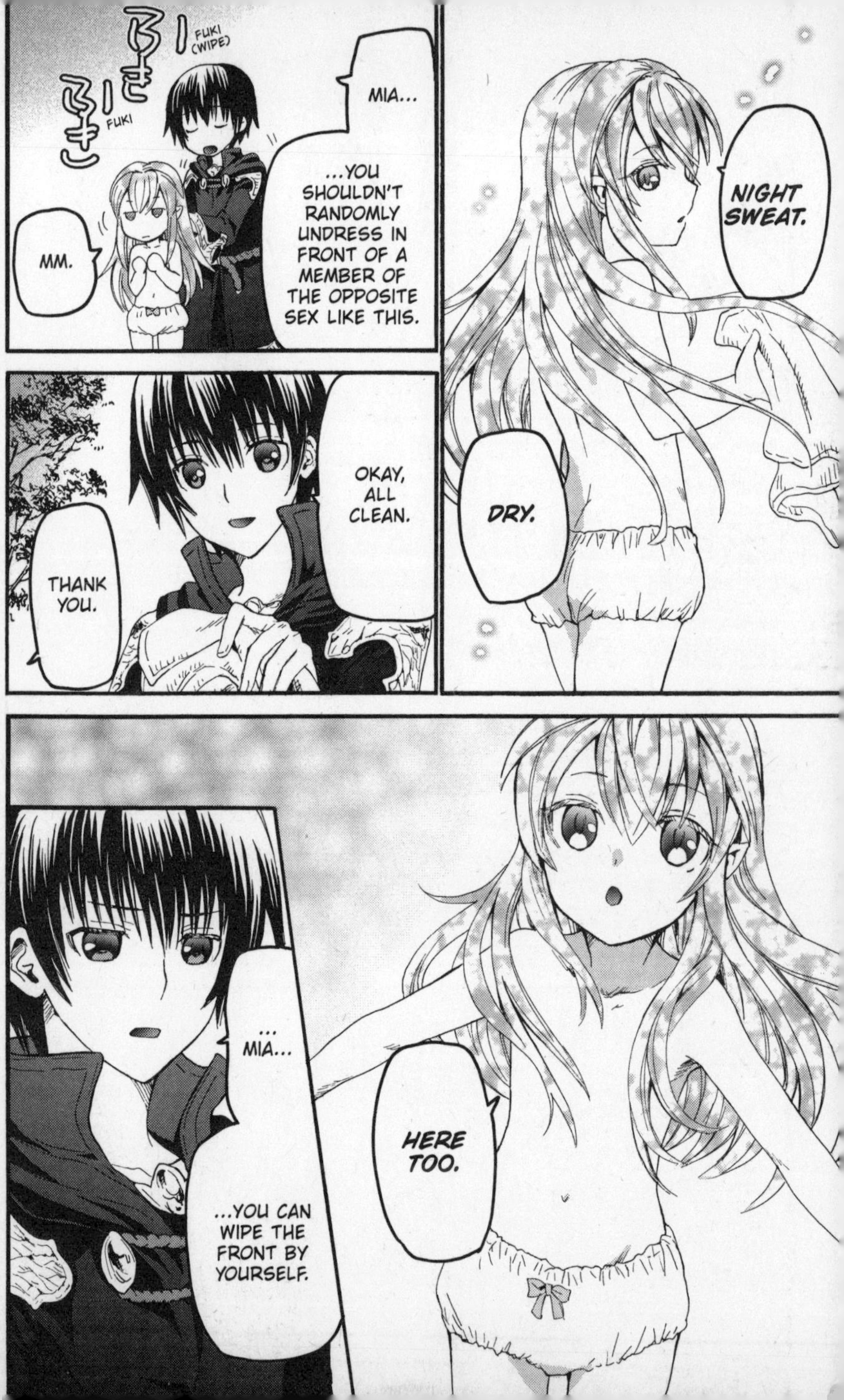

NIGHT SWEAT.
DRY.
MIA...
...YOU SHOULDN'T RANDOMLY UNDRESS IN FRONT OF A MEMBER OF THE OPPOSITE SEX LIKE THIS.
ふき FUKI (WIPE)
ふき FUKI
MM.
OKAY, ALL CLEAN.
THANK YOU.
HERE TOO.
... MIA...
...YOU CAN WIPE THE FRONT BY YOURSELF.

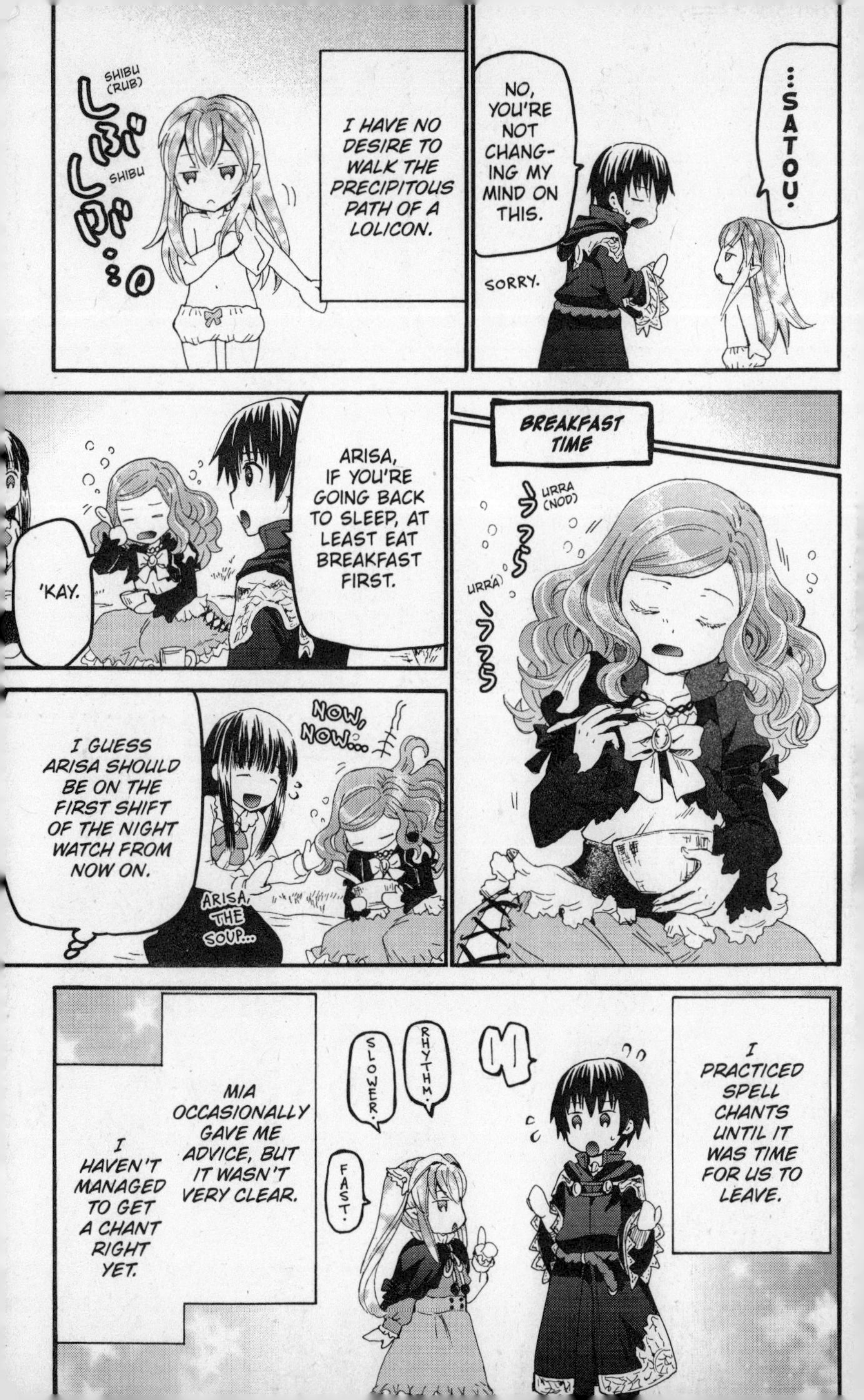
...SATOU.
NO, YOU'RE NOT CHANGING MY MIND ON THIS.
SORRY.
I HAVE NO DESIRE TO WALK THE PRECIPITOUS PATH OF A LOLICON.
SHIBU (RUB)
SHIBU
BREAKFAST TIME
URRA (NOD)
URRA
ARISA, IF YOU'RE GOING BACK TO SLEEP, AT LEAST EAT BREAKFAST FIRST.
'KAY.
NOW, NOW...
ARISA, THE SOUP...
I GUESS ARISA SHOULD BE ON THE FIRST SHIFT OF THE NIGHT WATCH FROM NOW ON.
I PRACTICED SPELL CHANTS UNTIL IT WAS TIME FOR US TO LEAVE.
RHYTHM.
SLOWER.
FAST.
MIA OCCASIONALLY GAVE ME ADVICE, BUT IT WASN'T VERY CLEAR.
I HAVEN'T MANAGED TO GET A CHANT RIGHT YET.

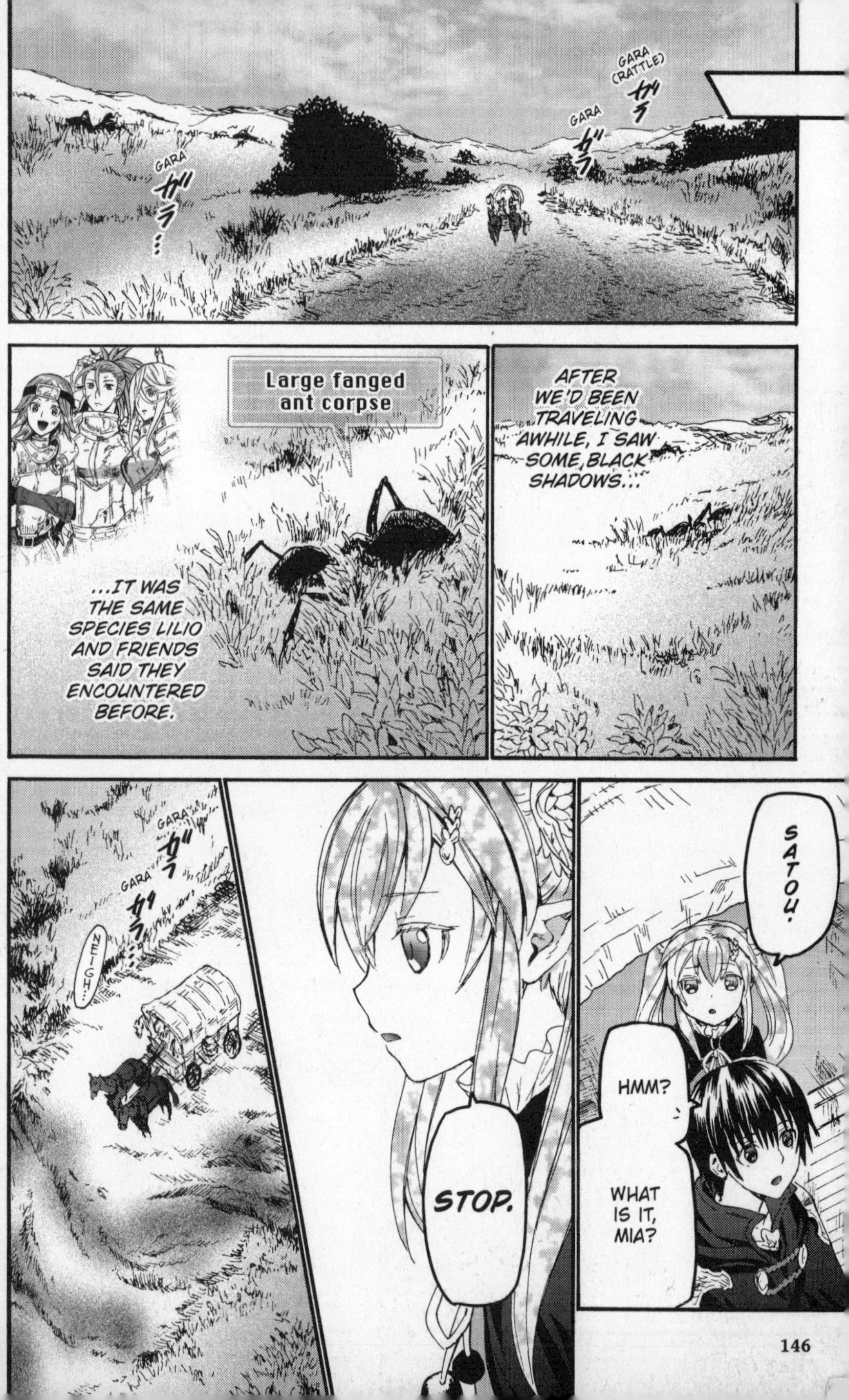
GARA (RATTLE)
ガラ
GARA
ガラ
GARA
ガラ…
AFTER WE'D BEEN TRAVELING AWHILE, I SAW SOME BLACK SHADOWS…
Large fanged ant corpse
…IT WAS THE SAME SPECIES LILIO AND FRIENDS SAID THEY ENCOUNTERED BEFORE.
SATOU.
HMM?
WHAT IS IT, MIA?
STOP.
GARA
ガラ
GARA
ガラ…
NEIGH…

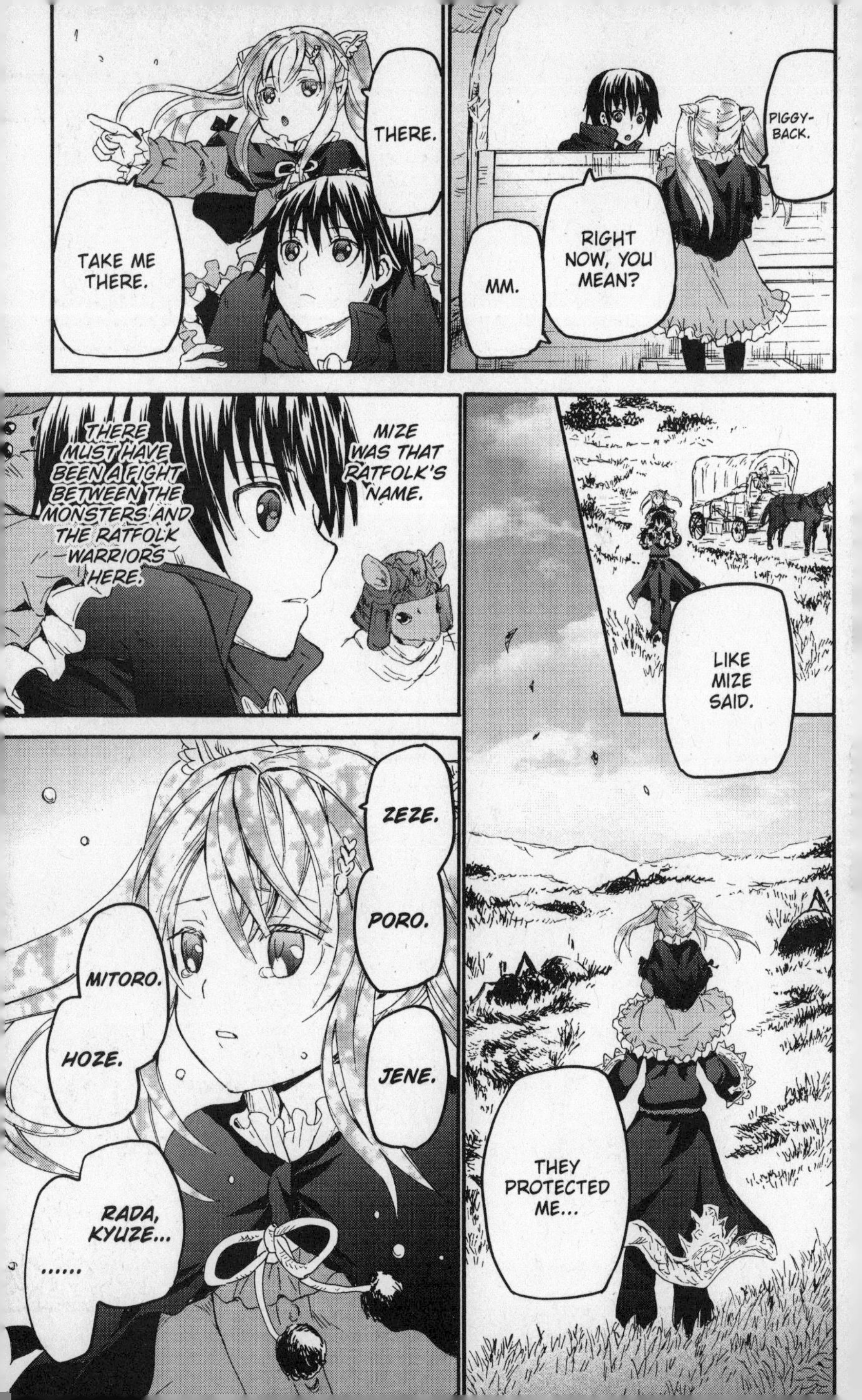
PIGGY-BACK.
RIGHT NOW, YOU MEAN?
MM.
THERE.
TAKE ME THERE.
LIKE MIZE SAID.
THEY PROTECTED ME...
MIZE WAS THAT RATFOLK'S NAME.
THERE MUST HAVE BEEN A FIGHT BETWEEN THE MONSTERS AND THE RATFOLK WARRIORS HERE.
ZEZE.
PORO.
JENE.
MITORO.
HOZE.
RADA, KYUZE...
......

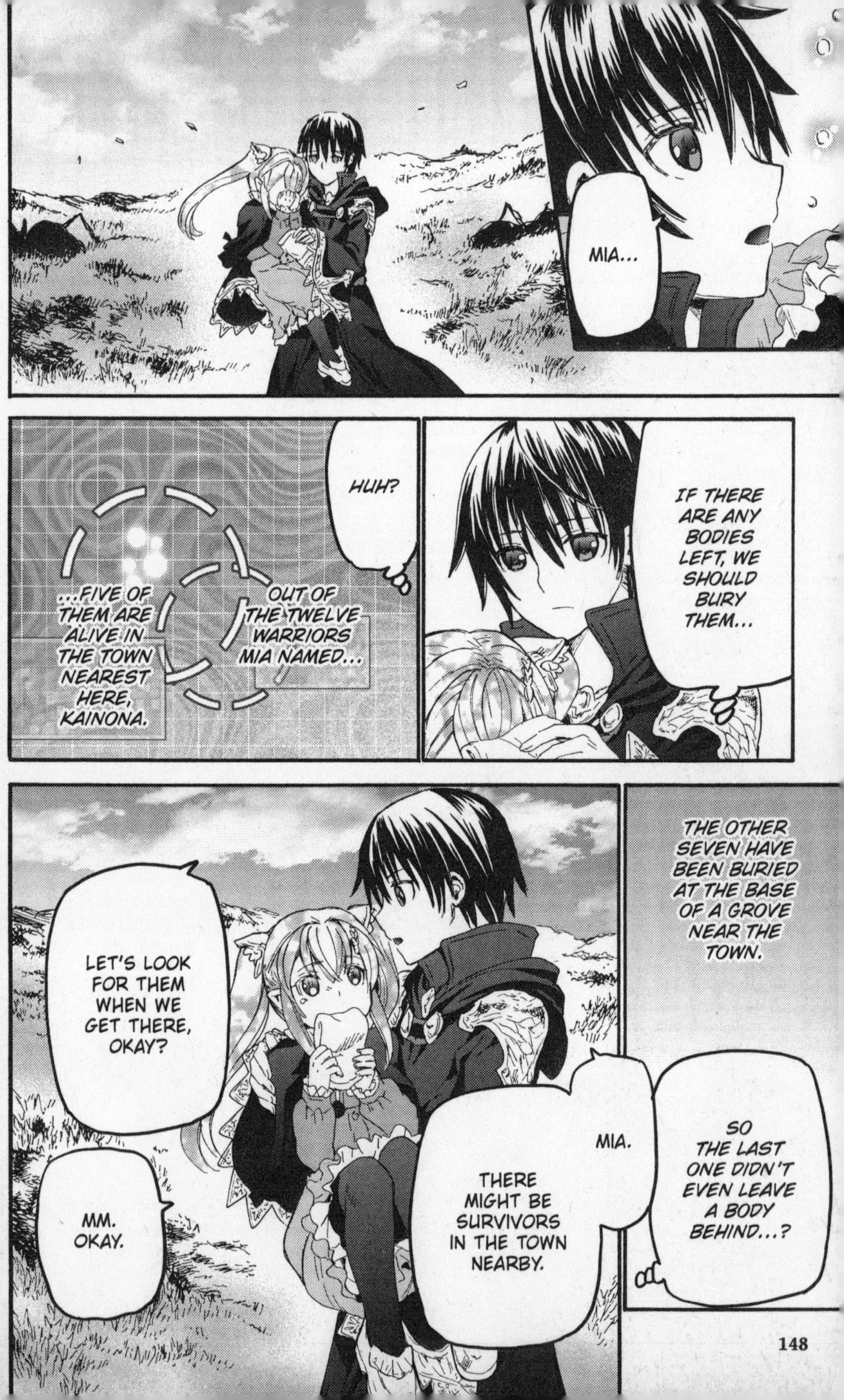

MIA...
IF THERE ARE ANY BODIES LEFT, WE SHOULD BURY THEM...
HUH?
OUT OF THE TWELVE WARRIORS MIA NAMED...
...FIVE OF THEM ARE ALIVE IN THE TOWN NEAREST HERE, KAINONA.
THE OTHER SEVEN HAVE BEEN BURIED AT THE BASE OF A GROVE NEAR THE TOWN.
SO THE LAST ONE DIDN'T EVEN LEAVE A BODY BEHIND...?
MIA.
THERE MIGHT BE SURVIVORS IN THE TOWN NEARBY.
LET'S LOOK FOR THEM WHEN WE GET THERE, OKAY?
MM. OKAY.

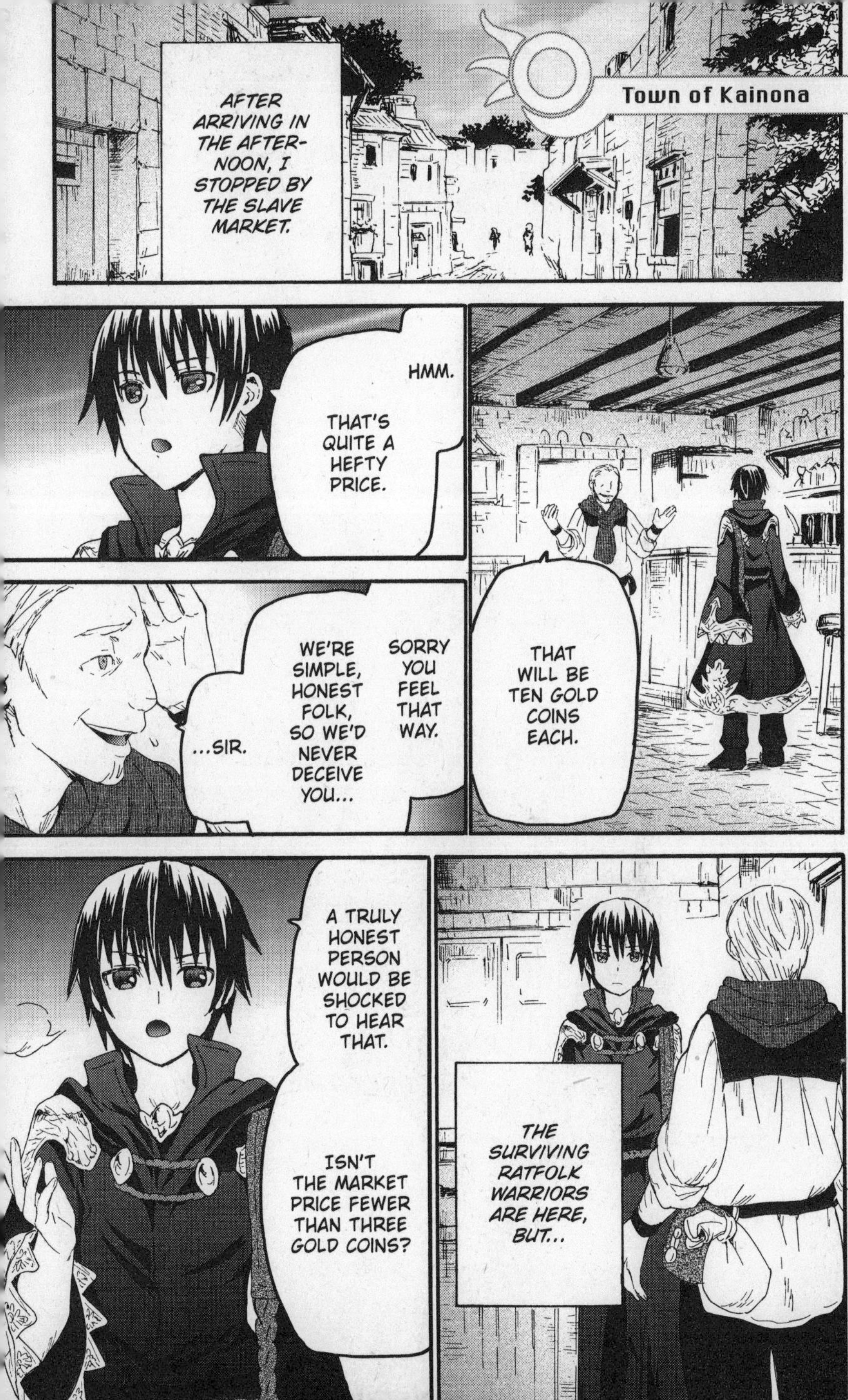
Town of Kainona
AFTER ARRIVING IN THE AFTERNOON, I STOPPED BY THE SLAVE MARKET.
THAT WILL BE TEN GOLD COINS EACH.
HMM.
THAT'S QUITE A HEFTY PRICE.
SORRY YOU FEEL THAT WAY.
WE'RE SIMPLE, HONEST FOLK, SO WE'D NEVER DECEIVE YOU...
...SIR.
THE SURVIVING RATFOLK WARRIORS ARE HERE, BUT...
A TRULY HONEST PERSON WOULD BE SHOCKED TO HEAR THAT.
ISN'T THE MARKET PRICE FEWER THAN THREE GOLD COINS?

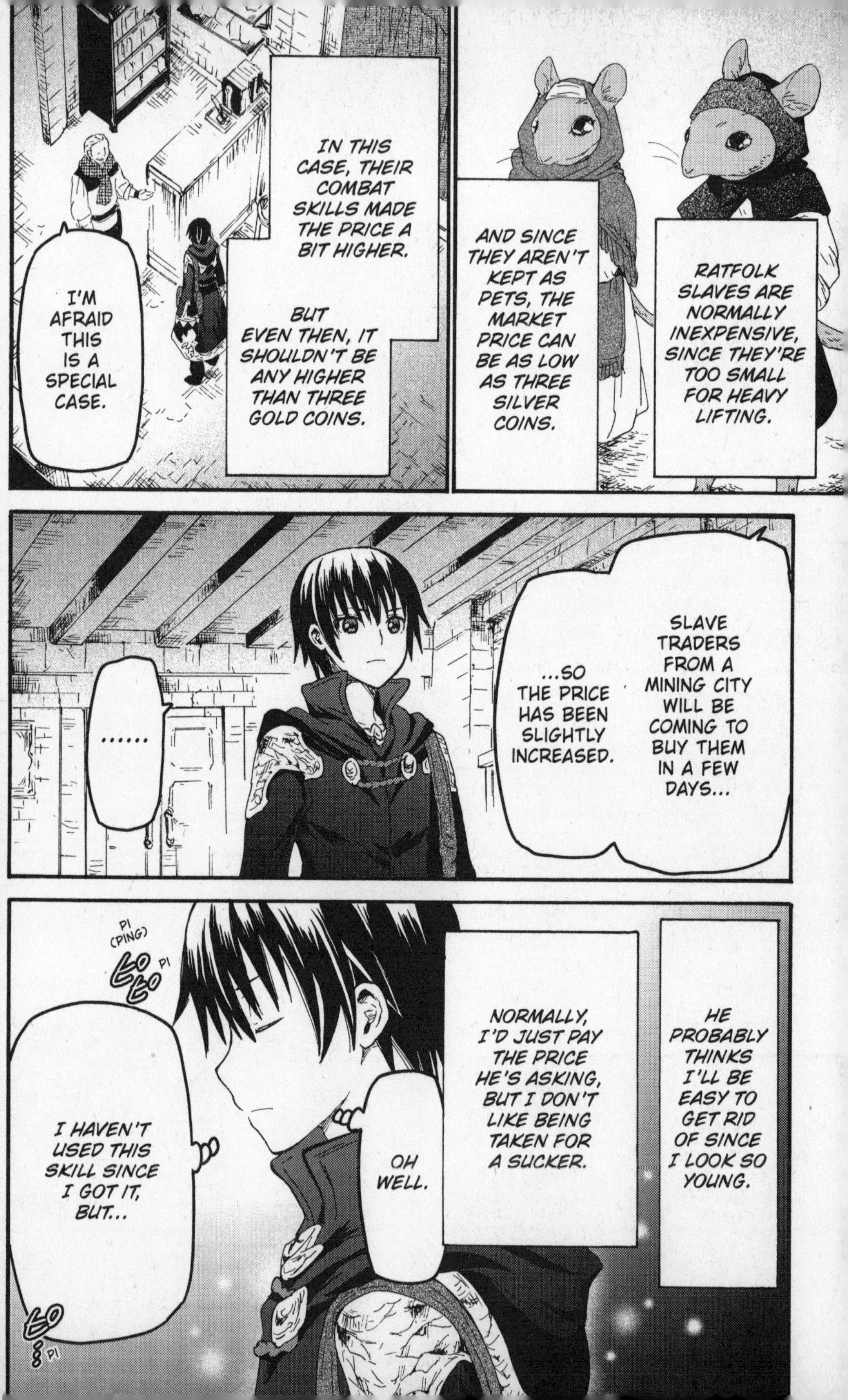
RATFOLK SLAVES ARE NORMALLY INEXPENSIVE, SINCE THEY'RE TOO SMALL FOR HEAVY LIFTING.
AND SINCE THEY AREN'T KEPT AS PETS, THE MARKET PRICE CAN BE AS LOW AS THREE SILVER COINS.
IN THIS CASE, THEIR COMBAT SKILLS MADE THE PRICE A BIT HIGHER.
BUT EVEN THEN, IT SHOULDN'T BE ANY HIGHER THAN THREE GOLD COINS.
I'M AFRAID THIS IS A SPECIAL CASE.
SLAVE TRADERS FROM A MINING CITY WILL BE COMING TO BUY THEM IN A FEW DAYS...
...SO THE PRICE HAS BEEN SLIGHTLY INCREASED.
......
HE PROBABLY THINKS I'LL BE EASY TO GET RID OF SINCE I LOOK SO YOUNG.
NORMALLY, I'D JUST PAY THE PRICE HE'S ASKING, BUT I DON'T LIKE BEING TAKEN FOR A SUCKER.
OH WELL.
PI (PING) PI
I HAVEN'T USED THIS SKILL SINCE I GOT IT, BUT...
PI PI

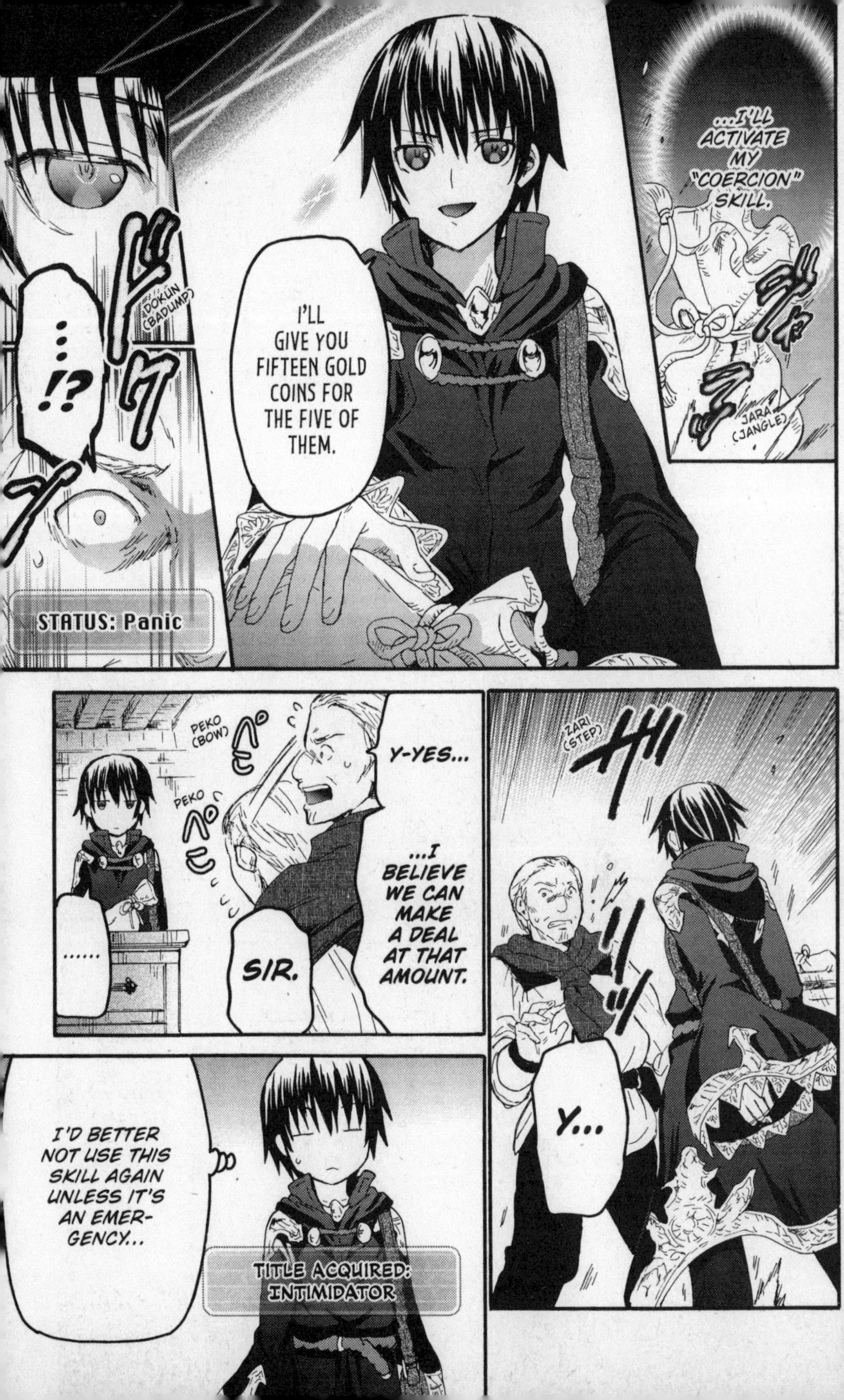
...I'LL ACTIVATE MY "COERCION" SKILL.
JARA (JANGLE)
I'LL GIVE YOU FIFTEEN GOLD COINS FOR THE FIVE OF THEM.
DOKUN (BADUMP)
...!?
STATUS: Panic
ZARI (STEP)
Y...
Y-YES...
...I BELIEVE WE CAN MAKE A DEAL AT THAT AMOUNT.
SIR.
PEKO (BOW)
PEKO
......
I'D BETTER NOT USE THIS SKILL AGAIN UNLESS IT'S AN EMERGENCY...
TITLE ACQUIRED: INTIMIDATOR

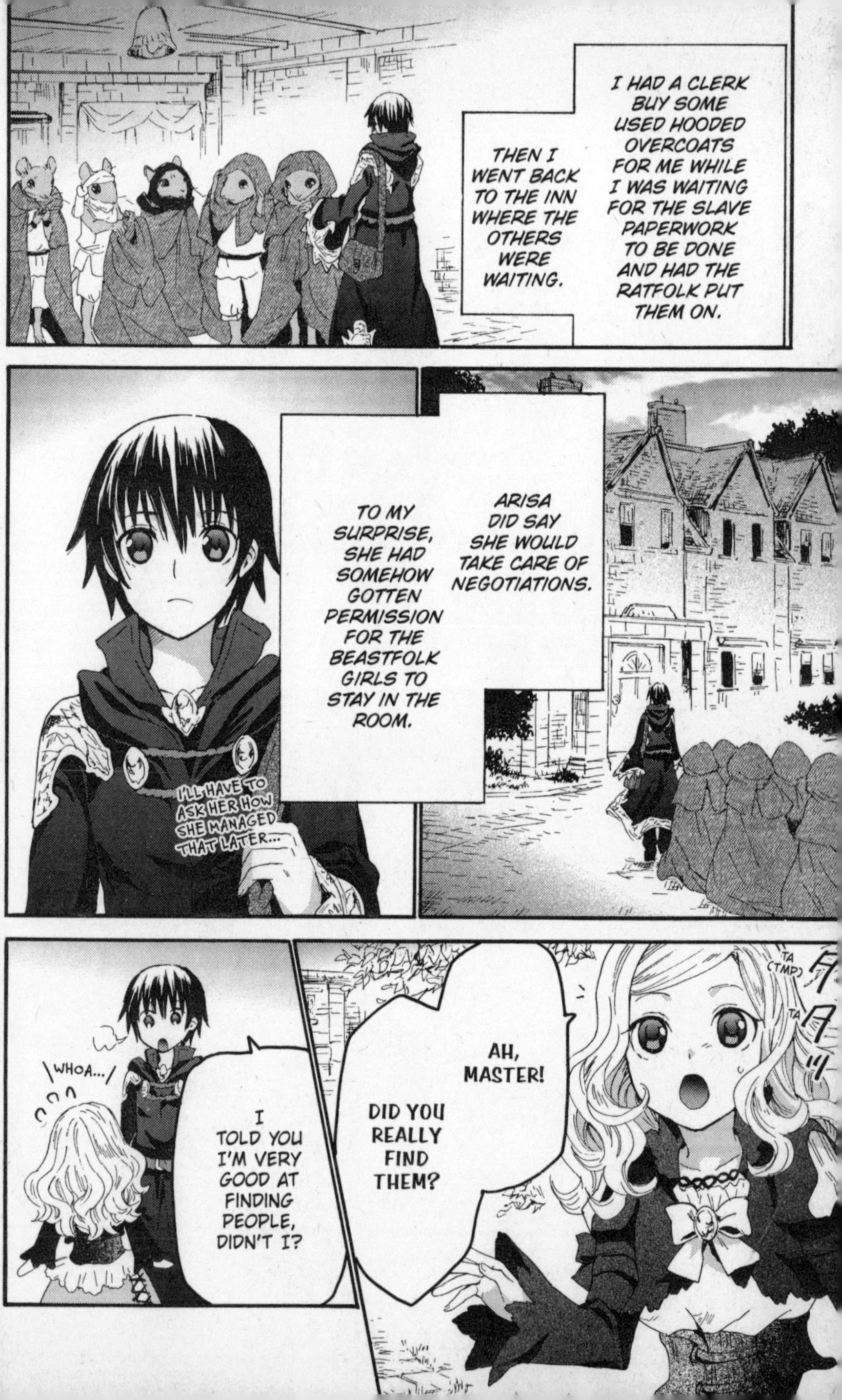
I HAD A CLERK BUY SOME USED HOODED OVERCOATS FOR ME WHILE I WAS WAITING FOR THE SLAVE PAPERWORK TO BE DONE AND HAD THE RATFOLK PUT THEM ON.
THEN I WENT BACK TO THE INN WHERE THE OTHERS WERE WAITING.
ARISA DID SAY SHE WOULD TAKE CARE OF NEGOTIATIONS.
TO MY SURPRISE, SHE HAD SOMEHOW GOTTEN PERMISSION FOR THE BEASTFOLK GIRLS TO STAY IN THE ROOM.
I'LL HAVE TO ASK HER HOW SHE MANAGED THAT LATER...
TA (TMP)
TA
AH, MASTER!
DID YOU REALLY FIND THEM?
I TOLD YOU I'M VERY GOOD AT FINDING PEOPLE, DIDN'T I?
WHOA...

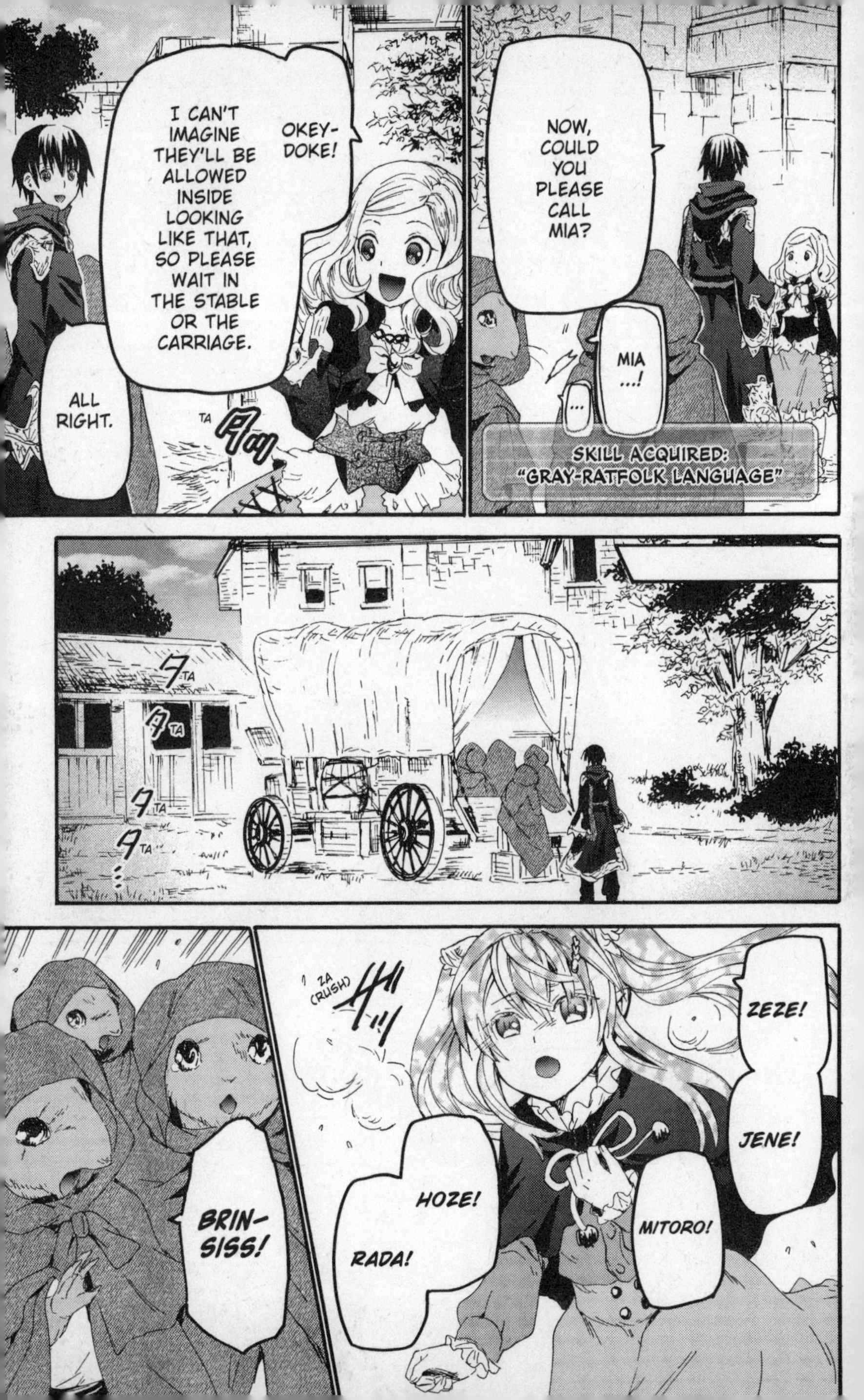
NOW, COULD YOU PLEASE CALL MIA?
MIA ...!
...
SKILL ACQUIRED: "GRAY-RATFOLK LANGUAGE"
OKEY-DOKE!
I CAN'T IMAGINE THEY'LL BE ALLOWED INSIDE LOOKING LIKE THAT, SO PLEASE WAIT IN THE STABLE OR THE CARRIAGE.
ALL RIGHT.
TA
TA
TA
TA
TA
ZA (RUSH)
ZEZE!
JENE!
MITORO!
HOZE!
RADA!
BRIN-SISS!

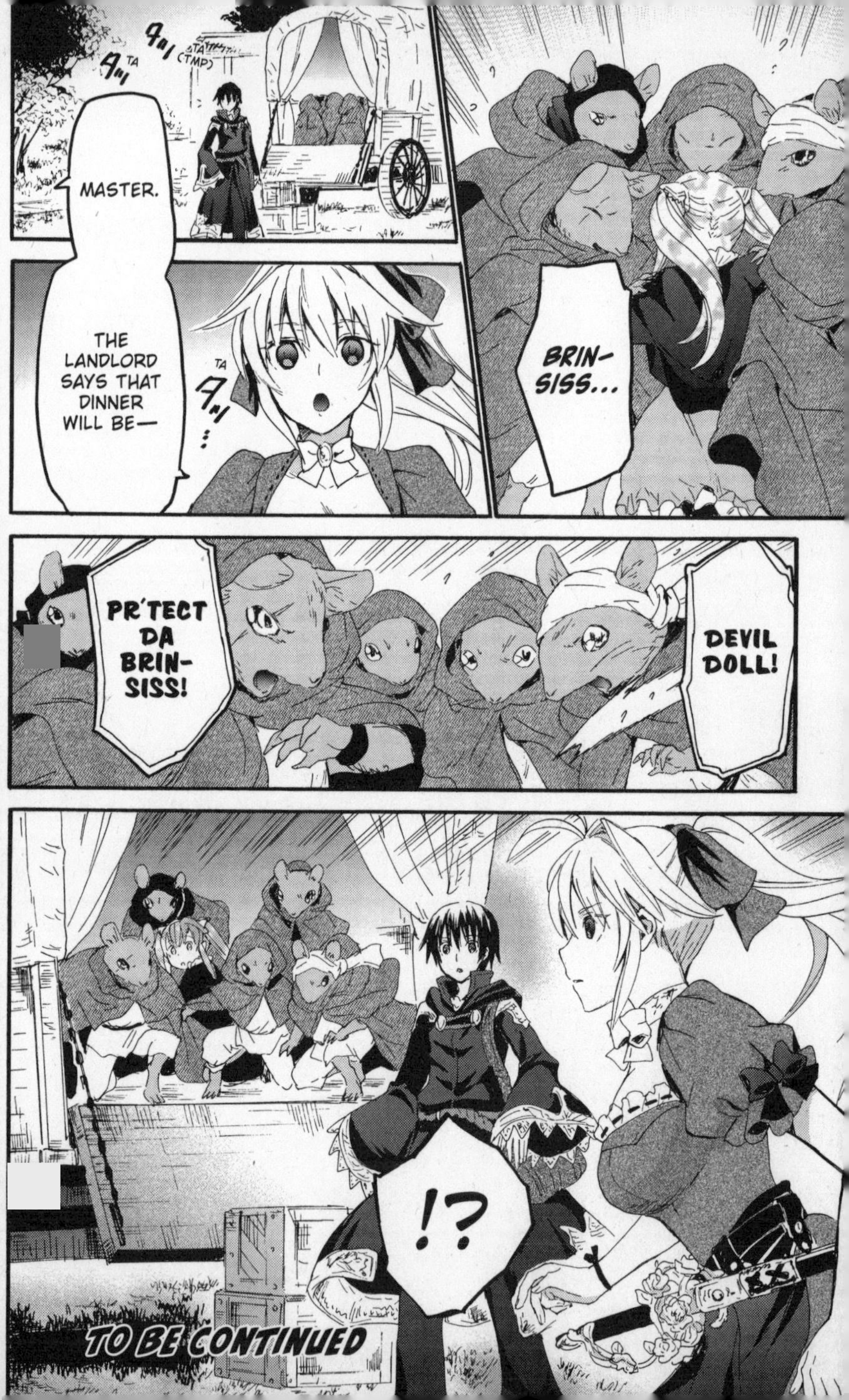
BRIN-SISS...
TA
TA (TMP)
MASTER.
THE LANDLORD SAYS THAT DINNER WILL BE—
TA
DEVIL DOLL!
PR'TECT DA BRIN-SISS!
!?
TO BE CONTINUED

RED DEER

From the name,
Satou was expecting
vivid colors, but
only the fur on their
chests is red. The
rest is the same color
as a normal deer's.

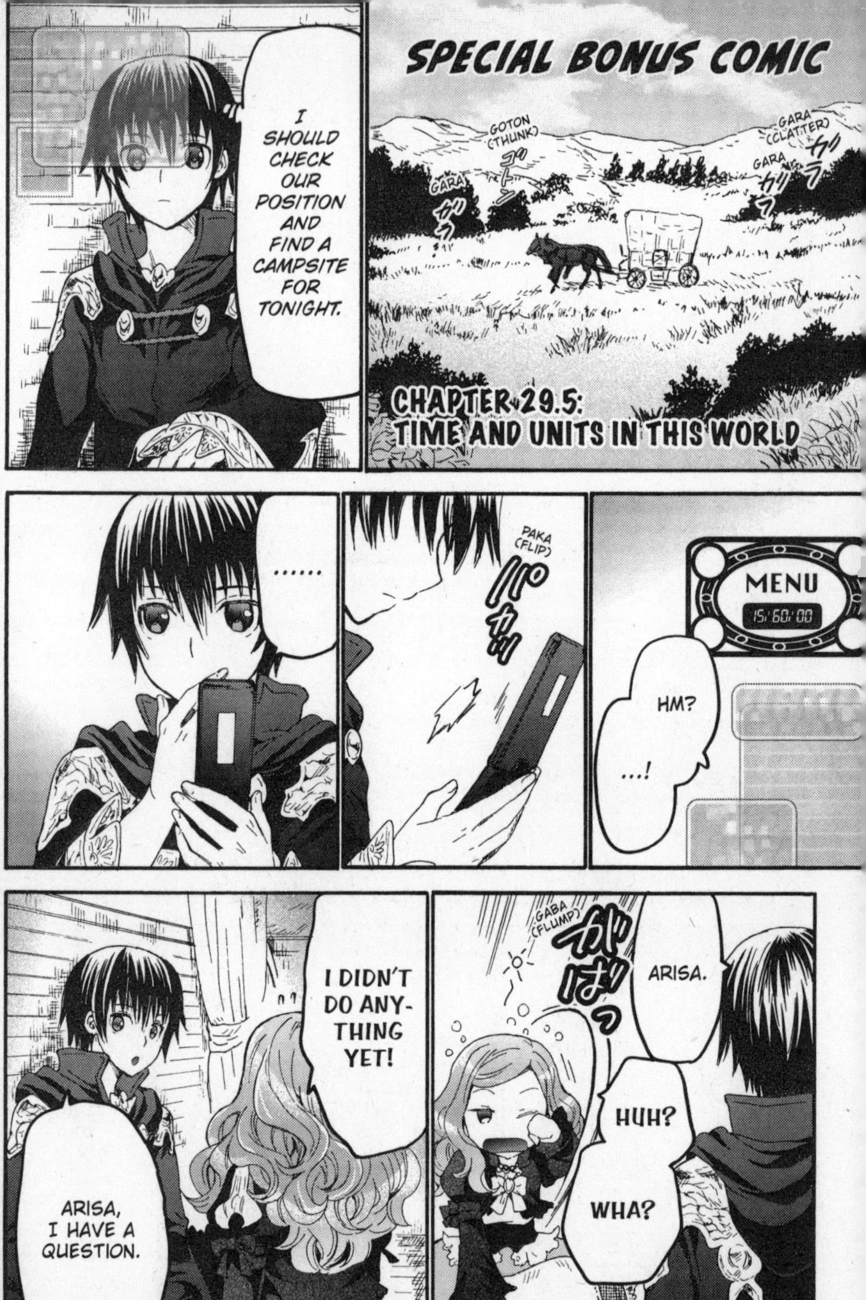
SPECIAL BONUS COMIC
GARA (CLATTER)
GARA
GOTON (THUNK)
GARA
CHAPTER 29.5: TIME AND UNITS IN THIS WORLD
I SHOULD CHECK OUR POSITION AND FIND A CAMPSITE FOR TONIGHT.
MENU
15:60:00
HM?
...!
PAKA (FLIP)
......
GABA (FLUMP)
ARISA.
HUH?
WHA?
I DIDN'T DO ANY-THING YET!
ARISA, I HAVE A QUESTION.

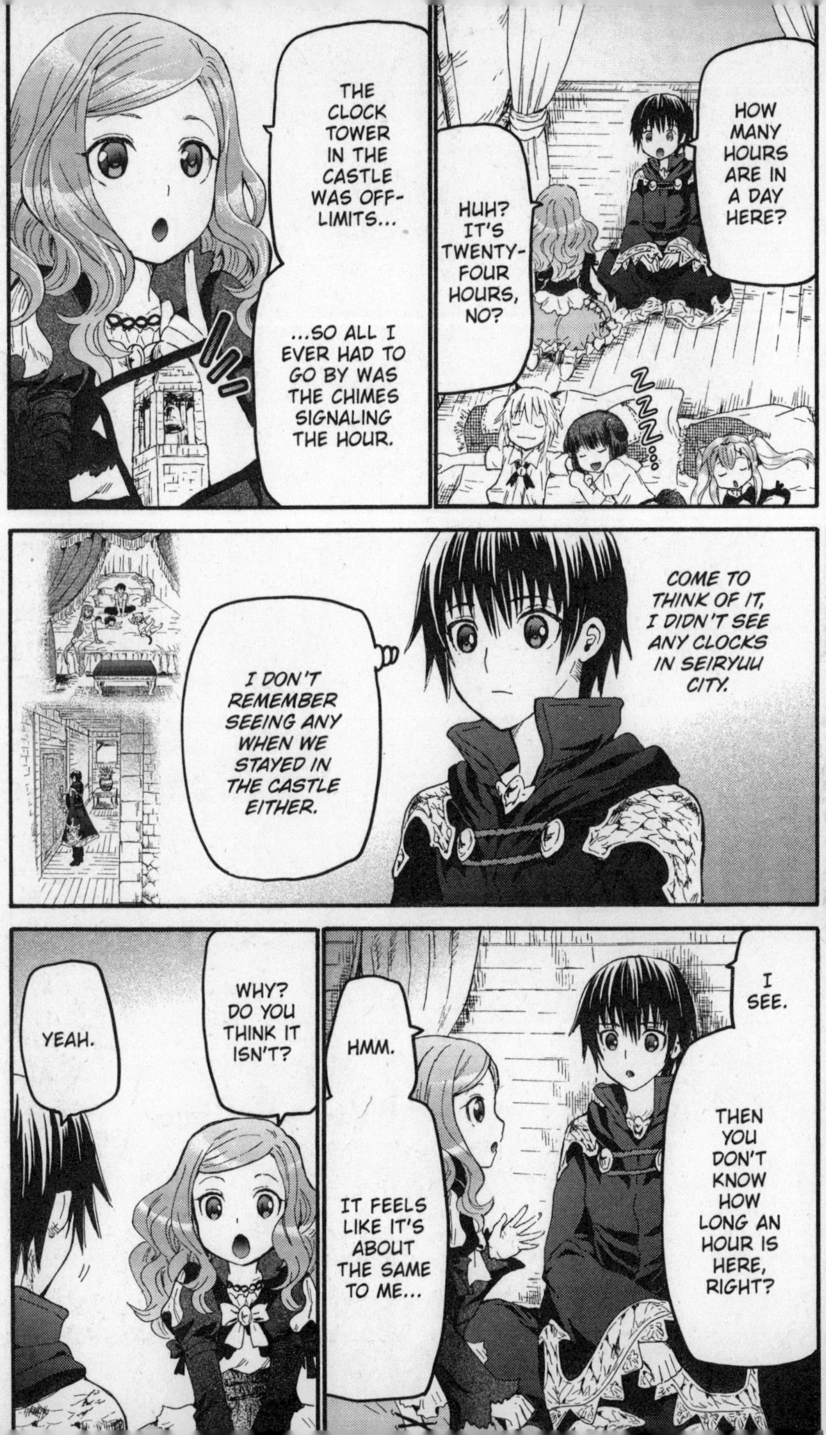
HOW MANY HOURS ARE IN A DAY HERE?
HUH? IT'S TWENTY-FOUR HOURS, NO?
THE CLOCK TOWER IN THE CASTLE WAS OFF-LIMITS...
...SO ALL I EVER HAD TO GO BY WAS THE CHIMES SIGNALING THE HOUR.
COME TO THINK OF IT, I DIDN'T SEE ANY CLOCKS IN SEIRYUU CITY.
I DON'T REMEMBER SEEING ANY WHEN WE STAYED IN THE CASTLE EITHER.
I SEE.
THEN YOU DON'T KNOW HOW LONG AN HOUR IS HERE, RIGHT?
HMM.
IT FEELS LIKE IT'S ABOUT THE SAME TO ME...
WHY? DO YOU THINK IT ISN'T?
YEAH.

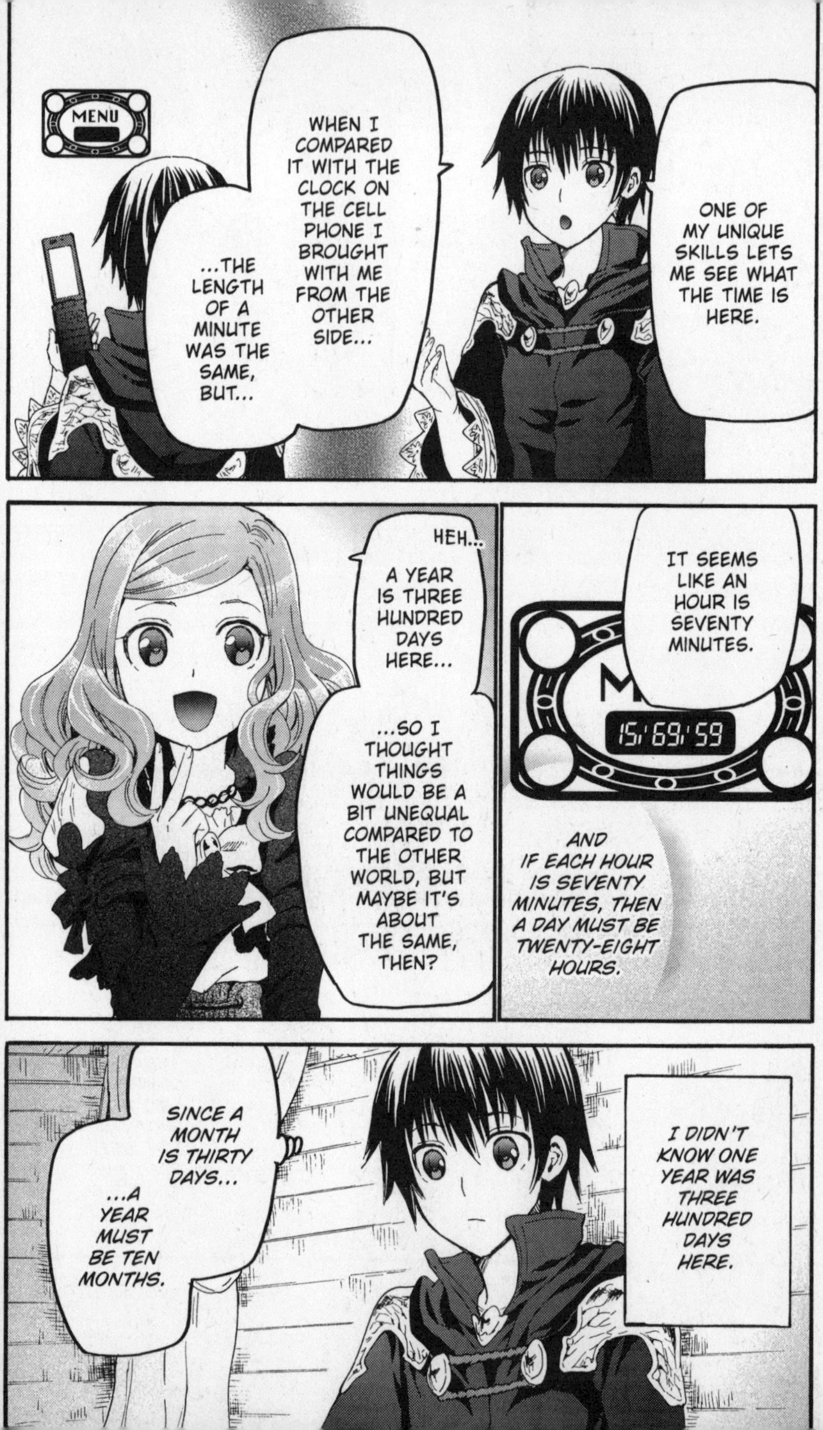
MENU
ONE OF MY UNIQUE SKILLS LETS ME SEE WHAT THE TIME IS HERE.
WHEN I COMPARED IT WITH THE CLOCK ON THE CELL PHONE I BROUGHT WITH ME FROM THE OTHER SIDE...
...THE LENGTH OF A MINUTE WAS THE SAME, BUT...
IT SEEMS LIKE AN HOUR IS SEVENTY MINUTES.
15'69'59
AND IF EACH HOUR IS SEVENTY MINUTES, THEN A DAY MUST BE TWENTY-EIGHT HOURS.
HEH... A YEAR IS THREE HUNDRED DAYS HERE...
...SO I THOUGHT THINGS WOULD BE A BIT UNEQUAL COMPARED TO THE OTHER WORLD, BUT MAYBE IT'S ABOUT THE SAME, THEN?
I DIDN'T KNOW ONE YEAR WAS THREE HUNDRED DAYS HERE.
SINCE A MONTH IS THIRTY DAYS...
...A YEAR MUST BE TEN MONTHS.

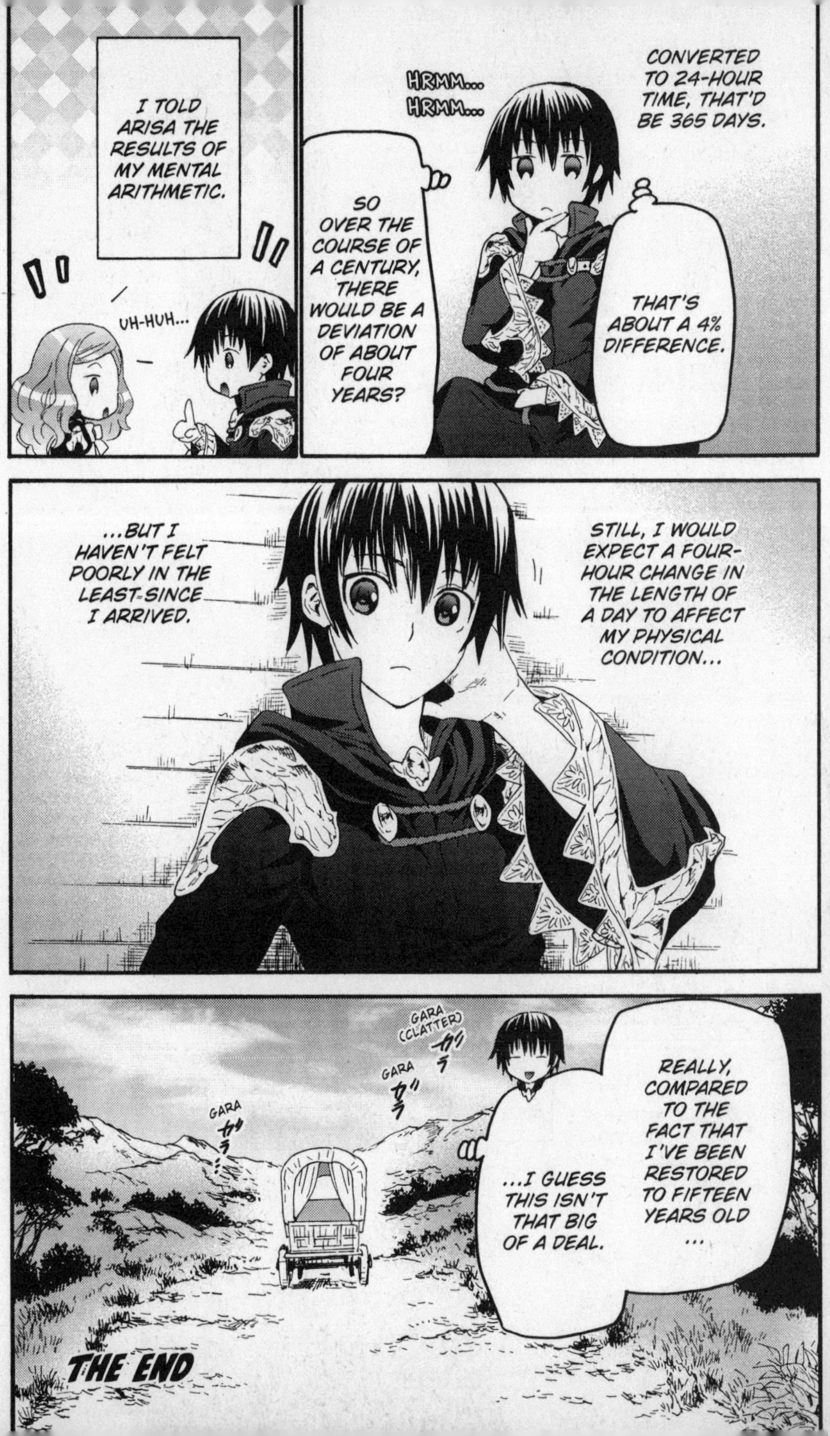
CONVERTED TO 24-HOUR TIME, THAT'D BE 365 DAYS.
HRMM... HRMM...
THAT'S ABOUT A 4% DIFFERENCE.
SO OVER THE COURSE OF A CENTURY, THERE WOULD BE A DEVIATION OF ABOUT FOUR YEARS?
I TOLD ARISA THE RESULTS OF MY MENTAL ARITHMETIC.
UH-HUH...
STILL, I WOULD EXPECT A FOUR-HOUR CHANGE IN THE LENGTH OF A DAY TO AFFECT MY PHYSICAL CONDITION...
...BUT I HAVEN'T FELT POORLY IN THE LEAST SINCE I ARRIVED.
GARA (CLATTER)
GARA
GARA
REALLY, COMPARED TO THE FACT THAT I'VE BEEN RESTORED TO FIFTEEN YEARS OLD...
...I GUESS THIS ISN'T THAT BIG OF A DEAL.
THE END

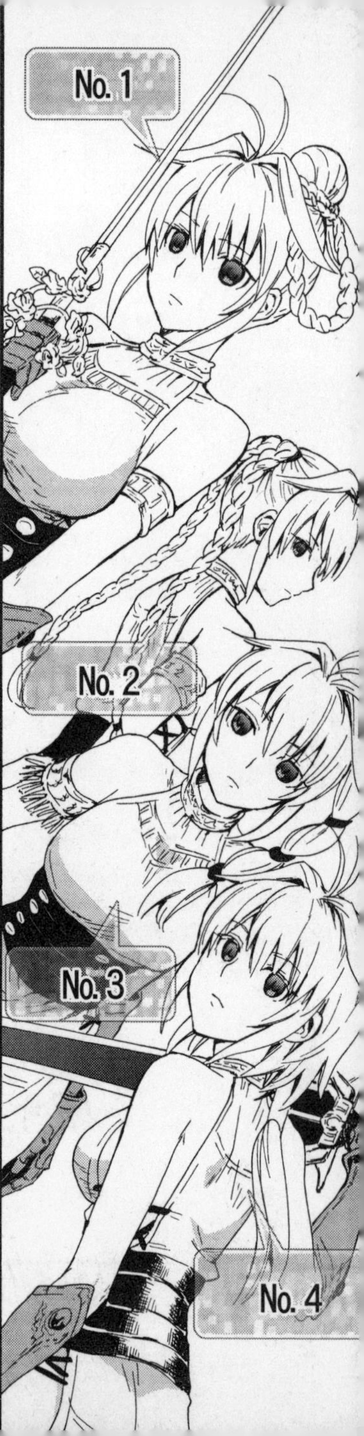
No. 1
No. 2
No. 3
No. 4

KINETIC VISION ↑↑

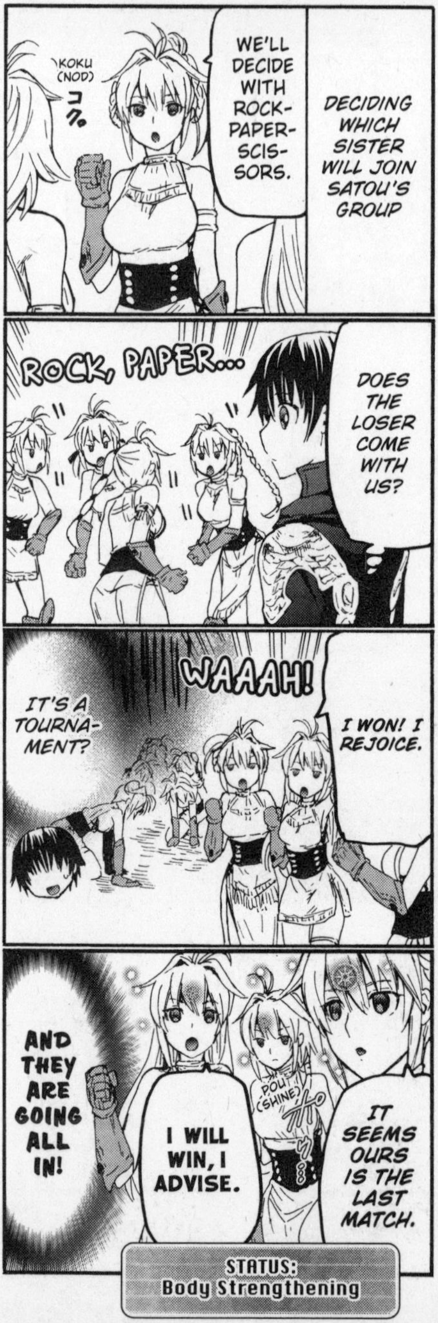
DECIDING WHICH SISTER WILL JOIN SATOU'S GROUP
WE'LL DECIDE WITH ROCK-PAPER-SCISSORS.
KOKU (NOD)
DOES THE LOSER COME WITH US?
ROCK, PAPER...
I WON! I REJOICE.
WAAAH!
IT'S A TOURNAMENT?
IT SEEMS OURS IS THE LAST MATCH.
POU (SHINE)
I WILL WIN, I ADVISE.
AND THEY ARE GOING ALL IN!
STATUS:
Body Strengthening

OTAKU CULTURE: WHERE FANS GET MORE ATTACHED TO THE CHARACTERS THAN THE SERIES

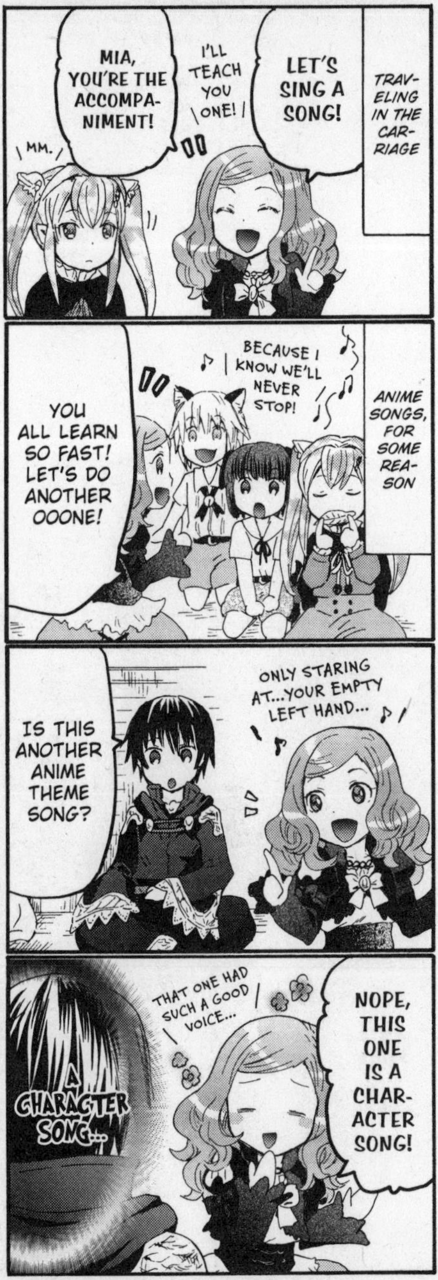
TRAVELING IN THE CARRIAGE
LET'S SING A SONG!
I'LL TEACH YOU ONE!
MIA, YOU'RE THE ACCOMPANIMENT!
MM.
ANIME SONGS, FOR SOME REASON
BECAUSE I KNOW WE'LL NEVER STOP!
YOU ALL LEARN SO FAST! LET'S DO ANOTHER OOONE!
ONLY STARING AT...YOUR EMPTY LEFT HAND...
IS THIS ANOTHER ANIME THEME SONG?
NOPE, THIS ONE IS A CHARACTER SONG!
THAT ONE HAD SUCH A GOOD VOICE...
A CHARACTER SONG...

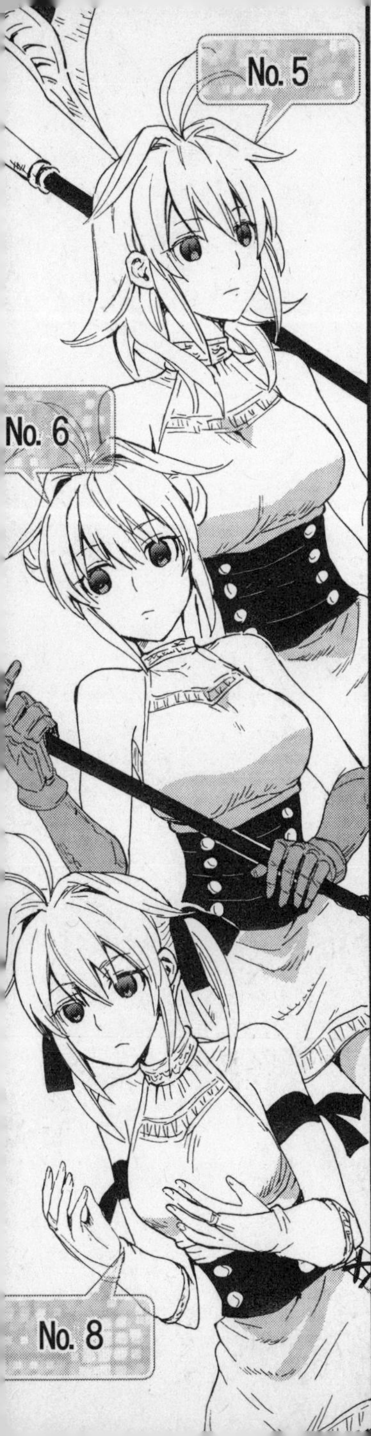
No. 5
No. 6
No. 8

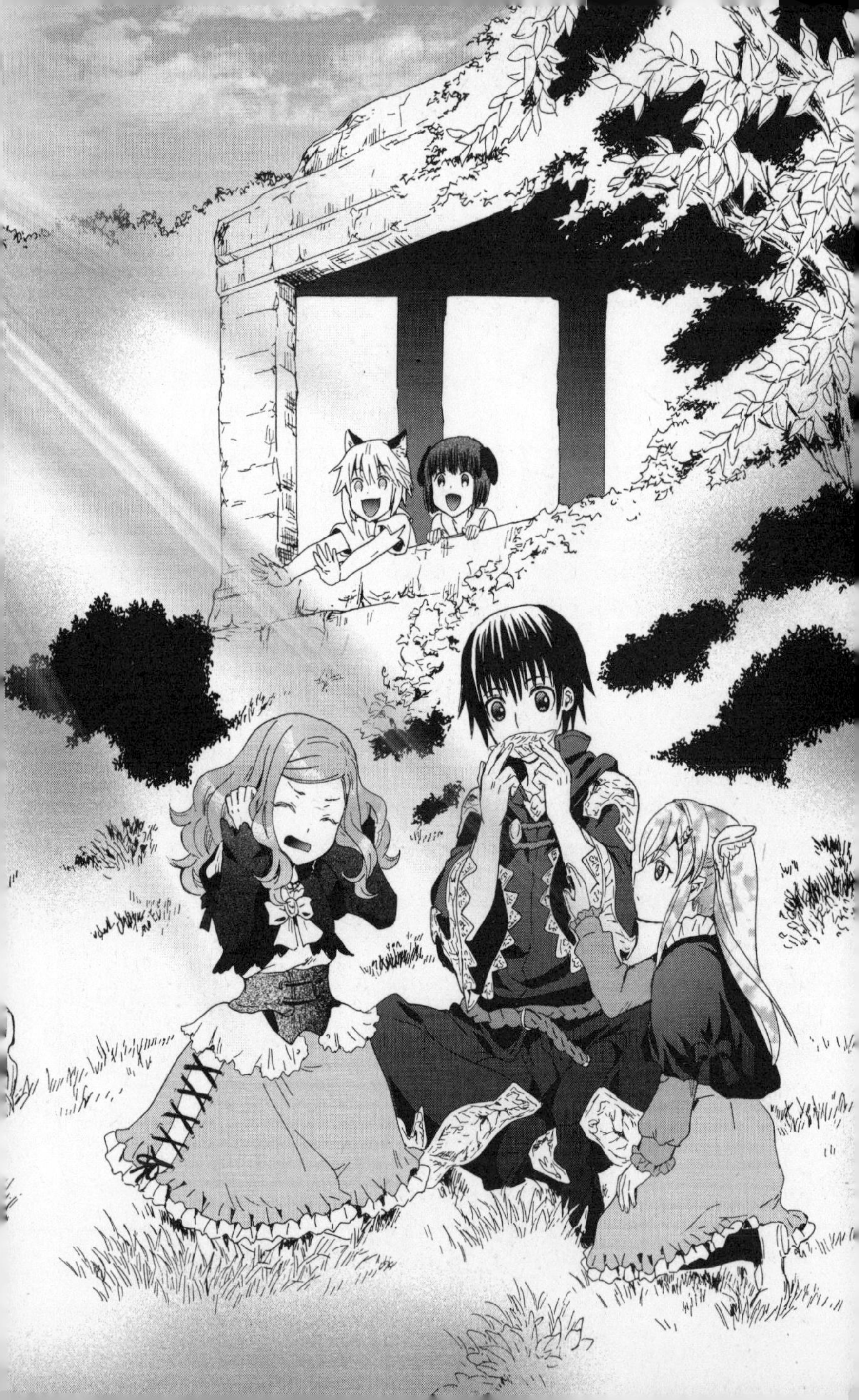

This is Volume 5.

Satou-san and friends have finally left Seiryuu City.

With their group as our guide, I think we'll start to see even more of the world of *Death March*.

I want to go ahead to look after them, but every time, I feel like I'm going to get left behind... I have to work harder.

I'd love to meet again next volume.

Thank you very much.

–Ayamegumu

...Special Thanks

● Manuscript production collaborators
Kaname Yukishiro-sama
Satoru Ezaki-sama
Yuna Kobayashi-sama
Hacchan-sama

● Editors
Toyohara-sama
Hagiwara-sama
Kuwazuru-sama
Arakawa-sama
Ishiguro-sama

● Binding
coil-sama

● Supervision
Hiro Ainana-sama
shri-sama

● Everyone who helped with the production and publication of this book

And you!

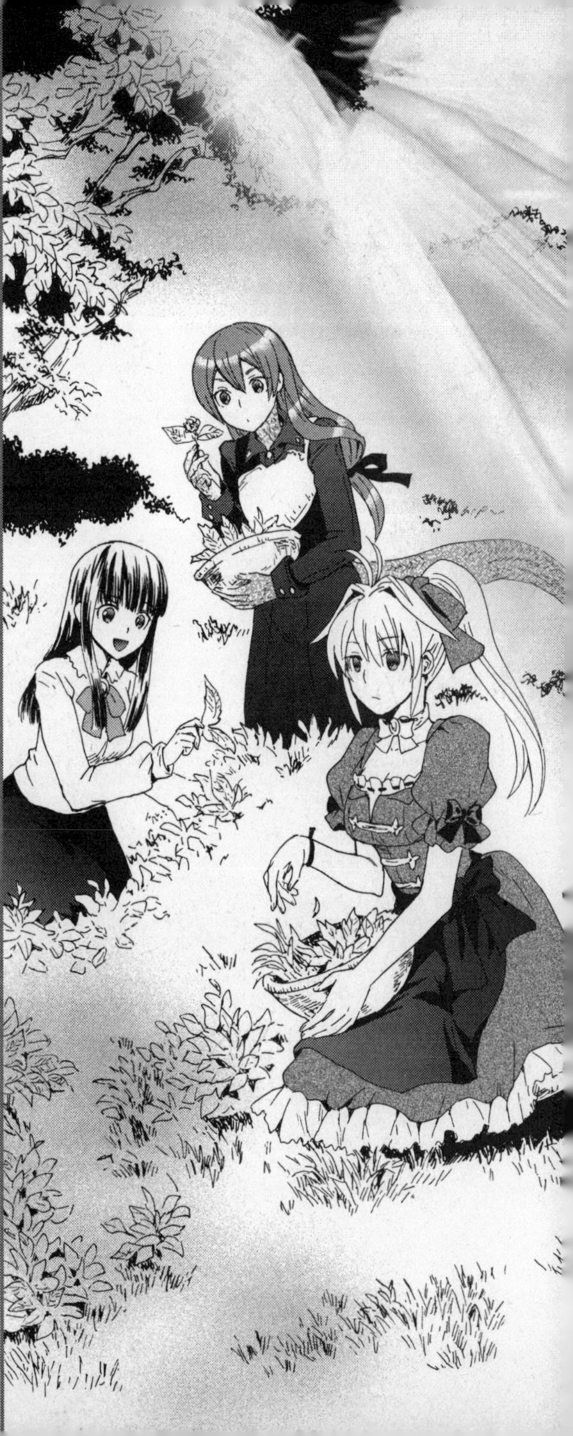

DEATH MARCH TO THE PARALLEL WORLD RHAPSODY 5

Original Story: Hiro Ainana
Art: AYAMEGUMU
Character Design: shri

Translation: Jenny McKeon ◆ Lettering: Rochelle Gancio

DEATH MARCHING TO THE PARALLEL WORLD RHAPSODY Vol. 5
©AYAMEGUMU 2017
©HIRO AINANA, shri 2017
First published in Japan in 2017 by KADOKAWA CORPORATION, Tokyo. English translation rights arranged with KADOKAWA CORPORATION, Tokyo through TUTTLE-MORI AGENCY, INC., Tokyo.

English translation © 2018 by Yen Press, LLC

Yen Press
1290 Avenue of the Americas
New York, NY 10104

Visit us at yenpress.com
facebook.com/yenpress
twitter.com/yenpress
yenpress.tumblr.com
instagram.com/yenpress

First Yen Press Edition: October 2018

Yen Press is an imprint of Yen Press, LLC.
The Yen Press name and logo are trademarks of Yen Press, LLC.

The publisher is not responsible for websites (or their content) that are not owned by the publisher.

Library of Congress Control Number: 2016946043

ISBNs: 978-1-9753-8088-5 (paperback)
978-1-9753-0203-0 (ebook)

10 9 8 7 6 5 4 3 2 1

WOR

Printed in the United States of America